# Philosophy's Journey

## From the Presocratics to the Present

### Second Edition

**Konstantin Kolenda**

*Rice University*

For information about this book, write or call:
Waveland Press, Inc.
P.O. Box 400
Prospect Heights, Illinois 60070
(708) 634-0081

*To the memory of Radoslav and Corrinne Tsanoff,*
*two great-souled people*

# Preface

Since the publication of the first edition of this book fifteen years ago, the aptness of the word "journey" in the title became more apparent to its author. The word is apt because it is natural for philosophy to be always under way; it has no fixed destination. The history of philosophy shows that the ambition to nail things down once and for all, to capture reality in one comprehensive theory or system, is illusory. That ambition is excessive because, as the entire career of the subject demonstrated, successive thinkers again and again come up with new comparisons, hypotheses and metaphors and propose corrective or alternative accounts of the world and of our place in it. New perspectives and different angles of vision result in enlarging the scope of comprehension without abrogating altogether the validity or usefulness of previously promulgated insights and intuitions. What at first seemed illuminating discloses problematic features and is either set aside or modified, thus serving as a stepping stone or a stimulus for a new idea.

One of the pleasures of studying the history of philosophy is to trace the development of an idea after it has been introduced. Philosophical mutations and transformations have their own intrinsic drama. If felicitous, a new idea is often explored in depth, ramified, refocused. In some cases it may require several generations of thinkers to exploit the implications of a train of thought. Not all its consequences or internal tensions can be explored at once, and it may take a sustained effort of brilliant minds to see the incoherence in an original idea or to probe its further possibilities by embroidering on it in unexpected ways.

Philosophy is what philosophers have made it. A venture into its history need not be seen as a trip into the musty, antiquated past. Nor is it a search for a "rational authority" of some great thinkers. The importance of philosophers whom we still read today does not lie merely in their discovery of new ideas or arguments. They have become a part of the history of the subject because they have expressed and formulated thoughts which may and often do occur to anyone who gives some thought to the matter. This is why Whitehead could say that all of the history of philosophy is but a series of footnotes to Plato. Some conclusions or implications of a provocative thought may appear compelling, while others may seem absurd. In either case something is gained. Minds long disembodied can teach us that some paths lead to a dead end. On the other hand, one may discover surprising kinships. To think, for example, Spinoza's thoughts after him may be to feel, in spite of the differences of cultural context, a common intellectual and spiritual bond.

It would be a mistake for a student of Western culture to follow David Hume's advice to consign to flames all books containing theological or metaphysical speculation. While they may fail in respects intended by their creators, many philosophical ventures have succeeded in other ways. As documents in the history of philosophy, they can be read with profit as exploratory thoughts, sometimes producing a growth in self-understanding and an appreciation of the intellectual progress in a given cultural epoch.

Some continuities and transitions are of special interest to a student of philosophy, since they also demonstrate the very nature of the subject. To a large extent philosophy is prolonged discussion. Once an important idea or an angle of vision has been introduced, it is likely to receive the attention of others, who may develop, criticize, or modify it. Philosophers may engage in building, unbuilding, and rebuilding a connected conceptual structure. The development from Socrates to Aristotle is a typical example; another is that from Descartes to Leibniz, and still another that from Locke to Hume. Tracing the paths of intellectual developments or hearing echoes of older views repeated in much later and different historical surroundings is one of the pleasures of studying intellectual history. It has its own life and drama, where the old characters reappear, sometimes unexpectedly, and where familiar *leitmotifs* are suddenly discernible in a new variation.

To be rational is to be guided by the best possible opinions generated by people whose competence we have good reasons to trust. In this sense, our expertise is an extension of that of others. This applies to philosophies we make our own. There is no better way of enlarging one's understanding and of illuminating one's present concerns than by acquiring some grasp of the thoughts which other human beings found important, illuminating, convincing or useful. The history of philosophy provides a panorama of such thoughts. This is why this introduction is using the history of philosophy as its base. Historical material, however, is not the sole content nor the main object of interest in this text. Some concepts and arguments in the history of philosophy stand out because they are still of interest today.

One lesson derived from studying the history of philosophy is that our views on what the world is like and what we want ourselves and our societies to be are amenable to changes, corrections, and even radical departures. The changing character of our interpretations does not square with the supposition that philosophy is a sort of archaeological enterprise, aiming at exhuming some alleged deep-lying foundations set down by some original law-givers, architects or builders. Those who accept this assumption will see themselves as vying with one another in the task of locating the site on which the edifice was built. They will try to devise the best possible tools with which the unearthing can be done. But more and more people have come to question this picture; they suspect that it is no more than a picture and that it holds us captive only because the succession of thinkers who comprise our tradition happened not to question it.

A serious questioning of this tradition was set in motion when philosophers began to pay closer attention to the functioning of language. This heightened sensitivity to different linguistic uses made us aware that our tradition unjustifiably favored the *referential* use of language and that meaning was made dependent on the possibility of reference to something nonlinguistic — objects, structures, essences, the thing-in-itself. Pragmatists in America, Wittgenstein in England, and Heidegger in Germany tried to break away from the assumption that language functions only in one way and that its main task is to produce knowledge understood as mirroring or corresponding to some pre-existent nonlinguistic reality. Pragmatists recommended that we regard ideas as plans of action. Wittgenstein thought of concepts as forms of life. And Heidegger suggested that our primary relation to what he called Being is characterizable in terms of care (*Sorge*) rather than of representational knowledge.

Casting about for new vocabularies that would give a fairer account of the way language enables us to cope with the world, contemporary philosophers are also forcing us to view the history of philosophy in a different light. If the enterprise to disclose the underlying foundations or essences of reality is inherently dubious, then it is possible to look at the theories and doctrines of our philosophical predecessors from a different direction. We will understand their arguments and pronouncements as *experiments in thought* that do other things besides what their authors claimed for them, namely, that they describe ultimate reality. Those other things would include recommendations as to how some particular aspects of the world and of our behavior in it might be characterized. If concepts do not constitute nets that capture Reality itself, but instead are either "plans of action" or "forms of life," and if some of them reveal our *attitude* to things rather than the things themselves, then we will gain a better understanding and appreciation of what our predecessors can teach us.

That philosophical theories have multiple or mixed objectives is confirmed by the fact that philosophers often draw ethical conclusions from their general views. Although in this book an effort is made to discuss prominent ethical theories in independent chapters, it is evident that positions in ethics tend to reflect a particular intellectual climate and are best understood when explored against the background of the authors' other beliefs. But the usefulness of ethical recommendations does not always depend on this connection and can be defended apart from it. It seems worthwhile to examine what Socrates or Kant had to say about morality, because what they had to say is pertinent to the situations in which we find ourselves today. Few discussions of the issue of civil disobedience are more discerning than the one found in Plato's *Crito*. Like all experiments in thought, ethical reflection has a cumulative effect, and we can understand contemporary views better if we look at them in the light of preceding analyses of moral experience. Like other conceptual changes, the changes in theories of what is good, right, or beautiful are a function of deepening insights and intuitions which at times revolutionize our thinking about different areas of experience. The history of such developments provides lessons in creative experimentation in which the images of a good, just, well-ordered society are accompanied by corresponding self-images of people who mustered enough imagination to modify and to refine received accounts.

The questions at the end of each chapter will help the student to focus on the main issues, arguments, and transitions. As the material accumulates, it may be useful to establish some comparisons and contrasts. Other questions intend to elicit the reader's own reactions, and the teacher may want to add still other questions, thus initiating further probing and discussion. The lists of suggested reading direct the student to the material that can deepen and expand philosophical exploration initiated by this text.

The change in the subtitle intends to underscore the continuity of contemporary philosophical thought with its historical antecedents. Since the first edition covered one of the periods — medieval philosophy — only briefly, a separate chapter on the influence of Christianity has been added. The concluding chapter is rewritten and expanded in order to introduce the reader to current intellectual ferments. The new currents, as can be expected, chart their course with the help of innovative vocabularies, but these vocabularies can be better understood against the background of previously held theories. Philosophy, we have said, is what philosophers have made it. The process of making, and remaking, is still going on.

Several of my colleagues have provided helpful comments and suggestions on the new material included in this edition, and my thanks for their kindness go to Steve Crowell, Street Fulton, Dick Grandy, and Don Morrison. Similarly I wish to express my appreciation to Minranda Robinson-Davis for struggling valiantly with transcribing dictated tapes and to Brian Oxley for his expert and cheerful handling of word processing chores.

I am grateful to Neil Rowe, the publisher of Waveland Press, for encouraging me to provide this revised and expanded version of *Philosophy's Journey*. Both of us hope that it will keep finding congenial travel companions.

# Contents

# Part II   Modern Philosophy                                  87

# Part III   Twentieth-Century Thought                         195

*Engraving of a Rubens drawing of Socrates*

# Ancient and Medieval Philosophy

# Chapter One

# Early Philosophical Ventures

## 1. The What and the How

Historians agree that Western philosophy as an independent, autonomous inquiry came into existence in Greece in the sixth century, B.C. Before the advent of some Greek thinkers who now are referred to as Presocratics (since they preceded Socrates), all ultimate explanations of natural and human phenomena were given in religious terms. The Greek religion was anthropomorphic. Gods were like human beings, except that they wielded superhuman powers. Mount Olympus, high above the clouds, was the place where the gods were believed to dwell and from there to direct the affairs of the world. There was, of course, a division of their spheres of influence: some gods controlled the sky, others the waters, and still others the bowels of the earth. The Greeks had a god of war and a goddess of love, a god of trade, and one of the arts. What happened on earth and in human history was ascribed to the action or the interference of gods. A change in the weather, especially if it was violent and unpredictable, was the work of Zeus; a storm at sea expressed Poseidon's wrath; a bountiful harvest of grapes showed forth the good will of Dionysus. Everything that happened was understood as a result of some divine agency. Ultimate questions had the form: who, or which god, is responsible for X? Religious myths were invoked to explain not only particular events, but also the origin and the general course of the world.

What is now referred to as the genius of the early Greek philosophers manifested itself in their ability to start asking a brand new kind of questions. Somehow they managed to set aside the customary explanations in terms of

3

divine, supernatural agencies. Not that they necessarily ceased to believe the religious stories and myths; it is unlikely that they could shake off altogether their own age-long, ingrained traditions and modes of thinking. Most of the new thinkers probably asked and explored new questions while holding some of the old beliefs. But it is also true that many of them began to show much greater interest in their inquiries than in the traditional mythical explanations.

The new explanations differed from the old ones in that they moved away from personalized toward impersonal accounts. The "who" was replaced by "what" or "how." Somehow it dawned on the bolder thinkers of the age that behind all the observed things and processes one might discover "the *nature* of things." Possibly, the Greeks were peculiarly prone to ask this question. The Greek religion, in spite of its anthropomorphic character, nevertheless recognized something called *nemesis, moira,* translated as fate or destiny, an inexorable force to which even gods were subject. Perhaps this conception facilitated a transition to an impersonal order of things, to the idea of "laws of nature."

Another factor often suggested as a reason why inhabitants of this particular part of the world were able to break through to new, unorthodox questions, is their geographical location. The cities of this area were centers of trade, and commerce often acts as the incubator of intellectual progress. Traveling all over the Mediterranean, traders had been exposed to varying customs, practices, and beliefs. Were all of them equally convincing? It must have occurred to some travelers that those varying and often contrasting accounts could not be true *together*. On the one hand this could encourage tolerance, but on the other hand it could also lead to a desire to discover *what was true* about the world, what did not vary from tribe to tribe, or from time to time. Even the very idea of some accounts being *true* may have had its origin here. Mythical accounts about gods and about the world, even when they are taken seriously by successive generations, do not necessarily concern themselves with the question of truth. Myth is something that is *told* and need not call for critical scrutiny, examination, or justification. The idea of possibly discovering the unchanging nature of reality behind the multiplicity of appearances and behind conflicting opinions is a most original and revolutionary idea in the intellectual history of humanity.

## Thales

"What is it?" is one of the most frequently heard questions. In many instances it is a request for information about the composition of a thing. "What is it made of?" "What kind of substance is it—wood, metal, mineral, glass?" "Is this real fruit, or plastic imitation?" The answer tells us something about the fundamental nature of the thing in question; we feel that we learn something important about it. This knowledge could also serve as an explanation of a thing's behavior. "No wonder it shattered to pieces when dropped on the floor—it was made of glass and not of metal!"

Suppose you ask the question: "Is there some substance or some basic stuff out of which *everything* is made?" Because he was the first to ask this question, Thales of Miletus is often referred to as the father of Greek philosophy. It is easy to see why he thought the question to be promising. If there *is* some substance, then we can claim to know at least one item which is universally and eternally true. Furthermore, the apparently unfamiliar things encountered for the first time would not be wholly unfamiliar, for one would at least be sure that they were manifestations of something which one already knew or was familiar with. Thus, the mystery and strangeness of things are removed, at least to a point—we know "what we are at" or what we are in reality dealing with. (A somewhat analogous, but of course a vastly more limited, discovery would be to find out that a medicine sold by different firms and under different, seemingly unrelated labels, turned out to have essentially the same content, e.g., aspirin.)

Thales not only asked the question, "What is the world made of?," he proceeded to answer it. The answer was bold and, to us, who live 25 centuries later, fantastic. Thales concluded that the primal stuff was water. We know today that he was wrong, but why is his conclusion of interest? It is of interest because this was not just a guess; it was a *reasoned* conclusion, and a conclusion is as good or as strong as are the reasons for it. What is of interest, therefore, is *why* Thales was inclined to propound his answer. Although we don't know what exactly led him to regard water as the basic stuff, some items can be mentioned as plausible explanations. Water was a familiar and ubiquitous element in Thales' experience. In his day Miletus was an important Greek commercial center on the eastern coast of the Aegean Sea. Thales noted how all living things depend on water for sustenance, and that all foods contain some moisture. Having spent some time in Egypt, he must have noted the crucial importance of the Nile for raising of crops in Egypt. He might have mused over the fact that water can take on such apparently dissimilar characters as liquid, ice, or vapor. He might have been aware of some old myths according to which the world came into existence from an initial watery chaos, and this could have suggested to him his philosophical conclusion, but the important feature of his reasoning is that it seeks support from what is impersonally observable and accessible to anyone.

Still, one might say, the available evidence is not only inconclusive, but also quite unconvincing, for some substances Thales himself encountered could not be reduced to water by any stretch of the imagination. These "negative instances" should be sufficient to kill the theory. No doubt they are, even though we should not forget that its implausibility is more evident to us, who are steeped in natural science, than it could be to those who were merely groping toward it.

## Anaximander

The difficulties with Thales' theory were not lost on his successors, nor should we assume that he was entirely unaware of them. In fact, these difficulties led Thales' pupil, Anaximander, to propound a view which, in its boldness, is no less astonishing than that of his teacher. Anaximander thought that neither water nor any other *known and definite* substance could be the primal stuff. Besides water, three other elements were regarded by the Greeks as basic or fundamental, namely, earth, air, and fire. If any one of these four is regarded as underlying the other three, there will be countless instances which won't fit the theory. But the difficulty, thought Anaximander, will not be just due to our inability to make proper observations. The difficulty is strictly logical. A *particular* substance cannot become other substances without losing its particularity, and if that occurs, how can it be *basic*? So, the only sensible conclusion, if we are looking for a basic substance, is that it must lack any particular character, is not determinate or determinable. Anaximander called it *apeiron*, "boundless" or "limitless," a substance which under some conditions may take on the character of water, earth, air, or fire, or of any of their combinations, but itself cannot be reduced to any of them. Anaximander applied a critical test to his teacher's doctrine, which consists, as is the case in most criticisms, in following through on some of the implications of the view advanced. If water is the primal stuff, then everything would have to be wet, or at least wetness should be discoverable in all things. But it is not. Furthermore, Thales claimed that "water" is capable of generating both the hot and the dry, but these characteristics are not compatible with wetness as an essential characteristic of water. Hence, by means of such a purely conceptual investigation, Anaximander could disprove his teacher's theory. At the same time, his own alternative was designed to avoid the difficulties which vitiated Thales' conclusion.

Unfortunately, Anaximander's concept of the boundless has difficulties of its own. Essentially, it is a negative concept—we are not told how we could recognize it if we should run up against it. In some ways, its reality is a demand of thought, a logical construct: there *must* be something which underlies all the familiar things and yet is different from all of them. The argument is analogous to a more recent argument propounded in the nineteenth-century in physics when it was discovered that light is propagated through wave motion. Some physicists concluded that the whole cosmos must be permeated by a material substance called ether. Light waves need a material medium in which to be propagated, hence there *must* be such a medium—a purely logical demand.

## Anaximenes

The argument for "boundless" did not seem to impress Anaximenes, a pupil and associate of Anaximander. He preferred to follow Thales' example and look among the known elements to land a candidate for the basic substance. Anaximenes thought that air is a more promising element. Why did he think so? "Just as our soul, being air, keeps us together in order, so also wind (or breath) and air encompasses the whole cosmos." Somehow, the importance of air for human existence led Anaximenes to think that that substance must pervade the universe and, as air sustains us, so it sustains and supports the whole cosmos. The idea suggests that humanity and the universe are kin; there is a unity pervading the microcosm and macrocosm.

As we have noted, the chief difficulty with the idea of a basic stuff was in the question as to how something, say X, can *become* Y. If Y is sufficiently different from X, we have a lot of explaining to do. Well, Anaximenes noted one phenomenon which seemed to furnish a clue. He was the first to notice that there may be a relationship between the quantitative and the qualitative aspects of things. Indeed, he may be credited with the performance of the first scientific experiment. Compress your lips and blow on your hand—the air feels cold. Now, blow gently with your mouth wide open—the air feels warm. The qualitative changes of phenomena, concluded Anaximenes, are due to the quantitative difference in substances. Rarefied air yields heat (the most rarefied, fire); condensed, thick air produces cold (the thickest air turns into earth).

## Pythagoras

The idea that the *arrangement* in space may determine the effects of a substance, or that quantitative differences can have qualitative consequences, could have been a germ of the new slant which came into Greek philosophy with the work of Pythagoras. Thales' philosophical speculations revolved around the question, "What is the world made of?" This general approach to philosophy was known in ancient Greece as the Ionian school. Pythagoras asked a new kind of question. To him it appeared that the *how* might be more important than the *what*. Born about 580 B.C. on the island of Samos off the Ionian coast, Pythagoras later settled in southern Italy. The ideas explored by his Ionian countrymen were probably not unknown to him, and he might have heard of Anaximenes' observations about the peculiar behavior of air. Nevertheless, the important shift in Greek philosophy from the *what* to the *how* was brought about by Pythagoras' further speculations.

His great discovery was that the inquiry into the basic *matter* of things may not be as fruitful as the inquiry into the *form* of things. He noticed, for instance, that regardless of what a stretched string is made of it will give off a harmonic octave if its length is doubled. The *numerical ratio* is what counts, not the material. The discovery behind this is that the ratio is not something seen or felt—it is comprehended by an act of thought. Pythagoras generalized this conclusion, believing that the knowledge of things comes from the study of patterns, relationships, numbers. What he had in mind can be seen from many examples. It does not matter, for instance, whether a key is made of steel or silver; if it has the right form or pattern, it will unlock the door. A pharmacist who knows the proper proportions of requisite ingredients will be able to prepare a medicine; his lack of this knowledge cannot be compensated by the possession of great quantities of the same ingredients. It was said that only three people in the world had the secret of making Coca-Cola; only they had the *formula*, although the materials might be known to everyone.

Pythagoreans were the first to discover a relationship between arithmetic and geometry. Using pebbles for points, they saw that two pebbles, when connected, constitute a line, and three pebbles make up a triangle. The theorem that the square of the hypotenuse is equal to the sum of the squares of the other two sides of a right-angled triangle is attributed to Pythagoras and bears his name.

In a later commentary on the discoveries of Pythagoras, Aristotle remarked that "since they show that the attributes and the ratios of the musical scales were expressible in numbers; since then all other things seemed in their whole nature to be modelled after numbers, and numbers seemed to be the first things in the whole of nature, and the whole heaven to be a musical scale and a number."[1]

Social and religious life is also governed by numbers, according to Pythagoreans. They believed that interpersonal relations can be characterized by numerical ratios. Thus, number four, or the first square, represents justice. The idea of retribution, "an eye for an eye, a tooth for a tooth" in a Pythagorean version would be "a two for a two." Marriage is symbolized by number five (two plus three), which is the union of the even (female) with the odd (male). As musical harmony depends on a certain numerical ratio among sounds, so the health of a person can be said to depend on a proper balance, a harmony of bodily ingredients. When they are "in tune" with one another, the person is well. When they are in discord and tension, illness sets in.

Pythagoreans believed that awareness and the right understanding of numerical relations enabled a person to peer, so to speak, behind the curtain of appearances and to know the reality of things. Mathematical knowledge was good for the soul because it purified it of the confusing and misleading impressions piled up by the senses. Pythagoras illustrated his scale of values in the following way. Three kinds of pursuits can be observed at Olympian games. There are those who sell and buy wares, those who compete in the arena, and those who merely look on. The latter group, the spectators, lead the best kind of life, for they are not involved in the cares of either making a profit or exhibiting their physical prowess—they are liberated from these burdens and can concentrate on observation, on looking around them, following *with understanding* what is going on. The Greek word "theoria" means "seeing all around" or "looking on." To live at the level of understanding, which for Pythagoras meant grasping the numerical, formal relations of all things, is to possess wisdom.

## 2. The Problem of Change

### Heraclitus

The philosophical promise of the question "What is the world made of?" can be fulfilled when at the end of the investigation we do come up with some substance which remains stable and unchanging throughout time. But suppose you are struck by the fact that *nothing* remains the same. Suppose that your observation of the world forces you to conclude that everything is in constant flux. This was the thought that impressed another interesting thinker from the Presocratic period, Heraclitus, born in 540 B.C. in Ephesos, and sometimes referred to as the "weeping philosopher," possibly because of his views. You cannot step into the same river twice, observed Heraclitus, because the next time neither you nor the river is the same as before. But if so, what *is* the river, and what are you?

The hold of the Ionian approach, however, was not easy to break. In spite of his discovery of the constant flux of everything, Heraclitus was nevertheless inclined to think that there ought to be one substance which makes up the universe. To him, the best candidate for that position was fire, but his analysis of fire struck out in a new direction. Heraclitus noted that fire is both a substance and a process: its very character depends on transformation. On the one hand, in order to be, fire must be fed. On the other hand, it yields other products: heat, smoke, and ashes. Seeing change or transformation all around him, Heraclitus saw in fire the model of all natural phenomena.

However, if everything in the world is constantly changing, if nothing remains the same as time goes on, can human thought rest on anything which remains stable and unchanging? Heraclitus believed that it could. He noticed that the very process of becoming, of transformation, binds the changing elements into a unity. In one sense, the bow and arrow are "opposed" to each other, for they pull in opposite directions, but the result is the process of tension which gives the whole weapon its characteristic function. In that sense, the bow and arrow also "agree" with each other. In fact, it is their opposition that constitutes their proper function. Here, we have a key to the whole universe, thought Heraclitus. Differences and disagreements among things nevertheless stand in effective unities, and in spite of his affirmation of universal flux, Heraclitus was still inclined to see that flux as unified by the very processes of mutual opposition and transformation. Hence, his proclamation that "the way up and the way down are one and the same."

Furthermore, the Cosmic Fire gives the totality of transformation a lawful and rational character. There is change, but the change is not haphazard. It is governed by *Logos*, or Reason, which permeates all reality. Like everything else, the human soul is touched by the sparks of Cosmic Fire, of which Heraclitus also conceived religiously, as an equivalent to God. Consequently, man can discern the lawfulness of things despite their constant flux. Hence, the capacity to think and to understand is the highest and best human attribute.

## Parmenides

To Parmenides, born about 515 B.C. in Elea, a city founded by Ionian refugees in southern Italy, the doctrine of constant flux seemed more problematic than it did to Heraclitus. There seems to be an inherent puzzle in the very idea of change, if one but stops and thinks about it. When something changes, it no longer is what it was; it becomes something else. But if so, does that original something still exist? Common sense is not bothered by this question, because it does not regard some changes as actually altering the things undergoing change. However, Parmenides wanted to go beyond common, practical sense. True, in our customary human perspective some things may appear to be permanent and stable, but if the march of time affects everything, then even the most stable things eventually disappear and cease to be. Thus, what can we say about their reality, their Being? Confined to *a* span of time, no matter how long, they still cannot be said truly to exist, to have *real* Being. Hence, Parmenides concluded that real Being does not change, it is always One, not many. Thought compels us to reject the panorama presented by the senses as disclosing the truth of things. The truth is unchangeable and eternal, it is Being, while the changing transformations are non-Being. Needless to say, nothing determinate can be said of Being, and

Parmenides himself speaks of it as *It*. "One path only is left for us to speak of, namely, that *It* is. In this path are very many tokens that what is, is uncreated and indestructible, for it is complete, immovable and without end."

*It* is accessible only by the power of thought. Indeed, Parmenides identified thought and reality. "Thought and reality are the same thing." He also added a darker saying. "Thinking, and that for the sake of which thought exists are the same." One interpretation of this might be that there is an identity of thought and of the content of thought. If so, Parmenides, like many other Greek thinkers of that time, tended to get his clues from mathematics, in which the reality of what is thought about is exhausted by the thought itself—it does not need to be tied to anything outside itself.

Zeno, a pupil of Parmenides, enriched his teacher's arguments by introducing his famous paradoxes. All of these paradoxes were designed to show that there are insurmountable logical contradictions in our effort to make sense of change and motion, and that therefore Parmenides' doctrine of the exclusive reality of the One was the only rational alternative. The race between Achilles and the tortoise is perhaps the most famous of Zeno's paradoxes. Known for legendary fleetness, Achilles should have no difficulty in overtaking the tortoise even if that slow animal is given a handsome handicap. When the race starts at a moment, *t*, Achilles requires a certain amount of time to get to the point where the tortoise starts its motion. But the tortoise, slow as it is, has nevertheless moved ahead a bit. To get to the new location of the tortoise, Achilles needs to use some amount of time, no matter how small, but the tortoise has not been resting either and has moved a little farther. So it is with the next fraction of time; although Achilles comes ever closer to the tortoise, he can never overtake it. Thus, when we see Achilles overtake the tortoise, some deception, some trick of the senses must have occurred. Hence, concluded Zeno, there is something wrong with our belief that motion is real.

It is worth noting that Zeno's paradoxes, even though there have been many refutations of them, have taxed the ingenuity of whole generations of philosophers and mathematicians to the very present. Articles on Zeno's paradoxes still appear in current issues of philosophical journals. Whatever their logical status, the paradoxes have been important in raising serious conceptual problems in the analyses of space, time, motion, and matter.

Parmenides met the problem of change head-on, in a logically uncompromising fashion. It is impossible, he believed, for A to become B and still somehow to remain A. If such a transformation is possible for A, then it cannot really *be*, concluded Parmenides. We have noted that similar considerations induced Anaximander to reject Thales' notion that the basic stuff is some *particular* substance—be it water, air, or anything else. There is no way for one particular substance to become *another* particular substance; hence, Anaximander's basic stuff is "boundless," indeterminate, not accessible to sense. The One of Parmenides also lies on the other side of anything particular and is similarly a *demand* of thought, something we cannot experience but must nevertheless recognize as real.

## Empedocles

The generation following Parmenides could not easily ignore the problems and puzzles about change to which he and Zeno had called attention. Feeling the impasse of the one-substance or one-reality doctrines, Empedocles appears to offer a compromise. Suppose that each of the four traditionally accepted elemental substances—air, fire, water, and earth—is indeed eternal and indestructible and that what we see in the world is the result of the mixture of these basic ingredients in various proportions. The possible combinations of such mixtures may be indefinitely large, hence allowing the world to have the undeniable richness it exhibits. Furthermore, different combinations of the same elements exhibit both identity and diversity, as Pythagoras demanded. Their sameness is due to the sameness of the ingredients, their "differentness" results from the differences in quantitative combinations. Indeed, Anaximenes' hunch that quality may be a function of quantity is followed up in Empedocles' account. New quality may emerge as a result of new mixtures of the four elements, and a particular thing is identical with its qualities. Still needed in this account is the reason *why* the mixtures form or fall apart. This, according to Empedocles, is due to two cosmic principles—Love and Strife, or Harmony and Discord. These principles account for the processes of attraction and repulsion. Where Love reigns, elements coexist harmoniously, in balance with one another, as in a healthy body. Where Strife sets in, the ingredients fall apart, and the body disintegrates. Empedocles believed that his account explains abnormal phenomena. When the forces of Love and Strife are in conflict, many freaks might appear on earth: neckless heads, arms without shoulders, cattle with human faces, or oxheaded human beings.

## Anaxagoras

Although Empedocles' bold move away from monism to some kind of pluralism appears to be breaking new ground, many questions are left unanswered. Why should there be only four eternal elements? What kind of reality do Love and Strife have—are they material forces, literally attracting and repelling, or are they altogether different in kind? Anaxagoras, still another important thinker of the time, thought that instead of just four elements, an indefinite number of them could be found in everything; he called them "seeds of existence." He also appears to be the first to have come up with a subsequently dominant distinction between matter and mind. Anaxagoras believed that there is an ordering principle, which he called Noûs, Mind, or Reason, which makes a *cosmos*, an orderly world possible. If an ultimate explanation of things cannot be found in either some basic substance or some eternal formal principle, then perhaps the phenomenon of change can be explained as an expression of some pervasive cosmic agency. Noûs was the name he gave such an agency. Subsequent philosophers, including Socrates and Aristotle, were not happy with Anaxagoras' Mind. Of Socrates' disappointment we shall learn later. Aristotle complained that "Anaxagoras uses reason as a *deus ex machina* for making the world, and when he is at a loss to tell from what cause something necessarily is, then he drags reason in, but in all other cases he ascribes events to anything but reason."[2] In Anaxagoras' thinking, Mind appears to be no more than a force, lacking the character of purpose or design ordinarily associated with minds. Nevertheless, his explicit introduction of the mental principle, as somehow basically different from material phenomena, gave a new direction to Greek philosophy.

## 3. The First Atomist

### Democritus

Although the early Greek philosophers were searching for ways of describing what happens in the world without falling back on divine intentions or acts of will—a type of explanation obviously borrowed from human experience, in which an event is ascribed to a person's act—there was still in all these accounts a trace of what might be called "animism." The favorite image of the world was still that it was like an animal, something animated from within. Thus, Thales' water is capable of generating other forms of itself; Anaximenes' air involves some kind of cosmic consciousness, and Anaximander's *apeiron* and Heraclitus' Cosmic Fire are credited with "steering" things. This directing and determining function is explicitly found in Empedocles' Love and Strife and also in Anaxagoras' Mind.

By contrast, the remaining philosophical contribution to be discussed breaks away from this quasianimistic tradition in a radically innovative manner. The doctrine of atomism, attributed to Leucippus (490-430 B.C.), but developed and clearly articulated by Democritus (460-360 B.C.) is the first fully worked out mechanistic-materialistic theory. Leucippus began by criticizing Parmenides' conception of space. For Parmenides, the notion of space presented a problem because he rejected the existence of non-Being. For him, space, or the void, as he called it, could not be nothing. Space, he thought, is part of the total *It*. But if there is no emptiness, no void between things, motion, as movement in empty space, cannot really take place. Leucippus thought that if we could think of space as a sort of receptacle which may be full in some parts, but not in others, Parmenides' difficulties would not arise. Given this concept of space, the doctrine of atomism could be advanced.

The key idea of this doctrine, as elaborated by Democritus, is that the ultimate ingredients of things are atoms—particles which are no longer divisible— literally, "non-sects." These atoms are material and infinitely varied in shape. Since they are very small, they cannot be seen by the human eye. Not only are they invisible, they also lack any of the characteristics discoverable by the senses: taste, smell, or touch. Their shapes differ, some exhibiting the regular features of geometric solids, others being irregularly shaped, with hooks, projections, and hollows. Being no longer divisible, they are indestructible and impenetrable. As if in a cosmic shower, they move through space with velocities corresponding to their size. In the course of motion they get entangled with one another, thus forming the composite structures which inhabit the world. Generation and destruction are merely the processes of the union and separation of atoms. Some combinations form large and lasting objects, such as seas and mountains; others form small and ephemeral things and creatures, including human beings.

The whole process is completely fortuitous; there is no need to postulate the existence of any design or regulating principles. Things emerge and events happen just because of the original nature of atoms, which in a purely mechanical fashion combine and recombine in the course of time. All phenomena, including those of human perception, are due to the motion of atoms. Seeing is due to the impact of tiny particles emitted by objects seen on the observer's eyes. Similarly with hearing, smell, or taste—all are instances of interaction between atoms and various sense organs. Indeed, it appears that here we have a reduction of all senses to only one—the sense of touch. The way in which the moving atoms "touch" us—outside and inside our skins—determines the particular mode of perception. Even such phenomena as thinking and remembering are given a purely materialistic-mechanistic explanation by Democritus. For him, as for the English philosopher Thomas Hobbes, a seventeenth-century proponent of a similar view, emotions are literally motions of tiny, nimble atoms through some parts of the body— head, heart, or liver. Memory is but a disappearing, dying movement of atoms gradually losing their initial momentum.

The description of atoms in terms of size, shape, and motion alone introduced a note which played an important role in the history of philosophy, namely, skepticism: human knowledge cannot reach beyond immediate perceptions. Mental states, including understanding and feeling, are just temporary and derivative conditions of organisms that have them. Even such things as colors do not exist independently: the rose has its red color only and literally in the eyes of the beholder. When some rose atoms do not impinge on any eye, there *is* no redness at all—only, we might say, potential redness. If an eye were placed in the area through which these atoms are moving, then the perception of redness would occur. Democritus' explanation of this phenomenon was to say that color perception, as well as all other mental events, happen "by custom"—they are not real, independent characteristics of the world. Their occurrence depends on subjects: hence, they are subjective, not objective. They do not remain in their characteristic mode apart from human beings.

Although the details of the atomistic doctrine were simply left to the imagination of the reader (after all, atoms were unobservable), this doctrine has a distinctly modern ring. In some respects it is a "process philosophy": things are reducible to, or the result of, motions. Even the properties of things that appear stable and unchangeable are shown to be events: being red is more like being noisy than like being solid. To us who are accustomed to speaking of colors as dependent on the length of the wave in which a particular light travels, this may sound congenial enough. And yet, the basic conceptual framework of such an explanation was born over two millennia ago. The philosophical path first cleared by Democritus was frequently traveled, and the mechanistic-materialistic approach had many variants. One attraction the doctrine had, even to Democritus, was that it seemed to do away with "superstitions" about entities and principles supposedly governing the world. This may be why Democritus was called "the laughing philosopher" by some of his contemporaries. His view liberated him from the fears and superstitions which often plagued believers in the various religious accounts of the world. If the world is a completely mechanical and fortuitous affair, if death is no more than the spilling out of consciousness-yielding atoms, there is no need to worry about the meaning or destiny of either humanity or the universe. There is no such thing as destiny, or purpose, or the ultimate meaning of things. The world is only atoms in the void, and its kaleidoscopic variations are just as temporal and groundless as is the motion of clouds driven by an indifferent wind.

## Questions

1. What changes in the explanation of natural phenomena took place in Greece during the sixth century B.C.? How can these changes be explained?

2. What were the various arguments for claiming that some substances are *basic*? What was plausible about these arguments, and what criticisms were offered against them?

3. What did Pythagoras understand by ''form?'' Why was the change of interest from basic stuff to form philosophically important?

4. What were Parmenides' and Zeno's arguments against Heraclitus' claim that everything is in flux? Do you agree with their conclusion that if something keeps constantly changing, then it cannot really be *known*?

5. How inclusive was Democritus' atomic theory—was it intended to explain *everything*? Are there some phenomena which in your opinion cannot be explained by that theory? Can Democritus' *theory* be explained in its own terms?

## Notes

[1] Aristotle, *Metaphysics*, Book I, Ch. 4, 986a. (*The Works of Aristotle*, 12 vols., translated and edited by J.A. Smith and W.D. Ross, London: Oxford University Press, 1908-1952.)
[2] *Ibid.*, Book I, Ch. 4, 985a.

# Chapter Two

# The Golden Age of Greek Philosophy

## 1. The Sophists: The Skeptical Challenge

The thinkers discussed in the first chapter obviously had high philosophic aspirations. Their questions were broad; their speculations bold. As we have seen, they were often internally inconsistent and mutually contradictory. Of course, a part of the philosophical impetus is furnished by the opportunity to point out conceptual errors in proposed doctrines. This critical tendency is human enough and not necessarily without benefit. Indeed, human civilization progressed because of frequent displays of critical spirit. The function of the critic is to appraise the views advanced—are they sound? To answer this, one must begin by looking for possible faults, for vulnerable places. But it would be premature and sometimes unfair to conclude from this that the critic is interested only in exposing weaknesses and in debunking what he examines. This may or may not be the case. The critic's motive cannot be determined simply from his success in discovering errors in arguments he examines. One's motive may be initially to understand the argument, but one may later discover errors, inconsistencies, and gaps in it—and these are *barriers* to understanding. It is especially important in philosophy to determine whether the proposed doctrine is sound, because the doctrine is presented *to the understanding* of the hearer or reader, and one cannot understand something which when examined, fails to make sense, either wholly or in part. Because of this, the critic's function is extremely important, even indispensable. If he is perceptive, his judgment can serve as a prism or filter through which a theory or doctrine can be passed. It may turn out, of course, that the view examined is indeed sound, not open to serious objections, and the critic himself may become a convert to the view. Indeed, he may be grateful for the enrichment of his knowledge and understanding.

This possibility presupposes that not all views will collapse when subject to criticism and that some views can be true and are worth knowing. One may conclude, however, that there are no such views. Having discovered again and again that there is something wrong with the views advanced and held, having seen that equally plausible views may nevertheless conflict with one another, and having many such theories to choose from, a person may reach the conclusion that none of them is really true or worth knowing. This conclusion may lead to an attitude of relativism and skepticism. A relativist believes that all views and opinions are relative to some starting points which are not questioned and that these starting points themselves cannot be shown to be true or false, or worth believing. Consequently, the conclusions based on them cannot be said to be true either—their truth depends on the truth of the premises. However, since the latter is not known to be the case, how can one be confident about the conclusion? If the starting points are arbitrary, exhibit a great variety, and are often inconsistent with one another, then none of the contending views deserve to be called true. Hence, skepticism results. Furthermore, if an apparently impeccable chain of reasoning leads to conclusions that palpably contradict plain facts of common sense, why should one take them seriously? If Zeno proves that according to logical reasoning Achilles cannot overtake a tortoise and we then see this happen, so much the worse for logical reasoning.

This was the conclusion of a group of men who called themselves Sophists. They appeared on the Greek intellectual scene sometime during the fifth century B.C., when many conflicting philosophical doctrines, some of which we have discussed in the first chapter, were already in circulation. Overwhelmed by the variety of proposed theories and confused by the discrepancies among them, the Sophists proceeded to discount their importance. They undertook to disabuse those who still believed that there was a right way of explaining the nature of things. "Sophist" means a wise man, but, paradoxically, those who called themselves wise men had little interest in truly understanding. Instead, they proposed to teach those who were willing to pay a fee in order to be successful in the world. The value of discussion, dialectic, and rhetoric lies in effective ways of persuasion; the winning of an argument depends on demolishing the opinion of the opponent. Since any opinion, with proper skill, is vulnerable and open to rebuttals, the advantage rests in greater rhetorical skills. A successful orator or speaker knows how to appeal to the prejudices of the audience, and so uses those arguments which are most likely to be effective. When he speaks to an audience with different preconceptions and attitudes, he of course changes his arguments—even if they contradict those used before previous audiences—because his only aim is to convince and to gain assent. There is no such thing as reasoning soundly, only arguing successfully. The Sophists felt that it did not matter whether or not your argument was sound—just as long as you won the argument.

The Sophists were instrumental in bringing about a shift from cosmic speculation to an interest in human capacities and needs. They believed that abstract intellectual interests do not deserve as much attention as theoretical philosophers tend to devote to them. Other things may be more important, such as how to proceed in life so as to gain maximum satisfaction in personal ambitions and endeavors. This satisfaction requires an acquisition of certain skills—it calls for education. In spite of their relativism and skepticism on broad and basic philosophical issues, the Sophists nevertheless believed in the value of education as a methodical process, requiring concentration on specific subject matter and attention to detail. Sophists were professional teachers, persons with special competence and a willingness to train others who sought this competence. The subjects they taught were practical— grammar, rhetoric, dialectic, mathematics, and harmonic theory. They were also willing to give instruction in arts and crafts; the Sophist Hippias, perhaps the first "do-it-yourself" enthusiast, appeared at the Olympic games splendidly dressed, boasting that he had himself fashioned every article of his gorgeous attire. The Sophists contributed to the realization that transmission of cultural values can be conscious and deliberate. By the same token, they helped to propagate the idea of a cultural and political unity of people who shared common values.

The emphasis on individual effectiveness and personal success was nevertheless bound to create difficulties for the Sophists. Having accepted the view that all social goals and arrangements are merely conventional and not rooted in any kind of natural order, they could not go on to argue that the accepted conventions are somehow right or good. They simply *are*; they are a sociological fact of a given period, and a wise person would follow them so as to reap great benefits for himself. Thus, they were in fact encouraging conformism. But this conformism was vulnerable, for it had no justification beyond itself. In fact, the final measure of things was a person's predilection. One of the most famous Sophists, Protagoras, proclaimed that "man is the measure of all things," meaning thereby that questions of knowledge must finally rest on the intellectual capacity of any given person. There is no higher recourse and no order of things beyond the conventional human order: "In respect to the gods, I am unable to know either that they are or that they are not, for there are many obstacles to such knowledge, above all the obscurity of the matter, and the life of man, in that it is so short." [1] This thoroughly skeptical remark is one of the very few lines remaining from Protagoras' writings. The mood of the line just cited is reminiscent of

Democritus, who similarly regarded as hopeless any pursuit of knowledge beyond the immediacy of sense impressions. Scholars speculate that Protagoras may have had some association with Democritus, perhaps by attending some of the latter's discourses on his famous atomistic doctrine.

A similarly skeptical view was advocated by another important Sophist, Gorgias, who taught that the truth about things is incomprehensible and that even if it could be comprehended, it could not be communicated. In practical matters Gorgias believed reasoning to be of some use, but primarily as an instrument of persuasion. He even advocated recourse to deception in rhetoric, because much of the success in persuasion depends on the power of suggestion and on the psychological peculiarities of one's listeners. From this it is but a short step to manipulation and coercion—why should they be shunned if they help to achieve the end sought?

## 2. Socrates: The Concept of the Soul

Socrates' position in philosophy can best be understood and appreciated against the background of the Sophist movement. Socrates himself was taken for a Sophist by many of his countrymen, but as Plato shows in his *Dialogues*, Socrates strongly resented being placed in that category. What is known about Socrates comes mainly from Plato's *Dialogues*. The most famous event of Socrates' life was his death, or rather, the few hours preceding the moment of his death. In the Dialogue entitled *Phaedo*, Plato describes the last hours of Socrates' life, after the Athenian Court had condemned him to drink a cup of hemlock (399 B.C.). Socrates has left no written work at all. His reason for not writing is interesting and reveals something about his view of the nature of reasoning. Socrates said, on one occasion, that as a conversationalist, a book is dead. When a reader questions what a book says and turns to it for a response, the book repeats the same answer over and over again. This remark could be taken as a dramatic illustration that the essence of thinking consists in live exchange; comprehension is a kind of growth, or development, and as such it cannot be *contained* in any finished statement. Perhaps this was also a reason why Plato chose to present Socrates' views in dialogue form, often leaving questions unanswered.

There is a problem in deciding which views are to be ascribed to Socrates and which were contributed by Plato. The problem arises not only because Socrates refused to write anything down, but also because Plato credits Socrates with originating many of the idea which Plato was ready to accept and to defend. Especially in Plato's earlier writings, Socrates dominates the scene and is the spokesman of ideas with which Plato obviously agreed and which he came to develop in his own way. Indeed even scholars find it extremely difficult to state with authority where Socrates' thought ends and Plato's begins. Some things, however stand out as obviously representing the Socratic point of view, and they deserve attention independently of Plato's further development of them.

Socrates was born in 469 B.C., the son of a stonecutter and a midwife. During his lifetime Athens passed through the glorious period of Pericles' rule, when the Parthenon rose in beauty and Phidias created his famous sculptures. Aeschylus had produced his great dramatic plays, and Socrates may have seen some of Euripides' and Sophocles' dramas on the stage. Socrates himself was later depicted satirically, suspended from the ceiling in a basket, in Aristophanes' play *The Clouds*. Socrates was present at its performance and enjoyed it. The flowering of arts coincided with Athens' military and political successes, but in the latter years of Socrates' life Athens declined in power and deteriorated politically. His death can be attributed at least in part to the political and moral upheavals which Athens was then undergoing.

According to some conjectures, Socrates supported himself by following his father's profession and did some work as a sculptor, but his notorious and preferred occupation was to engage his fellow men in conversation whenever and wherever he could find them: in the streets, at the marketplace, at banquets. In fact, Socrates was thought by many to be a Sophist, a teacher who charges money for instruction. During his trial Socrates denied that he was a Sophist and that he ever charged anyone for listening to what he had to say. He cited his well-known poverty as proof. Socrates' conception of his own activity was very different from that the Sophists had of theirs. This difference was extremely important to him and demonstrated some of Socrates' main philosophical and ethical convictions.

The dictum according to which Socrates proceeded was: "The unexamined life is not worth living." He rejected the Sophists' skeptical conclusions as premature. He warned against the mistake of "misology"—the hatred of reasoning. This mistake arises in the same way as does misanthropy. Having been disappointed again and again by a great many people, one may conclude that no one is good or trustworthy. However, this summary dismissal of the whole human race is unjust, for there may be some people who deserve trust and respect. Similarly with reasoning: having noticed again and again how arguments break down, one may conclude that no reasoning leads to sound and true conclusions. This, too, is a mistake. Both the misanthropists and misologists project their personal disappointments on the whole state of affairs which, in reality, may differ entirely from the way in which their disappointments prompt them to perceive it.

One principle to which Socrates frequently returns in his discussion is that a person who is aware of his ignorance on some point is better off than the one who is not aware of it. In a sense, this principle acknowledges what the Sophists made so much of: it is *disappointing* to discover one's ignorance. The difference between the Sophists and Socrates lies in the interpretation of this disappointment. The Sophists took it as a sign of the intellect's impotence, whereas Socrates saw in it a sign of intellectual health. For the question can be asked—and Socrates proceeded to ask it: Why should there be a disappointment upon discovering one's shortcomings? If a person experiences disappointment over his ignorance, this means that something in him or her has the desire to know and to understand. Thus, the Sophists fail to give the right interpretation of the human response to a discovery of ignorance. Socrates' claim is that to realize one's ignorance is to be better off than not to realize it; for then one is able to transcend one's ignorance. For what is it in me that judges and condemns my ignorance? How could I experience a disappointment over my errors and inconsistencies unless I had the impetus and capacity to correct them? To recognize one's error is to be no longer victimized by it. It is to be free to seek and possibly discover a better explanation, a truer understanding of things.

This conscious drive toward truth and understanding Socrates connected with the idea of the soul. Indeed, according to one important Socratic scholar, A.E. Taylor, "It was Socrates who, as far as can be seen, created the conception of the *soul* . . . something which is the seat of (a man's) normal waking intelligence and moral character."[2] Socrates' position regarding the possibility of knowledge may be compared with that of someone who remarks that not everything is wrong with the world as long as there are pessimists in it. This paradoxical observation takes into account what Socrates noted about the phenomenon of disappointment with one's own ignorance: the disappointment, like the pessimism, is a sign of health, since both *deplore* the observed condition. But to deplore something is to see it against the background of its contrast. The capacity to see the contrast and to be affected by it Socrates attributed to the activity of the soul.

Armed with this conviction of a positive tendency in human nature, Socrates went on to map out the procedures by which it may be helped to express itself. The context within which the affirmative action of the soul asserts itself is the gradual elimination of error. The work of the mind consists in the process of clarification. For example, consider an idea such as that of piety or justice. There are several possible definitions of it. Will they stand up when we subject them to examination using as standards those bits of knowledge which as far as we can see are sound and solid? One person may claim that the definition of piety can accommodate instances in which a son accuses his own father of murder, even though it is questionable that it was a case of intentional killing. Another may claim that justice is equivalent to the interest of the stronger. Yet another may defend a concept of moral rightness that allows him to violate a legally reached verdict of the court because he believes himself harmed by it. What consequences would the acceptance of such definitions have for the order and well-being of the society and of the individuals comprising it? Would life in such a society be worth living?

Socrates decided to devote his life to the exploration of the ways in which the concepts people use in thought and action are related to other beliefs they are also inclined to hold. He soon discovered that there is a widespread tendency to resist such an examination and clarification. When one's pet beliefs and prejudices are exposed as vacuous, the result may be embarrassment and resentment. A sluggish horse resents the gadfly that causes it to bestir itself. The same sluggishness and inertia are exhibited by our habitual modes of thinking, even though, when burdened by contradictions and inconsistencies, our vision is obstructed and our effectiveness is diminished. To be a human gadfly, which Socrates consciously chose to be, can be a dangerous profession. Indeed, Socrates' questioning offended many powerful Athenian politicians and guardians of conventional views, finally resulting in his condemnation and death.

Aristotle later summarized Socrates' most important contributions by saying that he introduced "inductive arguments and universal definitions" into philosophy. The Socratic method, as we see from Plato's dialogues, consisted in testing a given definition by asking its proponent to say which of its consequences and implications he would be prepared to accept. If the definition was poorly thought out, it would quickly turn out that even its proponent could not accept some of the consequences obviously entailed by it. In such a case one would have the choice of either keeping the definition and thus continuing to hold self-contradictory beliefs, or changing it so as to remove the difficulty. A definition which could survive such questions would be entitled to universal acceptance.

In contrast to the Sophists, Socrates dedicated himself to the task of replacing erroneous, internally inconsistent, and mutually contradictory beliefs by opinions which are in harmony with sound principles and will stand up under critical scrutiny. This he found to be a liberating and fulfilling activity. It also supported his view of the soul as the seat of intelligence and character. This is why he was inclined to link knowledge with virtue, and ignorance with vice. In the long run, *doing* what is right depends on *knowing* what is right. It was inconceivable to Socrates that a person could know the good and still not do it. His failure to do it would be a sign that somehow he did not quite see the whole picture accurately; he was deluded in some respect and so chose the lesser good, mistaking it for the greater good. Thus, to prefer what is worse to what is better is due to ignorance, to a fixation on some aspect of the total picture which prevents one from seeing it aright. It has been objected that Socrates was simply blind to the fact that people choose evil paths consciously, knowing full well that they are evil. However, the matter is far from being easily settled. The phenomenon of self-deception has been getting considerable attention in recent years. Even when doing evil, some philosophers claim today, one must convince oneself that somehow, in some sense one is doing good. Even a criminal may feel that he is "justified" in performing criminal acts; he wouldn't do them if he did not believe them to be right, at least for him. In cases like this, a Socratic comment, "He does not know what he is doing," is quite appropriate. He does not know, in the sense that he incorrectly thinks that only *his* aims are at stake and that his victim's aims are irrelevant.

Socrates' linking of morality with knowledge, a union of the true with the good, is rounded out by his conviction that somehow human nature echoes the reality of things. He objected to Anaxagoras' interpretation of Mind as the explanatory principle, because Anaxagoras did not inquire into the *value* of things and processes. To know anything properly we must also understand in what ways it is "for the best." Socrates saw in all things a natural bent to realize some good, some value. This principle of value is not limited to humanity—it permeates the whole universe. Although Socrates did not develop this idea in any detail, he nevertheless held it to be true—all the Greeks tended to see the whole cosmos as a living animal, animated by inherent purposiveness. Plato proceeded to elaborate these Socratic hints into a full-fledged philosophical view, of which, as we shall see, the Theory of Forms is the cornerstone. Socrates seemed satisfied to proclaim the human soul, with its craving for truth, goodness, and beauty, to be indestructible and immortal, because he was convinced that in being able to judge the body, to examine and question all its impulses and inclinations, the soul was superior and thus entitled to act as its guide. However, if the soul has this special role in determining what is right and good for the body to do, it must be lodged in a dimension different from the physical and therefore not subject to the laws of physical reality. In *Phaedo* Plato reconstructs Socrates' arguments for the soul's immortality. A fuller account of this argument includes views to which Plato himself probably contributed. Socrates' account of the soul also includes a statement of his moral convictions, and we shall return to both of these topics.

## 3. Plato: The Theory of Forms

Socrates' personal problems stemmed in part from the difficulties of his time. He saw Athens gradually losing its position of power and authority, of political and intellectual leadership. Among the concomitant phenomena was a loss of confidence in reason, in the ability to discover principles which would make the natural world intelligible and human affairs manageable. Plato was in full sympathy with Socrates' efforts to contain the spread of skepticism initiated by the Sophists. He was too young to have been one of Socrates' most intimate friends (he was 28 when Socrates died); nevertheless, the old man's trial and death had a profound effect on the pupil. Although he had been unsure about his career up to this point, Plato then decided to become a philosopher and to begin by recording his master's memory and philosophic views. The central figure in these early Platonic dialogues is Socrates. Plato's motive was to transform the intellectual and political climate of his time, but shocked by the extent to which society can become irrational and unjust, he concluded that nothing short of rethinking the whole foundation of knowledge and of political structure would cure Athen's ills. Nothing could remedy the situation until truly wise men became rulers and were given the opportunity to apply their wisdom to all human affairs.

Plato proceeded to found the first university, called the Academy, which flourished for 900 years. As director of the Academy for its first 40 years, he made it a center of intellectual activity. Not content with merely training young men for public offices, he also emphasized the study of mathematics, astronomy, harmonics, and other scientific and philosophical subjects. The study of geometry was a prerequisite for further inquiries, hence the inscription over the Academy's door: "No one without geometry may enter." The conviction that mathematics must stand at the center of the curriculum points to Pythagorean influence. As we have seen, the Pythagoreans believed that the study of numbers and relations was more likely to yield knowledge than was inquiry into what things are made of. Plato also believed that the discovery of principles and patterns should be the aim of philosophical investigations. This conviction was reflected in all subjects taught at the Academy, some of which Plato chose to discuss in his dialogues.

On some occasions Plato was tempted to think that, given an opportunity to educate a living ruler, he could teach him to be a philosopher-king. Such an opportunity presented itself when he was invited to the court of Syracuse. However, Plato's attempt to influence the thinking of King Dionysus ended in failure. It was the all-to-human politics and personal ambitions which stood in the way of philosophical instruction. Plato had to give up his project and barely escaped living out his life in slavery. His two trips to Syracuse must have contributed to his subsequent disillusionment about the possibility of bringing about immediate reforms in human affairs. Some of this disillusionment is reflected in the long, somber work *The Laws*, which was completed in Plato's later years. He died at the age of 80 while attending a wedding.

Plato's Socrates was impressed by the human ability to distinguish between a correct and incorrect account of things. How is it that persons can be led away from an erroneous conception toward a true one? How is it possible for a person to *accept* a correction, to *admit* that one was wrong in believing something? Socrates noted that the process of teaching requires the learner's active participation. There is a difference between a pupil's parrot-like "yes" and a thoughtful "Yes, now I see!" In one of the dialogues, *Meno*, Socrates shows that the capacity to learn is prior to the capacity to teach. In fact, he exaggerates his point by saying that in the teacher-learner situation, there is really no teaching going on apart from helping the learner to see for herself. The teacher is not putting anything in the learner's head; he merely helps her to realize for herself what is true. Obviously, the question of whether there is any teaching going on depends on what one understands by "teaching." If "teaching" means a literal imprinting of something on the learner's mind without even trying to understand what is going on and thus remaining completely passive, then one might agree with Socrates that a teacher does not teach. However, if "teaching" means helping the learner by asking her questions, making suggestions, and calling attention to some things that the learner has failed to notice, then obviously teaching is instrumental in the learner's coming to understand and know something.

In *Meno*, Socrates sets a problem to a slave boy who had never done any geometry. At first, the boy tries to guess what the answer might be, but Socrates shows him that the guesses are wrong. By leading the boy to see in detail what the various aspects of the problem are, through asking further questions and suggesting alternatives, Socrates succeeds in leading the boy to see the right solution to the problem. Throughout the discourse, Socrates is anxious to emphasize that each step in the progression from ignorance to correct understanding is the boy's own. Some of the steps are so minute that even the most obtuse pupil should be able to progress, thus leaving the readers of *Meno* with the feeling that it is unfair of Socrates to claim that he is not teaching the boy anything and that the boy's answers are "from his own head." However, the point that Socrates is trying to drive home is that without the boy's grasping for himself what each step, no matter how minute, *means* in this search for the right solution, the "teaching" could not possibly succeed.

For Socrates, this human capacity to understand, to see something in the right way, is extraordinary and fundamental. It is a remarkable capacity to be able to have an insight into the correct nature of some geometric relations, to be able to *see* them, not in the sense of visually perceiving a diagram on paper, but in the sense of understanding the relationships and being able to explain them. In fact, it is so remarkable that it requires an explanation. It is false to say that what a boy sees with his eyes, e.g., the diagram on the paper, simply *causes* the boy to have the corresponding understanding. For if this were so, the mere sight of the diagram would implant or imprint the requisite understanding. However, prior to the boy's grasping the relationship correctly—possibly with a "teacher's" help—the same visual structure did not generate such understanding. Imagine looking at a diagram of a geometrical problem prior to having it explained, and having understood it, looking at it again. What one sees with one's eyes is the same—the paper, the lines, the angles, the intersections—nothing has changed; the perceptual content is the same. However, the state of mind is different. Since this difference is not due to the change in perceptual, material circumstances, what does it amount to?

Socrates saw a need at this point to introduce a theory: the doctrine of recollection. We have already noted that in his view the capacity to understand and to judge is lodged in the soul. It is the boy's soul, then, that knows the truth about the geometric relations. But since the soul did not get this knowledge from the material, perceptual content, where did it get it from? From a previous encounter with the truth exemplified in that content, answers Socrates. This is the doctrine of recollection, or reminiscence. The process of teaching is the process of aiding one to remember correctly. As Socrates explained it, the concepts relevant to the boy's seeing the solution to the problem were present in him, but they were not properly understood by him. Socrates' questioning stirred these concepts and helped the boy to arrange them in the right order and in the right relationship. Yet, both his ability to say yes at each advance in the demonstration and his assent to the truth of what is being shown testifies to his previous contact with the truth as a disembodied soul. It is the soul that knows, and it is the soul that brings this knowledge to the person when he knows something truly.

This is the point at which Plato—with Socrates as his spokesman—invokes the Theory of Forms in order to supplement the doctrine of recollection. What does the soul know? The answer is: the Forms of anything. Thus, there must be a realm wherein the Forms reside. This realm is not material or temporal—it is eternal, outside of temporal reference. This is why the soul, since it exhibits knowledge of Forms, must also be eternal, or immortal. How otherwise could we explain its having knowledge?

It is important to understand the logical origin of Plato's Theory of Forms. It is invoked to *explain* some human capacities. When we have a concept of anything, this concept is not identical with the thing to which it refers. Consider any familiar object, say, a bed. Our concept of it is certainly not the object itself, for there are many beds and many kinds of them. Beds may be made of different materials and have very different shapes, yet they correspond to the same concept. Nor is the concept an image of a bed, and for the same reason—I can have images of very different beds, some big, some small, some rectangular, or some square. Yet I would still call them by the same general name "bed." How can I do this? Plato's answer is that I have a Form of Bed in my mind or my soul, and that Form tells me what the object is.

We can also see how this theory connects with the Socratic-Platonic quest for correct definitions. Before a child learns the meaning of "bed," he may use the word to refer to tables, benches, boats, or hammocks. Thus, he will make mistakes, because he does not truly understand the meaning of "bed." By removing all inappropriate connotations from his erroneous concept of bed, he will gradually refine it; he will *limit* the concept to only the right objects; in other words, he will delimit, or define, the word properly. Thus, clarity and understanding are reached through the process of removing error, and the ideal destination is the concept which is no longer contaminated by imperfections. Plato's Form of Bed meets this requirement.

The person who has worked his way out of confusions, contradictions, and misidentifications will be closest to the Forms and thus will be in possession of true definitions. This means that he will no longer mistake any particular thing in the world for its Form. The Form refers to all the things that exemplify it, but it is not any one or all of them. Plato's explanation is to say that the Forms exist in the Intellectual world, and only their manifestations inhabit the visible, material world.

To show what he means by this distinction, Plato invokes an analogy. We sometimes mistake the shadows of things for the things themselves. Of course, shadows have some features in common with the things of which they are shadows, for example, the shape. We can learn something about a thing by looking at its shadow. However, shadows are not the real things themselves; they are, so to speak, imperfect copies of those things. Think of the Forms, says Plato, as related to the things that exemplify them in the same way as real things are reflected in their shadows. If we introduce the notion of degrees of reality, the degree of reality of shadows is lower than that of things. Similarly, things are less real than their Forms. Any particular thing is like a shadow of its Form. It is a copy or imitation and, Plato adds, always less perfect than the Form itself. It is less perfect because it does not capture or manifest the total reality of the Form, simply because another part of that reality is realized in other things modeled on the same Form.

Following through on this line of reasoning, Plato concludes that in addition to the imperfect material world existing in time, there is also the timeless, perfect World of Forms. This timeless realm consists of eternal patterns of everything, which is defectively manifested in the temporal world. This includes not only the models of material things such as trees and beds, but also the ideal patterns and principles of relationships such as justice, courage, or beauty, which are to some degree at work in the actual, existing world. Human relationships and institutions often exhibit some degree of justice, and they can do so only because they are trying to approximate the ideal of Justice itself, which is lodged in the eternal Realm of Forms. To perceive beauty in a flower or in a human face is to be reminded of the reality of Absolute Beauty which is reflected only in part in the perceived material object and is not exhausted by any collection of actual, beautiful things. A wise person will conclude that all beautiful things only partake in a pattern which transcends them all and is more beautiful than any and all of them. This is the sense in which a philosopher might reject this world; she finds it inadequate when judged by standards accessible to her soul when the soul is impressed by the ideal of knowledge, beauty, and love.

Here, we are approaching the heart of Platonism: all things seen remind us of their origin and grounding in the realities unseen but comprehended by the power of thought. Philosophical activity aims at distilling from one's perceptions and one's total experience those aspects that are not at the mercy of time and change. When a mathematical discovery is made, its truth is not dependent on the time and place in which the discovery is made. The discovery *is* so dependent, but its truth is not. When one has the concept of an object, one knows what the object signifies, even though all actual objects answering to the specifications of the concept are destroyed. When one understands the workings of a certain law of nature, one can explain why some things happen the way they do. The events are in time, but the law itself is not. "Time is the moving image of eternity," said Plato. In order to understand how things in the world behave, we must go beyond them to realities which are reflected in the world. They are reflected imperfectly, but it is possible to discover what they are trying to reflect.

The function of Forms is multiple. First they provide the goal of all true definitions—showing us what anything really is. As such, they are ideals of knowledge. The philosopher's goal is to work his way through the shadowy world of temporal appearances to the luminous world of timeless truths. In addition, Plato's World of Forms also operates in a causal, dynamic way. Plato here follows the typical Greek tendency to regard the world as a living, animated being. What *moves* the world? What is responsible for the ceaseless change and activity in it? Again, the answer is the Forms. By virtue of their perfection, the Forms elicit in everything an impulse to imitate them. Things try to imitate their Forms. To the extent that they succeed in doing so, they participate in the Forms. This means that the world as it is cannot be wholly bad; there is at least as much good in it as is appropriated from the value and the beauty of the World of Forms. But it is not something which could be ever declared wholly good, because imitation and participation never come close to the full perfection of the objects of their participation and imitation.

The relationship between the two worlds imbues Platonism with a strain which has become dominant in the subsequent Western tradition. Life is a sphere of exertion, of dynamic activism. Life is *worth* living because it includes the potentiality of moving in the direction of ideals. Although sometimes a valley of tears, life is permeated by visions of love and beauty. Life is full of error, but only against the background of possible truth. In this dynamic, practical function, the Forms also provide us with our moral ideals, on which we shall reflect further in a later section.

## 4. Aristotle: The Purposive Universe

The continuity of Greek philosophy in its classical period was due in part to the personal relations of its three brilliant thinkers: Socrates, Plato, and Aristotle. Aristotle was a Macedonian, born in 384 B.C. in Stagira, where his father was the official physician to the king of Macedon. At the age of 17 he was sent to Plato's Academy in Athens, where he spent the next 20 years of his life. He was recognized by Plato as a brilliant student and thinker, but toward the end, the philosophical disagreements between teacher and pupil became rather serious. Nevertheless, the Platonic influence remained dominant in Aristotle's thought, although he rejected some of its basic doctrines.

Aristotle's life was destined to impinge on another important person, a young boy later designated by history as Alexander the Great. Alexander's father, Philip, the king of Macedonia, asked Aristotle to tutor his son, which Aristotle did for three years. At the age of 16, Alexander was made Regent of Macedon when his father left on an expedition against some Greek cities. After Philip's death, Alexander, at the age of 20, became the king of Macedon, which by then dominated all Greece, thus beginning his spectacular career as the conqueror of Persia. Aristotle returned to Athens and established the Lyceum, a school which rivaled Plato's Academy in achievement and influence. For 12 years, until Alexander's death in 323 B.C., Aristotle both directed the Lyceum and produced an amazing amount of philosophical and scientific research. In contrast to the Academy, the Lyceum included the pursuit of natural sciences and history. It had a large library and the first known biological laboratory; it is likely that his father's medical career had something to do with Aristotle's scientific and clinical interests.

The relationship between Aristotle and his famous pupil remained cordial. Alexander not only helped him to establish the Lyceum, but also sent specimens of plants, animals, and other curious objects from conquered territories. In addition, Aristotle collected manuscripts and maps. He held regular lectures, on both technical subjects for advanced students and popular subjects for general audiences. One of his great achievements was the classification of knowledge into various disciplines. Indeed, the divisions Aristotle introduced have remained intact to this very day. While at the Lyceum, he wrote treatises on logic, physics, biology, meteorology, ethics, esthetics, and many other subjects. Also among his interests was politics. He collected digests of the constitutions of 158 Greek city-states, in order to study and compare them. It is not surprising that Thomas Aquinas referred to Aristotle as "The Philosopher" and that Dante called him "the master of all who know."

After Alexander's death in 323 B.C., Aristotle's position became somewhat precarious, because of the strong anti-Macedonian feeling in Athens. In order to prevent Athenians from "sinning twice against philosophy," Aristotle prudently left the city. He died one year later in Chalcis, after a flare-up of a digestive disease. His will, which has been preserved, reveals him as a thoughtful provider, devoted to his family and friends and generous to his slaves, some of whom were to be freed and none of whom were to be sold.

Aristotle's philosophy expresses a fully developed, systematic world view. His intellectual debt to Socrates and Plato is obvious, but he proceeds to transform the insights of his predecessors into a highly organized conceptual structure. Aristotle was the first to demonstrate that philosophical thinking can result in a conceptual *system* in which all important ideas are related to one another in a logical way. Aristotle's example was followed by subsequent philosophers up to the very present, although in recent times there have appeared strong criticisms of this desire to produce philosophical systems. In fact, the very idea of a philosophical system seems repugnant to many thinkers. The nineteenth-century German philosopher Friedrich Nietzsche expressed a radical suspicion of what he called "the will to a system." The danger of which he warned, and which subsequently has been confirmed by many other philosophers, rests in the tendency of systematic thought to ignore actually existing differences and distinctions, forcing them into the philosopher's favored conceptual framework. As a result, we get a distorted account of experience.

Nevertheless, even those modern philosophers who believe that the reality of human experience is too rich and too multifarious to be captured in a neat, precise, and simple conceptual scheme still tend to agree that to understand things is to see how the concepts which we employ in our accounts are related to one another. In fact, philosophy could be seen as a kind of conceptual geography, showing us how we understand, or find our way in the world. Philosophy helps us to map out our conceptual territory — it can show us *how* we think about the world.

Aristotle was a most effective pioneer in this enterprise. He thought that the way we understand anything could be shown by means of questions we may ask about it. The kinds of questions we ask reveal the *categories* of our thought, the universal forms of predication. Consider some familiar thing, an oak, for example. In order to understand it, to make sense of what the word refers to, you ask a number of different questions. Each kind of question reveals what Aristotle called a category.

| *Question* | *Category* |
|---|---|
| 1. What is it? | Substance |
| 2. How tall is it? | Quantity |
| 3. How does it look? | Quality |
| 4. What is its bearing on others? | Relation |
| 5. Where is it? | Place |
| 6. When does (did) it exist? | Time |
| 7. How is it growing (straight, crooked)? | Posture |
| 8. What state is it in (shedding leaves)? | State |
| 9. What is it doing (growing, breathing)? | Action |
| 10. What is acting on it (wind)? | Being acted on, Passivity |

It is not difficult to notice that the first category, that of substance, plays a very different logical role from all the others. This category helps to pick out, to identify, the thing about which all the other questions are being asked. This distinction is reflected in a basic structure of our language. By means of language we can pick out a subject and attribute predicates to it. "The oak is tall." "The cloud is white." For Aristotle, the category of substance helps to connect our thoughts with reality. When we succeed in picking out something by means of a word, we are acknowledging its existence, its being. Reality, or being, manifests itself to us in individual substances, in particular things. Substance, "in the truest and primary and most definite sense of the word," is the individual. If there were no individual things—people, other living beings, physical objects—there would be nothing for language to describe; our thought would have nothing to hook on to. On the other hand, when we identify individual things, we do so by a word which has a common meaning. The word applies not only to that one thing, but also to many other things like it, if they exist. Thus, to say that an individual substance is a man places it into the general class of human beings. Human beings, in turn, belong to an even wider class of individuals, namely animals. Both animality and humanity are substances for Aristotle, but not in the primary sense; according to him, they are only secondary substances.

In examining individual substances we will discover that some of their attributes are essential to them, while others are merely accidental. Among the essential characteristics of an oak is its ability to absorb nourishment from the soil. That the oak happens to grow here, rather than two miles from here, is not essential to its being what it is. If carefully transplanted to another location, the oak would still be the *same* oak. However, it wouldn't be an oak if it did not have the capacity to nourish itself through its roots and leaves or if its leaves were shaped like those of a fir tree.

The connection between the primary and secondary substance of a thing is not easy to express. The difficulty lies in giving a satisfactory account of how we come to refer to the same thing by the same word. Aristotle uses the term *induction* here. Having observed some things repeatedly, we may notice that they have some common property. That common property, if it is essential to the thing in question, can be called its secondary substance, or a *universal*. So we may say that universals are found in particular things. We may remember that for Plato the very fact that the same general property can be found in many different individuals justifies the conclusion that that property is separable from particular individuals. This consideration led to Plato's Theory of Forms. Aristotle did not go along with his teacher on this point. To him, universals are not separable from particulars or, as he preferred to put it, from individual substances. Universals are always *in* particulars. The separation is possible in thought, but not in reality. Hence, for Aristotle, there is no independent Realm of Forms.

Aristotle also uses the concept of form and contrasts it with the concept of matter, but he insists on their inseparability. There is no matter without form and no form without matter. But matter is not identified just with some physical substratum. Indeed, Aristotle's concept of matter is wholly relative. Matter is not necessarily something material, physical, but it is the contextual condition which is then trans*formed*, given a new form. In one context something can be matter; in another, form. Consider our oak. What is its matter? Its matter is the ingredients which "give rise to it" and make it up— protoplasm, soil, mineral, water, air, sunlight. The form is the oak's natural shape and typical behavior. However, cut down the oak and make a statue out of it; the oak has become matter and the statue form. Should the oak be taken to the paper mill and converted into paper, it would then take on the *form* of paper. Again, the reams of paper may provide matter for books or newspapers.

The way things change or are transformed is open to further analysis. Aristotle believed that one can understand change better if one isolates what he called the four *causes* of change. For example, any process of making must start with a material to be worked. A sculptor needs wood for a statue. This wood constitutes (1) the *material* cause of the statue. The wood will remain mere material unless and until it is actually worked on by the sculptor. Hence, the sculptor's actual work constitutes (2) the *efficient* cause. The sculptor's design or the shape which he ultimately wants the piece of wood to have provides (3) the *formal* cause. Finally, the description of the process of this change would not be complete if we did not mention what the sculptor wanted to achieve, namely, the creation of a work of art fulfilling a certain purpose, something worth looking at and taking pleasure in, such as a statue for a temple. This Aristotle called (4) the *final* cause.

Although all causes should be mentioned in a true account of the change taking place, some may be more informative than others. There may be some question whether it is proper to refer to the material itself as a cause, for it merely takes into account that any process must start from something. But Aristotle did not think that all causes have equally important explanatory functions. For him, the final cause occupies a privileged position. If you don't know what the final cause of a process is, you are deprived of a particularly important piece of information. Suppose I describe to you an acorn in great detail, mentioning its appearance, its chemical composition, its molecular structure, etc., but I never mention to you that under normal conditions it will develop into an oak. Doesn't the failure to provide this bit of information affect your knowledge of what the acorn *is*?

Aristotle believed that the knowledge of final causes provides us with clues about the real nature of anything. To know what a thing is, is to know what it can become. To make this point, Aristotle also employed the terminology of potentiality and actuality. To know things is to know their potentialities, but unless these potentialities are actually present in them as their final forms, the things will never *realize* their potentialities.

The distinction between essential and accidental attributes of a substance is connected with still another basic Aristotelian concept, namely, *entelechy*. Some processes have a natural goal; the goal of an acorn for example, is to become an oak. This means that in each acorn there is a formal organizing force at work which leads it to its natural destiny. Aristotle calls this energizing life force entelechy, the principle of growth in which the essential nature of a substance is being gradually realized. In natural processes the formal and final causes appear to overlap or coincide. The end for the sake of which an acorn exists is to achieve the form of an oak. Here, Aristotle's distinction between matter and form, and potentiality and actuality reinforce one another and merge into the concept of entelechy.

Aristotle also thought that to know the final form of a substance is to know its soul. He extended the notion of soul to all living beings. "Soul" is the name for the particular kind of entelechy, or principle of growth, inherent in a substance; it is its essential characteristic nature. For plants, this nature consists in the ability to absorb nourishment from their environment and to use it for sustenance. Thus, a plant could be said to have a nutritive soul. Animals, in addition to this, also have a sensitive soul, since it is essential to their nature that they be able to both feel and move themselves. The souls of human beings since they are also animals, share these characteristics with the rest of the vegetative and animal kingdom, but in addition, they possess another basic feature, namely, rationality. Hence, Aristotle defines human beings as rational animals.

For Aristotle, the world manifests a hierarchy, a dynamic order of forms seeking to express their natures or souls. The matter of each substance is "pulled" in the direction of its corresponding form. Thus, the whole universe is pervaded by purpose. The Greek word for "purpose" is "telos"; hence, Aristotle's universe can be described as teleological. Telos is at the same time a cause of and a reason for a process. In substances lacking explicit rationality, the telos is unconscious; nevertheless, its presence explains why anything becomes what it is. In that sense, natural processes are rational, for they exhibit an order which can be understood by describing the purposive causes at work.

The physical metaphor of "pull" is very helpful in understanding Aristotle's system. In fact, as we shall see later, with the rise of modern science in the sixteenth and seventeenth centuries, this metaphor was replaced by that of "push," in which the efficient causes were given greater prominence, and Aristotle's final causes fell into disrepute. For Aristotle, however, to know the determining forms or final causes of things is to know how the universe works. As a dynamic entity, the universe as a whole must have a final cause as well. Since this cause is immaterial, Aristotle described it as Pure Form and also referred to it as Prime Mover, or God. The whole universe is a hierarchical structure of entelechies or natural processes. At the lowest end of the spectrum are undeveloped substances in which matter is dominant and form only rudimentary. As we proceed along the hierarchical scale, the formal aspect grows in importance and exerts greater dominance over the matter which it organizes. The control of form over matter increases as one proceeds toward higher natural forms.

It is logical to conclude, believed Aristotle, that at some level of reality the form reaches a state of complete dominance over matter. Falling back on the distinction between potentiality and actuality, we may describe the situation by saying that at the highest level of reality, there is no unrealized potentiality and that the substance in question is indeed Pure Actuality. This is another term for God. Since every potentiality is already realized in God, God is not moving toward further realization. However, God's very presence in the scheme of things acts as a teleological pull on all lower hierarchically arranged substances; *they* are moved by God. The Prime Mover provides the inspiration, the reason for all the activities going on in the universe. True, God is not moved by the world and in that sense does not love it, because loving would indicate some need, some unrealized possibility. But the world is drawn toward God; it is inspired by God's perfection. The closest truthful thing that we can say about God's mode of being is that it consists in thinking about thinking; God is contemplating the unchanging perfection fully realized in himself. Since there is no unrealized matter in God's nature, no changes take place in him and the passage of time does not affect his being; God is eternal.

To the extent that we can understand the causes of things, including their potentialities and natural development, we can think God's thoughts after him. Knowledge, then, is the highest form of activity—it is a natural activity for the human kind of being. All human beings by nature desire to know, declared Aristotle. Worthwhile knowledge is not only theoretical, providing us with the information as to how things work and how they interact to form a cosmos, it is also practical, telling us what we must do in order to live up to our rational nature. Reason can be used not only to find out what the case is, but also to determine what we ought to do. In the realm of ethics and politics, man can also discover which particular goals and ends are humanly worth pursuing. Since Aristotle's contributions to this inquiry are no less interesting and important than are his contributions to the theoretical inquiries, we shall return to them when dealing with the questions of ethics.

It is no exaggeration to say that Aristotle and his intellectual predecessors *invented* Western philosophy. They discovered that the heart of philosophizing is *argument*. By "argument" is meant not the heated defense of one's favorite view, but a desire to test the claims made in order to be sure that they stand up under critical scrutiny. When a claim is put forward or a doctrine propounded, some other things will logically follow, and if we can see that these further conclusions or implications cannot be true, then we are obliged (*logically* obliged) to reject the original claim or doctrine. The form of the argument is this: If $X$ is true, then $Y$ and $Z$ would have to be true as well. But if either $Y$ or $Z$ is not true, then $X$ cannot be true either. The argument, however, need not stop here. A criticism may serve as a stimulus to a new theory, one which will not suffer from the difficulties of the old. The work of the early philosopher-scientists shows many marks of such a progressive refinement of original hypotheses.

Philosophical argument and discovery involve a movement from one position to another. If A says something, but B objects, a conversation or argument thus gets started. The Greeks' word for this was *dialectic*. That concept has been absorbed into the philosophical vocabulary, acquiring in time a variety of special technical meanings. However, in its original form it should be seen as a contrast to mythical, static thinking. Myths are not to be argued with; they are to be accepted without question. They intend to *tell* something and do not call for an intellectual response. To put forward a philosophical thesis is, however, explicitly to *invite* such a response, and this response, argument and counterargument, as we have noted, is the heart of philosophy.

A dialectical process is generated even when a person tries to think something out for herself or when, as Plato suggested, "the soul is conversing with itself." A serious process of deliberation may consist in examining what objections could be raised against the view or opinion one is inclined to hold. The dialectical exchange is clearly at work when two persons engage in a critical dialogue—reacting to each other's statements by means of objections, counterarguments, and rejoinders. There also seems to be a transpersonal, or historical, dialogue in which a mind addresses itself to problems left behind by remote contemporaries or by immediate predecessors. Sometimes the criticism may be directly and consciously addressed to views formerly propounded, but sometimes those views are no longer identified with any particular person. The views may be simply "in the air," in the climate of opinion, even though not clearly understood or articulated. Once expressed, however, no matter how tentatively, an idea may contain a germ of further thought which may grow into a fuller, more illuminating point of view.

Another important point to keep in mind is that the nature of the question tends to determine the range of appropriate answers. We have noted, for instance, that total reliance on the question "Who, or which god, is responsible for such and such an event or process?" rules out certain answers. The question *presupposes* that a reference to intentions or actions of gods is expected in an answer. In contrast, the questions "What is the world made of?" or "How is the world run and ordered?" invite very different sorts of answers. This is why important intellectual breakthroughs come when it occurs to someone to ask new and different questions.

Another way of putting this is to say that questions are not conceptually neutral. They may involve or presuppose certain basic concepts which then, not surprisingly, crop up in the answers the question generates. Once the question is asked, a variety of answers may be given, but in some sense, if they are answers at all, they will reflect presuppositions built into the question.

When philosophical inquiry revolves around one key question or, in other words, when one basic concept dominates the inquiry, the philosophical analysis is likely to be one-sided. Once adopted, a concept has its own inertia, and this tends to make us blind to counterexamples and limit us to only one way of looking at things. Even today, we are just as guilty of this tendency as were the early Greek thinkers. What is important, however, is that the questions asked by the Greeks initiated an ongoing inquiry which contributed to a more penetrating and more effective understanding of the world in which we live. The process of inquiry may, of course, significantly transform the original questions. Our sophisticated concepts of matter and energy, for example, are a far cry from the initial gropings for the basic stuff, but the scientific quest for the underlying reality of all phenomena was inaugurated by the Greek philosopher-scientists, who were bold and imaginative enough to ask brand-new, unheard-of, questions.

The discovery of the philosophical method, centrally important as it was, does not constitute the only great achievement of the Ancients. They also initiated inquiries whose main *substance* has had a tremendous influence on all subsequent thought. When Plato concluded that what we are aware of in the world are mere appearances and that reality is to be found behind or beyond appearances, in the World of Forms, he set into motion two opposing tendencies. One tendency was to regard the verdicts of the senses, the immediately available phenomena of perception, with suspicion and even with skepticism. The other tendency was to give the entire course of human existence an idealistic slant: what distinguishes us from other beings is our capacity to pursue *ideals* such as truth, beauty, and goodness. The Platonic conception of life is *aspirational*, envisaging the human career as an effort to attain perfection through rational insight and enlightened action. The pre-Socratic notion of Mind as the ordering cosmic principle was *humanized* by Socrates and Plato; each person was seen as a bearer of rationality and a potential witness of the ultimate meaning of the universe. This emphasis on each individual's capacity to participate in that meaning through proper thought and actions has become the cornerstone of all subsequent philosophical and religious versions of affirming the supreme worth and dignity of every human being.

Plato's idealistic-perfectionist tendency was muted by his depreciation of material phenomena. Not only was matter radically distinguished from the forms which it could embody, it was also seen as a barrier to perfection, as an obstacle to be overcome. Socrates, as we shall see, complained about the constant distracting demands of the body. That deprecating note can be regarded as an obverse of the idealistic thrust. Because mortal life is often difficult, disappointing, and painful, one may look upon it as inferior to the possibilities which the mind and the heart can envisage.

This Platonic otherworldly note, relegating the material world to an inferior status, is transmuted by Aristotle into something different. Coleridge had remarked that every Western philosopher after the Greek classical period could be labeled as either a Platonist or an Aristotelian. This extremely broad generalization may not be very helpful in any specific case, but it calls attention to a basic difference of philosophic vision. When Aristotle insisted that form is to be sought *in* matter, he thereby elevated the status of the material world. The word "nature" points to a synthesis of the material and the formal aspects. It is *natural* for things to be what they are; by exhibiting a certain form, shape, pattern, or function, they serve the purpose of endowing matter with meaning and value. Aristotelianism is *naturalism*; it emphasizes the possibility of things to actualize their potentialities. To the extent that a thing or a being does actualize its potentialities, it reaches its natural and characteristic state.

Consequently, it is fitting and proper to pay attention to natural forms and to seek fulfillment of natural capacities. We can learn what things are and what they can become by observing their development. The work of the naturalist, or the scientist, is therefore to be valued for disclosing to us the natural order of things. Indeed, the positive connotation which the word "nature" has for us has something to do with its etymological Latin connection with birth, origin, new beginning, life, and fulfillment. "Nature" is one of the keynotes of Western philosophy. It embodies the vision of the world in which we are at home, to which we naturally belong, and in which we are called upon to fulfill our highest potential. No less important than the Platonic idealism, this vision is positive and affirmative, although the focus shifts away from eternity and otherworldliness toward life and development in time.

This does not mean that Aristotle repudiated the Platonic picture altogether. As we have seen, the concept of God as Pure Form is still a necessary aspect of his philosophical system. The idea of perfection still governs this world, and human activities should be governed by it. But the entire sweep of the cosmic drama displays excellences of various kinds, from the simple to the most complex, hierarchically arranged on the scale of value.

Both Plato and Aristotle were rationalists. They believed that we can understand the things and phenomena in the world by grasping their universal essences. The epistemological problem about which the two great masters had serious disagreements concerns the relation of universals to the particulars which they represent or embody. Indeed, as we shall see, the problem of universals has exercised philosophers for centuries, our present age included. It is a difficult problem because it is connected with so many other key philosophical distinctions, and partly for that reason the difficulty of the problem accounts for its lasting fascination.

## Questions

1. Why did the Sophists think that their activity was valuable? To what extent do you agree with them, and in what ways would you criticize them?

2. Why did Socrates emphasize the importance of recognizing the extent of one's ignorance, and why did he attribute such a great weight to self-knowledge.

3. What considerations led Socrates and Plato to the conclusion that knowledge is really recollection?

4. What is Plato's Theory of Forms and how did he arrive at it? What roles do Forms play in Plato's philosophical system?

5. What is Aristotle's doctrine of the categories? What is their function?

6. How did Aristotle criticize Plato's Theory of Forms? How do changes in the world occur, according to Aristotle? Compare the basic similarities and differences in Plato's and Aristotle's general points of view.

7. What is the role of God in Aristotle's system?

## Notes

[1] Protagoras, as quoted by Theodor Gomperz in *The Greek Thinkers*, 4 Vols., translated by Laurie Magnus, London: John Murray, 1969, Vol. 1, p. 448.

[2] A.E. Taylor, *Socrates*, New York: Doubleday, 1953, p. 132.

# Chapter Three

# Greek Ethics

## 1. Socrates: Persons in Community

Ancient classical philosophers did not regard ethics as a separate domain of inquiry. For them, to discover the nature of human beings was also to discover how they should act. This is particularly true of Socrates. The soul, in his view, is not only the theoretical center of a human being, allowing her to know and to understand; it is also the *active* center, enabling her to do what she judges right. This intimate connection between knowing and doing is perhaps the most characteristic feature of Socrates' philosophy, succinctly summarized in his dictum: "Virtue is knowledge." Nowhere is this connection better illustrated than in Plato's account of crucial moments in Socrates' own life. It would not be an exaggeration to claim that the view of the human self as essentially a *moral* self was Socrates' discovery. We are indebted to Plato for showing us in vivid detail how this view of humanity came into existence.

The obvious place to start is Socrates' conception of his mission in life. Puzzled by the oracle's claim that he was the wisest of all men, Socrates decided to find out in what this wisdom could possibly consist. This enabled him to discover an important phenomenon: there is a tendency on the part of many, perhaps most people, to pronounce judgment on matters in which they are not competent to judge. Being competent in one area makes them think that they are entitled to judge in other areas as well, forgetting, or not realizing, that their competence may not reach *that* far. Just because I am a good carpenter does not mean that I can fix radios. A successful businessman is not necessarily

**41**

a good judge of politics or education. Socrates pointed out that to claim competence where one does not have it is careless—one does not take proper care to find out other things which would possibly make one a competent judge on matters about which one, in the present state, is ignorant. Socrates regarded this carelessness and the resultant ignorance as moral faults. It is something that one can and should remedy, by taking steps to remove one's ignorance. At least one should recognize one's ignorance and refrain from basing one's actions on it.

This point is tellingly illustrated in Socrates' encounter with the young man Euthyphro, who in the name of his concept of piety was willing to accuse his own father of murder. In the ensuing discussion it became apparent that Euthyphro had no idea of what piety consisted in, but this did not stop him from running to court to accuse his father of a heinous crime. In addition, Euthyphro's carelessness was demonstrated in his hastiness to label his father's action as murder, although the facts of the case raised serious doubts whether the label was at all applicable. Socrates believed that in bringing Euthyphro to see the glaringly inadequate basis of his action, he would shock him into a realization of the wrong he would be committing. In other words, Socrates pointed to the presence of *personal responsibility* connected with human action. If a part of our essential nature is the capacity to act, then responsibility for our actions is an inevitable corollary. Some actions are such that the agents must *take* responsibility for them. At this point Socrates regarded it as fit and proper to invoke the concept of the soul, for this concept calls attention to the fact that a person, a self, is also a decision-making center and thus accountable for the consequences of his decisions and actions.

When Socrates criticized his fellow citizens either for judging and acting on matters in which they had no competence, or for neglecting to take care of things for which they were clearly responsible, he was reminding them that these ways of behavior endangered the very core of their being, the well-being of their soul, and their moral health. Indeed, he made it his life's vocation to help people realize the close connection between reasoning soundly and acting rightly. If only he could bring his fellow citizens to exercise greater care and thoughtfulness in going about their affairs, the benefit to all would be worth the trouble. He discovered, however, that people have a tendency to regard any critic with resentment, especially if he calls attention to some possible dangers and faults in their customary ways of thinking and acting. In addition, if this kind of criticism occurs in troubled times, as in periods of political instability and insecurity, the hostility toward a person who emphasizes moral integrity may indeed become intense.

The circumstances of Socrates' incurring the wrath of many Athenians and his subsequent condemnation and death were undoubtedly complex, and Plato's account of the events is probably slanted in favor of his teacher. Nevertheless, most scholars agree that the court verdict against him was unjust and probably due, at least in part, to the personal resentment of some powerful political figures. In the *Apology* Plato gives us a picture of how Socrates defended his conviction that his "gadfly" activity was motivated by a desire to benefit not only each individual on whom he tried to exert his influence, but also Athens as a social and moral community. Socrates believed that the moral and political health of a society depends on the moral soundness of each individual citizen. This is why he went about trying to see what he could do to help as many people as possible to attain a proper understanding of important matters.

Socrates' procedure is distinctive in its reliance on individual, person-to-person encounters. The only way to reach people is to treat them as persons capable of independent judgment. We have seen that the theoretical doctrine of recollection also put the responsibility for rational judgment on the individual thinker. Until I can see for myself that something is true, until I have an "Aha, now I understand!" experience, I am relying on someone else's authority. The important thing about the doctrine of recollection is that it calls for a *personal* recollection—it is *my* soul that has to respond to the challenge of the problem, and it is I who must be the judge.

However, to *judge* something as right or wrong is to do more than just take a stand. Socrates' great contribution to the very concept of morality was his realization that judgment necessarily involves a reference to a *community* of persons. To conclude that something *is right* is to claim that more than just one person likes or wants it. There is a difference between saying "I like it" or "It is fine with me" and saying "This is the right thing to do" or "This ought to be done." One can ask whether something is a *right* thing to do only if there are *common* standards by which this rightness can be determined. If something is right in *these* circumstances, it is right in all other circumstances which are sufficiently similar. If a person does not believe that there are such common standards, the question cannot even be asked. Thus, when we say, "Yes, it is right; you ought to do it," we signal by these words that there are some common standards to which we believe the hearer to be committed as well. The hearer may, of course, reject the advice by saying that there is no such standard and that therefore he does not have an obligation to perform the action in question. But even in rejecting the speaker's conclusion, he understands it the way the speaker intended it, namely, that the question of right does presuppose a possibility of appealing to common standards.

This analysis indicates that the quest for the right thing to do is the quest for the *common* good. The person who urges others to do the right thing must herself be concerned about bringing it about; otherwise, she is not justified in even urging others to do what is right. In other words, a moral critic must speak from the position of a personal commitment to the common good. One must also demonstrate this in some manner, for otherwise one forfeits the right to be a critic, a person who urges others to do what they ought to do.

As Socrates insisted during his trial, he went about his business of persuading Athenians to change their ways because he believed to be doing it in their own interest, or in the interest of the entire Athenian community. Of course, that interest was also his own, since he was a member of that community. Nevertheless, whether a man is really committed to the common good may not be evident from what he says, especially if there is a suspicion that he has some ulterior motive or derives a personal benefit from being a critic. One of the benefits may be, of course, a sense of self-importance, or power, or pride which the individual may feel as the result of chastising others. Are there some ways of showing that these are not the reasons for which a person is engaging in the business of criticism? Did Socrates show that these were not his reasons, and if so, how did he do this?

Consider Socrates' behavior in jail after he was sentenced to death. Some of his friends arranged for his safe escape; all that was needed was his consent, which he refused to give. His best friend, Crito, tried to convince Socrates that to escape was the right thing to do. Crito argued that by remaining in prison, Socrates was not only succumbing to an unjust verdict, but also jeopardizing the future of his family, depriving his friends of continued companionship and counsel, and finally, failing in his obvious duty to save his own life. Socrates did not deny that these were powerful arguments; he did believe, however, that all of them taken together were not quite strong enough to overbalance one additional obligation which Crito had failed to mention, namely, his obligation to Athens as a community. Socrates realized that all the transactions between individuals and society must be conducted within the framework of a moral bond. This bond is established when some rights and obligations become reciprocal. The state, the society, provides the individual with some goods which only the group can provide: security, protection, education and an institutionally supervised exchange of services and transactions. By virtue of being a beneficiary of all these, the individual in fact incurs an obligation to respect and protect the framework of social practices.

This respect also includes the willingness to submit to a judgment the society may make about the fate of a citizen if it is displeased with him. If the laws of the state allow a member of the community to be put to death and if the verdict is arrived at in a lawful manner, then a moral, law-abiding individual is obligated to obey the verdict. If he does not, he is doing violence to the society by putting himself outside its laws. Of course, he has a perfect right to insist that he is innocent and that the society is making a serious mistake in imposing on him such a verdict. If, however, he has been given ample opportunity in court to defend himself, to try to persuade and convince his peers that he is innocent, and still has failed to change their minds, it would be wrong for him to take the matter into his own hands, even with the help of willing friends. Taking the matter into his own hands would demonstrate that his membership in the Athenian community was only conditional, subject to basic reservations: he is willing to obey the law only when the community agrees with him as to what is good for it; in other words, only if the community takes *his* opinion to be the ultimate opinion of what is right. If a person were to join a community on this basis, would there *be* a community? If everyone were to say: "I cooperate with you only as long as you accept *my* judgment as to what is good for you," a moral bond among individuals could not come into existence. Hence, it would be "right" for every individual to do what he thought right, for he would not be committed to anything but his own will — he would be the ultimate judge.

Under such conditions there would be no morality. If there is to be morality, individuals have to show, in their actions and not just in words, that they are acknowledging an authority not restricted to their own judgment and will. The person acknowledging such an authority must, of course, believe in its capacity to function morally in the long run. If Socrates had no hope and no expectation that Athens would continue as a viable society, that it would continue to pursue humanly desirable goals, but had to assume that its citizenry would turn into a band of anarchists and criminals, then his situation would be quite different. An individual who has lost all faith in the future moral health of his society has no reason to persist in his loyalty to it. However, it happens only very rarely and only in extreme cases that an individual arrives at the conclusion that the community is no longer worthy of allegiance and support, that it is no longer capable of being a moral community. This is not to say that it could not occur or be justified. A person may find himself in a situation where he no longer has any trust in the good will of his fellow men. If he is right about this and the members of his group are in fact totally amoral, he would be a fool to treat them as capable of establishing a moral bond with him and with one another. Yet, as long as he has not arrived at such a drastic judgment, he should respect the right of the community to demand from him the fulfillment of *his* obligations.

Socrates' opinion of Athens at the time of his trial was not negative. He did think that in this particular judgment about him, the Athenian society was morally incompetent. Indeed, Socrates was convinced that in time the Athenians would recognize their error and would repent. His conception of the Athenian community went beyond the presently existing one. There may not even be a need to wait for the arrival of the next generation. Those who err today may see their mistake tomorrow. One important way of recalling them to their senses is to demonstrate that in their midst there are persons, like Socrates, who are aware of the value and importance of respecting the moral bond.

This was an additional reason why Socrates wanted to remain in prison. His loyalty would be just another demonstration that a moral community is something *worth* saving, sometimes even at the expense of one's own life.

Socrates operated from the conviction that evil should not be repaid with evil. Obviously, the state was about to do him harm, ultimate harm. But this does not give him the right to harm in return. Actively participating in Crito's scheme to escape from jail by bribing the jailer would amount to deliberate wrongdoing. There are some things that neither friends nor society can compel a moral man to do. If by way of penalty the state commanded Socrates to kill someone, he would refuse (he actually had disobeyed an unjust order to participate in the arrest of a military leader). Thus, the moral community cannot command Socrates to *do* evil, although he may not be in a position to stop the society itself from doing evil, especially if he is the victim.

Socrates was the first Western philosopher to see clearly that morality rests on the reciprocity of rights and duties. Moral community can exist only when this is recognized. In that sense Socrates can be regarded as having created the concept of morality. We have noted before that according to some historians, he should be credited with inventing the very notion of the soul. The soul is the most intimate, precious, and irreplaceable aspect of man. A seat of understanding and knowledge, it also was thought to guide and determine a person's actions. Plato's description of various aspects of a person assigns the superior role to the rational element. A human being is not only an individual, rational animal but also a *social* animal. The considerations that should govern social relations are perhaps most dramatically and forcefully demonstrated in the *Crito*, where Socrates shows how the essential well-being of a person depends on his proper relations to others. It would not be far from the truth to declare that Socrates invented the notion of *moral community* as well. The possibility of living a good life, of searching for truth, security, and welfare, hinges on the ability of human beings to assume obligations toward others. However, to assume an obligation is to recognize that some limits must be set on one's self-assertion. Socrates introduced the notion of moral debt: if I owe something to others, it is not up to me to decide unilaterally, without a good reason, that I do not owe it to them. This was his description of his situation as recorded in the *Crito*. As a citizen of Athens, he had acquired certain obligations toward his community, and he believed that it would be wrong to abrogate them unilaterally. This is why he refused to escape from prison. What is involved in incurring a moral obligation has also been one of the key topics explored in moral and political thought ever since Socrates' pioneering efforts, and we shall encounter this problem again.

# 2. Plato: The Quest for Harmony

The Socratic conception of the soul assigned it a guiding and controlling role in human life. Although immaterial and distinct from the body, the soul was nevertheless a source of authority, prescribing the good and rational life. Plato's dialogues contain further attempts to describe what the soul is and how it acts. The Socratic influence is always pervasive; in most instances Socrates remains the main spokesman, but some of the views about to be discussed probably represent Plato's development of his teacher's ideas.

Plato recognized the presence of several different aspects of human personality. In the dialogues he actually speaks, somewhat misleadingly, of various *parts* of the soul. Perhaps these aspects can be best identified by describing their functions: (1) the appetitive, (2) the spirited, and (3) the rational.

1. Human beings naturally exhibit a desire, an appetite, for some things—they have bodily needs. These needs and desires range from the most fundamental—food, sex, physical comfort—to the most refined pleasures of the senses. The attractions supplied by the material side of our being are almost endless in their variety; a connoisseur of pleasures can vary his tastes indefinitely.

2. There is in us an ability to assert ourselves in a certain way, to concentrate our will, our energy in a certain direction. This capacity should be recognized as independent of appetites, thought Plato, because it is often mobilized against some of them and may even override them. Ambition provides a good support for the claim of the independence of this will-energy aspect: the ambitious person acts mainly from sheer ego-drive. One's actual objectives may not be very important; they may change drastically and fundamentally, but the ambition itself persists unabated.

3. We have the ability to compare, contrast, and evaluate the various appetites and drives which motivate us. Since this comparison involves a sort of overview, it enables us to determine the course which appears to us more desirable. I need not be at the mercy of my appetites and ambitions; they may be allowed to express themselves, but they may also be suppressed and controlled. This is the work of the rational element of the soul.

It should be clear that Plato's description of the three elements, or aspects, of the soul also involves an evaluation of them. Since the rational element is in a position to maintain a general overview, it is naturally entitled to leadership. It can prevent a person from acting blindly, randomly, or haphazardly. Reason and spiritedness are closer to each other than are reason and the appetites, because the commitment of the will in some definite direction provides at least a degree of control over the appetites. Consequently, the lowest on the scale is the appetitive element, for it is always at the mercy of a particular momentary attraction.

Each aspect has its corresponding moral virtue. If no appetite exercises a dominant influence but each is given due recognition, the appetitive aspect of the soul can be said to be in a state of *temperance*, or moderation. If the spirited aspect is directed toward the right objective, the resulting virtue is *courage*. If the rational element coordinates the rest of the motivational forces within a person in the right way, that person possesses the virtue of *wisdom*. There is also an additional, overall virtue which Plato designated as *justice*. This is the state of the soul in which each of the elements has reached the level of its corresponding virtue. A person who is temperate, courageous, and wise will also be just. She achieves a proper balance of the elements of her soul; all of them discharge their appropriate functions well.

In the light of such an analysis of human personality, morality enjoins us to strive toward a kind of harmony in which each aspect is properly related to all others. This state of harmony is not easy to attain, for there is a tendency, especially on the part of the two lower aspects, to go their own independent, often obstreperous, ways. Plato illustrates this effectively in the *Phaedrus*, where he equates the rational element to a charioteer trying to control two horses with very different temperaments. One of them, representing the spirited element, or the will, may respond to mere admonition. The other, representing passions or the appetites and expressing their unruly tendencies, tries to pull the chariot off course. The driver has to use all his skill and knowledge to keep the chariot going in the direction *he* wants and sets, and although he must rely on the horses to get anywhere at all, he needs to remain in full control of them.

This illustration shows that Plato does not deny the need to satisfy the appetites. Pleasure is a legitimate goal of life, provided that its pursuit is controlled by and subordinated to other goals which are dictated by reason. What is called for is discrimination and judgment. To be sure, as Socrates frequently warned, bodily pleasures can easily be distracting and may crowd out a person's higher aspiration. Furthermore, one should note that some pleasures are nothing positive in themselves; they are attendant upon some activities, like reading or rowing. Sometimes, they depend on the transition from a lack or a pain to a neutral state of calm; pleasures of food or sex arise from antecedent discomforts. There are, of course, positive pleasures, derived from the contemplation of beautiful objects. Recalling the Theory of Forms, we should realize that, as Socrates so eloquently describes in the *Symposium*, an instance of beauty is never self-sufficient in itself, but has its attractive character by virtue of participating in the Form of Beauty itself. The whole process of moral education consists in being gradually led from seeing beauty in particular things—flowers, human faces, social arrangements, celestial order—to seeing one absolute timeless Form, in which the particular manifestations partake in only a limited degree. This is true of all worthwhile experiences; they point to the ideal but never quite reach it. The ideal toward which all human action reaches out is the Form of the Good itself. This is why human life is a constant quest, a journey toward greater and greater perfection, a quest in which the state of justice—with its corresponding corollaries of wisdom, courage, and temperance—provides the aspirational dynamics of action.

Plato believed that his analysis of the individual soul could be applied, by analogy, to the society as a whole. The state, he said, is the individual writ large. The needs and capacities of a human group may be described in analogous ways. First, there are the material needs—food, clothing, and shelter. How can they be best taken care of? By entrusting these concerns to those whose talents and skills can be most effective in providing them. Instead of having each person provide for his or her own food, clothes, and housing, it is more desirable and efficient to have a group of artisans or technicians perform the various productive and technical functions. A good state will see to it that there is such a group and that it discharges its function well.

Since a state exists as a political entity among other states, it may sometimes find itself in opposition to others, either when it has ambitions of its own, or when it is called upon to defend itself against aggression. In other words, the will of the society as a whole should have a corresponding expression in actual physical force. Who will supply it? Again, those who by virtue of special talent and special training can perform the proper task wholeheartedly and effectively. Therefore, the state needs a class of warriors who, in order to be always prepared to undertake its special tasks, must refrain from dissipating their energies and time on other activities and occupations. The warriors should be physically tough and mentally alert, and their training such as to prepare them to be the executors of the state's will.

The state also needs to be governed. The multiplicity of material needs, and the political goals and ambitions have to be supervised and coordinated, fitting them to one another and to the general well-being of the state. Also in this realm, the experts and the professionals need to be entrusted with a special task. Since this task is the most difficult and the most important, the preparation for the work of a governor or a guardian will take a long time. The guardians must have as much knowledge and wisdom as can possibly be acquired. In this area, too, the possession of special talents is a prerequisite for the necessary training. The training should begin with fundamentals, such as mathematics, and should wind up with the deepest and most intensive philosophical studies. In Plato's plan, the life of future guardians until the age of 40 should be filled with the acquisition of the necessary prerequisites for the discharging of their functions. It takes a long time to acquire such a comprehensive wisdom, believed Plato. Yet without such persons at the helm, the state is at the mercy of unreason. "Until philosophers are kings, or the kings and princes of this world have the spirit of philosophy, and political greatness and wisdom meet in one . . . cities will never rest from their evils . . . and then only will this our state have a possibility of life and behold the light of day."[1]

This comprehensive scheme for an ideal government was worked out by Plato in his most famous dialogue, *The Republic*. In addition to emphasizing this tripartite scheme, imported from his idea of the individual soul, Plato described in detail the procedures to be used in selecting people for assignment to each class, in regulating their life within that class in relation to other classes, and in specifying the nature of their training. Among some of the many startling provisions was, for instance, the abolition of the family for the guardian class. The raising of children would be in the hands of the state in order to allow for the impartial selection of children for membership in a particular class according to their talents. Even the choice of mates would not be left to the individuals, but would be arranged for them by the guardians, with an eye toward the most effective furthering of the state's ends. Thus, the bravest and strongest warriors would be allowed to mate more than others, in order to ensure the best stock of future warriors. (Plato appears to be the first to conceive of scientific eugenics.) Some decisions would be made by lot, but the guardians would also be allowed to engage in some prearranging in order to ensure that the results would be to the greatest advantage of the state. Thus, *The Republic* advocates the so-called noble lie. Plato also proposed the idea of abolishing private property for the ruling class, on the grounds that this would remove a temptation to rule unjustly.

These, and many other recommendations of Plato's *Republic*, have made it an object of severe criticism. In a famous recent study by a contemporary philosopher, Karl Popper, Plato heads the list of the enemies of the "open society." It would be difficult to contend that such criticisms are entirely undeserved. Not only the details of Plato's utopia, but also the basic scheme of such a rigid division of functions within a society invite serious questions. Is this rigidity not in conflict with the very idea of an individual soul as a harmonious function of several different aspects? Should the virtue of wisdom be so truncated in artisans and warriors as to result in virtually transforming them into mere functionaries? Is it possible for persons to be arrested in the performance of a definitely limited function? Even if it were possible, is it desirable for this to happen?

No doubt many things are wrong with the conclusions and recommendations of *The Republic*. Nevertheless, we may admit that Plato was not altogether wrong. Some of his key insights are fundamentally correct, for instance, his view that the benefits for the society will be greatest when each contributes his or her best talents to it. The division of labor has its application on the political level as well. Special skills are needed if the necessary tasks are to be fulfilled properly. This is why each aspiring politician today has to convince prospective voters that he is *qualified*, that he "can do more" than other candidates. Second, Plato's scheme assigns a crucial role to education. Education is important because on its character and quality depends the well-being of all members of society. Third, for Plato, the task of governing is the highest honor and the greatest responsibility. Those who are entrusted with it can be expected to give themselves fully and wholeheartedly to the task. This means that they have to forego certain pleasures and satisfactions open to those with less weighty duties to perform. "Noblesse oblige" — the occupancy of a higher position imposes special obligations — it has its price. The lot of a guardian is not an easy one. Nevertheless, since it combines a life-long pursuit of knowledge with the exercise of socially important decisions, it calls for the deepest respect and honor. Plato's idea of morality and of politics is an aristocratic one, but in the exalted sense of this word; in each realm his aristocratic idea calls for the rule of the best. An aristocrat to Plato is one who *deserves* his position.

## 3. Aristotle: The Functional Definition of the Good

Aristotle's ethical theory is in harmony with his general philosophical point of view. He conceived of the world, we may recall, as dynamic and purposive. Everything has a final cause, an end for the sake of which it exists. The goal of knowledge is to discover what that end is. This applies to human beings as well. If we describe human nature correctly, we will also know what sort of things we should aim for, for the definition of humanity will also include a description of its "final cause" or of the potentiality which it can actualize.

What do human beings aim for? Happiness, answers Aristotle. However, the Greek word, *eudaemonia*, which is often rendered in English as "happiness," is a comprehensive term and cannot be equated with pleasure. Pleasure is indeed a part of happiness, it helps to make it complete, but it would be false to claim, thought Aristotle, that people seek nothing but pleasure. An accurate description of the goals human beings pursue and find worth pursuing calls for a richer catalog of activities. The simple category of pleasure as an end to be sought is equally applicable to animals, inasmuch as animals also avoid painful feelings and delight in pleasant sensations, as a purring cat so eloquently testifies. Remembering Aristotle's view that each kind of being has a corresponding soul, we should ask ourselves what capacities or potentialities are inherent in each kind of soul. If human soul has other dimensions besides the vegetative, these dimensions should not be ignored.

Aristotle identified the special feature of humanity when he defined human beings as *rational* animals. To live an appropriate life, we must live at the level of rationality. This includes the capacity to perceive the kinds of activities which will fulfill us *as* human beings, thus securing eudaemonia, well-being, happiness. The perception of what Aristotle called virtuous activities is not simply a matter of intuition, even though he thought that it includes an element of intuition, of direct seeing. Good is what good people do, what they perceive and enact in their lives. However, rationality can also supply them with an intellectual comprehension of the nature of the virtue to be pursued.

This perception of particular virtues occurs within a context of a peculiar conceptual structuring. To see that something is a virtue is to see its position between two opposites. This may seem surprising, for we tend to speak of values in dualistic terms: good *vs.* evil, right *vs.* wrong, pleasure *vs.* pain. Aristotle noticed that a virtuous disposition can be contrasted with two different vices and that the two vices are extreme opposites of each other. For example, consider the virtue of courage. There are two different ways in which a person may fail to manifest it. On the one hand, one may be cowardly, afraid of something of which there is no reason to be afraid. On the other hand, one may be rash, exhibiting foolhardy boldness in the face of palpably overwhelming odds. It would be wrong to ascribe courage to such a person. If we were inclined to use the word so broadly as to include rash acts as well, then we would have to qualify a person's behavior by adding that in spite of the apparent bravery, it is nevertheless foolish or stupid. In other words, we would exclude this kind of "courage" from desirable, virtuous acts, acts which we would expect of ourselves and recommend to others. Thus, the virtue to be sought lies between the two opposing vices.

We should be careful, however, not to fall victim to confusion at this point. Aristotle's doctrine is not a praise of mediocrity. Just because the virtue of courage is contrasted with two opposing vices—cowardice and foolhardiness—its value is not neutralized by this "middle" position. As Aristotle puts it, "in respect of its substance and the definition which states its essence virtue is a mean, with regard to what is best and right an extreme." This double opposition to the corresponding vices is the heart of Aristotle's concept of the Golden Mean. This concept helps us to arrive at an identification of virtues proper to humanity.

Besides courage, Aristotle names *temperance*, which on the one hand is opposed to insensibility—a complete lack of appreciation of pleasures derived from the senses—and intemperance on the other—the tendency toward excessive indulgence, like gluttony or an inordinate fondness for drink. Courage and temperance, we may recall, ranked high in the ethics of Socrates and Plato, and Aristotle follows his predecessors in giving them prominence. However, he adds others as well; his list is more extensive than theirs. He praises liberality, placing it between meanness or stinginess and excessive generosity and prodigality. The rich man who is reluctant to part with his money even for worthy causes suffers from a moral defect, but so does the man who neglects to meet his obligations to his family in order to appear a great benefactor. Aristotle also believed that a person ought to exhibit a proper self-respect in his action. This virtue, which he called "magalopsychia" and which may be translated as great-souledness, highmindedness, or rational self-esteem, he contrasted with humility on the one hand and conceit on the other. Perhaps influenced by Christian ideals, we tend to think of humility in essentially positive terms, but to Aristotle humility might be a form of self-abasement, and he concluded that if a person has no proper respect for herself, she is morally deficient. But so is the one who falls into the opposite vice of inordinate conceit about her own worth. Another interesting virtue of the Aristotelian catalog is what he called "good temper." Aristotle's ideal was a human being who is even-tempered, not easily given to anger, to the vice of irascibility, but who also is not so placid and emotionally immovable as to fail to assert herself in any circumstances—in other words, a person who suffers from spiritlessness. Again, modesty is a virtue, in contrast to shamelessness on the one hand and bashfulness on the other.

"Virtue, then, is a state of character concerned with choice, lying in the mean, i.e., the mean relative to us, this being determined by a rational principle, and by that principle by which the man of practical wisdom would determine it."[2] Aristotle also thought that in determining the right position with respect to the opposing vices people must take into account their personal tendencies and inclinations. Knowing that we are generally attracted more to one extreme than to another, "we must drag ourselves away to the contrary extreme; for we shall get into the intermediate stage by drawing well away from error, as people do in straightening sticks that are bent."[3] Furthermore, virtuous dispositions require cultivation; morality is acquired by establishing reliable habits, and one learns how to be moral by constantly trying to act morally. Aristotle also reminds us that "it is no easy task to be good," and that "goodness is both rare and laudable and noble." In all instances, morality calls for *judgment*. There is no better way of making this clear than quoting once more from Book II of Aristotle's *Nicomachean Ethics*. To act morally is to do something "to the right person, to the right extent, at the right time, with the right motive, and in the right way."

Aristotle's catalog of virtues indicates various ways in which, according to him, people can perform their proper function as human beings. The virtues define the ends for the sake of which human persons exist. For this reason it is not improper to amend Aristotle's definition of a human being as a rational animal by adding that such beings are also *moral* animals, or that their rationality is partly expressed in their morality. To this should be added another important feature of human life, namely, its social character. People are also *social* animals. We need others in order to live a full life. We should recall here Aristotle's peculiar concept of matter, as contrasted with form. Matter, for him, as we have noted, is any contextual condition which can be transformed, given a new form by some agent. One such necessary contextual condition for morality is society. The virtues mentioned above—courage, liberality, good temper, modesty—can be expressed in a social setting, when directed toward other human beings; we could not express our full potential if deprived of the company of other persons. This is seen in the fact that one of the severest features of being put in jail is that a person is isolated and denied natural human relations with other people.

The need to express our potentials in a social setting indicates that we are also *political* animals. We seek to express ourselves as citizens, as participants in a common life, as contributors to lawmaking and administration. One of the guidelines of life in society is the principle of justice; corrective justice requires reparation of wrongdoing, and distributive justice requires that goods be allotted in proportion to deserts. Yet, because of this rational capacity, we may also see how the idea of strict justice must sometimes be supplemented by the virtue of equity—the ability to recognize that the spirit of justice is more important than the letter of the law. Persons who accord others even more than their full right deserve to be called equitable.

Aristotle did not underestimate the importance of material goods as a necessary underpinning of a good life. To act effectively a person needs some property. One also has to be part of a smaller social unity, such as a family, in order to give an individual style to one's mode of living. On these grounds Aristotle rejected Plato's idea of a propertyless and communal life style for the guardian class. These provisions would make them lesser human beings and hence less capable of governing well.

Among the "matter" which could be used to form one's life style Aristotle also included good fortune, such as having good looks or special talents. Endowed with such gifts, a person can lead a happier life. Good birth can be also a factor. In fact, Aristotle accepted the then prevalent view that some persons are not quite capable of reaching their full human potential, and hence deserve to be treated as slaves by their betters. The approval of slavery on Aristotle's part can perhaps be attributed to a certain blindness; having seen that many slaves were physically well built and seemed to show no interest in "civilized" activities, Aristotle may have concluded that this was something inherent and not, as we would put it today, culturally conditioned. To

Aristotle's credit, it must be admitted that he did not believe that it is right to enslave people who are already free; before his death he freed some of his slaves whom he regarded as capable of living in freedom. Also, he provided that none of his other slaves should be sold after his death.

The good of human life, then, is eudaemonia, happiness in the full-blooded sense of satisfaction derived from living on all levels of human excellence, including family, friendship—based not on utility but on the desire for mutual perfection—and participation in civic affairs. All of these relations, although necessary for a good life, do not exhaust the possibilities for rational living. In fact, the ability to think, to contemplate, to use reason not in some pragmatic or instrumental sense, but as pure, self-justifying activity, is the crown of a happy life. Perhaps the perfection of pure thought is in part derived from the fact that its "matter" is itself, not something extraneous to it, like some practical problem requiring a solution. We may remember that for Aristotle, God's perfection consists in his thinking about thinking; his Pure Activity is not interrupted by cares, concerns, and desires. In being able to spend at least part of his time at the level of contemplation, a person comes close to God, to divine perfection. Pure contemplation is not competitive; it feeds on itself and is therefore most continuous and most "God-like." To indulge in it is to realize that "the activity of philosophic wisdom is admittedly the pleasantest of all virtuous activities."

## 4. Epicureanism: Seek Pleasures Pure and Simple

Greek philosophers believed that the search for wisdom would result in knowing not only what is the case, but also how we should act. In helping us to realize what human nature is, philosophy can also tell us what would be the naturally desirable things to do. This conclusion is clearly evident in Aristotle's functional definition of humanity. As rational beings, people are equipped with the capacity to discover the truth about things; the very same capacity can show us what activities we should undertake.

This unity between the general philosophical outlook and the prescription for desirable action is even more prominent in Epicureanism. Indeed, the logical connection between the two objectives of thought appears to be even more intimate in the case of this early type of Hellenistic philosophy, as Greek philosophy after Aristotle is called. The classical philosophical doctrines, propounded by Socrates, Plato, and Aristotle, developed when Greek city-states, even though suffering from internal and external threats, still relied on their own cultural and moral resources, proclaiming high-minded social, political, and religious ideals. However, as the power of Athens declined, so did the positive, affirmative character of her ideals. With the loss of political independence came a loss of intellectual and moral self-confidence. Very soon, Greece was to become a province of the spreading Roman Empire. It should not be surprising to see the emergence of points of view which sought to bring people to terms with a reality which appeared in a much less glorious light than the classical Greek philosophers were wont to believe.

Epicureanism derives its name from Epicurus and his school, which he founded in Athens about 306 B.C. Known as the School of the Garden, it continued in existence for many years, even though it never achieved the prominence of Plato's Academy or Aristotle's Lyceum. The influence of Epicurus' teaching was, however, considerable. Although most of his numerous writings have been lost to posterity, his philosophy was widely followed. It was restated in a long philosophical poem by Lucretius (98-55 B.C.), *On the Nature of Things*, a masterpiece of Latin literature.

Epicurus believed that the true account of the nature of things is contained in the doctrines of Democritus. Everything in the world is the result of some fortuitous cluster of atoms falling through the void. The variety of things and beings results from the different ways in which atoms hang together for awhile, by virtue of the way their shapes allow them to conjoin with other atoms. Epicurus thought that atoms have some capacity for spontaneous motion, but even *that* motion was certainly not governed by any design or purpose.

This thoroughgoing materialism had no place for purpose in the universe; things simply happen, without any plan or design. To be sure, some combinations of atoms result in what we call life or sensation. The atoms which display themselves in such ways are, of course, so small that they are invisible. They cannot be seen, but they tell us what seeing is: an impact of smooth, round, highly mobile and nimble particles on the clusters of atoms we call eyes. A similar explanation is given for hearing, smell, or taste. Thought is also a form of sensation, a march of delicate atoms through the interstices between other, grosser atoms of our bodies. A contemporary materialist theory of mental processes would locate them in the brain, but Epicurus himself was inclined to think that the mass of atoms responsible for all mental phenomena was located in the breast.

As long as sensation-producing atoms course through our body, we exist as persons. But when they are stopped, due to the disease or destruction of some vital organs, the person disappears. The coarser atoms still remain, of course, as a corpse, but they, too, will soon be separated from their temporary home and will form other combinations in the world. Who knows, some of the atoms making up our soul may become ingredients of another person's life. However, that is as far as the notion of immortality makes any sense; there is certainly no survival of the *person*.

The interesting point about this doctrine is that Epicureans did not regard it as depressing or gloomy. On the contrary, it liberated humanity of all the superstitions of religion. There may possibly be some beings infinitely happier than ourselves, living perhaps in less precarious, less turbulent corners of cosmic space. But in what sense are they happier?

Epicurus' answer is straightforward. Every sensation, thought, experience *is* the way it feels. How does a thing strike you? Is it pleasant, comfortable, soothing? Or is it painful, jarring, disturbing? (The question "How does it strike you?" should be taken literally in this philosophy.) It is the momentary truth that counts. The happy life consists of a succession of such momentary pleasant feelings. The unhappy life is full of painful bumps, collisions, inner and outer conflicts, and frustrations. If so, there is only one prescription for moral wisdom: avoid painful states and seek pleasant ones, for they are the only punishment or reward you can get—if it at all makes sense to speak of rewards and punishments. It really doesn't, because there is no one around to bestow awards or mete out punishments. Nevertheless, it is possible to learn about the likely succession of sensations. A wise person will discover that intense pleasures are frequently followed by acute pains, as in overindulgence of various sorts. Thus, the Epicurean advice would be: don't expose yourself to the dangers of overindulgence. Furthermore, if you allow yourself to become dependent on luxuries, which almost by definition are not easy to obtain, you will be "hooked," and you will suffer "withdrawal pains" when luxuries are not available.

The state of mind a wise person cultivates is that of *ataraxia*: repose, tranquility, calm contentment—not the contentment of a glutton after a bulging meal (with subsequent discomforts inevitably to follow), but that of a sensible person easily pleased with a bowl of wholesome porridge. For in addition to physical sensations, i.e., those directly dependent on the senses, there are also satisfactions of the mind, like that of two friends engaged in a quiet exchange of ideas or serenely contemplating the inevitable course of events around them. Thus, Epicurean philosophy has little, if anything, to do with the contemporary notion of an Epicurean as connoisseur, gourmet, or even lusty gourmand. The pleasure principle is the only principle worth taking seriously, but Epicurus believed that it can truly pay off when the pleasures are low-keyed, when they are pure and simple. Of course, since there are no other standards to look to, Epicurus could offer no criticism of anyone whose pleasure needs are vigorous and for whom *ataraxia* has no attraction. At most, he could offer a prediction that the seeker of violent pleasures is likely to come to grief. If, however, the response to this should be "So what?", Epicurus could merely shrug his shoulders. If the judgment rests on the actual character of momentary pleasures, there can be no argument over tastes.

When Epicurus speaks of natural desires, he means those which, in his experience, have tended to leave him even-keeled, calm, and subject to no subsequent reversals or pitfalls. Pain is unnatural only in the sense that experiencing it is accompanied by the desire to escape it. It stands condemned the minute it appears. Wise are those who manage to avoid the unnecessary bumps and jars which life, unwittingly, of course, is bound to put in their path. They avoid involving themselves in responsibilities, especially in the public arena, for such an involvement is more likely to expose them to unavoidable blows. Nor will they be scared by bugaboos of supernatural superstition conjured up by religious believers. For an Epicurean, the quietude of contentment, adorned by a friendly conversation, is the only worthwhile thing in the cosmos of meaningless motion of matter in space.

## 5. Stoicism: Accept Your Place in Nature

One of the unconvincing features of the Epicurean account of the nature of things is its insistence on the absence of any ordering principles. Nature is the result of fortuitous combinations of atoms. Seeing a great degree of orderliness in the behavior of things around us, we may find the Epicurean outlook obviously false. This was the conclusion of the Stoics. This school of philosophy also had its origin in Athens. Founded by Zeno (334-262 B.C.) (Zeno the Stoic is not to be confused with his predecessor, Zeno the Eleatic, the discoverer of the famous paradoxes about motion) and first defended in his school on the Stoa (a painted porch in Athens), the school exerted a strong influence for several centuries. It also had some famous representatives among Roman citizens: Cicero (106-43 B.C.), Epictetus (A.D. 60-117), and Emperor Marcus Aurelius (A.D. 121-180).

Stoicism shared with Epicureanism its materialistic bias, but the materialism of the Stoics had a curious form. The Stoics could account for the orderliness of phenomena only by assuming that there must be a real universal force which imposes its character on the world. This force they called God. However God, too, was material, operating in the world as a fine, invisible substance which permeates all things and all beings. Since fire comes closest to representing such a volatile, mobile, and powerful force, the Stoics spoke of God as Cosmic Fire. Pervading everything, God also determines the laws of nature. Hence, the order of things is at the same time natural and rational. The combination of these two attributes was also expressed in the Stoics' conviction that everything that occurs happens necessarily and is governed by reason.

On the basis of this general philosophy, the Stoics formulated their ethical views. In fact, these views were but an extension of that philosophy. Human nature and human life are also governed by Cosmic Fire. Hence, everything that happens to us and everything we do follows inevitably from the rule of Reason. The objective of thought is to discover our role in the scheme of things. That role has to fit in with the rest of our surroundings. Reason, then, is seen as the fate, or providence, which assigns to us the particular role we are to play. A wise person will recognize this role and accept it. If one is born rich, one will not see one's situation as any better than that of one's neighbor who happens to be born poor. In neither case is there a cause for exultation or depression. Neither station in life is preferable to the other, considering the whole scheme of things, into which each role fits according to the inexorable laws of Reason. To be excited about one's position, be it high or low, is not to see things aright. We must adjust our thought to the reality as it is, and we must accept it.

Those who fail to do this are victims of delusions. Their delusions typically express themselves in certain passions: envy, jealousy, or hatred. These emotions will disturb their peace of mind and make their existence painful. Pain, the Stoics agreed with the Epicureans, can be distracting. Therefore, we should cultivate the virtue of *apathy*, the state of mind in which we are not dominated by passions and desires. The highest moral asset for a Stoic is self-control. Stoics will not be aroused; neither the images of bliss nor the spectacles of suffering move them. "Disease is an impediment to the body, but not to the will, unless the will itself chooses. Lameness is an impediment to the leg, but not to the will."

First of all we should cultivate in ourselves the capacity to resist the lures of the senses. This capacity also fortifies us against any misfortunes. Stoics value fortitude, the unbroken spirit in the face of calamities, be they their own or those of their neighbors. They avoid undue attachment, even to their own families. When his wife dies, a Stoic does not grieve excessively, for her death belongs to the course of nature or is in the hands of providence. Should he give vent to weak emotions, he would fail to recognize the inevitability of things and would thereby disturb his soul unnecessarily. We cannot control our fate, but we can control our *attitude* to that fate; let us be, therefore, courageous and self-possessed.

It is not difficult to see that this kind of ethical view is cognizant of human vulnerability and exposure. It is a philosophy which helps you to keep a stiff upper lip with the odds stacked against you. It enabled the slave Epictetus to endure the breaking of his leg with a calm remark to his angry master: "I warned you that my leg would break if you twisted too hard." Stoicism can be an effective weapon against the evils of persecution because it recognizes the fact that suffering is a normal aspect of the human condition. In this respect, Stoicism had a strong influence on the spread of Christianity.

In its later forms Stoicism shared with Christianity still another conviction, namely, universal human brotherhood. If iron laws of fate govern all, then all human beings are equally subject to it. There are no privileged participants in the cosmic drama. The emperor, as a person assigned a definite role in that drama, has to play *his* role, just as his lowly subjects have to play theirs.

Thus, Marcus Aurelius thought of himself as a citizen of the cosmos, on equal footing with all men. Zeno, the first Stoic, said: "All men are by nature equal; virtue alone establishes a difference between them." He was later echoed by a Roman Stoic jurist: "All men, according to natural right, are born free and equal." This side of Stoic philosophy tends to bring out the importance of justice, of right social relations, and had a strong influence on the notion of universal natural law, as it was formulated in the Roman code of juris-prudence. The idea that the legal code provides not just practical solutions to felt needs of administration, but also reflects the rational structure of the universe, originated with the Stoic philosophers.

The Stoic suppression of emotions is reminiscent of Socrates' suspicion that a person in the clutches of passion will not be able to see things aright. The Stoics, however, went far beyond the injunctions of Socrates and Plato that passions should be controlled. Apathy is literally a passion*less* state of mind. The Stoic's mind is controlled by reason alone. But even if it were possible to eliminate emotion altogether, would it be desirable to do so? It seems that a Stoic cannot be even *committed* to his ideal of rationality, because commitment is characterized by some emotional tone as well. As Spinoza later observed, wisdom consists not in getting rid of all passions, but in trying to replace emotions that are irrational by those that are intelligent and appropriate.

There is also a logical difficulty in the Stoic determinist philosophy. If everything is bound to run its inevitable course, does it make sense to claim that we can have control over our attitudes? Aren't our attitudes just as determined as everything else? The Stoic dictum "The fates lead the willing; the unwilling they drive" suggests that a wise person will not fight her fate, but will submit to it. But is the act of submission really her own? Questions like these are bound to intrude themselves, and they are equally relevant to any other fully deterministic philosophy.

When the confidence of classical philosophical thought began to falter in the Hellenistic period, the ancients still looked to philosophers for ethical enlightenment, although such enlightenment amounted to no more than consolation. Even if one's ambition to achieve knowledge is frustrated, we should still look for ways to adjust rationally to the verdict of our philosophical conclusion. Epicureanism and Stoicism, different as they were, still saw in philosophy the guide to life. Even in extreme adversity, thoughtfulness may help us to distinguish between desirable and undesirable courses of action. Each school, however, raises general questions which are also applicable to other schools of thought with a similar basic philosophical orientation. By adopting a purely materialistic view of the universe, the Epicureans questioned the very possibility of rational thought, not to speak of ethical thought. By adopting strict determinism, the Stoics made questionable the notion of human freedom. These general problems haunt subsequent philosophers who accept analogous starting points.

## Questions

1. Why did Socrates believe that there is an intimate connection between knowledge and virtue?

2. Why did Socrates insist on the importance of both *personal* integrity and *common* moral standards? What was his view of the proper relation between the individual and society? How convincing do you find this view?

3. What were Plato's views about the various parts, or aspects, of the soul and of their proper relation to one another?

4. How did Plato apply his theory of the individual soul to his theory of the proper political order of a state? How successful do you find this application?

5. What is the goal of human life, according to Aristotle?

6. Provide an analysis of some virtues and some vices in terms of Aristotle's doctrine of the Golden Mean. Can you think of some examples to which the doctrine is not applicable?

7. What is a good life, according to the Epicureans? Contrast this conception with that of Aristotle. How would you explain the difference between them?

8. What are the strong points of Stoicism? What are its weaknesses?

## Notes

[1] Plato, *The Republic*, Book V, 473d. (*The Dialogues of Plato*, 4 vols., translated by B. Jowett, London: Oxford University Press, 1953.)

[2] Aristotle, *Nicomachean Ethics*, Book II, Ch. 6, 1107a. (*The Works of Aristotle*, 12 vols., translated and edited by J.A. Smith and W.D. Ross, London: Oxford University Press, 1908-1952.)

[3] *Ibid.*, Ch. 9, 1109b.

# Chapter Four

# Philosophy Christianized

## 1. The Arrival of Christianity

Daily we are reminded that something important has happened about two-thousand years ago. Every time we affix a date to a letter or a check we write down a figure which points back to an event that was deemed important enough to signal a new beginning. Historians have adopted a notation according to which events fall into two temporal spans, B.C. and A.D., the first referring to everything that happened before the birth of Christ, and the second to the particular year in the era of "Our Lord." Recognizing that this division of history revolves around an event which gives a special status to one particular religion, those who find this partiality problematic have recently proposed that more neutral terms be used: B.C.E., standing for "Before Common Era," (thus replacing B.C. as referring to the birth of Christ) and C.E., standing for the Common Era (thus replacing A.D. - Anno Domini). Although this notation seems less invidious, it nevertheless identifies the beginning of the Common Era with the rise of Christianity.

The history of the world was profoundly affected by the life of Jesus of Nazareth, and the effect was multidimensional. Its philosophical dimension has come to the surface only after Christianity as an institution came to dominate the life of Europe. The emergence of Christianity as a potent historical force can be understood better in terms of the social and political situation of the times. It came into existence when the Roman and Hellenistic civilization found itself in an ever deepening crisis. That crisis was complex and had to do with Rome's inability to keep its empire together, to defend itself against

63

external enemies, to feed its inhabitants, and to keep order among its far-flung components. In spite of its initial successes, the empire could not generate leadership equal to all these challenging tasks. The despondent mood of the times was characterized by a third century (C.E.) commentator.

> You must know that the world has grown old, and does not remain in its former vigor. It bears witness to its own decline. The rainfall and the sun's warmth are both diminishing; the metals are nearly exhausted; the husbandman is failing in the fields, the sailor on the seas, the soldier in the camp, honesty in the market, justice in the courts, concord in friendships, skill in the arts, discipline in morals. This is the sentence passed upon the world, that everything that has a beginning should perish, that things which have reached maturity shall grow old, the strong weak, the great small, and that after weakness and shrinkage should come destruction.[1]

Not surprisingly such a state of affairs encouraged a surge of beliefs that would help people to cope with the spiritual malaise. Traditionally, the Roman empire did not impose its rather formalistic religion on its citizens, who therefore were free to embrace religious beliefs and practices that seemed to answer better to their needs. Seeking some kind of certainty and security, people were attracted to religions that promised relief from the difficulties of life. Exotic cults and mystery religions had a strong appeal. Imported from Egypt, for instance, was the worship of mother goddess Isis and her family. From Iran came Mithraism, centered on the belief that the world is the eternal battlefield between the forces of good and evil.

At a time of trouble and turmoil an intervention of some extraordinary power may appear attractive. Hence a religion with a messianic message is likely to be successful. Judaism, as a religion in which a personal relation of God to his people is emphasized, has proved to be a binding force and succor for a people, which, being located at a crossroads of trade-routes, found itself subject to invasions and exiles by conquering neighbors. An elaborate moral and dietetic code has helped to cement the Jewish peoples' identity during prolonged periods of adversity, recognized in the spiritual and literary utterances of the Bible. When Jesus proclaimed himself as the founder of the New Kingdom, which promised liberation and salvation not just to one people but to all suffering humanity, his message was eagerly received by multitudes. By taking an anti-formalist and anti-ritualistic position, and by embracing the cause of the truly down-trodden—prostitutes, tax collectors, and simple fishermen—Jesus struck a responsive chord among the citizens of the decaying empire. His exhortation to moral reform and personal righteousness echoed the stance of the Stoics, who strove to mobilize their spiritual resources as a defense against external calamities. Since there seemed to be no hope for worldly improvement, and since secular authorities and institutions proved cruel and corrupt, the only remedy was to throw oneself on the promises of supernatural powers, to which prophets and messiahs declared themselves to be connected.

The message of Jesus was seen as a threat both to the Jewish and to the Roman authorities because it appeared to aim at establishing a new political order. This perception led to his execution and to the initial and persistent persecutions of early Christians. But these calamities only added to their conviction that the worldly powers are inimical to the life of the spirit and helped to intensify the activity of the converts to the new religion. Its revolutionary, apocalyptic, and eschatological message tended to attract adventuresome and vigorous individuals, transforming some of them into fanatics and martyrs. Seeing the growing appeal and the organizational strength of the new religion, Constantine the Great, in the year 325, put a stop to the prosecution of Christians and made Christianity the official religion of the Roman Empire.

Once a movement becomes organized it seeks ways of reaching a wide spectrum of society and of attracting those who are influential and powerful. As a consequence, the initial appeal of Christianity to people who understood its message in simple and direct terms was extended to those who responded to its being articulated in more sophisticated terms. This involved relating the Christian world view to other beliefs which it sought to supplant or supplement. As a formulation of a desirable way of life, the new religion had to come to terms with rival formulations, or at least it had to relate itself to already developed conceptions. This is the territory on which religion meets philosophy. The original disseminators of Christianity, such as St. Paul, could up to a point concentrate on the story of Jesus told without resorting to philosophical language, even though the strength of the story included a powerful mystical vision as well. But when the propagation of the message passed into the hands of St. John, who moved in a different world from that of St. Paul and emphasized the importance of conveying that message to Gentiles as well, the process of propagation acquired a new dimension. That dimension was distinctly philosophical, as is testified in St. John's famous proclamation, "In the beginning was the Word."

St. John used "Word" in a technical sense derived from Greek philosophy. The center of religion was no longer just a personal encounter with a mysterious figure called Jesus, but began to move into the conceptual territory already explored in the Greek classical tradition. Thus Christianity acquired a distinctly philosophical dimension, and conversely, philosophy became Christianized. Since the Logos doctrine had a long tradition, by connecting the newer religion with that tradition, St. John's Gospel helped to transform both. Beginning with early Christian thinkers and extending into the period we call Middle

Ages, the relationship between the two acquired an increasingly complex elaboration. As we shall see, the founders of the Christian doctrines, the so-called Church Fathers, and later on the Scholastics, devoted their energies to showing how the Christian faith would understand, revise, and interpret certain key positions developed by classical Greek thinkers.

Since the central thrust of the Christian religion was to see human existence as radically dependent on and conditioned by a supernatural reality, and since the Greek thought has already produced some definite theories about the relationship between the temporal and eternal, it was only to be expected that this relationship would need to be re-examined in the light of the Christian world view and its particular doctrines. Plato and Aristotle had developed some impressive views about the role of God in the world. Since Christianity was more God-centered than was either Platonism and Aristotelianism, Christian theologians could not escape the task of dealing with some problems already encountered in Greek philosophical thinking. Indeed, as we shall see, a great portion of the intellectual energy of medieval philosophy was directed at these problems. Since the idea of God lies at the center of the Christian religious view, its philosophy as theology had to revolve around that center. It is therefore not surprising that intellectuals who felt the force both of Greek classical thought and of the Christian message would attempt to bring about a synthesis of the two. One impressive example of such an attempt is the philosophy of Plotinus.

## 2. Plotinus: The One and Its Radiance

Plotinus (205-270) was the greatest of the Neoplatonic philosophers. By ascribing superior reality to the World of Forms, Plato relegated the material world to an inferior status. The depreciation of the temporal world was underscored during the difficult times in which Christianity came into being. Plotinus shared the sense of inadequacy and insufficiency of the natural aspects of human life; he is reported to have been ashamed of his body. It is no wonder, then, that, like Plato, he did not look to the senses to provide real knowledge. But Plato at least thought that the sense world, in virtue of imitating the Forms, provided clues to knowledge. In contrast, Plotinus emphasized oracular, mystical aspects of Platonic thought, no doubt encouraged by the recent popularity of mystery religions. As a student of Ammonius Saccas of Alexandria, who for a while professed to accept Christianity, Plotinus must have been affected by the claim of that religion that reality owes its existence and nature to one primary source and principle. In Plato that principle was ambiguously lodged in the World of Forms or the Form of the Good, which, although eternal, received embodiment in the world through the intervention of the Demiurge, the divine Artificer.

Plotinus' version of Platonism unequivocally made God, the One, the center of reality, from which everything else emanates or radiates, losing in perfection as the distance from the One increases. Because at the level of embodied human existence the awareness of God's reality is blurred, that reality cannot receive an adequate description. For that reason Plotinus also spoke of the One as It. No quasi-temporal or quasi-spatial concepts can be used to refer to It, indeed, no predicates at all can apply to It, although of course, It is a positive and dynamic Reality, the source of all that is. Timelessly, It, the supreme Existent, unbounded Life and Power, spontaneously energizes all that surrounds It.

The first *derived* reality Plotinus calls Noûs. This notion contains what could be called the Divine Mind corresponding to Plato's World of Forms. In Clement's of Alexandria and Origen's Christian adaptation of Neoplatonism, Noûs is equivalent to the Logos of St. Johns Gospel, the Second person of the Trinity, the Word Principle incarnated in Jesus Christ. The second level of derived reality is what Plotinus calls Soul, an intermediary between Noûs and the world of sense. Soul is the principle of life and growth. This Aristotelian notion is given by Plotinus a universal function; immaterial and immortal, Soul is diffused everywhere. It energizes the next, material level of reality, furthest removed from It or the One or God.

Individual souls of human beings are, as it were, "parts" of the Universal Soul. Connected with the body, the activity of the soul in turn represents three levels, the characterization of which bears a strong similarity to Plato's. The lowest part of the soul is animal and sensuous, closely linked up with the body. The logical, reasoning part enables human beings to exercise rational self-control over their bodies, a capacity which distinguishes humanity from all other life. Finally, the third and highest part makes it possible for the soul to reestablish its connection with Noûs, and through Noûs with God. Since the order of reality is downward from the soul to the body, it seems more correct to speak of the body being in the soul, rather than, as the popular understanding has it, the soul in the body.

Plotinus has many names for the One. Referring to the One as It, he intends to underscore the inadequacies of language to describe the One. But he also calls it "the Good" and does not hesitate to use the personal pronoun "He." But Plotinus constantly reminds us that all the words attempt to say the unsayable, to eff the ineffable. In this respect he anticipates the thought of a contemporary philosopher of religion, Paul Tillich, who was prepared to speak of God *beyond* God or God as the Ground of Being. This is clearly what Plotinus wants to communicate. "When you think of Him as Mind or God, He is still more: and when you unify Him in your thought, the degree of unity by which He transcends your thought is still greater than you imagine it to be. For He exists in and by Himself without any attributes. Substance needs Him in order to be One; but He does not need Himself; for He is Himself.'' Resorting to the impersonal pronoun, Plotinus talks of God in the way reminiscent of Aristotle. ''It has life in Itself and all things in Itself. Its thinking of Itself is Itself, and exists by a kind of immediate self-consciousness, in everlasting rest.''[2]

The Aristotelian train of thought is further in evidence when Plotinus asks himself, in reflecting on Noûs, why Noûs exists as a distinct reality. ''Why did It not remain by Itself?'' Plotinus' answer is not altogether different from Plato's explanation of why Demiurge decided that the World of Forms would spill out toward matter and its unorganized chaos. ''It must be a radiation from It while It remains unchanged, just like the bright light which surrounds the sun, which remains unchanged though the light springs from it continually . . . . Nothing can come from It except that which is next greatest after It. Noûs is next to It in greatness and second to It; for Noûs sees It and needs It alone; but It has no need of Noûs.''[3]

Individual souls, as parts of Universal Soul, need both the Noûs and that which Noûs needs, namely, the One. Plotinus sees Noûs as existing independently of its individual knowers. ''We are not Noûs; we are conformed to it by our primary reasoning power which receives it.'' While Noûs is a self-contained activity, soul has two aspects; its inward aspect is directed toward Noûs, and its outward aspect toward the material world. This is also the case with individual souls. Their special distinction is that they can return to the source from which they radiate, namely the One. That the label ''Neoplatonism'' is quite fitting can be seen from clear echoes of Plato's *Symposium* in Plotinus' description of the process by which the return to the One is initiated. ''Let him who can, follow and come within, and leave outside the sight of his eyes and not turn back to the bodily splendors he saw before. When he sees the beauty in bodies he must not run after them; we must know that they are images, traces, shadows, and hurry away to that which they image.''[4]

The mystical call of Plotinus can be easily translated into the Christomysticism of St. John and St. Paul. All three share the conviction that the sensible world is but an image of the Divine Mind, which holds the world together through the power of Logos and which draws all creation toward Itself by a sort of centripetal attraction. According to Porphyry, Plotinus' disciple who has put together his master's writings under the title *Enneads*, Plotinus experienced a mystical union with God four times during the last six years of his life. His last reported words were: ''That which is divine in me departs to unite itself with the Divine in the universe.''[5]

## 3. Augustine: The Primacy of Divine Will

St. Augustine's life (354-430) dramatizes the forces which made Christianity a powerful alternative to philosophies of classical Greece: Jerusalem v. Athens. His education included an exposure to ancient pagan wisdom, transmitted by such writers as Cicero, inducing the young Augustine to become a teacher of rhetoric. For a number of years he was a follower of the Manichean Doctrine, according to which the evils of the world are inherent in its material nature. As he explains in his *Confessions*, this doctrine seemed to exonerate the sinner: ". . . it had seem to me that it was not we who sin but some unknown nature within us and it soothed my pride to be guiltless and, having done something evil, not to have to confess I did it in order that you might heal my soul which sinned against thee; I loved to excuse myself and accuse that unknown something in me that was not I."[6]

This confession on Augustine's part provides a clue to what is special in the Christian outlook as compared with that of the ancient Greeks: a consciousness of a *personal* relationship to the ruling cosmic powers. Indeed, these powers themselves are seen as personal; the world is an expression of divine *will*. This conception calls for a restructuring of attitudes appropriate for such a personal relationship between God-person and the human person. As long as the source of the world is understood in terms of an impersonal power or principle, the response to it will lack the requisite intensity. As Augustine has just described it, it encourages to view our motives as likewise impersonal, making self-exoneration easy. But to view the Divine Power as an expression of a personal will is to see one's own doings as willful reactions to the requirements of the Divine Will. Hence the plausibility of the idea of sin.

Already prepared to be receptive to this idea by his Christian mother, Monica, at the age of thirty Augustine fell under the influence of St. Ambrose, the bishop of Milan, where Augustine went to teach rhetoric. The friendship led to Augustine's baptism in 387, and thus he embarked on a Christian career culminating in his 35-year service as a bishop of Hippo. A part of that service was a composition of writings which were ten times larger in volume than those of Aristotle. Besides his famous *Confessions*, these writings contain the equally famous *The City of God*. Like St. Paul before him and St. Thomas Aquinas after him, Augustine has left an indelible mark on Christianity as the apologist and defender of faith against all manner of heretics. What has become known as Augustinianism, echoed by such future "knights of faith" as Pascal and Kierkegaard, stresses devotional inwardness as the crucial feature of religious faith.

When the appeal to faith is central, the role of reason becomes problematic; little, if any, room seems to be left for argument and rational demonstration. When reason is made subordinate to faith, is this subordination a *philosophical* act, or does philosophy cease to be relevant? A believer will speak of *higher* understanding, achieved by belief, but the order of the two is now reversed. It is not understanding that leads to belief, but the other way around: "except ye believe, ye shall not understand" (Isaiah 7, 9). No act of reason can bring about the belief; it happens only as a result of divine grace. It is at this point that the contrast between the classical Greek philosophy and Christianity comes into a sharp focus. The search for wisdom is replaced by experiencing a direct personal encounter with God, mediated through Jesus Christ. The primacy of the intellect is replaced by the primacy of the will. For Augustine, even sense perception involves an activity on the part of the soul and is in that sense the function of the will.

Nevertheless, philosophy is not easily separable from faith, and the apologist for it cannot escape the need to deal with some problems, prominent among which is the problem of evil. If God is all-good and all-powerful, why is there evil in the world? Why are human beings, the crown of divine creation, prone to sin? St. Augustine's treatment of the problem was one of the most acute and proved to be most influential, still being acceptable to many present-day Christians. The philosophical side of the issue turns on the need to escape a dilemma. Of course, God could create a man incapable of sinning, but would such a man be free—would he have the freedom of choosing either good or evil? So it seems that the creation of such a man would not be admissible. On the other hand, if the created man does turn out to be a sinner, can God, his creator, escape the responsibility for this result? St. Augustine's answer was that God gave human beings the freedom of choice and that the choice to sin is a deliberate perversion of one's will. The possibility of choosing the good is always there, but if one allows one's will to turn away from this possibility, there is only oneself to blame. Whether or not this solution is satisfactory is still a subject of lively debate among both believers and nonbelievers; nevertheless, it provided a point of view which many Christians could and did embrace.

The ultimate dependence on divine grace was defended by Augustine in the face of a different view embraced by Pelagius and his followers, all of which were subsequently declared by the church to be heretical. Pelagius attributed more efficacy to the human will as such, and regarded the act of divine grace as merely an *aid* to making the right choice. Augustine disagreed. Perhaps colored by the recollection of his own fall into youthful escapades, he tended to identify original sin, passed on from Adam, with sexual lust, akin to a volcanic eruption of the powers of darkness. There seems to be a Neoplatonic component in Augustine's view, according to which evil is nothing positive; it is a privation, lacking the attribute of existence as such. Still another argument advanced by Augustine and later echoed by Leibniz was that God *permits* evil for the sake of a larger good; though man is responsible for evil, God creates the good.

Even in God, wisdom and goodness depend on His infinite power which subsumes under itself all knowledge as well. Should God cease to exist, everything would disappear as well, because He sustains the world in its existence. But this Neoplatonic element in Augustine's view did not collapse into pantheism; faithful to the Christian doctrine, he insisted on distinguishing between God and His creation. Whatever is good and true is not intrinsically so, but only because God wills it. The aim of humanity and of all philosophy is to be one with God, thus partaking of the knowledge contained in God's understanding and achieving a blessed relationship with the creator of the world.

God is also a creator of time, which is nothing apart from his creation. He made the world out of nothing, and the temporal properties we ascribe to phenomena in the world are subjective impressions accompanied by a general awareness of time's passage. Since God exists eternally, we cannot ask about what He was doing *before* the creation of the world; the question does not make sense. Before the creation there was nothing and time did not exist because time depends on movement and differentiation. The preferred Greek classical theory viewed cosmic history as cyclical, but for Augustine there can be only one world, and Christ died but once for its salvation. With his birth there came the possibility of world's redemption, and the end of the world will be preceded by the Last Judgement, after which heaven and hell will go on forever, with nothing else coming into being. One problematic consequence of this news is the eternal damnation of sinners, a consequence not easily squared with God's infinite goodness.

Since human happiness is not something obtainable in this world, Augustine did not show any interest in the physical world—a topic to which the Presocratics and Aristotle gave a great deal of attention. The role of the state, the City of Man, was of interest to Augustine primarily as aiming at the City of God. Following the Gospels, he was prepared to leave to Caesar what was Caesar's and accepted the society and its modes of organization under the Roman Empire as not centrally significant aspects of life. This attitude was a corollary of seeing the most important feature of life in the individual's relation to God (a theme later revived and intensified in the writings of a modern Augustine, Søren Kierkegaard). In the light of this view, one can imagine Augustine not to experience the siege of Rome by vandals, during which he died at the age of 86 reciting penitential Psalms, as an unequivocal spiritual crisis. Earthly empires come and go, but the City of God remains unshaken.

# 4. Aquinas: Reason and Revelation

The centuries between the deaths of St. Augustine (430) and the birth of St. Thomas Aquinas (1225) witness a collapse of civilized conditions in Western Europe and are often referred to as Dark Ages. After the division of the Roman Empire into Western and Eastern, the city of Rome ceased to be an administrative, political, and intellectual center. Frequent rebellions in various parts of decentralized empire made life difficult and precarious. Under such conditions Christianity offered at least spiritual refuge. Emphasizing human short-sightedness and short-handedness, the need to show humility and dependence and to appeal for help to supernatural powers, Christianity in time became the dominant force in western Europe, not only regulating the spiritual domain but also exercising political authority. In time, the Popes of Rome became the equals of kings, and many important military campaigns such as the Crusades were initiated in the name of religious convictions. As the Christian religion became institutionalized, often organized into a militant church, it also needed more precise formulations in order to reassure itself and it adherents that they all believed the same doctrines.

Those who are referred to as Church Fathers had the task of formulating the common Christian creed but, as is usually the case when the work is done by a committee, disagreements and differences of opinions were difficult to avoid. The same was true about the councils of bishops who were called upon to provide a uniform, orthodox and catholic creed. Both terms—"orthodox" and "catholic"—were originally meant to indicate the rightness, correctness and truth of the professed doctrine. It took several councils—of which the Council of Nice and Council of Trent were the most important—to hammer out such final doctrines. Those whose views failed to prevail had to be distinguished from the correct believers. Since some of the dissenters were frequently unwilling to abandon their convictions, they had to be declared heretics by the upholders of the prevailing opinion; and so the Patristic Period, during which the main Christian doctrines received their formulation, also produced a goodly number of heretics whose views deviated from those of orthodox believers. Some of the questions that needed to be settled were clearly philosophical. For instance, there was the doctrine of the Trinity—God presented himself in three persons: God the Father, God the Son, and God the Holy Spirit. Is Christ, God the Son, the same as the Father? If so, did the Father send Himself to die on the Cross to redeem humanity? There appears to be a theological problem as to how one being can exist in three persons; the Church Fathers had to find some convincing way to solve this problem. The Nicene Creed, still recited today by many Christians, contains the formulation which prevailed.

Christian theology grew in extent and volume during the so-called Scholastic Period in the early centuries of the present millenium. The name derives from the Latin *schola* or "school." All existing schools were run and organized by the church and were frequently attached to cathedrals and monasteries. Not surprisingly, the subject matter taught in the schools was almost wholly confined to religious teaching and the religious conduct of life. But deeper issues of a philosophical sort also engaged the intellectual energies of theologians.

Some of these issues were inherited from antiquity, such as the problem of the Universals. Does the universal "man" have a separate existence from individual men? In the Christian framework the problem takes on an additional significance, for it can be tied to the question of sin and salvation. If there is one universal nature of man, then perhaps the propensity to follow Adams's unfortunate choice is understandable, for his choice literally infected the universal "man." On the other hand, the problem of the Divine Trinity could then perhaps have a plausible solution: the universal nature of God is present in all Three Persons. Nevertheless, these arguments were not without their own difficulties, and consequently the problem of universals received divergent treatments.

Disputing the *realists*, that is, those who believe the universals to have independent and real existence, was a group of thinkers who called themselves *nominalists*. Nominalists were of the opinion that all real existence and substantiality is individual and concrete in character. A universal is a mere name, *nomen* in Latin. There is nothing corresponding to the term "humanity" over and above the existing individual men. The problem for nominalism, however, is that it leaves the unanswered question of why the individuals are grouped under the same name. If we apply this solution to the problem of the Trinity, we are forced to conclude that the three persons are quite distinct from one another and have nothing in common. Hence, we cannot possibly speak of one God. It is not surprising, therefore, that Roscellinus (1050-1125), the upholder of the nominalist view, was threatened with excommunication unless he denounced his philosophical view. Roscellinus chose to comply with the demand of the Church.

A way out of the impasse between realism and nominalism was also proposed during this period. One of the most famous scholars of the time, Peter Abelard (1079-1142) suggested that the universals do not represent some essential component of all individuals belonging to a class. The mind has the capacity to form concepts by abstracting from individuals their common characteristics. So, the universals exists only in the mind and not in reality. Hence, this doctrine was called "conceptualism."

These theological disputes demonstrated that it is difficult for religious ideas to escape philosophical attention. In fact, the philosophical tendency of religion is directly responsible for the existence of the term "theology." The two etymological components of this word make clear that reasoning (*logos*) about God (*theos*) cannot be kept out of religious consciousness. It is difficult, if not impossible, to keep religious consciousness from waxing philosophical when conditions become propitious. Among such conditions is the need to convert those who still do not see the light when the basic tenets of faith are presented to them. The presentation must be followed by explanation. Such explanations, when seriously pursued, tend to become systematic, thus giving rise to arguments and demonstrations.

St. Thomas' prominent position in the Catholic church is primarily due to his success in bringing together two possible approaches to religious faith. Choosing Aristotle as his intellectual mentor, St. Thomas proceeded to develop formulations of Christianity that intended to preserve the revealed message of personal intervention and Divine Grace while rendering a rational account of the natural world. The great achievement of St. Thomas is to have produced a powerful account of how revelation and reason can exist side by side, mutually supporting one another. Just how successful this synthesis was is itself a philosophical question still being debated both in theological and philosophical circles. But it is undeniable that he succeeded in practical terms. In spite of oppositions and setbacks, Thomism dominated the Catholic church at least from the time when he was elevated to sainthood in 1323 until the present. His prominence was confirmed as recently as 1879 in Pope Leo's XIII encyclical, "On the Restoration of Christian Philosophy."

Thomas Aquinas (1225-1274), an Italian from Naples, entered the Dominican order and then went to the University of Paris, where he fell under the influence of the Dominican scholar, Albert the Great. Albert was of the opinion that secular learning was important for developing the capacities of the human mind, and that this activity could contribute to, rather than detract from, one's religious faith. Aquinas outdid his teacher in this respect, for he set himself the task of reconciling the philosophy of Aristotle, which by then had reached Europe via the Arabic scholars in Spain, with the tenets of the Christian faith. His prodigious writings include *Summa Theologiae*, which is longer than all the extant works of Aristotle. During the last twenty years of his relatively short life (he was 49 when he died in 1274) he dictated over sixty books, among them extensive commentaries on Aristotle and on various Christian books.

The guiding idea of Aquinas' system is a view of the world as a vast teleological edifice in which everything has its proper function and place. This point of view is still applicable even when in place of a world-indifferent God, as Aristotle saw him, we have the God of Christian revelation. In both perspectives the world manifests a divine purpose, and each thing and each creature reflects this purpose in its own proper way.

The purposive design of things Aquinas believed to be one of the proofs of God's existence. There were other proofs, some of them also reminiscent of Aristotle. Consider the proof from motion: in order to move anything, the thing itself must be put into motion by something else; thus, to account for any motion, we have to trace it back to other moving things; but the series must begin with something that does not depend on being moved by something else—it must be able to originate motion by itself—that is, there must be a prime mover. This is what everyone, including Aquinas, understands to be God. A similar argument is used by him to show that there must be a first cause, since in the end there must be a cause that is not dependent on a preceding cause.

Another proof of God's existence was suggested to Aquinas by the idea of perfection. If something possesses a degree of perfection, the presence of that perfection must be explained. How? Aquinas answers that a greater perfection must exist which is capable of explaining the presence of a degree of perfection in something else. So, as long as there is any perfection in the world, there must be a maximum perfection which accounts for the reality of many lesser perfections. Aquinas also makes a distinction between the possible and the necessary being. Every existing thing is only contingently so—it comes into being and disappears—hence, it is possible for it not to exist. Furthermore, contingently existing beings may bring other beings into existence. But not everything can be contingent and merely possible. To account for the actuality of merely possible beings, there must also be a necessary being which does not receive its reality from another being. That being, once more, is God.

Aquinas also agreed with the basic conclusion of St. Anselm (1033-1108), according to whose famous ontological argument God's essence implies his existence. If we describe God as "a being than which nothing greater can be conceived," then it is clear that a being that exists only in the mind is certainly not as great as a being that also exists in reality. Hence, the very definition of God guarantees that he exists and that God cannot be conceived not to exist. But since in Aquinas' view the human intellect is too weak to grasp nature-transcending truths, he thought that the ontological proof requires supplementation by other truths derived from God's effects in the world. From our understanding of the world we can conclude the existence of God, but not vice versa.

By starting from observed things, from nature, Aquinas constructed a *natural* theology, according to which it is possible to move from nature to God. Of course, he added, what we can say about God can be only analogical. The predicates we apply to Him are not univocal in meaning with the predicates we apply to man. God's wisdom or goodness is different from human wisdom or goodness because God transcends everything that is natural. Reason can lead us only *towards* God, but the final truth about him can only be revealed and must be taken on faith. So reason can lead a believer only a part of the way; the final step lies beyond reason, and the primacy of faith is restored. Furthermore, faith is possible only through divine grace, which must be freely given and does not depend on any act of the believer. Thus, Aquinas believed himself to have brought about a reconciliation, a synthesis of reason and faith.

The Thomistic solution fed the tendency of the scholastic philosophy to depend on logical deductive argument, making argument and disputation one of the characteristic features of that philosophy. The final conclusions of these arguments, however, were not available to examination; they depended on faith. Consequently, when the reasoning led from these conclusions back to observable things, the conclusions became unquestioned premises. The believer had to start with them, and no other mode of reasoning was acceptable. Theology became an authoritative, limiting perspective. There was no other way of philosophizing, and one had to accept the dogmas of the church. Theology set limits to philosophical exploration.

The late scholasticism during the fourteenth century has produced thinkers who questioned some of Aquinas' philosophical arguments. Prominent among them was Duns Scotus (1266-1308), a Franciscan who taught at Oxford. He objected to Aquinas' claim that merely analogical predication can give us knowledge of God. Instead Scotus taught that such notions as "being," "true" and "good" have to be taken unequivocally, whether applied to God or to anything in nature. Otherwise knowledge of God and his order is impossible; it would convey *different* meanings. To be sure, our knowledge of God is only general; we do not know Him in His individuality and perfection.

Concerning the problem of the universals Aquinas believed that universals have an existence which is independent of individual manifestations. But he countered Aristotle's denial of the independent reality of universals by claiming that they exist in God's mind, prior to his creation of their manifestations (they exist *ante rem*). In the world, as Aristotle taught, universals exist only in particulars, and in the human minds they emerge only after the appropriate abstraction from individuals has occurred. Scotus, however, defended the view that we need to acknowledge the reality of what he called *haecceitas*, thisness, of embodied universals. Humanity, for instance, is not just a conceptual entity. One might say that the reality of a universal is "contracted" or "limited" to an individual difference manifested in a given person. This, Scotus believed, preserves the *essence* of humanity in each individual manifestation, and does not reduce individuality, as Aquinas seems to have been doing, merely to a spatio-temporal and bodily location. Scotus' insistence on combining individual things with their essences through his concept of haecceity made it possible to claim that sense perception can reveal common essences, a view later echoed in C.S. Peirce's claim that general characteristics have real existence, a view he dubbed "Scottist realism."

Carrying this epistemological theory back to the widest universal "being," and thinking of "being" as univocally applicable to things in the world *and* to God, one can see Scotus' ultimate interest in infinite, transcendent beings. In other words, his epistemology is theological, or God-centered. Somehow, in our accounts of the nature of humanity and the world, we must include God. Conscious of the presence of God in the world, a believer will also find in God's being the call to act in the divinely prescribed way. Ultimately, the voice of intellect merely translates the will of God. Thus, Duns Scotus embraced a *voluntarist* view, which, echoing St. Paul and St. Augustine, declares the will to be nobler than the intellect. Scotus comes close to saying that good is whatever God wills. Since God is not constrained even by reason, we cannot establish rationally what the creation would have to be; we must defer to God as an absolutely free agent. This means that philosophy needs to be supplemented by faith by accepting what God has chosen to reveal.

William of Ockham (1290-1350), a student of Scotus, was equally certain that God was all-powerful and the creator of the world. He did not think that natural reason alone is sufficient to know God. While speaking of God, we cannot distinguish between His will and His intellect—both characterizations refer to *the same* reality. In the dispute about the universals, Ockham sided with the nominalists against the theologically modified realism of Aquinas. Ockham's celebrated "Razor," namely, that "what can be explained on fewer principles is explained needlessly by more" was applicable to the theory of universals. If that theory is unnecessary to account for our ability to name things, then it should be abandoned. Aquinas thought that in knowing universals, the human mind, up to a point shares the content of God's mind. But if nominalism is true, no such sharing can take place. One consequence of this criticism of rational, natural theology was the doctrine of double truth. We can get one kind of truth when we stick to our observation of things in the world. Divine truth, however, has no connection with what we can know from such observations. By shifting the interest of philosophy from universal or common natures to individual things, Ockham was moving toward an empiricist epistemology. To him intuitive knowledge was concerned with a singular thing as existing and present to the senses of the observer. Whatever abstractive knowledge we can gain depends on such first-hand observational knowledge. This empiricist and nominalists drift, emphasizing the need for immediate experience, tended to leave behind scholastic metaphysical speculation and steered toward the emerging modern science and toward separating philosophy from theology. One consequence of this separation was that the intellectually curious were less and less inclined to turn to matters to which only faith is relevant and to concentrate more and more on the concretely available matters at hand. They also found the rationalistic approach, typified by Aquinas, increasingly implausible and helped to direct the inquiring minds to secular matters.

In addition to these skeptical but fideist Christian critics of Aquinas, the waning Middle Ages also saw the emergence of many prominent Christian mystics. The experience of a unity with God is not a function of reason but a result of feeling and piety. God who is "above being," as Meister Eckhart said, must also be above knowledge and thus accessible only through a mystical experience. Thus, mysticism contributed to the decline of the philosophical approach in the matter of deepest concern to the medieval mind, namely, the reality of God.

## 5. Christian Ethics

To present God in personal terms is to give prominence to the ethical dimension. The first truth of Christianity is that God sent his only begotten son to suffer and to die on the cross because he *loved* the world and was concerned about every single human being. That love is universal, extended to *all* people in the world regardless of their race, nationality, or status. God's love is also indifferent to the particular cultural or intellectual beliefs that people might have. Similarly, Christian love is neutral with regard to philosophical or political views a person might embrace. The emphasis is on practice, attitudes and feelings rather than on logical doctrines or intellectual positions. Christian ethics commands to live in the light of the *example* set by Jesus, who communicates to human beings God's vision of His Kingdom. In this way, ethical message is an integral part of the entire gospel message.

The famous authors of the Gospel — Matthew, Mark, Luke, and John — record the life of Jesus in the rich context of beliefs and teachings to which Jesus reacted as he preached and exemplified his message. Not surprisingly, therefore, there is in the New Testament a certain eclecticism and acknowledgement of a pluralism of ethical standards. The evangelists reacted to contemporary ethical beliefs as articulated in the texts of the Old Testament, the teachings of the rabbis, Stoic philosophers, and sayings of other sages. The best way to capture the content and the spirit of Christian ethics is to concentrate on concrete pronouncements, parables, and examples as they are presented, with some not always consistent variations, in the actual texts of the four evangelists.

Throughout, there is an insistence on distinguishing between the material and the spiritual aspects of human existence, reminiscent of Plato's dualistic view of all reality. The spiritual dimension is more important than the physical.

"Man cannot live on bread alone" (Matthew 4:4, Luke 4:4).[7] "Surely life is more than food, the body more than clothes" (Matthew 6:25). Human beings, in contrast to animals, have the sense of the sacred and they should not dishonor it. "Do not give dogs what is holy; do not throw your pearls to the pigs" (Matthew 7:6). To put material comfort and pleasure ahead of spiritual and moral values is to turn away from Godly life. In John 6:27 we read: "You must work not for this perishable food, but for the food that lasts, the food of eternal life." Similarly, the Kingdom of Heaven is characterized in Matthew 13:45 as follows: "A merchant looking out for fine pearls found one of very special value; so he went and sold everything that he had, and bought it." Mere observance of rules and token lip service to ethical values will not do: "Alas for you lawyers and Pharisees, hypocrites! You give tithes of mint and dill and cumin, but you have overlooked the weightier demands of the Law: justice, mercy and good faith" (Matthew 23:23). "For where your treasure is, there will your heart be also" (Luke 12:34). "Beware! Be on your guard against greed of every kind, for even when a man has more than enough his wealth does not give him life" (Luke 12:15).

Ethical *activism* stands out in the gospel's characterization as desirable for humanity. The capacity to act ethically and to be seriously concerned about spiritual matters is stressed again and again, clearly indicating that human will is free to do so. A Christian life is expected to bear fruit, where by fruit is meant a certain kind of life. "What will a man gain by winning the whole world at the cost of his true self?" (Matthew 16:25 and Luke 9:25). All these exhortations contrast ethical and spiritual exertion with a life of indifference, inactivity and stagnation. Such a life is explicitly deprecated in the parable of talents (Matthew 25:14-30). The nineteenth-century German philosopher J. G. Fichte called moral stagnation "the sin against the Holy Spirit." Some of the Gospels' injunctions also emphasize that ethical motivation seeks no extraneous rewards but sees the performance of duty as being its own reward — a view on which Immanuel Kant based his entire moral theory. "When you have done all that has commanded you, say, 'We are servants and deserve no credit; we have only done our duty'" (Luke 17:10). "You receive without cost, give without charge" (Matthew 10:8).

The central commandment of Christianity to love your neighbor as yourself (Matthew 23:37-39, Mark 12:28-34 and Luke 10:27-28) has as its background the clear awareness that suffering is ubiquitous. That suffering was exacerbated by the unstable political conditions of the world: crumbling empires, wars of conquest, constant danger of pillage and slavery — in addition to other evils and dangers that beset mortal creatures everywhere. War against evil is Jesus's explicit mission according to Luke 4:18: "He has sent me to proclaim release to the captives and recovering of sight to the blind, to set at liberty those who are oppressed" — slogans still at the center of what is today called "liberation theology." As Jesus explains his task in a message to John the Baptist (Luke 7:23): "The blind recover their sight, the lame walk, the lepers are made clean, the deaf hear, the dead are raised to life, the poor are hearing the good news." Those who labor and are heavy-laden are promised rest. (Matthew 11:28-30).

The Gospels are acutely aware of the dominance of wickedness and injustice in the world, and the Beatitudes (Luke 6:20-23) propose ways of dealing with them. Jesus has no illusions that evil is easily conquered. In a world where egoism is rampant, to proclaim the brotherhood of all humanity and to command the love of enemies is to ask for trouble from those who insist on clinging to their exploitative wicked ways; ". . . As lawlessness spreads, men's love for one another will grow cold. But the man who holds out to the end will be saved" (Matthew 24:12-13). The opposition to evil ways must be resolutely militant: "I have not come to bring peace, but a sword" (Matthew 10:34). Temptations to sin are unavoidable, but woe to those who succumb to and acquiesce in them. Jesus is also aware of the tendency to sidestep the task of eradicating evil, in oneself and in others, by dwelling on its causes rather than concentrating on its elimination. When asked who is to blame for a person's blindness, Jesus answered: "It is not that this man or his parents sinned, he was born blind so that God's power might be displayed in curing him" (John 9:3). Focus on remedies, and do not dwell on explanations: they are easily turned into excuses for doing nothing.

Like Socrates before him, Jesus is convinced that evil cannot be fought with evil as fire cannot be quenched by fire, thus turning away from the Mosaic justice of "eye for eye and tooth for tooth." "Do not set yourself against the man who wrongs you. If someone slaps you on the right cheek, turn and offer him your left. If a man wants to sue you for your shirt, let him have your coat as well . . . . Give when you are asked to give, and do not turn your back on a man who wants to borrow" (Matthew 5:39-42). The Gospel underscores what has become known as the Golden Rule and has been given a highly sophisticated form in Kant's formulation of the Categorical Imperative. "Always treat others as you would like them to treat you" (Matthew 7:12). In Luke 3:10-14, Jesus admonishes his followers to share clothing and food, the tax collectors to collect no more than the assessment, and tells the soldiers: "No bullying; no blackmail; make do with your pay."

The injunction to love one's enemies is indeed revolutionary and most problematic for a civilization in which a world without enemies is inconceivable. Hatred of enemies was, and disconcertingly still is, the order of the day. But Jesus's stance is unequivocal: "Love your enemies and pray for your persecutors . . . . If you love only those who love you, what can you expect? Surely the tax-gatherers do as much as that" (Matthew 5:44-46). Christian ethics is not marked by provincialness or tribalism. Jesus says, according to Luke 4:43, that he "must give the good news of the Kingdom of God to the other towns also," for this is the purpose for which he was sent. The Samaritan who comes to the aid of the wounded Levite exemplifies the spirit of love which ignores tribal barriers (Luke 10:29-37).

Another key ethical norm is forgiveness. "If your brother wrongs you, reprove him, and if he repents, forgive him. Even if he wrongs you seven times a day, and comes back to you seven times saying, 'I am sorry,' you are to forgive him" (Luke 17:3-4). That we tend to be partial to ourselves, minimize our shortcomings and maximize those of others, is no secret to anyone. The parable of the man with a log in his eye trying to remove a speck from the eye of another (Matthew 7:1-5 and John 7:24) has daily confirmation.

Christian ethics is incompatible with complacency; unceasing personal effort is required. So the rich young man who led a decent life was nevertheless admonished to exceed the limits of comfortable beneficence, to sell his possessions and to follow Christ (Matthew 19:19-22). Jesus commends the poor widow who put two copper coins into the chest of the temple treasury: "This poor widow has given more than any of them; for those others who had given more than enough, but she, with less than enough, had given all she had to live on" (Luke 21:3-4). Ever-active vigilance and preparedness characterize a righteous life, because even if the spirit is willing, the flesh may be weak (Matthew 26:41). To recognize one's shortcomings and imperfections, the virtue of humility is needed.

Jesus calls himself the good shepherd because his mission on earth is to show how human beings can "have life and have it abundantly", referring to the abundance of qualities which make life worth living: love, compassion, generosity, forgiveness. The possession of these qualities is not the function of material wealth or intellectual prowess. No matter what one's external circumstances or innate talents, one can still live worthy and admirable life filled with meaningful projects. By holding the possibility open for every single human being, Christianity provided a comprehensible ethical code for its followers. But whether the validity of this code depends on accompanying theological doctrines or not is an open question. To call a person "a real Christian," in the common meaning of that expression, is to say something about that person's character, behavior, and attitudes, not about the intellectual or doctrinal of beliefs. When in the eighteenth century Kant came to examine the Christian religion, he concluded that its message is primarily and essentially ethical. The concentration on the ethical dimension may be one of the consequences of a world view which, as does Christianity, interprets ultimate reality in personal terms.

## Questions

1.  What was the historical context in which Christianity came into existence?

2.  What are the essential feature of Plotinus' doctrine of emanations?

3.  How does Augustine deal with the problem of evil?

4.  What is the relation of faith to divine grace, according to Augustine?

5.  What does Thomas Aquinas mean by analogical predication?

6.  How does Thomas Aquinas solve the problem of universals?

7.  How should one deal with the presence of evil in the world, according to the Christian Gospels?

8.  What does Jesus mean by saying that a Christian can "have life and have it abundantly?"

## Notes

[1] Cyprian, Ad. Demetr. 3, quoted in W. R. Inge. *The Philosophy of Plotinus*, New York: Longmans, 1929, Vol. I, pp. 25-26.

[2] Plotinus, *The Enneads*, quoted in *Mysticism*, F. C. Happold, Baltimore: Penguin, 1963, p. 206.

[3] Ibid., p. 207.

[4] Ibid., p. 210.

[5] Quoted in W. R. Inge, *The Philosophy of Plotinus*, New York: Longmans, 1929, Vol. I., p. 121.

[6] St. Augustine, *Confessions*, V. X. 18. Trans. E. B. Pusey, New York: Dutton, 1950.

[7] This and the following quotations from the New Testament are taken from *New English Bible*, Oxford: Oxford University Press, 1961.

# Part I

# Suggested Further Reading

Abelard, Peter. *The Letters of Abelard and Heloise*, translated by Betty Radice. Baltimore: Penguin, 1974.

Allan, D.J. *The Philosophy of Aristotle*. Rev. ed. London: Oxford University Press, 1963.

Bailey, C. *The Greek Atomists and Epicurus*. New York: Oxford University Press, 1928.

Bambrough, R. *The Philosophy of Aristotle*. New York: New American Library Mentor Classics, 1965.

Barnes, J. *The Pre-Socratic Philosophers*, 2 vols. New York: Odyssey, 1966.

Barrett, C. K. ed. *The New Testament Background: Selected Documents*. New York: Harper Torchbooks, 1961.

Bettensen, H. ed. and translator. *The Early Christian Fathers*. London: Oxford University Press, 1956.

Bourke, V. J. *Aquinas' Search for Wisdom*. Milwaukee: Bruce Publishing Co., 1965.

Brumbaugh, R. S. *Plato for the Modern Age*. New York: Collier, 1964.

Burnet, John. *Early Greek Philosophy*. New York: Meridian, 1957.

Burnet, John. *Greek Philosophy from Thales to Plato*. New York: Macmillan, 1960.

Cornford, F. M. *Before and After Socrates*. Cambridge: Cambridge University Press, 1932.

DeWitt, N. W. *Epicurus and His Philosophy*. Minneapolis: University of Minnesota Press, 1954.

Dodds, E. R. *The Greeks and the Irrational*. Berkeley: University of California Press, 1960.

Dodds, E. R. ed. and translator. *Selected Passages Illustrating Neoplatonism*. London: SPCK, 1923.

Epictetus. *Enchiridion*, translated by T. W. Higginson. Indianapolis: Library of Liberal Arts, 1964.

Epicurus. *The Letters, Principal Doctrines, and Vatican Sayings*, translated by R. M. Geer. Indianapolis: Library of Liberal Arts, 1964.

Ferguson, J. *Moral Values in the Ancient World*. London: Methuen, 1958.

Festugiere, A. J. *Epicurus and His Gods*. Oxford: Blackwell, 1955.

Friedlander, P. *Plato: An Introduction*, translated by Hans Meyerhoff. New York: Pantheon, 1958.

Gould, John. *The Development of Plato's Ethics*. Cambridge: Cambridge University Press, 1955.

Grube, G. M. A. *Plato's Thought*. Boston: Beacon Press, 1958.

Guardini, R. *The Death of Socrates*. New York: Meridian, 1962.

Guthrie, W. K. C. *The Greek Philosophers: From Thales to Aristotle*. New York: Harper Torchbooks, 1960.

Guthrie, W. K. C. *The Sophists*. Cambridge: Cambridge University Press, 1971.

Guthrie, W. K. C. *Socrates*. Cambridge: Cambridge University Press, 1977.

Hadas, Moses, ed. *Essential Works of Stoicism*. New York: Bantam Books, 1961.

Hawkins, D. J. B. *A Sketch of Medieval Philosophy*. Westport, CT: Greenwood Press, 1968.

Huby, P. *Greek Ethics*. New York: St. Martin's, 1967.

Irwin, T. *Plato's Moral Theory*. Oxford: Clarendon Press, 1977.

Jaeger, W. *Aristotle: Fundamentals of the History of His Development*. London: Oxford University Press, 1934.

Kenny, A. *The Aristotelian Ethics*. London: Oxford University Press, 1978.

Kirk, G. S. and Raven, J. E. *The Presocratic Philosophers*. Cambridge: Cambridge University Press, 1960.

Leff, G. *William of Ockham*. Totowa, NJ: Rowman and Littlefield, 1975.

Long, A. A. *Hellenistic Philosophy: Stoics, Epicureans, Sceptics*. London: Duckworth, 1986.

Mure, G. R. G. *Aristotle*. London: Ernst Benn, 1932.

Nettleship, R. L. *Lectures on the Republic of Plato*. New York: Macmillan, 1958.

Randall, J. H. *Aristotle*. New York: Columbia University Press, 1963.

Randall, J. H. *Plato: Dramatist of the Life of Reason*. New York: Columbia University Press, 1970.

Rist, J. M. *Stoic Philosophy*. Cambridge: Cambridge University Press, 1969.

Rist, J. M. *Epicurus: An Introduction*. Cambridge: Cambridge University Press, 1972.

Ross, W. E. *Aristotle*. New York: Meridian, 1959.

Taylor, A. E. *Socrates*. New York: Doubleday, 1952.

Taylor, A. E. *Plato: The Man and His Work*. New York: Meridian, 1956.

Taylor, A. E. *Aristotle*. New York: Dover, 1955.

Veatch, H. B. *Aristotle: A Contemporary Appreciation*. Bloomington, IN: Indiana University Press, 1974.

Versenyi, L. *Socratic Humanism*. New Haven: Yale University Press, 1963.

Wheelwright, P. ed. and translator. *The Presocratics*. New York: Odyssey, 1966.

Winspear, A. D. *Lucretius and Scientific Thought*. Montreal: Harvest House, 1963.

*Immanuel Kant (1724-1804)*

# Modern
# Philosophy

# Chapter Five

# The
# Rationalists

## 1. Descartes: Minds are Distinct from Bodies

Descartes is often credited with originating modern philosophy. But he did not invent modernity single-handedly. When he came on the scene, Europe has gone through a period called "Renaissance" which lasted almost two centuries, roughly between 1350 and 1550. The word "Renaissance" means rebirth. What was it that was being reborn? The most immediate and correct answer is classical learning. Aristotle's thought, as we have seen, was already known in Europe and had been effectively fitted, by Aquinas, into the Christian framework. Plato's writings, however, had not been available, at least not in the original. When they did arrive in Europe, first of all in Italy, they had a tremendous impact. The dialectically lively and free-wheeling arguments of Socrates, the dramatic structure of the dialogues, their poetical vision and moral earnestness, could not fail to impress those who read them. What a contrast between them and the dry, pedantic, scholastically doctored and syllogistically presented Aristotelian doctrines!

The chief reason for the impact of classical Greek writings was their decisively and unashamedly humanistic flavor. Here, one felt no weight of the supernatural pressing at all points on the human mind demanding homage and allegiance. Humanity was the center of interest—human capacities, talents, worries, problems, and possibilities. This was what was being reborn with the help of classical learning—humanity's interest in itself, freed of the ever-present preoccupation with sin and corruption. It has been said that medieval man philosophized on his knees, but Renaissance man dared to stand up, to rise to his full statute as Man. He was no longer willing to use Church Latin as the medium of learning and expression. He wrote in the language of his own people—Italian, English, French, or German.

Interest in the multiple possibilities of human nature including a lyrical, poetic self-expression was gaining momentum steadily, affecting all areas of life. New paintings showed great interest in human form. Even while depicting religious scenes, Michelangelo shows us the glorious aspect of the human body. The details of daily life—food, clothing, musical instruments, landscape, Greek and Roman ruins, things new and old, those directly visible, and those remote in time—are painted and lovingly examined, because they present the panorama of human concerns and possibilities. The very idea of landscape to be enjoyed, of nature to be beheld aesthetically and with pleasure, was born in this period. The globetrotter, a traveler, traveling for the sake of travel also appeared on the scene. Add to this the excitement of the new discoveries by the explorers and circumnavigators of the globe—Magellan, Vasco da Gama, Columbus, and many others. The discoverers of new lands brought home stories about strange peoples and customs, exotic foods, plants, and animals. Rome acquired a giraffe for its zoo and mourned in a city-wide procession the death of its favorite elephant. The accounts of travelers were avidly read, and the promise of profit and personal wealth frequently displaced the concern for supernatural rewards.

Representatives of the Renaissance manifested this new spirit of discovery, invention, and emancipation. There was Leonardo da Vinci (1452-1519), a universal genius, who exploited the possibilities of life through his multifaceted activities as painter, writer, scientist, and engineer. His *Mona Lisa* with her smile, tantalizing the viewer with her inscrutable human depth, and his bold attempt to invent a flying machine, are but two examples of his desire to explore nature within and to conquer it without. Pico della Mirandola (1463-1494), in his work characteristically entitled *Oration on the Dignity of Man*, sums up this liberation of human powers by ascribing to God the following sentiment:

> We have set thee at the world's center that thou mayest from thence more easily observe whatever is in the world and mayest fashion thyself in whatever shape thou shalt prefer.[1]

Descartes was also a beneficiary of the rise of modern science. Like many of his predecessors and contemporaries, he was conscious not only of the expansion of the earthly horizon; the world itself seemed to explode in space. One of the important elements in maintaining the dominance of the Christian view was the belief that the earth was the center of the universe. As long as this was unquestioned, it was plausible to interpret some events in some localities, such as the birth of Christ, as having cosmic meaning. The universe was man-centered because it was earth-centered. However, this image began to change. The change was due at first to the relatively small discovery that it was not the sun that revolved around the earth, but the other way around. To us today this may seem not very important, but it had a weighty significance for the authority of the church when Copernicus and Galileo made these discoveries. These discoveries not only contradicted what was found in the Bible, but also tended to upset the whole cosmic order and hierarchy of heavenly bodies. But even though the new investigation made the church authorities nervous enough to demand a recantation from Galileo on pain of excommunication, the full repercussions were not quite realized, even by those who made the discoveries, except perhaps for one man, Giordano Bruno, another extraordinary personality representing his time.

Bruno was the first to see that the Copernican view does not end in the discovery that the earth is not the center of the universe. The new astronomy shows, he concluded, that it is meaningless to speak of "the center of the universe." It has no center, but projects from any point into infinity, with stars, suns and galaxies proliferating in all directions. This infinite universe filled Bruno with awe and wonder, shattering the familiar and honored beliefs about the earth-bound meanings of human destiny and salvation. Compared to the infinite scope of the cosmos, how significant was the birth of Jesus of Nazareth? Implications like these must have worried the bishops who condemned Bruno to be burned at the stake when he refused to recant his heretical views on the spatial relationships of heavenly bodies. The year was 1600, almost two thousand years after another champion of free thought, Socrates, had been condemned to death by the guardians of traditional beliefs.

The new science, although stimulated by astronomic discoveries and the invention of the telescope, was not limited to the exploration of heavenly bodies. The workings of nature within narrower ranges were also the object of growing interest. Francis Bacon's (1561-1626) call to scientific investigation, to the setting up of research laboratories, was heeded by scores of curious natural philosophers, as scientists were then called. Bacon himself was surprisingly unaware of many important discoveries of his day, including the discovery of the circulation of the blood by his own physician, Harvey. The microscope and the barometer were invented, spermatozoa and bacteria were discovered. Boyle (1627-1690), the first great chemist, formulated the famous law named after him, which describes the relationship of temperature, volume, and the pressure of gases. The work of Copernicus, Kepler, and Galileo helped to pave the road to the discoveries of physical laws expressible in mathematical equations. Standing on the shoulders of these scientific giants, Newton was able to formulate the famous laws of motion which ruled both the fall of the apple from the tree and the movements of stars in their orbits.

For Galileo, the universe was written in the language of mathematics. The significance of this was that the scientist no longer needed to refer to

Aristotelian "purposes" or entelechies to describe natural phenomena. Aristotle's *anima* or soul was replaced by a neutral *vis*, force, as in the now familiar formula $f = ma$. The philosophical repercussions of natural science took a long time to work themselves out. Indeed, it is doubtful whether the consequences of the new world view have fully exhausted themselves even in our own present lives. Descartes' philosophy was one of the cornerstones of that view.

The two centuries stretching from Descartes to Hegel witness another exuberant flowering of Western philosophical thought, this time not confined to the Greek peninsula, but including all of Europe. Historians agree that the revival of Greek classical learning during the Renaissance was one of the chief influences on modern European philosophy. We have also noted that the expansion of geographical and cosmic horizons, brought about by global voyages and by the Copernican revolution, helped to stimulate intellectual ferment analogous to that experienced by the ancient Greeks, who in their travels reacted to the varieties of cultural life in the Mediterranean world. Those of the Modern Era shared the Ancients' expectation that the world could be understood and explained if it were subjected to proper scrutiny and inquiry. That spirit of intellectual daring ended the domination of all learning by the Church, which, while allowing philosophical exploration within the limits of religious doctrine, tended to inhibit bolder independent inquiries. Not all theologically dominated thought was fruitless and barren; medieval philosophy contributed arguments and ideas which deserve attention and study, although the discussions were, for the most part, conducted within the confines of official dogma. Among the more interesting contributions was the medieval philosophers' treatment of the problem of universals. Besides that, proofs of God's existence, the relation between reason and faith, the separation of heresy from orthodoxy, and the problem of evil absorbed most of the intellectual energies of medieval thinkers. Modern philosophy began to establish its own special position in the history of European thought with the advent of thinkers who, like Descartes, saw the need for, and the possibility of, laying down new foundations for all knowledge.

René Descartes (1596-1650) was a gentleman scholar. His father was wealthy enough to provide a good education for his son, first in the Jesuit college of la Flèche in Maine, and later in Paris, where René, equipped with money and a valet, pursued his studies independently. After a period of service in the army, which enabled him to travel to various parts of Europe, Descartes settled in politically liberal Holland, where he wrote his most important works, including *Discourse on Method* (1637), *Meditations* (1641), and *Principles of Philosophy* (1646). The Latin name for Descartes is Cartesius, hence "Cartesian philosophy."

Having been invited by Queen Christina to help establish a Swedish academy of sciences, Descartes moved to Stockholm, where he met an untimely death. Accustomed from childhood to linger in bed until noon—some of his main insights supposedly came to him while in a supine position—Descartes could not quite take the bitter cold Scandinavian mornings, especially when the busy queen would discuss with him the plans for the academy at 5 a.m. On one of those mornings, at the age of 54, he caught pneumonia and shortly thereafter died. Descartes was said to have been of cheerful disposition. He liked to dress well, enjoyed the company of intellectual friends, and led a quiet, well-ordered life. His sensible, rational, practical philosophy is convincingly described in the opening pages of the *Discourse on Method*.

Descartes' education included good training in mathematics and logic; indeed, in later years, he made some important mathematical discoveries. He was the first to apply algebra to geometry, thus inventing analytic geometry. But Descartes had higher ambitions for the mathematical method. Why should not its rigor and precision be applied to philosophical questions? If, as Galileo thought, the universe is written in the language of mathematics, then mathematical methods are best suited to all important human inquiries. This supposition was shared by many characteristic thinkers of the day, including the other two great Rationalists, Spinoza and Leibniz. Spinoza wrote his main work, *Ethics*, in the geometrical manner, and Leibniz was known to mathematicians as the discoverer, along with Newton, of calculus.

Descartes' procedure in philosophy points out an interesting feature of the modern approach. Both Aquinas and Descartes were Christians and did not question their faith, but Descartes, unlike Aquinas, was not primarily interested in reconciling philosophy and faith. Without abandoning his faith, Descartes turned to philosophy to answer *all* of his questions; in other words, he regarded the human mind as the instrument of knowledge and discoverer of truth. His method was radical and thoroughgoing; it started with complete skepticism, but it was a methodological, not dogmatic skepticism. In other words, Descartes did not claim, as did other skeptics, that all knowledge is unreliable or impossible; instead, he proposed to examine all his beliefs and their sources in order to test their validity and reliability. Should it happen that none of his beliefs were found to be trustworthy, then he would be justified in becoming a skeptic. But, if his examination should present him with knowledge which could not be doubted, his method would lead him to truth. Furthermore, having discovered some indubitable truth, he could then use it as a criterion of truth, as a test of the truth of other propositions.

There is a certain beauty, elegance, and even a hint of dramatic suspense in the way Descartes conducted his investigation. He tried to be as cautious as he could possibly be in scrutinizing the sources of possible knowledge. First is the source of sense perception. Can we rely on it? Possibly yes, in most cases. Yet isn't everyone familiar with situations in which he was deceived by his senses? You think you see a man, but then you come closer and notice that it is only a bush. You think you hear the voice of a crying child, but it turns out to be a tomcat on his nightly promenade. The water feels hot to your fingers, but only because they were freezing cold, and so on. The instances of sensory illusion and deception are just too numerous to be ignored. If so, how can one be certain of any instance of sense perception? For all one knows, even the perception which seems most reliable will turn out to be a fraud in the next moment.

Then consider the reasoning involved in calculation. We all know how to reckon sums or do multiplications; in the simple cases, we seem to have no qualms, but in more complicated ones we are not confident and often make mistakes. To reassure ourselves, we may do them over, but even then, correct results are not guaranteed. If we can make mistakes in more complex calculation, could we not make them in simple ones as well? In fact we do. It is not easy to draw a line between cases that are clearly simple and those that are not. So here, too, we cannot claim certainty in any given instance.

Consider next the normal conviction that the objects we are surrounded by, such as the diverse furniture of our daily experience, really exist. Here I sit at the table with a pen in my hand, traveling over the firm surface of a writing pad. I look up, see the flowers of the garden, the trees and buildings in the distance. Can I doubt whether all these exist? Of course I can, countered Descartes. On many occasions, I thought that the multiple objects around me, attractive, enticing or sometimes frightening and threatening, had a real existence. They seemed real enough, for they made me tingle with delight or break out in a cold sweat. But then the next moment I wake up and say, "Thank God, it was only a nightmare," or perhaps, "Alas, it was only a dream." For all I know, I might suddenly wake up and find that the sky, the earth, and all other features of my supposedly waking experience have vanished like a dream. So here, too, certainty cannot be had.

At this point skepticism seems triumphant, but one should not jump to conclusions. Indeed, relief and sudden illumination are just around the corner. In a way, the insight comes as a surprise by a slight shift in one's object of attention. Consider now the subject that is undergoing all these experiences, perceiving, catching himself in his mistakes, doubting, dreaming, awakening, thinking. Whatever the content of my thinking, and it may be quite varied, as we have just seen, there is no denying that I, the thinker of these thoughts, exist. Can I think and not exist? If I did not exist, I would not think. So Descartes runs into one proposition that he could not possibly doubt. *Cogito ergo sum*: I think, therefore I exist. Here we have the famous Cartesian *cogito*.

Thus, skepticism is defeated. There is at least one proposition which is true and which is known with absolute certainty. This break in the clouds of skepticism turns out to be much more than a sunny interval. In fact, to change the metaphor, the tactical retreat into doubt has paid off in a most positive way. Descartes believed that he had found a position from which he could counterattack, rout the enemy, and carry off a resounding victory on behalf of reason. How did he do it?

Once more, he carefully examined what he had. The *cogito*, the proposition "I think, therefore I am," has a peculiar feature. It is known clearly and distinctly. It is intuited without any possible doubt, and it is distinctly set off over and against any other proposition. Since this is the feature which brings out the truth of the *cogito*, it can be used as a criterion for any truth. Thus, Descartes had what he was looking for: a way of distinguishing knowledge which is certain from that which is not. True propositions are those which can be thought clearly and distinctly. In this, Descartes had a rock upon which he could construct the rest of his philosophical edifice.

There are further truths to be discovered in contemplating the proposition "I think, therefore I am." Since what I am thinking about, for instance my physical surroundings or even my body, is separable from the act of my thinking, I am right in concluding that a thinking substance is distinct from everything else. I know myself directly and immediately as a thinking substance. Thus it follows, Descartes concluded, that "this ego, this soul by which I am what I am, is entirely distinct from the body and is easier to know than the latter and that even if the body were not, the soul would not cease to be all that it is." [1]

Next, Descartes turns to the fuller content of his mind or soul. He finds that the absolutely certain *cogito* proposition (together with the criterion of truth, which it carries on its face) occurs in the context of other thoughts. Along with discerning truth, his soul also encounters or entertains doubt, uncertainty, hesitation. In other words, it is not perfect. It judges itself to be so. But here again, a question intrudes itself. How could the ego, the soul, judge itself imperfect without a standard for such a judgment? Whence does the very idea of perfection come into my soul in order to condemn me as imperfect?

One answer to this last question is clear. Knowing myself as a doubting, uncertain being, I could not possibly be the source of the idea of perfection. I simply do not qualify. Yet that idea is in my mind. Since every reality must be accounted for, and the idea of perfection is real (otherwise I could not judge myself as imperfect), my task is to find its source. Aside from myself, this source could possibly be the world, all of those things distinct from myself, that provide the content of my experience. The same objection, however, that disqualified me as a possible source of the idea of perfection also

disqualifies the world. Many things I find around me strike me as less good
or less beautiful than they could be. Even I could think of some ways of
improving them. Hence, it follows that the world does not furnish me with
the idea of perfection.

Only one possibility remains: the source of that idea is God. There are
obvious echoes here of St. Thomas Aquinas' argument that any existing
perfection must come from a perfection which is greater than itself; hence,
there must be a reality more perfect than anything existing in the world,
including humanity. That reality accounts for whatever perfection can be
encountered in the world.

Having connected the idea of perfection with its source in God, at this point
Descartes produces a version of the famous ontological argument which was
first formulated by St. Anselm. What is the reality corresponding to the idea
of perfection? First, it cannot contain any limitation, because a limitation would
be a sign of imperfection. As unlimited, God cannot be dependent upon
anything else. Second, God cannot be composed of parts. This conclusion
is derived from the fact that I myself am composed of mind (an intelligent
nature) and body (a corporeal nature); my partial dependency on the latter
is manifestly a defect. Since God could not possess this, or any other defect,
His reality is not a composition; His substance is single, simple, and infinite.
Obviously, all things which are composite and finite stand in a relation of
dependence to God. Everything depends on Him and could not subsist without
Him for a single moment.

Now comes "the ontological move." *To on*, in Greek, means reality, being,
existence. Of course, one might object, so far we have been moving within
the realm of mere possibilities; we were analyzing concepts. Not so, counters
Descartes. If God is perfection, then the idea of His existence is contained
among His necessary attributes. To conceive of perfection, and yet to conceive
of it as nonexistent is to conceive an impossible contradiction in terms. A
nonexistent perfection would not be perfect. It is as if one were to offer the
following description: "An excellent car, comfortable, safe, economic and
beautifully made; it is deficient in only one respect, it does not exist." Would
this do as a description of a perfect automobile? We should be warned,
however, that this example, although it shows the form of Descartes' argument,
is misleading. When Descartes talked about perfection, he was careful to note
that he was not talking about the perfection of any *finite* thing, be it an
automobile or an island. In fact, the ontological proof is applicable only to
one entity, that of God. For only God is infinite and contains no limitations.
With this proviso, the argument is as conclusive as any valid proof in geometry.
That three angles of a triangle must be equal to two right angles follows from
the very concept of a triangle. Of course, it does not follow that a triangle
should exist. But the concept of God includes His existence, just as triangularity

includes the idea of three angles being equal to two right angles. The failure to see this is a mistake in logic, not a mistake in faith. Thus it came about that Descartes' investigations led him to prove the existence of a being who for other believers was but an object of faith. Whether the God discovered by Descartes is the same God worshipped by Christians is another question.

At this point we are certain of two items: one, the existence of thinking substances; and two, the existence of God. Indeed, when Descartes established the existence of God, he remarked that now the criterion of truth is *guaranteed*. There is some question whether or not Descartes was arguing in a circle here. He used the criterion of clearness and distinctness to prove the existence of God, and then he proceeded to say that this criterion is true because God exists. The logic of the issue is too complex to be discussed adequately in a short exposition of Descartes' thought. One possibility of avoiding the issue, however, would be to say that the entire argument which we have tried to trace is a seamless whole and constitutes an analysis that lays out the whole conceptual setting of logically related and mutually supporting concepts.

One final item must be included before Descartes' reconstruction work is complete. Although the existence of bodies and of the external world has been mentioned, the epistemological status of our knowledge of that world has not been considered. Can we say that aside from God and ourselves as minds, the material world exists in its own right? Yes, we can, said Descartes, using the following argument: We have perceptions; they must have a source. This source could be either ourselves, or God, or some third reality. It could not be ourselves, because most perceptions persist no matter how hard we try to think them out of existence or deny their reality. They stubbornly intrude themselves on our experience and persist in their being. God could not be directly manifesting Himself in external things, because by now we know that God is no deceiver; if He were directly present in all things, we would be aware of His presence in them. But we are not, so God is not the source of our perceptions. Then, the only remaining possibility must be true, namely, that the external world exists in its own right. Thus the rational demonstration of what can be known is completed. The methodological doubt has paid off handsomely.

What is striking about this whole procedure is that it is boldly self-confident. It reminds us of the affirmative, optimistic use of reason on the part of the classic Greek philosophers. In that sense, both philosophical approaches, the ancient and the modern, are highly rationalistic. Furthermore, its connection with religion, although important, is secondary. For, we must not forget that this is also the age of rising natural science, in which Descartes was deeply interested. He himself had conducted many experiments, especially in anatomy. His hope was that the mathematical method would produce great results when applied to the study of matter.

While the essential attribute of minds is thought, the essential attribute of matter is extension in space. Descartes even believed that all other properties of matter were sense-dependent. A piece of wax changes almost all its sensory properties when placed near the fire—all but extension. That does not change. Thus, the study of matter is the study of the arrangement of space, the proper study for mathematical physics. Significantly enough, this was the aspect of Descartes' discovery that became of central interest to future investigations of natural philosophers. They believed that the workings of the world should be explicable in terms of efficient causes, with no reference to final causes or purposes. Consistently enough, Descartes himself thought that all animals, except of course human beings, were machines, or automatons. Descartes exerted a strong influence on modern science and mathematics, but his approach raised other issues, many of which are centrally important to contemporary philosophy. Some of them were taken up by Descartes' immediate successors. Before turning to them, it may be useful to compare his views to those of his illustrious rationalist predecessor, Plato.

Plato's philosophy proclaimed the dualism of appearances and Forms. Descartes's dualism affirmed a radical distinction between bodies and minds. In some ways, the two dualisms have much in common. For Plato, knowledge can be had when the soul disregards the appearances and looks beyond them to the World of Forms. For Descartes, bodies can be known only indirectly; the existence of the external world requires a rational proof, and the criteria for proving any truth are accessible to the mind alone. Bodies are defined as unthinking substances. For both philosophers, the capacity to think, to apprehend truth, is lodged in the mind, in the rational aspect of man. Descartes, like Plato, believed that the existence of minds is conceivable without the existence of bodies. Both were rationalists, and both thought that philosophical knowledge is akin to mathematical knowledge.

In spite of asserting the primacy of minds over bodies, Descartes, unlike Plato, had no doubt that we can get reliable knowledge about matter. Since for him the essence of matter is extension and since extension is an arrangement in space, to know the essence of material things is to study the mathematical relations governing those things. Like Galileo, Descartes believed that the universe was written in the language of mathematics, and he was attracted to the newly emerging mechanical models in physics. For Descartes, even animals are pure automata, and therefore animal physiology is but a branch of physics or mechanics. This side of Descartes' philosophy was in agreement with and confirmed the prevailing hope of his contemporaries that all natural phenomena could be subjected to scientific-mathematical investigation.

Descartes' radical dualism, however, saddled him with the thorny problem of explaining how two wholly distinct substances could interact. All material objects, including human bodies, have extension. That is, they exist in space, but mind has no existence in space, and thought has no extension. Nevertheless, it is obvious that bodily states, for example cold or hunger, do affect mental states. Conversely, thought may lead to bodily action. If the two substances, the mental and the material, are fundamentally distinct, how can they interact?

Descartes was bothered by the problem and could not quite solve it. The solution which occurred to him, in connection with his anatomical studies, was so obviously wrong that it is difficult to take it seriously. In studying the components of the brain, Descartes discovered a centrally located organ, the pineal gland. Since at that time the function of the gland was not known, Descartes thought that this may be the point of the connection between mind and body. This means, however, that in order to affect the gland, which is located in space, the mind would have to be also located in space, and vice versa, that the gland should share with the mind the attribute of thought.

Be that as it may, the problem of interaction constituted a serious gap in the logic of the Cartesian system. Some of Descartes' contemporaries tried to remedy the situation by overhauling the entire system in a fundamental way. The philosopher Geulincx thought that since, as Descartes taught, everything depends on God, there is really no need to worry about the way in which the interaction between minds and bodies takes place. On the occasion on which a bodily change takes place, a corresponding idea occurs in the mind. This doctrine was called "occasionalism." Clearly, this solution leaves much to be desired. The problem is fundamental, and an entirely new reconstruction, or a new system, was needed to remove the difficulty. One such system, rivaling, or in the eyes of many, surpassing, Descartes', is found in the philosophy of Spinoza.

## 2. Spinoza: All Being is One

Baruch, or Benedict Spinoza, lived his philosophy. His career demonstrates perfectly the new mood of spiritual independence and bold intellectual initiative. In Spinoza's case, this independence proved costly. Born in Amsterdam in 1632, Spinoza belonged to a family of Jews who had fled to Holland to avoid persecution in Portugal. His orthodox parents saw to it that he was well versed in the Old Testament and the Talmud. They wanted him to become a Rabbi. However, Baruch's studies inclined him to seek his own truth to the extent that he began to voice strong doubts about his ancestral religion. Since he persisted in his criticism, he was finally excommunicated from the synagogue and abandoned by his family. He fled to the Hague, where, in gratitude to some Christian friends who sheltered him for a time, he adopted the name "Benedict." As a Rabbinical student, he had learned a trade; his was lens grinding. This became his daytime occupation, supplied his livelihood, and satisfied his interest in optics. At night he worked at his philosophy. After he published a work on Cartesian philosophy, his fame began to grow, and he was offered a chair at the University of Heidelberg, which he refused, preferring to retain his independence. After his death in 1677, his most famous work, *Ethics*, was found in his drawer. All those who knew him testified to the kindness, gentleness, and humaneness of this quiet man who made philosophy the guide of his life.

Spinoza was a true son of his age in his belief in the efficacy of the mathematical method. Indeed, he carried this method even further than had his predecessors by writing his main work in geometrical style, stating axioms and definitions and deducing theorems. Spinoza thought that all knowledge should have this thoroughly logical deductive character. It appears that suggestions toward the new approach resulted from his becoming aware of logical flaws in Descartes' system.

According to Descartes, there is one infinite substance, namely, God, and two distinct finite substances: the mental and the material. When reflecting on these distinctions, Spinoza was detained by the notion of substance itself. What does it mean when we really think it through? Remembering, perhaps, that even for Descartes the infinite substance, or God, contained no limitation, Spinoza thought that the only correct logical conclusion to draw from this was that there can be only *one* substance. It belongs to the *definition* of substance that it is self-caused, self-dependent, self-existent, and free. These multiple references to "self" are logically implied in the concept of substance as not limited and not determined by anything outside itself.

If this view about substance is correct (and it is, Spinoza believed, for we were merely drawing out its logical implications), then further consequences must follow. It is clear that the notion of finite substances is a contradiction in terms. If something is finite, then it cannot be substance; this means that its reality, its being, cannot be characterized independently of that which is substance. Another way of putting this is that "finite substances" and all their "modes" or "modifications" are only *aspects* of the one self-existent substance. In other words, all reality is one.

This does not mean that Descartes' distinction between the mental and the material does not hold. It still does, except that the status of these dimensions is altered. Instead of being regarded as independent substances, they should be seen as *attributes* of the one substance, namely, God. So, if we think of the world as Nature, as the order of existing things, then, in effect, we are also thinking of God, of one of His attributes. Hence Spinoza concluded that it is quite proper to speak of God or Nature, *Deus seu Natura*, in the Latin text of his *Ethics*. Among the attributes of God are found both thought and extension, but bearing in mind the infinite reality of God, we must take the word "among" seriously. It so happens that we, being mental-corporeal beings, are aware of only two of God's attributes. Thus, we can read, so to speak, only two pages in the volume of God's work, which is infinitely rich in attributes.

Whether we approach anything from the corporeal-material side or from the mental side, we are still referring to a mode of God's being. As far as our experience is concerned, everything can be seen from these two directions. This is Spinoza's double-aspect theory, or psychophysical parallelism. According to this doctrine, the order and connection of ideas are the same as the order and connection of things. When we get to know something, its mental side is accessible to us. But in addition to the mental side, each thing also has a physical existence. To every mental occurrence there is a physical correlate; conversely, to every physical event there corresponds a mental side. This means that there are no events which are merely physical or merely mental. Spinoza's double-aspect theory, or psychophysical parallelism, is reminiscent of Aristotle's move in his criticism of Plato: form has no existence independent of matter; we always encounter matter *in* some form and form in some matter. Analogously, Spinoza argued that to each physical phenomenon there corresponds a psychical, or mental, side.

Note that this doctrine avoids the problem of interaction. If everything has two aspects which are parallel to each other or always exist side by side, we need not worry how one *affects* the other. They do not affect each other, but with a change in one, a corresponding change in the other also occurs. This has an important consequence for Spinoza's ethical theory, as we shall see later on.

We have noted at the outset that God, or Nature, is free, self-caused. To this we can add a corollary that nothing else is free. Every modification of substance, every event in the world is determined and follows logically from "God or Nature." To understand an event, we must trace its connection with other events, and a proper understanding of any event will show that, given these contextual connections, it could not have been otherwise. Thus, Spinoza's view is thoroughly deterministic. If we were to allow some final causes and purposes to display themselves in the scheme of things independently of God's nature, then we could not connect all things and events in their actual order, we could not explain them. Hence, the presence of final causes or purposes would make the world irrational. The explanation of things must proceed by efficient causes alone, recognizing that they operate with necessity and ultimately display God's own nature and reality.

In the light of this metaphysics, what is Spinoza's theory of knowledge? According to him, there are three kinds of knowledge: (1) sensitive, (2) scientific, and (3) intuitive. Sensitive knowledge is our knowledge of things as they affect our senses. It is a knowledge of surfaces without any depth—

the immediate verdict of perception without interpretation, explanation, and analysis. Obviously, even though such knowledge may be correct up to a point, it will be obscure, limited, and unreliable. It will consist of vague notions and opinions and will not reveal anything essential or permanent. At this level the mental attribute of God's nature is only minimally at work in us, operating merely as passive imagination.

When we move to the next level, the imagination merges into active reason. At the level of scientific knowledge, the obscurity of initial impressions is gradually replaced by an orderly vision in which the logical connections among things can be perceived in terms of principles and laws. The abstract ideas of physics and mathematics are employed to widen the human horizon of intellectual vision, thus allowing us to share in God's true arrangement of nature. Here, Spinoza does not abandon Descartes' criterion of truth. The clearness and distinctness of ideas provide their validation.

However, science is not enough. No matter how clear and true the particular items of knowledge are, there must come a point where they must merge into a whole. This can come only as a result of intuition. Somehow, the logical connections must merge into a unity of complete order. Until we reach this point, the necessity of the particular relationships of things to one another will not be experienced. Intuition yields the perception of such a necessity, in which we perceive that things are the way they have to be, as expressing God's own order. "The more we understand particular things, the more do we understand God." We must endeavor to put aside all our biases and partialities, for God in us thinks impartially and impersonally. Needless to say, such a vision will have unsurpassed beauty, higher than mathematical elegance and scientific conclusiveness. For then we will be able to see things, as Spinoza puts it, under the form of eternity. "The human mind, in so far as it knows itself and its body under the species of eternity, thus far it necessarily has knowledge of God, and knows that it exists in God, and is conceived through God."[2] Knowledge, then, in effect, is a union with God. One consequence of this view is *pan*psychism, the theory that the universe is permeated by mind through and through, thus making it amenable to rational analysis and understanding. Moreover, since all phenomena are interconnected and on the physical level are subject to the law of causality, God, or Infinite Substance, or, in Spinoza's appellation, *Natura Naturans*, permeates all reality. To understand things truly is to see them as God sees them, under the aspect of eternity. This philosophy combines Aristotle's naturalism—the respect for the natural order of things (*Natura naturata*)—with Platonic idealism, urging us to aspire to highest perfection through understanding of and sympathy with all things. It is not surprising that Spinoza's lofty idealism inspired many of his readers, among them Goethe. There is a definite mystic overtone in this philosophy; not without reason was Spinoza later called a "God-intoxicated man."

Spinoza entitled his main work *Ethics* for a good reason. The greater part of the book is concerned with questions of human conduct. His objective was to discover the good life for humanity. But this cannot be determined independently of discovering how we fit into the scheme of things. This, in turn, calls for a correct determination of what that scheme is. Having done this, Spinoza devotes his full attention to what a truly philosophical life should be like. Although these conclusions are an integral part of Spinoza's entire system, we may postpone them until we deal with some representative theories of modern ethics in Chapter 8.

## 3. Leibniz: Each Individual Mirrors the Universe in Its Own Way

Gottfried Wilhelm von Leibniz (1646-1716) performed brilliantly in the worlds of both thought and action. Engaged successfully in many scholarly activities, Leibniz had stimulating personal contacts with other illustrious personalities of his time, including Spinoza, whom he visited in Holland. His great ambition was to bring about a reconciliation between Protestantism and Catholicism; he also proposed an alliance of all European states. Philosophy was not his exclusive interest; he studied jurisprudence, mathematics (besides calculus he also invented a calculating machine), history, theology, and philology. In his philosophical works, he addressed himself to questions raised by all prominent philosophers, both of ages past and of his time. His works include *New System of Nature* (1696), *New Essays on Human Understanding* (written in 1704 but not published until 1765), *Theodicy* (1710), and *The Monadology* (1714), which is the best known of his works. For many years he worked as a librarian of the Hanover Library and wrote the history of the House of Brunswick. Undoubtedly the greatest German philosopher before Kant, Leibniz nevertheless died a forgotten man, his passing going unnoticed even by the Society of Sciences in Berlin, which he had helped to found.

Perhaps Spinoza's preoccupation with the unity of all being satisfies the craving to see things under the aspect of eternity. It is comforting to know that somehow all things are one, that ultimately there is only one reality, one substance, namely God. The pantheistic note of Spinoza's philosophy undoubtedly has an attraction for those who cannot rest content until the finitude, the contingency of things and beings is taken up into a larger whole, finally encompassing all there is. In Spinoza's philosophy we may have the closest approximation to those teachings of the East which emphasize the unreality of any particular thing or self and want to shift our attention to the Brahman, the World Soul, in which the illusion of all particularity and temporality is dissolved.

In regard to this tendency, Leibniz is a true son of the West. He affirms the theme which was so dear to Socrates' heart and which also constitutes the philosophical core of the Christian religion, namely, the ultimate importance of the individual soul. It is not surprising, however, that Leibniz does this in the context of the views and doctrines prevalent in his time. In fact, like Spinoza before him, he examines critically some of Descartes' basic distinctions and points out their logical flaws. Although he found much of the Cartesian and Spinozistic mode of thought congenial, Leibniz saw the need for a fundamental revision of their key points. He directed his arguments against both Spinoza's notion of substance and Descartes' characterization of matter.

Recall that for Descartes, the essence of matter was extension. But extension is essentially a mathematical concept, applicable primarily to geometry. Does this reveal the true nature of material substance? Not at all, says Leibniz, for it completely ignores the active, dynamic component of all material things. Anticipating later developments, Leibniz prefers to say that matter is what it does. The energetic, behavioral aspect of things gives a clue to their real nature. Take a keg of sand and a keg of gunpowder. Their extension or dimensions may be the same, but set a match to both and see what happens. This illustration brings home what Leibniz thought worth calling attention to, namely, power, force, or energy. We must look to these concepts to give us a true characterization of things. They should not be understood in the physical sense alone. Leibniz's prototype here is the Greek word *to dynamicon*. He attributed to this concept two aspects—passive and active. "Passive power properly constitutes matter or mass; active constitutes entelechy or form."

There are, says Leibniz, also other grounds for dissatisfaction with mere extension as the characteristic feature of matter. Here, he anticipates an argument also used by Berkeley against Locke. It is possible to demonstrate, says Leibniz, "that the ideas of size, figure and motion are not so distinctive as is imagined, and that they stand for something imaginary relative to our perceptions." In other words, "we may doubt whether they are actually to be found in the nature of the things outside of us." In pointing to the relativity of spatial characterizations, Leibniz effectively undermines their status as ultimate. Instead, ultimacy should be ascribed to something else, namely, force.

Note how interesting and far-reaching this move is. If the measurement in space does not really reveal the most fundamental nature of material things, and if instead we must speak of forces or energies, as modern physics also tends to do, then it becomes very difficult to take any mechanical account of the world seriously. Leibniz recognized this and christened the ultimate units which manifest a certain persistent form of behavior and a unique career, not *atoms* as did Democritus, but *monads*. The term "atom" is still dominated by a concept of spatiality, and its behavior is wholly mechanistic. Although all atoms are naturally and inherently in motion, their movements and situations are determined from the outside, by the movements of other atoms. "Nought happens for nothing, but everything from a ground and of necessity," said the early Greek atomist. Even Epicurus was not satisfied with this view, and suggested that atoms have at least the potential for a swerve, of initiating some motions of their own. Still, this highly limited degree of initiative was not purposive and did not realize any design for Epicurus; thus, it was compatible with a purely mechanical interpretation of events, which, consequently, are endowed with no meaning and signify nothing.

Leibniz's monads are very different from this. In fact, they are the centers of meaning and value. Each monad is a unique expression of the universe, mirroring it from its particular standpoint. This is Leibniz's famous Monadology. The relationship between the mental and the material ceases to be a problem because there is no way of characterizing the material except in terms of some activities. Some of these activities are clearly such that their characterization as "mental" is obviously correct. Thus, human monads are properly called "souls," because of the nature of their activities. Besides souls, that is, monads which exhibit consciousness, there are also those which appear to lack it. But here Leibniz tended to agree with Spinoza and therefore accepted the double-aspect point of view. Even the monads which exist on levels far below those of human consciousness should be attributed some capacity of perception, no matter how limited. Leibniz called it *petites perceptions*, small perceptions. This appears to be consistent with his own view that everything which exists exerts some force, some effort, in maintaining itself in existence. Such exertion cannot be devoid of all self-awareness and feeling. Interestingly enough, a contemporary philosopher, Alfred North Whitehead, expressed a similar view in his *Process and Reality*, a distinguished speculative philosophical system of our century.

Much more can be said of a monad than that it perceives or has feelings, or is conscious. In the course of its existence, it expresses its unique career, which, as we have just said, at the same time reveals the universe from its characteristic perspective. Thus, Leibniz managed to affirm the world from two directions: it is meaningful in its totality and in its every detail, every single detail being a phase in the life of a monad. Leibniz accepted the conclusion of his predecessors that the presence of all finite and contingent beings cannot be explained by reference to any collection of other contingent beings. He believed that "the sufficient or ultimate reason must needs be outside the sequence or series of these details of contingencies, however infinite they may be." Hence, "the ultimate reason for things must be a necessary substance in which the detail of the changes shall be present merely potentially, as in the fountainhead, and this substance, we call God.'' God's free action, then, must be invoked in order to produce the final explanation of why everything is as it is. All the details of the world are linked together throughout, and ''there is but one God and this God is sufficient.'' Every individual career exists potentially in God, but each monad brings its potentiality into actuality in its own way.

Leibniz realized that if every single action and event in the world is following out a career inscribed in its inner core and prescribed by God's will, then it cannot be that the monads *cause* each other's actions. As Leibniz put it, ''one created monad cannot have a physical influence upon the inner being of another.'' Strictly speaking, monads do not affect one another at all; they are ''windowless,'' each following out the course designed for it by God. But the realization of that design is not wholly up to God. Leibniz claimed that ''created things derive their perfections through the influence of God, but their imperfections come from their own natures, which cannot exist without limits. It is in this latter that they are distinguished from God. An example of this original imperfection of created things is to be found in the natural inertia of bodies.''[3]

If monads are ''windowless,'' that is, do not affect one another causally, why does there appear to be such a coordination of natural processes, an orderly and regular succession of events, with many entities cooperating and seemingly affecting one another? Leibniz's answer to this is his doctrine of *pre-established harmony*. As a symphonic work fills the air with all its harmony and beauty because each musician independently plays his own notes, so the action of the universe is an orchestration of independently pursued individual goals. The musicians do not cause one anothers' sounds, yet the activity is orderly and intelligible. Another way of illustrating the pre-established harmony is to imagine a watchmaker's shop in which clocks and watches of various shapes and sizes are perfectly synchronized to show the same time. This second illustration is less fitting, because of the obviously mechanical operation of each component. By contrast, each monad displays a purposive dynamism which requires a reference to the fuller surroundings, to the context of the action of other monads, in order to be understood. Indeed, Leibniz is prepared to say that we can think of each monad as a universe in itself, provided we do not forget that all monads are ''only the aspects of a single one as seen from the special point of view of each monad.''

The Leibnizian cosmos is bustling with activity, but it is harmonious, purposeful, meaningful activity. Leibniz also said that this is the best of all possible worlds, a verdict which later on we shall see squarely contradicted by Schopenhauer. On what grounds did Leibniz proclaim this optimistic conviction? How can it be squared with the obvious presence of evil and suffering in the world? Leibniz was aware of the problem which his view presented, but he also thought that it contained a solution to the problem of evil.

According to Leibniz, evil is threefold: metaphysical, physical, and moral. "Metaphysical evil consists in simple imperfection; physical evil is suffering; moral evil is sin." Physical suffering is a natural ingredient in life. It is a counterpart to pleasure, which is a sense of rising perfection. Moreover, pain on the whole is the exception rather than the rule. Leibniz was astonished that people are sick only occasionally, and are not always ill. Moreover, suffering is largely the result of sin, thus pointing to moral evil, which is essentially a sense of being limited by the weaknesses and imperfections of created beings. Indeed, Leibniz appears to reduce moral evil to metaphysical evil. The existence of anything sets a limiting condition on the existence of any other existing thing. If there were only one thing in our entire space, then any other thing created afterward would be limited by that thing to the extent that it could not occupy its space. Thus, this principle of limitation of creation is applicable throughout. Once a certain course has been followed, it imposes certain conditions on subsequent possibilities and developments. When we appraise anything, we must take into account all conditions under which it exists. We must not ask what kind of world is possible, but what kind of world is *compossible*, that is, what best arrangement is compatible with everything else that also exists. Leibniz emphasizes his doctrine of the "compossibility" of God's attributes. In being both all-good and all-wise, He chose to create the world which is better than any conceivable alternative. We may recall here that for Plato also, the imperfections present in the world are simply due to the imperfections of the materials with which God had to work. To Leibniz the natural inertia of bodies was one example of this original imperfection of created things.

Since the world cannot be other than finite, limited, and imperfect, some evils in it cannot be eliminated. To have the necessary sterile conditions to minister to patients' health, the hospital must exterminate living bacteria. One person's good fortune sometimes involves the misfortune of another. In judging things fairly, however, we must not stop at the immediate picture, but must look to its context and its further consequences, some of which may be beyond anyone's ken but God's. To make this point, Leibniz observed that if we isolate a patch on a painting, it may present to us a chaotic, even ugly, sight, but if the rest of the canvass is uncovered, one sees a masterpiece in which the seeming blemishes merely enhance the beauty of the design. Thus, Leibniz, although not as impressed by the unity of everything as was Spinoza, nevertheless enjoined us to look at things in their wider context in order to perceive their proper place and value. He also observed that perceived evils are often exaggerated because they are seen from a subjective, partial perspective. Here, too, he agreed with Spinoza that to see things aright is to disengage oneself from personal bias.

These considerations have a bearing on Leibniz's theory of knowledge. He distinguished between the truths of reason and truths of fact. The former are those which cannot be denied without self-contradiction; they are tautologies, that is, true under any conditions. The existence of a square triangle is a logical impossibility. But truths of fact are different. The opposite of a truth of fact is possible. However, there is also the principle of sufficient reason. Even facts can be fully explained; that is, it can be demonstrated that, given the rest of the situation to which they belong, they could not be otherwise. Of course, to *show* the sufficient reason of anything may require knowledge that is not available to the person seeking its explanation. But if we remember that everything follows its course, harmonized with everything else, we may at least know how to look for a complete explanation and thus understand why it was certain that something had to be the way it was, even though it was not logically necessary. The complete knowledge of the sufficient reasons for anything and everything can of course belong only to God. However, we can at least move in the direction of that knowledge and exchange knowledge which is confused and obscure for knowledge which is clear and distinct.

Leibniz held a most interesting view about the difference between necessary and contingent propositions. Consider a subject-predicate sentence. In necessary propositions the truth is analytic; we know that the proposition is true by merely inspecting the meanings of the subject and the predicate. "The square is four-sided." The predicate is seen *in* the subject as a part of its meaning. In contingent or empirical propositions, the inspection of the meanings of the subject and predicate will not suffice. "The flower is blue." The predicate "blue" is not part of the meaning of "flower." There are flowers of other colors as well. Nevertheless, if the empirical proposition is true, then its truth will be analytic to the mind which knows the sufficient reason why it is true. Thus, although for us the proposition "Napoleon lost the battle of Waterloo" is not analytic, for the outcome of the battle could have been otherwise (e.g., if Napoleon had not suffered from a cold during the battle), nevertheless from God's point of view, who sees all of the circumstances, including Napoleon's talents and weaknesses, the loss of the battle of Waterloo belongs to the subject "Napoleon" just as certainly and necessarily as for us ordinary mortals three-sidedness belongs to the logical subject "triangle."

The principle of sufficient reason, when added to the conclusion that this is the best of all possible worlds, justifies our belief that whatever appears reasonable will be found to be so. "Nature makes no leaps," believed Leibniz. It works according to the principle of continuity. It provides a place for everything that can fit into a rational framework. All change is continuous. This is why we can think of nature as a plenum, as a "great chain of being." All kinds of species both in the flora and fauna have been included in the world of living things, thus allowing for the greatest possible scope of divine creativity and good will.

This conviction, we can now see, is a common characteristic of all rationalistic philosophers. The world is intelligible because it is rational in structure, and it is rational because it is the work of an understanding and benevolent God. Leibniz disagreed with the voluntarists, who claimed that the principles of goodness, justice, and perfection are effects of God's will alone. Rather, he thought, all His principles follow from His understanding. The primacy of reason over will, even in God, is affirmed.

Leibniz's monadology preserves Spinoza's double-aspect theory by acknowledging the presence of a physical and a mental pole in every entity. But in addition, Leibniz emphasizes the uniqueness of every monad. The nature and the history of each single monad—be it a planet, a plant, or a person—displays its own induplicable individuality while at the same time manifesting and mirroring the universe as a whole. This doctrine, when applied to human existence, underscores the typical Western view of each person as irreplaceable and intrinsically good. The universe cannot be indifferent to the fate of any individual, since the career of that individual reflects the career of the whole universe as well. This view fitted nicely into Leibniz's religious convictions and prompted him to proclaim his doctrine of preestablished harmony, according to which the whole cosmos is an expression of God, or Monad of Monads. By calling attention to the active, dynamic character of all beings, Leibniz's process philosophy anticipates the later tendency to look at matter as a form of energy—a thing *is* what it *does*. For Leibniz, all of nature is a ''great chain of being'' peopled with an infinitely rich variety of individuals, each in its way contributing to the plenum, to the fullness of things in the fullness of time. Since every view is a view from a perspective, each perspective, with its corresponding concomitant consciousness and feelings, is of intrinsic value to the one who has it. As we shall note later, A. N. Whitehead constructs a metaphysical system which echoes some of Leibniz's basic views.

## Questions

1. How did Descartes move from his initial skepticism to the discovery that he is a thinking substance, that God exists and that there is an external world? Which steps in his argument appear to you questionable?

2. Is it possible to arrive at some truths by beginning with a universal doubt?

3. What was Spinoza's theory of psychophysical parallelism? Is it as universally applicable as he claimed it to be? Must every physical entity also have a mental side?

4. What is the highest kind of knowledge, according to Spinoza? Is there a similarity between his views on this matter and those of Aristotle?

5. What is a Leibnizian monad? How does a monad differ from an atom, from a soul? Why did Leibniz believe that monads are "windowless?"

6. What were Leibniz's grounds for claiming that this is the best of all *possible* worlds?

7. Why did Descartes run into the problem of interaction between minds and bodies? In what ways did Spinoza and Leibniz try to deal with this problem?

## Notes

[1] René Descartes, *Discourse on Method*. New York: Liberal Arts Press, 1950, p. 21.

[2] *Spinoza's Ethics*, Part V. Prop. XXX, translated by Andrew Boyle. New York: Dutton, 1967, p. 216.

[3] G. W. Leibniz, *Monadology*, par. 42, translated by R. L. Latta. Oxford: Clarendon Press, 1898.

# Chapter Six

# The
# Empiricists

## 1. Locke: Ideas are Copies of Things

John Locke (1632-1704) recognized the multiple function of philosophy. At Oxford, where he lived for 30 years, he studied Aristotle and Descartes and obtained a medical degree. He was also active in practical affairs as a personal physician and advisor to a leading politician, the Earl of Shaftesbury.

Locke's interest in medicine was stimulated by his friendship with Robert Boyle, the famous experimental scientist. Similarly, Locke's main philosophical book, *An Essay Concerning Human Understanding* (1690), grew out of his year-long discussions with several friends. The result was a work which provided the foundation for the school of thought known as British Empiricism. In addition to these original contributions, Locke produced important works on political philosophy, some of which played an influential role in subsequent struggles for religious tolerance and political liberty. Many key phrases of the American Declaration of Independence are echoes from Locke's treatise on civil government.

The new thing in Locke's approach was his starting point. The Rationalists, following Descartes' lead, had been searching for principles which reason could discover independently of the contents of experience. The Cartesian *cogito* is a typical illustration of this method. The particular contents of what I am thinking play no role in my discovery of my essence as a thinking substance. Similarly, when the concept of substance was brought into play, it was examined by both Descartes and Spinoza with the objective of finding its logically necessary properties. This approach struck Locke as unsatisfactory. Restricting oneself to a logical analysis of some basic, abstract concepts is likely to lead to the postulation of ideas which lack any connection with experience. It encourages the temptation to talk about alleged innate ideas, present in all minds, which is both false and dangerous. It is false because these so-called innate ideas are not present in the minds of philosophically untutored persons or in children; it is dangerous because somebody who occupies a special position may use his influence to make people think that they have these ideas, while nothing of the sort is really the case. For Locke, the whole approach to knowledge appeared to be in need of a thorough overhaul, and he proceeded to work out an alternative to the rationalistic method.

The key word in Locke's theory is "idea," but his use of this term is very different from Plato's. For Locke, an idea is "whatsoever is the object of the understanding when a man thinks." Thinking is impossible without some objects of thought. Indeed, Locke's view of the human mind is that at birth it is a *tabula rasa*, a blank tablet on which nothing as yet has been written. To illustrate further, Locke says, "The understanding is not much unlike a closet wholly shut from light, with only some little openings." Only when ideas enter through these openings can the closet become illuminated, or the tablet furnished with letters that convey some meaning.

What are, then, ideas and how do they originate? They come from two sources, says Locke—sensation and reflection. Some examples of ideas coming from sensation are: yellow, light, heat, cold, soft, hard, bitter, sweet. Once such ideas have entered the mind, it is possible to reflect on them, but not before. It is also possible to distinguish the mind's reaction to received ideas from the ideas themselves. This is reflection. Locke speaks of these operations of the mind as internal sense and gives us examples: perception, thinking, doubting, believing, reasoning, knowing, and willing. In a sense, then, Locke reverses Descartes' order. The thinking of the self cannot occur in a vacuum; it *follows* the entrance of some particular idea. This concept, as we shall see, will have important consequences for the entire empiricist position, but it will not become definitely evident until David Hume appears on the scene.

Locke distinguishes between simple and complex ideas. Simple ideas can come from either sensation or reflection, or simultaneously from both sources. The notion of simple ideas is interesting and important from the epistemological point of view. They constitute the ultimate building blocks of which all experience is made up. One could perhaps look at them as atoms of all knowledge. Locke says that "the mind can neither make them nor destroy them." In receiving them, the mind is purely passive; it must take them as they come and recognize them for what they are. They cannot be broken down into simpler ideas or analyzed; they represent "one uniform appearance or conception in the mind.'' Think of any particular smell or color; it is simply given. Locke believes that ''nothing can be plainer to a man than the clear and distinct perception he has of these simple ideas.''

Locke went on to give examples of simple ideas. Among ideas which come from only one sense he includes any given color, sound, or smell, or a sensation derived from touch, heat, cold, or solidity. The last example may seem surprising. Locke defines solidity as ''that which hinders the approach of two bodies when they are moving one towards another.'' He also claims that solidity is distinct from both space and hardness. To get a feeling for the idea of solidity, Locke invites us to perform an experiment: place a stone between your hands and try to join them, and then you'll know what solidity is. Regarding all simple ideas, Locke remarks that we have names for only some of them. Our senses bring us such a richness and variety of simple ideas that we could not possibly coin distinct names for all of them. Some simple ideas can come from two or more senses, such as the ideas of space, figure, and motion. We can be informed, by either sight or touch, that an object is moving. Similarly, the outline of a figure can be seen or it can be traced with a finger while one's eyes are closed.

Locke gives perception, thinking, willing, remembering, judging, etc., as examples of ideas that come from reflection. There are also simple ideas that can come simultaneously from both sensation and reflection. The presence of some object may be experienced in a particular way; some things strike us as pleasant, others as painful. Since the mind registers immediate reactions to these objects, both sensation and reflection are involved in discerning these ideas, namely, the ideas of pain and pleasure. Further examples of ideas which come simultaneously from both sensation and reflection are power, succession, existence, and unity. The last two are especially interesting since, according to Locke, they are ''suggested to the understanding by every object without and every idea within.'' In other words, whatever idea is presented to the mind, we grasp it as constituting one thing, a unity. Also, its presence, when reflected on, conveys the idea of its existence. From this it seems to follow that whatever is perceived or experienced, exists. But some of the consequences of Locke's analysis were not quite apparent to him, as Berkeley and Hume were to point out later.

Let us now turn to complex ideas. How do they come about? They are made by the mind out of simple ideas. In addition to being a passive receptacle for simple ideas, the mind can also be active. Once furnished with simple ideas, it can operate on them: (1) by combining several simple ideas into a compound one, (2) by setting them side by side and comparing them, thus perceiving a relation between them, and (3) by abstracting from them something they have in common.

One may wonder at this point why Locke did not regard reflection as an activity of the mind, especially if we remember that he regarded the notion of existence as present in all simple ideas and hence, as abstracted from them. It seems, however, that Locke thought of such ideas as directly given and that reflection consisted merely in acknowledging them, for which the three modes of operating with ideas were not necessary. According to Locke, there is something involuntary about our having to accept such notions as existence and unity, while the active faculty of repeating, joining, varying, and multiplying the received simple ideas is voluntary.

Locke divided the complex ideas, voluntarily made by the mind, into three classes: (1) modes, (2) relations, and (3) substances. The first are due to the simplest operation of the mind, the ability to compound, or to add to one another, simple ideas of the same kind; hence, we have the notions of dozen or score. But when several distinct simple ideas, e.g., power, figure, and delight are combined, the operation of the mind can yield the concept of beauty, which Locke called a mixed mode.

Complex ideas of relations constitute a rich domain. By looking beyond a simple idea and seeing how it stands in regard to another, the mind can form ideas which express the perceived relationships. Examples of this are: son, father, uncle, friend, enemy, subject, professor, islander, master, superior, older, contemporary. We shall say more about the ideas of relations after examining the last domain of complex ideas, namely, substances.

The complex idea of substance presents Locke with a difficulty. Reflecting on the etymological origin of the word, he begins to suspect that perhaps his initial commitment to the acceptance of only the direct content of experience imposes important limitations; for the very idea of substance, conceived of as a substratum, as something supporting or underlying the experienced qualities or properties of the thing, is by definition something outside and beyond the immediately perceivable properties. Consequently, Locke begins by admitting that our general idea of substance is obscure and recites the story of an Indian trying to appease the child's question, "What supports the world?" A great elephant, in turn supported by a broad-backed tortoise, in turn supported by what? Something I-know-not-what is the only possible answer.

A similar difficulty exists for anyone trying to get to the bottom of the idea of substance. In the end, we are forced to be satisfied with the following: something I-know-not-what, which is the bearer of certain qualities, or, an unknown cause of the union of certain qualities. To be sure, in real life we don't seem to be troubled by the difficulty. We think of such substances as man, horse, gold, or water as several simple ideas coexisting together. Nevertheless, Locke the philosopher sees that this commonsense readiness to speak of substances merely covers up the obscurity and confusion of probing questions about the accessibility of something which we call "substance," which is more than just the collection of directly perceivable simple ideas.

The concept of substance is troublesome for Locke in an even more fundamental way. He realizes that he owes his readers a fuller account of the source of ideas. Sensation and reflection, after all, occur only in the mind. But do ideas have their reality in the mind alone? Since Locke says that the mind neither creates nor destroys simple ideas, he needs to give some reason for this independence and reality of the items which enter our experience. To deal with this question, Locke introduces his famous distinction between the primary and secondary qualities. Underlying this distinction is the view that ideas themselves are only representations of something existing independently of them. What is that something? Powers, answers Locke, powers of objects. Things have certain qualities, and these qualities are powers which can be experienced by minds in two ways: when a quality is perceived the way it is in the object, the mind perceives the primary qualities; on the other hand, when a quality is perceived in a way different from the quality itself, the mind perceives a secondary quality. Ideas are in the mind; qualities are in bodies. "The ideas of primary qualities of bodies are resemblances of them, and their patterns do really exist in the bodies themselves, but the ideas produced in us by these secondary qualities have no resemblance of them at all." [1]

Examples of the secondary qualities are colors, sounds, tastes, etc. The redness of the rose is not in the rose, but only in the eyes of the beholder. When there is no one in the forest, the sound of the falling tree does not exist. What does exist is only the powers of the physical events to produce the experience of sound in the mind. Without the mind on which to exert this power, the sound, as the idea of secondary quality, does not exist. With primary qualities, it is different; when experienced, they represent qualities as they are in the object. Examples of these are: solidity, extension, figure, motion, rest, and number. "The particular bulk, number, figure and motion of the parts of fire are really in them, whether anyone's senses perceive them or no; and therefore they may be called *real* qualities because they really exist in these bodies. But light, heat, whiteness, or coldness, are no more really in them than sickness and pain in manna." [2]

Note the Cartesian-Newtonian background of this distinction. Figure, motion, and number are objects of mathematics and physics. Moreover, the powers that produce the ideas of secondary qualities in us are really the function of primary qualities. If our senses were acute enough to discern the minute particles of bodies, then we would experience the world very differently — all of our sensations would be different from what they are now. Locke even claims that "the now secondary qualities of bodies would disappear, if we could discover the primary ones of their minute parts." Whether this follows may be questioned, but it nevertheless indicates that the supposed contrast between the primary and secondary qualities is not as radical as one might initially suppose.

Of even greater importance is the question of whether we really do have the knowledge of *bodies* when we know their primary qualities. Locke assures us that these qualities are the same in the objects as they are in the perceiving minds. But recall that, according to him, no collection of qualities really acquaints us with the substance of the thing in which these qualities are united. The most we can say is that the secondary *and* primary qualities only *represent* the objects existing outside. Ideas are copies of things. Even if we are willing to say that the idea of a primary quality of X represents X itself, we still are not in a position to claim that the relation of representation really holds. For, remember, ideas are in minds; qualities in bodies. There is no way for a mind which experiences the idea of X to inspect directly whether the idea really connects it with the power that produces X. This indicates that Locke's views follow the basic pattern of Cartesian mind-body dualism and are beset by the problems of that epistemological position. Minds can know only ideas, not the way in which these ideas connect with something outside them. Locke admits as much when he says that there can be no science of bodies: "We want perfect and adequate ideas of those very bodies which are nearest to us . . . certainty and demonstration are things we must not, in these matters, pretend to."[3]

Hence, knowledge built on the immediate messages of the senses cannot really tell us where these messages come from and whether, in fact, they come from anything at all. The basic difficulty with the copy theory of perception is that in order to say that an idea is a copy of something, there must be an independent way of getting at that thing. Otherwise, we cannot really say that we are actually dealing with a copy. This is a logical, not empirical, point, because the notion of an idea is *defined* in such a way that its connection to that to which it refers or which it is supposed to represent, cannot be expressed by means of the theory itself. To know that a picture is a picture of Thomas, I must be able to see Thomas himself and not just his picture. To say that an idea represents the power of X, I must have access to the power itself, independently of that idea. But the terms of the theory forbid such direct acquaintance with the powers themselves. I can know them only *through* the ideas in the mind. Hence, in spite of trying to find a new departure point, Locke still is following Descartes, who declared that only the mind is known directly and that the reality of bodies is inferred and must be proved. In place of such a proof, Locke merely asserts that ideas of primary qualities resemble the qualities themselves, but he offers no reasons for this contention. As we shall see later, the distinction between the primary and secondary qualities, the latter admittedly existing only in the mind, will be sharply attacked by Berkeley.

That Locke was uneasy about some of the consequences of his theory is clear from the rather unsuccessful distinctions he made in his theory of knowledge. He thought that there are three kinds of knowledge: (1) intuitive, (2) demonstrative, and (3) sensitive. "We can have knowledge no farther than we have ideas." When I see a circle, I intuit it as such; I cannot mistake it for a square. This is intuitive knowledge. We have demonstrative knowledge when we perceive agreement or disagreement between ideas. Obviously, demonstrative knowledge presupposes the complex ideas of relations. Interestingly enough, Locke contrasted mathematical knowledge to the knowledge of bodies by attributing to the former a higher degree of certainty. We need not be bothered with the question of whether the ideas compared refer to anything existing at all. We only need to examine in what relations they stand to one another. The beauty of mathematical knowledge is that it is only of our ideas. Sometimes, comparison of ideas requires intervention of other ideas; this is what is involved in reasoning leading to demonstrative knowledge, as in proving mathematical theorems by means of axioms and definitions. It should also be noted that for Locke, both moral reasoning and theological reasoning are of the demonstrative sort. Both yield genuine knowledge, but they do not concern knowledge of facts derived from experience. The idea of a Supreme Being as well as that of morality are capable of demonstration "from self-evident propositions by necessary consequences" and are "as incontestable as those of mathematics."

The third kind of knowledge, which Locke calls "sensitive," is invoked to allay the theoretical doubt about the real existence of things. Locke admits that it does not reach the degree of certainty available in the first two kinds, but his appeal here is to common sense alone. "I ask anyone whether he be not invincibly conscious to himself of a different perception when he looks on the sun by day and thinks on it by night, when he actually tastes wormwood or smells a rose, or only thinks on that savour or odor."[4] We are provided by our senses with an evidence that puts us past doubting, observes Locke.

Yet, at other moments, Locke sees the difficulty clearly, for he asks: "How shall the mind, when it perceives nothing but its own ideas, know that they agree with things themselves?" In answer to this question he reaffirms the certainty of all complex ideas *except* that of substances. The reason for this is that all other ideas are "not intended to be copies of anything, not refer to the existence of anything, as to their originals." They are combinations of ideas "which the mind by its free choice puts together without considering any connection they have in nature." This is not the case with substances. Here, the mind obviously tries to reach beyond its own depth, but alas, not very successfully. We must be satisfied with an inferior, unclear sort of knowledge in the case of material objects. An analogous situation exists with regard to minds, or spirits. If there is thinking, understanding, willing, and knowing, then there must also be a substance in which these activities subsist. The idea of such an immaterial, spiritual substance is not any *less* clear than in the case of a material substratum. However, considering the difficulties with the latter, we find little comfort in this analogy.

Locke concludes on a note which is meant to be reassuring, and yet it strongly suggests latent skepticism. "Sensation convinces us that there are solid extended substances; and reflection that there are thinking ones; experience assures us of the existence of such beings; and that the one has the power to move body by impulse, the other by thought; this we cannot have any doubt of. Experience, I say, every moment furnishes us with clear ideas both of one and of the other. But beyond these ideas, as received from their proper sources, our faculties will not reach."[5] Whether they reach even that far was the question examined in further detail by Locke's empiricist successors.

Locke's philosophical fame is also due to his contribution to political theory. His second treatise *Concerning the True Original Extent and End of Civil Government* was a reply to *Leviathan* by Thomas Hobbes (1588-1679). Espousing a materialist epistemology, Hobbes claimed that human beings are essentially creatures of desire and are governed by the craving for power, "a perpetual and restless desire for power after power, that ceases only in death." Humanity in its original state was engaged in a constant warfare of all against all. Consequently, in the state of nature, as Hobbes puts it, human life was "solitary, poor, nasty, brutish, and short."[6] The only way in which this strife can be contained is through the emergence of a power to which individuals surrender their wills in order to be safe from the natural aggressiveness of their neighbors. Hence, the state, called by Hobbes "the Leviathan" and controlled most effectively by an absolute monarch, is born out of dire necessity. Only when such a central power comes into existence can one expect a degree of peace and prosperity.

Locke disagreed with Hobbes. The actual state of nature, according to him, was quite different. Living together and acquainted with the God-given law of nature, human beings were helpful and well-disposed to one another. Recognizing their equality in a community, they respected each other's life, liberty, health, and possessions. In this original state of nature, property was acquired by "mixing one's labor" with material objects, thus making one's own the products of such an activity. A plot of land no one owns acquires an owner when he cultivates it. To avoid injustices that can be brought about by those who do not respect natural law, the community can band together to create a civil society, a "body politic." The existing rights are enhanced through a social contract, by which a government, consisting of the legislative and executive branches and safeguarding checks and balances, is established.

Furthermore, if the sovereign power resorts to force which is unjust and unlawful, the people may resort to a revolution. Almost a century later Lockes's views, as articulated by Thomas Jefferson, played an important role in the American Revolution.

## 2. Berkeley: Material Substance Does Not Exist

George Berkeley (1685-1753), born in Ireland and educated at Trinity College, Dublin, wrote most of his important works while still a young man. He developed his philosophy in the *Essay Towards A New Theory of Vision* (1709), *The Principles of Human Knowledge* (1710), and the *Three Dialogues Between Hylas and Philonous* (1713). After spending eight years in London, where he associated with Swift and many other famous English writers, he traveled a good deal on the Continent, chiefly in Italy. In 1729 he went to America, intending to establish a college in Bermuda, where the clergy for New England was to be trained and the conversion of Indians facilitated. However, this attempt ended in failure. After four years in America, he had to leave without obtaining his objective, because money for the project was not appropriated. Yet Berkeley had exerted some influence on the New World through his association with its leaders of thought and education. In 1734 he was appointed Bishop of Cloyne and served in that office for almost 20 years.

The intellectual drama of British Empiricism was enacted with surprising brilliance and perhaps with unexpected results by the young man who was to become the Bishop of Cloyne. When Swift introduced him to his then more prominent relative, Lord Berkeley, he is supposed to have remarked to the Lord, "It is a much greater honour to you to be related to him, than it is to him to be related to you." Thus, Swift foretold both the future fame and notoriety, of his young friend.

Having followed Locke's argument, we may have some idea of promising areas of further analytical searching. This certainly appeared so to Berkeley. He chose to examine two points of Locke's doctrine: (1) the notion of abstraction, and (2) the distinction between primary and secondary qualities. Locke claimed that abstraction is one of the mental operations which yields complex ideas from simple ones. By observing several individuals, the mind may discover that they have a common property. Thus, a new complex idea arises which does not refer to any of the individuals, but to the abstracted common property. It should be noted that by a similar process of detaching properties from objects in which they are observed, Plato arrived at his theory of forms, and the medieval philosophers affirmed the reality of universals. Now, the issue comes up again, but this time within the empiricists' framework.

Berkeley accepts Locke's starting point: let us examine what the particular components of our experience really are, and let us not admit anything which cannot be traced back to some simple, indestructible idea. But if we are true to this injunction, we have to admit that we never have in our minds something corresponding to Locke's supposed abstract ideas. In actual fact, when I examine an idea present to my mind, says Berkeley, I always run into some particular idea. The triangle I am thinking of is either oblique or rectangular or equilateral, or scalene. I cannot think of one that is either all or none of them at the same time. Berkeley challenges anyone to conceive an abstract idea. For his part, he cannot do it: "I cannot by any effort of thought conceive the abstract idea above described. And it is equally impossible for me to form the abstract idea of motion distinct from the body moving, and which is neither swift nor slow, curvilinear nor rectilinear; and the like may be said of all of the abstract general idea whatsoever." [7]

Note that Berkeley interprets Locke's view that our ideas are in the mind almost literally. An idea is a kind of image; either I have it or I don't. If I do have it, it may have definite but particular characteristics. If this is so, the notion of an abstract idea must be a blur of all the different properties that are subsumed under a general concept. Not surprisingly, it is not easy and probably impossible to imagine such a blur. Berkeley's point is that an abstract idea would have to contain logically incompatible characteristics, such as a motion which is both swift and slow. It is no wonder Berkeley believed that abstract ideas must involve self-contradictions.

It is not that Berkeley denied the usefulness of general words. Without such words, language would be unmanageable. Every particular stick or stone would have to have its proper name. We can go on employing general words, but we must understand their functions clearly. There is nothing to which an abstract idea corresponds (so far, Berkeley is a nominalist), but there need not be any entity corresponding to that idea in order for us to have a general word. According to Berkeley, "a word becomes general by being made the sign, not of an abstract general idea, but of several particular ideas, any one of which it indifferently suggests to the mind." He also says that "an idea which considered in itself is particular, becomes general by being made to represent or stand for all other particular ideas of the same sort." [8]

Whether Berkeley's own definitions do away with the difficulties in offering a correct account of the function of general words is doubtful. The relationship of "standing for" or "representing" other ideas is problematic and has been a focus of searching investigations up to the present time. What is important is Berkeley's correct observation that if we think of mental activities as events or episodes, we are misrepresenting what is actually going on. An attack on this whole approach to "mental events," which carries Berkeley's criticism further, is found in the recent work of contemporary philosophers, which we shall come to later in the book. Berkeley anticipates these contemporary investigations by asking us to look closely at the way language actually works instead of populating the realm of the mental with imaginary inventions. In the very same context in which he attacks Locke's account of abstract ideas, he reminds us that the function of many words is very different from "standing for" or "representing" something. Again, he anticipates our own century, which has been alerted by some philosophers to the so-called "emotive meaning." According to Berkeley, "the communicating of ideas marked by words is not the chief and only end of language, as is commonly supposed. There are other ends, as the raising of some passion, the exciting to or deterring from an action, the putting the mind in some particular disposition." [9] A typical example of such a passion-raising word for Berkeley is the word "good."

Whatever general consequences follow from Berkeley's attack on abstract ideas and whatever difficulties his own account may contain, his specific objective has still to be discussed. Indeed, his attack on abstraction was just a softening-up move, a way of laying ground for his main offensive. This offensive consisted of charging Locke with being untrue to his empiricist premises by accepting the meaningfulness of the idea of material substance. It may be illuminating at this juncture to recall once more Descartes' belief that the existence of the external world needs to be proved, that the mind is easier to know than the body, and that the character of the latter is something derived from more immediately available data. It is also helpful to recall Locke's own scruples about substance—something I-know-not-what. Starting from Descartes' premises, material substance is problematic, and Berkeley's insistence on this point is understandable.

Locke thought that the mind gets a foothold in the objective world by being aware of primary qualities, the ideas of which are the same as (or as he also put it, resemble) the qualities themselves. But Berkeley is not convinced. When we think carefully about the matter, we notice that the so-called primary qualities are reducible to the secondary ones, which, as Locke himself had said, are only in the mind. Berkeley laid the ground for this line of thought in his theory of vision, which in some ways anticipates contemporary discoveries in psychology. In visual sensations we actually never encounter space or magnitude. These characteristics are not absolute, but relative to the particular perspective. The actually seen size of a thing does not remain put, but varies from moment to moment, depending both on how we approach it, and on the angle of vision. Distance is never *seen*; it is merely suggested by other experiences. Figure and motion, Locke's primary qualities of material objects, do not exist "without the mind in unthinking substances." We cannot "conceive the ideas of the extension and motion of the body without all other sensible qualities." Figure is so many visible points; motion is either swift or slow and changes with the position of the sense organs. Primary qualities do not remain the same, "because to the same eye at different stations, or eyes of a different texture at the same station, they appear various." In short, "when we do our utmost to conceive the existence of external objects, we are all the while contemplating our own ideas." As recent psychological experiments have shown, the perception of depth is not direct, but involves the interpretation of some other visual clues.

Note the consequences of the disappearance of the distinction between primary and secondary qualities. The notion of the substratum, in which primary qualities are supposed to reside, is also eliminated. This means that the belief in the existence of material substance is without foundation. So, the notion of matter is either unintelligible, says Berkeley, or self-contradictory. It is self-contradictory because to believe in its existence is to claim that it is possible to perceive something which is admittedly unperceivable. But if we dismiss this idea from our minds, which indeed we must, because, as has been shown, it never has been in the mind, what can be said to exist? According to Berkeley, two realities — (1) perceptions, and (2) minds, or as he also calls them, *spirits* that have those perceptions. Hence, Berkeley's famous dictum: "to be is to be perceived." But since he also claims that in addition to the perceived ideas there are also perceiving minds, the dictum should be supplemented by "to be is to perceive."

At this point it is tempting to remind Berkeley of Locke's realization that the difficulties about the concept of substance may be just as applicable to spiritual or thinking substances as to material substances. Locke tried to make use of the analogy by saying that since we are directly aware of ourselves as spiritual substances, in which our thoughts reside, there must be a material substratum in which qualities exist. Neither Locke nor Berkeley was very careful on this point, and it took another empiricist, this time a Scot, David Hume, to think through the consequences of the doctrines of his predecessors.

Having demolished the idea of material substance, Berkeley is now ready to expound his positive views. That there was a need for something to fill the conceptual vacuum is evident from some of the reactions which Berkeley's demolition job precipitated. When asked for his opinion of Berkeley's doctrine, Samuel Johnson replied, kicking a stone, "I refute him thus." This "refutation" shows, however, that Johnson did not understand the doctrine. To forestall such misunderstanding, Berkeley had listed no less than 13 possible objections to his views and proceeded to answer them. These answers also helped to highlight his own positive philosophy, as contrasted with his critical arguments.

The key distinction Berkeley makes in the early part of his treatise is between the passive ideas and active minds or spirits. This distinction had already been employed by Locke, who also believed that the reality of ideas consists simply in being received. Ideas can do nothing of themselves; they are passive, inert.

Only minds and spirits can operate on them, transforming them into complex ideas and producing knowledge. Berkeley accepts this point and makes it even more explicit: all perceived ideas of sensations "are visibly inactive; there is nothing of power or agency included in them. A little attention will discover to us that the very being of an idea implies passiveness and inertness in it, insomuch that it is impossible for an idea to do anything."[10]

Where, then, does the power, the activity, the agency reside? It resides in spirits or minds, answers Berkeley, and there are two basic forms which the activity of spirit takes: understanding and will. It does not escape Berkeley's attention that having agreed with Locke that all our knowledge is knowledge of ideas and having drawn a sharp distinction between ideas as essentially passive and mind as essentially active, he is raising the question as to whether minds can be *known*. He admits that minds or spirit are not perceived. "Such is the nature of spirit, or that which acts, that it cannot be of itself perceived, but only by the effects it produceth."[11] Thus, the existence of spirits or minds is inferred from their activities. (This may remind us of Descartes' "I think, therefore I am.") Berkeley is even willing to admit that this peculiar way in which the existence of spirits must be affirmed does not really entitle us to say that we can have an *idea* of spirit. We cannot form such an idea, because all ideas "being passive and inert, they cannot represent to us by way of image or likeness, that which acts." In referring to spirits, therefore, it may be helpful to use some other term. Berkeley's choice is *notion*. We get the notion of soul or spirit when we reflect on such operations of the mind as willing, loving or hating. These are active operations, and we are directly aware of them. Indeed, these operations appear to constitute the basic model of causal agency and real existence for Berkeley, and he once more ridicules the idea of material substance: "When we think of unthinking agents or of exciting ideas exclusive of volition, we only amuse ourselves with words." This emphasis on volition, on agency as legitimating a claim to existence appears to parallel Leibniz's conclusion that all reality is dynamic, an activity of monads. But Leibniz did not deny the physical aspect of monads; he merely saw them as coupled in various degrees with the mental aspects, obviously following Spinoza's doctrine of psychophysical parallelism and modifying it by his own notion of continuity between these two aspects.

With the acknowledgement of the reality of spirits, Berkeley's thought receives a markedly anthropomorphic-theological tinge. The activity of human beings as beings that think, will, plan, design, and perceive goals furnishes a clue to the heart of the universe. That heart is also a Spirit, whose essential nature is also active, but which, in contrast to finite spirits, transcends them in potentiality and power. At this point Berkeley joins his eighteenth-century contemporaries, for whom nature appeared purposively and intelligently designed. What we call "laws of nature" is the way the Author of nature, or the Infinite Spirit, arranges the ideas in which they are experienced by finite spirits. Coupled with the religious conviction that the order and connection of these ideas is for the benefit of finite spirits, the observed regularity and beauty of phenomena can be seen as the expression of God's goodness and wisdom. Since matter, as the intermediary between God and man, has been shown to be a nonentity, a conceptual mistake, the finite spirits could experience their ideas, the world, as a much more intimate union with God. God is the creator and conserver of all existence. "In Him we live and move and have our being." This is indeed literally true, thought Berkeley, and he saw the importance of his philosophy in the elimination of the illusory, and thus unnecessary, barrier between God and humanity. He was probably also alarmed by the trend of the times to read nature as a manifestation of indifferent neutral forces, interpreted along strictly secular scientific lines. Berkeley believed that the Cartesians and the new scientists, who followed the mathematical approach to understanding the physical world, were unwittingly laying ground for atheism. In this respect, his fears were not unfounded, and he should perhaps be regarded as one of the early resolute warriors in the conflict between science and religion, which flared up quite violently in the nineteenth century and which is far from being solved today.

Against those who might conclude that Berkeley's philosophy eliminates the need for science, he argued vigorously that nothing of the sort follows from his views. Scientific investigation and explanation remain intact and should be pursued as usual. The only thing that is required is a revision of our thinking about science. Samuel Johnson's stone-kicking refutation missed the point, because Berkeley never suggested that the order of our experiences will either disappear or become unpredictable and chaotic. As in the case of vision, certain ideas incline us to expect other ideas to follow, and so in all other perceptions certain perceptions function as signs, or as Berkeley also puts it, "marks and prognostics of other ideas." In other words, some ideas guide or incline us to expect other ideas, which is another instance of God's benevolence toward us. So it is He who arranges the ideas in the order in which they appear and thus admonishes us what to expect or to avoid. He thinks them in the order in which nature appears to us. Physics is Divine Psychology. This interpretation of the order of nature does not suffer from the rigid determinism of mechanistic science. It even makes miracles intelligible. On special occasions God may suspend His customary way of ruling the world, thus allowing a miracle to take place. Berkeley remarks, however, that while possible and appropriate for God's purposes, miracles are seldom used.

If someone were to conclude from the dictum "to be is to be perceived" that things cease to exist when no one perceives them, his conclusion would not necessarily be correct. When I cease looking at the flower, it does not necessarily disappear, because another person may be perceiving it. If no finite spirit happens to be around, however, it is still possible for the flower to exist as perceived by Infinite Spirit. The only possibility that is excluded is for the flower, as a set of perceivable ideas—for this is what the flower actually is—to exist with *no* spirit at all experiencing these ideas. That, as Berkeley thought he demonstrated, is a self-contradiction. A satirical way of putting Berkeley's point is found in a popular limerick:

> *There was a young man who said*
> *God must think its exceedingly odd*
> *If he finds that this tree*
> *Continues to be*
> *When there is no one about in the quad.*

> *Dear sir, your astonishment's odd*
> *I'm always about in the quad*
> *And that's why the tree*
> *Will continue to be*
> *Since observed by yours faithfully, God.*

This humorous presentation of the doctrine should not however, be regarded as being equivalent to a refutation. Berkeley's objective was philosophical understanding, not a denial of obvious facts, perfectly understood and accepted by everyone. Indeed, the notion of matter, of material object, is still intelligible and useful. Berkeley does not recommend a reform of language in which the reference to thing-words would be eliminated, provided that references to things and material objects are regarded as just shorthand for anticipated perceptions. "Think with the learned, and speak with the vulgar." This, another of Berkeley's famous mottoes, should not be construed as a criticism or rejection of ordinary language. "Vulgar" in this connection means the common daily speech of nonphilosophers. There is nothing wrong with it as such, and we should continue to use it. We will not be misled by it as long as we do not superimpose upon it an indefensible metaphysical interpretation. When a common man says that the coins he had put in the piggy bank still exist, he means that if he were to rattle the bank, it would emit a characteristic noise; or if he were to break it, the coins would spill out. This is all he needs to say, in order to give meaning to the words, "The coins still exist even though I don't perceive them." In this sense, they obviously do exist, but not as some independently perceivable substantial reality. Berkeley does not think that his philosophy leads to skepticism. "We are not for having any man turn skeptic, and disbelieve his senses; on the contrary, we give them all the stress and assurance imaginable." [12]

There is, of course, a distinction between ideas that are perceived and those that are merely imagined, but produced by the independent activity of finite spirits. There is a great difference between the real fire and the idea of fire as it is merely thought of, or between dreaming that one is burned and actually being burned. The distinction, however, exists *within* possible experience. It differentiates between two different types of it. The ideas of sense, says Berkeley, "are more strong, lively and distinct than those of the imagination." They are not excited at random, as is often the case in human reflection, imagination, and especially daydreaming, but exhibit a steadiness, order, and coherence. This fact about ideas received from sensation testifies to the wisdom and benevolence of their author and is not to be attributed to the inert, unintelligent, and unintelligible entity called "matter." That entity does not exist.

## 3. Hume: Minds are Bundles of Sensations

The third act of the intellectual drama of British Empiricism was written by David Hume (1711-1776). Born in Edinburgh, Scotland, he studied there at the University and later served as a librarian, during which time he wrote a highly popular history of England. During the last years of his life (also spent in the Scottish capital) he was famous and surrounded by admiring friends. But fame had not come to him at once. His *Treatise on Human Nature*, published in 1739 and later recognized as one of the masterpieces of philosophical literature, failed to create a stir; it "fell still-born from the press," as Hume himself disappointedly remarked. In contrast, his *Essays, Moral and Political*, which appeared two years later, were an immediate success. Besides this book and a rewritten version of his first book under a new title, *An Enquiry Concerning Human Understanding* (1748), he also wrote *Enquiry into Morals* (1751), *Political Discourses* (1752), and *Dialogues on Natural Religion*. The latter was published posthumously because Hume was afraid that the book would offend the religious sensitivities of his contemporaries and had prudently held it back.

Hume did not always remain at home. He made several trips to France, where, after achieving fame, he was a highly celebrated figure. His wit and irony were congenial to the spirit of the Enlightenment. He also played a part in public life, as a secretary to the British ambassador in Paris and later as undersecretary of state. His equanimity of spirit and kindliness of disposition accounted for his many friends.

Hume accepted the basic premise of the Empiricist school: all knowledge is derived from experience and is built up from particular ideas. Berkeley, we recall, recognized a distinction between ideas of sensation and those created by the minds themselves in memory or imagination. The difference for

Berkeley lay in the greater vivacity, strength, and steadiness of ideas derived from the senses. Hume thought that the contrast was great enough to require a change in vocabulary. Both kinds of knowledge materials could be called "perceptions." But the original data of sense perceptions should have a name of their own, and Hume called them *impressions*. In contrast, *ideas* are only *copies* of original impressions, that is, they are contemplated in thought, memory, daydreaming, or imagination. Of course, the content of the copy is the same as that of the impression from which it is derived, but the *manner* of perception is different, and Hume agrees with Berkeley that this is a matter of the difference in liveliness or vividness.

The use of different words for the two kinds of perceptions enabled Hume to state the basic principle of Empiricism more explicitly. When an idea is entertained, it is not evident from its mere presence in the mind whether it is to be trusted. The question we need to ask and to answer is, "From what impression is this idea derived?" When such an impression cannot be produced, the idea is illegitimate, untrustworthy. The distinction between impressions and ideas also makes it possible to give meaning to words which refer to something which does not exist, such as Pegasus. The impression of a Pegasus cannot be produced, because such an animal cannot be encountered in experience. But we can have impressions of horses and of wings; if we combine the copies or ideas of these impressions, we have the idea of Pegasus. Thus, the ability of the mind to combine ideas to create still further ideas is not denied, but the test of referring the component ideas to their corresponding original impressions enables us to know whether the word itself refers to something that is perceived or whether it is a free-floating combination of ideas made by the mind.

Hume also accepted the distinction made previously by both Leibniz and Locke. Leibniz talked about truths of reason and truths of fact, the former being based on the principle of noncontradiction and the latter on some act of confirmation by experience. Locke also found that the relations between two ideas can be known with greater certainty than the relation of an idea to a thing or substance which it represents. Hence, mathematical knowledge for him as for Leibniz, was rationally demonstrable. But when it comes to physics, Locke said that there is "no science of bodies." For Leibniz, the distinction between truths of reason and truths of fact, or as it was later called, between analytic and synthetic truths, was dissolved in the mind of God, who, having perfect knowledge of sufficient reasons for each fact, sees each fact as logically following from its total history. Locke did not take this path, although he conjectured that if we were to know all the minute connections among the primary qualities of things, we would also know why secondary qualities are what they are. Presumably, the knowledge of these minute relations among the components of primary qualities will reveal further truths about the substances themselves. But Locke did not press this line, concluding instead on a skeptical note that substance "is a supposed I-know-not-what."

Hume makes this implicit skepticism explicit. He accepts the distinction between the relations of ideas and matters of fact, as he preferred to call them, but he then raises a further question: On what is the reasoning concerning matters of fact founded? He answers: It is founded on the relation of cause and effect. Locke's skeptical reflections were originated by his inability to give an adequate account of substance, as a substrate of all distinct things. Hume sees a further problem. We talk of objects affecting one another, of events making up a chain of causes and effects, and of nature comprising an order of causally connected phenomena. Thus, the notion of causality is a pervasive idea underlying all our descriptions of natural events and our explanations of the behavior of objects that surround us.

When in doubt about the meaning and legitimacy of an idea, such as the idea of cause, we know what to do: apply the empiricist test. From what impression is this idea derived? Let us examine it, says Hume, and see what impressions are actually to be found in any instance of what we call a causal relation. What do we actually observe in any causal relation? First, we observe a temporal relation of *succession*; the effect follows the cause in time. Second, the cause and effect are *contiguous*; they are close to one another in space. And third, we observe something which Hume calls *constant conjunction*; we observe *repeatedly* that cause and effect are conjoined—as far as we know, no exceptions are observed. Thus we now have *all* the impressions of which the idea of cause is a copy: (1) succession in time, (2) contiguity in space, and (3) continual conjunction.

But what we fail to find is a *necessary* connection between the two events; we merely find an *empirically observed* continual conjunction between them. "When I see, for instance, a billiard ball moving in a straight line towards another; even suppose motion in the second ball should by accident be suggested to me, as the result of their contact or impulse; may I not conceive, that a hundred different events might as well follow from that cause? May not both these balls remain at absolute rest? May not the first ball return in a straight line, or leap off from the second in any line or direction? All these suppositions are consistent and conceivable." [13] The impression corresponding to the necessary connection cannot be found in any causal relation; hence, we cannot say that in Hume's example the billiard ball *must* move the way it does; it merely does so. In other words, we cannot discover any reason why it does so, because to discover such a reason would be to discover an impression that would tell us *that* the connection is necessary. But such an impression is not to be found; hence, causal explanations are not *rational* explanations. There is no foundation for the claim that natural science, as the explanation of why events go together as they do, is based on reason. Look as hard as you may, you will never find a necessary connection between two events. But if you cannot connect two simple events in a rational way, how can you talk about the science of physics or of any natural sciences as such? This is what strict empiricism leads to when its premises are followed through to their logical consequences.

Hume's search for a necessary connection between causally connected events was thorough. He was willing to examine situations in which the likelihood of encountering the impression of a necessary connection between cause and effect is presumably the greatest. We know, for instance, that we ourselves can cause changes in our environment. At least, we can cause our limbs to move. For example, examine what happens when you raise your arm. You will it to go up: cause. It is going up: effect. You perceive the cause; you feel and observe the effect. But do you experience a necessary connection between these two events? asks Hume. He answers: "We learn the influence of our will from experience alone. And experience only teaches us, how one event constantly follows another; without instructing us in the secret connection, which binds them together, and renders them inseparable." If we think of necessary connection as established by some special power, we do not find the operation of such a power in ourselves. "We may, therefore, conclude from the whole, I hope, without any temerity, though with assurance, that our idea of power is not copied from any sentiment or consciousness of power within ourselves, when we give rise to animal motion, or apply our limbs, to their proper use and office. That their motion follows the command of the will is a matter of common experience, like other natural events: but the power or energy by which this is effected, like that in other natural events, is unknown and inconceivable." [14]

As Berkeley had already discovered before Hume, effects are different from their causes and are not discoverable *in* them. Hume added that they are not discoverable *between* them either. Thus, the predictions we make about the way things will behave in the future are not derived from reasoning. But if they are not, how are we to explain our usually successful predictions of the course of events? Hume's answer to this is similar to that given by Berkeley when he was accused of undermining fundamental human beliefs about things. The analysis of the relation of causality was not intended to show that what we see happening doesn't really happen, as Parmenides and Zeno tried to show by their arguments. Of course, we do predict and predict successfully, but we must not claim for our knowledge of events more than experience actually allows. In other words, as philosophers, we must not postulate entities or processes that in fact cannot be located in our experience. Furthermore, alternative, correct explanations of our confidence in the orderly succession of events can be found, and Hume proceeds to offer such an explanation.

To say that our expectation of future regularities is not based on reason is not to say that it is not based on anything at all. In fact, it is based on feeling, habit, custom, and *association of ideas*. Having experienced a constant, unvarying conjunction of two events, a habit is established in our minds. We are *set* to expect the repetition of the past conjunction; it is a matter of feeling. After a man has observed many times that a certain effect is followed by another event, he pronounces them to be connected. "What alteration has happened to give rise to this new idea of connection? Nothing but that he now *feels* these events to be *connected* in his imagination, and can readily foretell the existence of one from the appearance of the other." Hume also tells us that "the mind is carried by habit upon the appearance of one event, to expect its usual attendant, and to believe that it will exist."

Thus, the great guide of human life is not reason, but custom. "It is that principle alone which renders our experience useful to us, and makes us expect, for the future, a similar train of events with those which have appeared in the past." My belief that the sun will rise tomorrow is not *known better* than its opposite, but is *felt* more *strongly*, concludes Hume. In its beliefs about matters of fact, the mind is carried by feeling and custom, and all these operations of the mind which lead us to expect familiar conjunctions in and among things "are a species of natural instincts, which no reasoning and process of the thought and understanding is able either to produce or to prevent." Hume also says that "belief consists not in the peculiar nature or order of ideas, but in the *manner* of their conception and in their feeling to the mind."[15]

Hume's analysis amounts to saying that causality is something which reveals something about *ourselves*, and not about the world. *We* associate certain ideas, heap them together in our minds, establish habits, and follow them out customarily in our experience. This, of course, involves a denial that we have objective knowledge about the world. If real connections between two single events cannot be known, who can speak of the laws of nature? The result is skepticism about the nature of the external world.

But Hume's demolition job is not yet complete. Having shown that we have no knowledge of how things hang together in material phenomena, he proceeds to apply the same arguments to spiritual phenomena. Recall that Locke had been uneasy about our manner of knowing either the material or the spiritual substances. He said that we are not any better off in one realm than in the other, and he showed that we are poorly off in trying to get a science of bodies. Berkeley thought it fair to recognize that we don't have *ideas* of spirits, but only *notions*. How true, agreed Hume, only that resort to something called notions is a dubious move, because it has no place in the whole framework of empiricism. Once more apply the fundamental test and see what happens. From what impression is the idea of spirit, soul, or self derived? When you apply the test, you get a surprising result: you won't find any such impression. Perhaps other peoples' situation is different, suggests Hume, but as for himself, he knows what he has and doesn't have. "When I enter most intimately into what I call *myself*, I always stumble on some particular perception or other, of heat or cold, love or hatred, pain or pleasure, I never can catch myself at any time without a perception and never can find anything but the perception."[16] The same arguments that undermine the possibility of knowing the objective connectedness within and between things also undermine the possibility of knowing the objective connectedness of ideas in some entity which we label spirit, soul, self, or mind.

Thus, Hume completes his skepticism. Not only is the existence of bodies unknowable, but the existence of minds as well. For Hume, the mind is only a customary fiction. According to him, "the mind is a kind of theatre, where several perceptions successively make their appearance; pass, repass, glide away and mingle in an infinite variety of postures and situations."[17] For Berkeley, matter did not exist, but he still had two types of realities, ideas and spirits, or minds. Hume's analysis leaves us nothing but impressions and ideas. The content of minds is just a bundle of sensations, exhibiting only as much connectedness among them as is found in actual experience. The presence of a *single* self, however, holding these sensations or ideas together, cannot be inferred. The connection between the occurrence of thoughts and the postulation of a substance in which this occurrence is supposedly taking place is not logically guaranteed, in the way it is for Descartes. Indeed, when aware of impressions or ideas, I am not aware of any self in which they supposedly reside. I think, therefore I cannot be. Empiricism reverses the Cartesian dictum, winding up in skepticism.

Needless to say, if the existence of finite spirits cannot be made sense of, then the idea of the Infinite Spirit is no better off. In addition to the general arguments just considered, Hume also critically examined the familiar arguments for God's existence, especially the then-popular argument from design, and found them all wanting on additional grounds. Knowing that his skeptical conclusions in the field of religion would shock his contemporaries, he refrained from publishing his *Dialogues on Natural Religion* in his lifetime. However, the conclusions of his *Enquiry* were hardly less shocking. "If we take in our hand any volume, of divinity or school metaphysics for instance, let us ask: Does it contain any abstract reasoning concerning quantity or number? No. Does it contain any experimental reasoning concerning matter of fact and existence? No. Commit it then to the flames, for it can contain nothing but sophistry and illusions."[18]

But what of the entire empiricist structure which went up in flames when subjected to Hume's critical onslaught? Hume himself did not doubt that his arguments were sound. What did this mean for philosophy and for the prospect of using reason in arriving at truth and at good life? Hume did not despair. Philosophy is not all of life. When it leads you to skeptical conclusions, you can turn away from it and lead a life that is not encumbered or threatened by abstruse speculation. Moreover, according to Hume, morality is not based on reason, but on passion, feeling, and sentiment. "Reason is and ought only to be the slave of the passions, and can never pretend to any other office than to serve and obey them. It is not contrary to reason to prefer the destruction of the whole world to the scratching of my finger." [19] After leaving his study where he did his philosophy, Hume, the man, could still return to his quiet, peaceful life and enjoy a game of backgammon. Be a philosopher, he said, but amidst all your philosophy, be still a man.

This was Hume's way of facing his own scorching skepticism, because of which he was often referred to as the terrible Hume. But philosophy did not come to an end. Hume's predicament was not inevitable. His great achievement was that he boldly and courageously followed out the logical consequences of the empiricist position. There was a possibility, however, that the premises of this position were not as solid as they initially appeared to Locke. Perhaps it was time for philosophy to retrace its steps. And so it is not surprising that another philosophical giant, Immanuel Kant, came to remark that it was Hume who aroused him from his dogmatic slumber.

It is important to note, at least in a summary way, that although the British empiricists map out a conceptual territory of their own, their basic premise is essentially Cartesian. Like Descartes, Locke undertakes to discover what is going on when a person thinks, or what is present to his understanding at any given time. The key term for the empiricists is "idea," the typical model of which is an item of sense perception. Thus, I have an idea of redness while looking at a red flower, or an idea of solidity when I try to squeeze an inflated football. Starting with this model, the empiricists tried to assimilate to it other kinds of ideas, even such ideas as "unity," "existence," or "willing" (the latter, for Locke, coming from what he called "reflection"), but, as we have seen, the results were not very convincing. Hume introduced a further refinement by limiting the notion of idea to a memory or image of an "impression" previously received in actual experience. But that refinement did not solve basic problems, which began to arise very early, even in Locke's originally perceptive, yet perplexed, mind.

The big culprit was the idea of substance; somehow it refused to fit into the empiricist framework. Because of the very meaning of the word, substance could not be present to a man's mind when he thinks. It insisted on staying outside or beyond the reach of the senses and reflection. How, then, can one get hold of or understand substances? Locke's treatment of the question verged on outright skepticism, although he would not quite admit it, even to himself.

His distinction between primary and secondary qualities did not quite work, because, as Berkeley pointed out, the ideas of primary qualities, being *ideas*, can be *only* in the mind. Thus, the substratum of qualities remained elusive. Berkeley saw the problem more clearly than did Locke, but his solution, namely, to attribute the emergence of ideas in finite minds to the activity of Infinite Spirit, had no rational support, although it satisfied Berkeley's religious beliefs. (Berkeley's position here is not unlike Leibniz's to the extent that both of them emphasized the active character of reality, although the former stopped short of embracing monadology and appeared to be satisfied with a more orthodox account of the relation between the finite spirits and the Infinite Spirit.) Berkeley believed to have proved conclusively that the notion of material substance was self-contradictory, and, given the premises from which Locke had started, the conclusion did follow.

The plot of the empiricist drama thickened when Hume wanted to determine what kind of sense could be made of the concept of causality in terms of the empiricist theory of knowledge. He concluded that, since we do not have an impression of a necessary connection between causes and effects, the belief in causal connections among things is due not to reason but to feeling. We are accustomed to expect certain effects from certain antecedents because we have observed them invariably conjoined, but we have no *reason* to think that they will be conjoined the next time. This conclusion was no less startling than Berkeley's claim about the nonexistence of material substance. It brought in its wake a persistent debate about the grounds on which we establish the validity of physical laws. In logic this has become known as the problem of induction. Every lawlike statement goes beyond the actually known or tested instances; hence, each proof of propositions of the form "*All X*'s are *Y*'s," since it is based on a *limited* sample of *X*'s and *Y*'s, is formally invalid. To save inductive arguments from this fallacy, some philosophers tried to introduce premises such as the "uniformity of nature." But how is such a premise to be justified? It seems that the conclusion that nature is uniform can be based only on incomplete inductive evidence. As we know, Hume accepted his skeptical conclusions with equanimity, as befits a philosopher. Nevertheless, the state of affairs at this juncture of the modern philosophical journey seemed to cry out for a drastic reorientation, and that was provided by Kant.

## Questions

1. According to Locke, what is really going on when a person perceives a physical object? Give an analysis of such a perception, utilizing all of Locke's important distinctions.

2. Why did the concept of substance appear problematic to Locke, and how did he attempt to deal with this problem? Do you find his attempt successful?

3. What was Berkeley's argument for claiming that material substances do not exist, and which of Locke's important concepts did he employ in his argument? To what extent do you find Berkeley's position plausible, and in what ways would you criticize it? Do you think that Samuel Johnson's attempt to refute Berkeley is successful?

4. Compare Berkeley's idea of God with that of Leibniz.

5. How did Hume analyze the concept of cause-effect relationship? Why did he claim that causal explanations are based not on reason but on feeling, habit, custom, and the association of ideas?

6. Do you agree with Hume that the notion of personal identity requires the possibility of having what he called the *impression* of a self? Do you accept his conclusion that a self is but a bundle of sensations? If not, what other analysis do you find more satisfactory?

7. Can Hume's skeptical conclusions be traced to the original empiricist position outlined by Locke? Which aspects of that position do you find particularly questionable?

## Notes

[1] John Locke, *An Essay Concerning Human Understanding*, Book II, Ch. VIII, par. 15, edited by A.C. Frazer, Oxford: Clarendon Press, 1894.

[2] *Ibid.*, Book II, Ch. VIII, par. 17.

[3] *Ibid.*, Book IV, Ch. III, par. 26.

[4] *Ibid.*, Book IV, Ch. II, par. 14.

[5] *Ibid.*, Book II, Ch. XXIII, par. 29.

[6] Thomas Hobbes, *Leviathan*. Indianapolis: Bobbs-Merrill, 1958, p. 107.

[7] George Berkeley, *Principles of Human Knowledge*, Introduction, par. 10, *The Works of George Berkeley*, 8 vols., edited by A.A. Luce and J.E. Jessop. London: Thomas Nelson, 1948-1957.

[8] *Ibid.*, Introduction, par. 12.

[9] *Ibid.*, Introduction, par. 20.

[10] *Ibid.*, par. 25.

[11] *Ibid.*, par. 27.

[12] *Ibid.*, par. 40.

[13] David Hume, *Enquiries Concerning the Human Understanding* and *Concerning the Principles of Morals*, edited by L.A. Selby-Bigge. Oxford: Clarendon Press, Part I, Section 25, 1966.

[14] *Ibid.*, Part I, Section 7.

[15] *Ibid.*, Part I, Section 5.

[16] David Hume, *Treatise of Human Nature*, Book I, Part IV, Section 6, edited by L.A. Selby-Bigge. Oxford: Clarendon Press, 1896.

[17] *Ibid.*

[18] David Hume, *Enquiry*, Part III, Section 12.

[19] David Hume, *Treatise of Human Nature*, Book II, Part III, Section 3.

# Chapter Seven

# Kant and His Successors

## 1. Kant: Mind Makes Nature Possible

Immanuel Kant (1724-1804) brought about a revolution in philosophy while leading a quiet, relatively uneventful life in his native city of Königsberg in East Prussia. At first a student, then lecturer, and finally a professor at the University of Königsberg, Kant produced his monumental works only late in his life. The *Critique of Pure Reason* appeared in 1781 and was followed by other works, including the *Critique of Practical Reason* (1788) and the *Critique of Judgment* (1791). These three *Critiques* have exerted a profound influence not only on all subsequent philosophy, but also on the entire intellectual climate of the Western world.

Kant never traveled farther than 50 miles from Königsberg, never married, and his mode of life was methodical, to the extent of enabling his neighbors to set their clocks by the exact timing of his habitual afternoon walks. He had the reputation of being a sprightly lecturer and a spirited conversationalist. But his books, on which he spent most of his intellectual energy, are too closely argued to be easily read. Nevertheless, their contents have transformed the entire philosophical scene, and there is a general agreement that, as in the case of Plato, one can do without Kant, but not as well.

Both the Rationalists and the Empiricists looked upon the mind as something active. The Empiricists, especially, sought to contrast the inert, passive ideas with the active minds. They recognized that complex ideas arise as the result of the mind's operation with or on ideas. Knowledge arises when the mind, having been furnished with ideas, proceeds to inspect them and issue judgments as to what truths they can yield. In other words, in order for knowledge to arise, the mind must make a contribution of its own, and without this contribution there can be no knowledge.

This conclusion may have been foreshadowed or even implied in the analysis offered by Kant's predecessors, but it took his painstaking labors to show that further progress in philosophy would call for a radical shift in focus. Instead of continually asking what can we know, what are the possible objects of experience, we must ask an indispensable preliminary question: How is knowing brought about, or how does the mind work when it yields knowledge? At the cost of oversimplification, one may get a clue to Kant's new approach to philosophy by saying that before him, philosophers looked at the world as something wholly independent of the mind and were trying to think of the best way of allowing the independently existing realities to reveal themselves. Kant, however, realized that this picture was all wrong, that nothing can reveal itself unless the mind first acts on it, prepares it, presents it in the proper garb, thus making a cognitive contact with the presented reality possible.

Such metaphorical illustrations can be misleading and should not be pressed too far. A better understanding of what they are trying to show can be achieved after some specific details of Kant's analysis are laid bare. But already they help us to see that there may be something clearly wrong with Locke's starting point, namely, thinking of the mind as a *tabula rasa*, capable of accepting and accommodating anything, in any way. Here may lie the great mistake of empiricism, and here may be the foundation of the skepticism which Hume expresses. Kant's "Copernican revolution" consisted in reversing the assumption that all knowledge must conform to objects. Could it not be the case that in order to be known, the object must conform to certain conditions set by the subject? To explore this possibility, Kant launched his investigation, which he himself labeled "Critical Philosophy"; hence, the word "critique" in the titles of his important works.

Let us begin with a distinction that had already been used by Kant's predecessors. It has been labeled in different ways, but the essential point is the same. Leibniz distinguished the truths of reason from the truths of fact. Both agreed that the former category relied on the principle of noncontradiction; a denial of a truth of reason is self-contradictory. But the truths of fact require confirmation by experience. Kant calls the first type of judgment "analytic" and the second type "synthetic." He also brings in two technical words to describe the way in which each is known. Analytic judgments are known *a priori*, that is, prior to or independent of any act of confirmation by experience, whereas synthetic judgments are known only *a posteriori*, that is, after some act of confirmation, such as looking or listening, has taken place. Whether it is true that it is raining outside, I can know only by experience, that is, by looking out of the window, sticking my hand out of the door, or listening to the patter on the roof. But in order to assent to the truth of the proposition "All sisters are female," I need not perform any act of verification. If I know the meaning of the words "sister" and "female," I know that the former logically includes the latter; a male sister is a contradiction in terms. Kant also observes that an analytic judgment does not yield any new knowledge, but that a synthetic judgment does. Unless I am teaching someone the language, I do not inform him of anything when I tell him that all sisters are female. If he knows the language, he already knows that. But if I tell him that it is raining outside, I do give him some information which he may not have had prior to being so informed.

The question Kant proceeds to ask is this: Are there some judgments that are synthetic, that is, convey some information, and yet are not *a posteriori*, based on some particular experience, but are *a priori*, that is, are known to be true without our having to verify them? In other words, are there *synthetic a priori* judgments? Consider an example: "All events are caused." Is this statement true? Yes. Do we need to ask whether any particular event has a cause? No, we don't. But if this is so, there are at least some synthetic *a priori* judgments. Indeed, the one we have mentioned and many others besides, are presupposed by natural science; so the question is not whether, but how, synthetic *a priori* judgments are possible. Here, Kant offers an analysis.

There are two concepts that play a very special role in our accounts of things and events—space and time. Kant says that they are not discursive concepts; they are not learned in the same way as are other elements of our discourse. The concept "oboe," for instance, comes after our having encountered and singled out some object corresponding to the word "oboe," but we don't single out space as one of the ingredients of the world. Whatever else we single out, it must be in space, but space is not something we can set side by side with other objects.

The concept of space is entirely different. It is *something*, namely, the condition of all possible material objects, but it is not itself an object. We can think only of *one* space, says Kant, for if we think of particular volumes of space—rooms, stadiums, planets, galaxies—we still think of them as being part of one space. We could not think of objects, no matter how small or large, unless we already had a concept of space at our disposal or in our minds.

Similarly with the concept of time; all events presuppose the concept of time because they happen in it. When we think of an object, we think of it as existing and having some duration in time, no matter how infinitesimally short. Hence, we cannot think of any actual objects in the world without the concept of time.

Kant believed that these peculiarities in the function of the concepts of space and time justify our regarding them as different from all other concepts. Indeed, Kant thought that they deserve a special name; he called them "pure forms of sensibility." "Sensibility" refers to the mode in which all objects accessible to us through the senses present themselves. The reference to form is intended to bring out their purely formal character; no matter what the particular size or shape of an object, it formally exists in space and time. Finally, the word "pure" indicates that we deal with *a priori* concepts, which we do not learn from experience, and which all our experience presupposes. This means that the mind brings spatiality and temporality to experience; they are not derived from it, as the empiricists supposed. (For Locke, time was the experience of the succession of ideas.) Kant remarks that even mathematicians did not appreciate the peculiar features of the concept of space. "They did not recognize that this thought space renders possible the physical space, that is, the extension of matter itself; that this pure space is not at all a quality of things in themselves, but a form of our sensuous faculty of representation." [1]

Having noted that space and time enjoy a special status, Kant believed to have explained how mathematics is possible. Space and time are not nonentities, but neither can they be identified with any particular contents of space and time. Kant says that "the intuitions which pure mathematics lays at the foundations of all its cognitive judgments which appear at once apodictic and necessary are space and time."

This quotation includes more of the terms Kant uses in a technical sense, but that sense is not difficult to grasp in the light of his essential intention. The term "intuition" does not refer to some special gift of grasping hidden connections, but simply to the awareness of a sensory contact with something. Thus, in this technical sense, I intuit the color or fragrance of a flower when I am looking at it or smelling it. This, of course, would be a synthetic intuition; but there are also pure intuitions, and geometry is based on them. When I say that given three lines, it is possible to construct a triangle, I say something true about the *a priori* concept of space; for it could be the case that space would not allow the construction of a triangle from three lines. This is a way of saying that although the concept of space is *a priori*, a pure form of sensibility, it nevertheless dictates certain specific, formal conditions to which all objects must conform. These conditions could be different if our concept of space were not what it actually is. Among other things, it makes the truths of geometry possible. Truths of geometry are thus synthetic *a priori*. Another example Kant gives is the axiom that the straight line is the shortest distance between two points. It cannot be analytic, he says, because the concept of straight is not analytically contained in the concept of short.

As space provides the *a priori* conditions for geometry, so time provides such conditions for arithmetic and pure mechanics. Counting and other operations of arithmetic are possible because the pure form of time allows a successive advance from one moment to another, thus generating determinate time-magnitudes. The concept of motion also presupposes the representation of time. In either case, we need not think of any particular empirical units being added or bodies moving. When the empirical features are abstracted, we are still left with the pure, nonsensuous representation of time. Propositions of arithmetic are also therefore synthetic *a priori*. The number twelve cannot be derived from a mere analysis of the numbers seven and five, and yet "seven plus five equals twelve" is a necessarily true proposition.

Kant entitled his new doctrine of space and time "Transcendental Aesthetic." Both words need an explanation. "Aesthetic," in Kant's use of the term has nothing to do with art or artistic perceptions. It simply refers to the realm of sense perception, which was the original meaning of the Greek word. A person under an anaesthetic is made insensitive to sensory stimuli; the original meaning still survives in this word. (It was much later than "aesthetics" began to be used as referring to the theory of art.) "Transcendental" is an important word in Kant's philosophy, for it summarizes his main insight. Space and time are transcendental forms because they transcend any particular sensory content. Nevertheless, they are present in every instance of sense experience and, indeed, make it possible. Thus, "transcendental" does not mean something lying outside experience; it is found within experience, as its fundamental and indispensable condition. Part of the intent of the "Copernican revolution" was to call attention to such transcendental conditions of all our experience.

Kant now moves on to a further dimension in which transcendental elements, which he calls "categories of the understanding," are to be acknowledged. Kant entitles this investigation "Transcendental Logic." The realm of sense, including the pure forms of space and time, if it is to disclose to us a world, or, in other words, if it is to become experience, needs to exhibit further features; in addition to pure forms of sensibility, the mind also manifests pure concepts of understanding. Their status and function are analogous to those of space and time. By means of the "categories," as Kant calls these pure forms of understanding, the world of objects and the various distinctions we make within it are made possible. How are these categories discovered?

Interestingly enough, Kant finds them by paying close attention to some features in the use of language and to some distinctions within this use made by classical logic—hence the term "transcendental logic." Consider, for instance, the statement "All dogs are friendly." Kant notes that such a statement could be looked at from four different angles, so to speak. It involves judgments about quantity, quality, relation, and modality. What does he mean by this? When judged from the angle of quantity, the statement above qualifies as *universal*; it refers to *all* dogs. The statement could be changed to "Some

dogs are friendly,'' which would yield a *particular* judgment. When changed
to a statement which refers to only one dog, e.g. "Fido is friendly," it yields
a *singular* judgment. All three distinctions (which could be called "sub-
categories") fall within the category of *quantity*, which specifies the quantitative
range of the applicability of the statement. Next, consider *quality*. Here, the
statement is looked at from another direction, as either *affirming* or *denying*
something. The judgment "All dogs are friendly" is changed with regard
to quality if we put a "not" in front of "friendly." Kant has still a third
distinction within the category of quality, namely, infinite judgment, but since
it complicates his analysis unduly and is questionable from the point of view
of more recent logic, we may omit it.

With regard to *relation*, it is also helpful to modify Kant's account, without
undermining his basic intent. A relation is *categorical* when something is
predicated of a subject, as in our example friendliness is predicated of dogs.
But when we say: "Fido hides bones," we are describing a cause-effect
relationship; Fido causes the bone to be hidden. Kant labeled such a relation
*hypothetical*. This label appears plausible when we translate cause-effect
statements into if . . . then statements. For example: "All metals conduct
electricity" can be expressed: "If something is a metal, then it conducts
electricity."

Last, consider *modality*. Here, Kant recognizes three types of judgment:
(1) *problematic*, (2) *assertory*, and (3) *apodictic*. Sometimes we assert something only tentatively: (1) "Fido *may* be friendly," or we can say simply,
(2) "The cat is on the mat." Sometimes the modality may be unconditional:
(3) "Triangles must have three sides." Again, doubts may arise about the
logical status of problematic judgments. But Kant's intent is still clear; he
wants to call attention to another aspect in which judgments can be examined.

Now comes the central claim, for which we are to some extent prepared
by the transcendental aesthetic. How can we make these different types of
judgment? Kant answers: Because we are in possession of pure concepts which
enable us to categorize our experience in these ways. Within the category
of quantity we have the concepts of *unity, plurality*, and *totality*, which account
for our ability to make universal, particular, and singular judgments. If we
had no concept of unity, we could not refer to all individual items as belonging
to *one* class. The concept of plurality enables us to refer to some particular
items belonging to a class of similar items. The concept of totality makes
it possible to indicate that the judgment is exclusively about one single
individual. Similarly, the other categories have their underlying pure concepts.
Within the category of quality we think in terms of *reality* and *negation*. Within
the category of relations we think either with concepts of *substance and its
predicates* or in terms of *causality*. Within the category of modality we think
in terms of *possibility, existence*, and *necessity*.

Note what happens when we do lift these concepts from the rest of our conceptual inventory and recognize their special role. Like space and time, they are not derived from particular experiences; rather, they are the means by which experience comes into being. But if so, it was an obvious mistake for the Empiricists to want to derive all concepts from some impressions, to locate them among the ordinary furniture of the world. The Empiricists were looking for them in the wrong place; they are not in the world, but in the mind as it deals with the world.

However, one must be very careful here; one must not continue to think of pure concepts of the understanding as if they were somehow independent of all experience. In illustrating Kant's doctrine, commentators often resort to examples which, while helpful to some extent, can also be misleading. It is said, for example, that the categories could be thought of as analogous to eyeglasses which give everything one sees a special color. Kant repeatedly emphasizes that the categories are *logical* categories: they are *ways* in which we see the world, not instruments which transform or distort the world. They are *a priori*, but not *temporally* prior. It is not the case that the mind at birth is equipped with the categories themselves with sense experience added later. The discovery of categories is a result of a logical analysis of experience. They are declared to be pure not because they somehow can exist and operate by themselves, but because they are present in *all* experience as its indispensable conditions.

When seen in this new way, the deep difficulties which Locke and Hume had with the concepts of substance and cause disappear. Both concepts are categories of the mind. Substance is not something I-know-not-what, but the power of the mind to hold together an indefinite number of properties. The idea of subject or thing is a logical idea. It enables us to separate or isolate from the welter of experience some collections of properties which constitute more or less permanent unity. Thus, when we refer to a substance we are not referring to something *in addition* to its properties, but to all of its properties *as unified*. Similarly with cause. In affirming the synthetic *a priori* proposition "All events have causes," we simply give recognition to the fact that an uncaused event would not be acceptable to the mind. We *must* think causally about our experiences. Our rejection of the claim that something was uncaused comes not because we are stubborn or incurably subjective, but simply because such an event is *unthinkable*. It is contrary to what we *can* think; hence, it defines for us the manner in which thinking is possible. When this becomes clear, we will no longer be inclined to look for an impression of a necessary connection.

Returning now to the conviction, already expressed by Rationalists and Empiricists, that the mind is something active, we should now add the Kantian qualification. Logical powers of the mind are not psychological powers. Hence, they are not special processes and activities, although Kant is sometimes inclined to use expressions which suggest that they are. Once more, the functions of pure forms of sensibility and of the categories are transcendental, but they do not subsist independently of experience; they are disclosed in it. Note how Kant derived the categories. He made an inventory of judgments we actually make, and he discovered in them certain invariable *forms* without which we could not make judgments. Just try to say something about the world, yet refrain from making use of one of the aspects of the category of quantity, i.e., to say something without specifying the range of your reference. Or, try to make a statement that does not specify the subject, thing, or substance about which something is being said. Even though one may have doubts about the particular set of distinctions Kant actually made within the concepts underlying all our discourse, his essential discovery that we do rely on some concepts of this special character still stands.

Turning now to the question of the nature of the self or mind that is active in thinking, we see Kant dealing with other perennial issues. What is the self that does the thinking and has experience? Clearly, Hume's search for an impression of the self was a mistake. To correct this mistake, Kant coined the term "transcendental unity of apperception." Again, we should try to understand his point, although a less formidable vocabulary would be helpful. Transcendental unity of apperception is all that remains of Descartes' *cogito*. Kant resorts to the term "transcendental" in order to indicate that he is not talking about the empirical self, something that can be discovered in sensation or reflection. Hume was right on that point; try as we may, we can never catch any such thing while thinking of ourselves. What do we find? The ability to focus on our experiences as unified in our own perceptions of them. Hence, there is a self that holds all of the experiences together, sees them in the order of their succession, remembers past events, and anticipates the future. Furthermore, it is while perceiving and thinking of the world with all its objects, distinctions, and processes that this unity of the self is experienced. The "I think" accompanies all of our perceptions, says Kant. This means that the self and the world arise together, simultaneously. There is no self without the world, and no world — in the sense of organized unified structure — without the self. Mind makes nature possible, and the self exists as the experiencer of that nature. We cannot think of one apart from the other, contrary to Descartes, who claimed that the mind is easier to know than the body and that he could think of himself as existing while everything else had perished. Nevertheless, we may see Descartes and Kant as the two pivotal figures in the modern intellectual drama.

When Descartes arrived at his famous dictum, *Cogito, ergo sum*, he pointed to the domain which was long to be the central focus of study, namely, human mind. For Descartes, the undeniable fact was human existence as that of a thinking substance, *res cogitans*. When Kant arrived on the scene, he claimed to have discovered that the thinking mind yields knowledge because it has a complex logical structure by means of which the phenomena of the world are organized. Thus, one might say that the Kantian doctrine of the categories completes the Cartesian quest for the identification of the essential features of the thinking self. Descartes' *cogito*, in Kant, becomes the Transcendental Unity of Apperception, synthesizing space and time as pure forms of sensibility and the 12 categories of the understanding. To relate Descartes and Kant in this way is, of course, to offer an oversimplified and probably in some ways misleading, account. Furthermore, to appreciate fully the distance between them is to have some awareness of the twists and turns the philosophical journey actually took, thanks to the initiative of all the intervening philosophers of both the rationalist and empiricist schools.

The function of the unity of apperception can be described in greater detail, thought Kant. Since the main "activity" of the self is holding together, connecting the logical and the sensory contents of experience; the proper description for this "activity" is *synthesis*. In making a judgment the mind spontaneously and simultaneously brings together aspects from each one of the four categories; it makes a judgment *through* them. Furthermore, the synthesizing operation can be observed in three different phases: *apprehension, reproduction*, and *recognition*. This feature of the mind can perhaps be illustrated by reference to a context. Think of yourself as waking up. You open your eyes, drowsily, nothing as yet is in focus, you don't know where you are, what the objects surrounding you are, or what time of day or night it is. Then your mind beings "to click," your sense content takes on meaning: this is a window, that is a chair, I am in a hotel, I arrived yesterday, etc. The first grasping of connections in your surroundings is "apprehension." Yet, you could not go on thinking unless the apprehended objects were being continually "reproduced" in your mind, unless you "remembered" that a moment ago you saw a clock which told you that it was 8 o'clock. (Another good illustration of the synthesis of reproduction is the fact that while listening to someone's speech, we keep "reproducing" the first word of the sentence in order to understand the whole sentence when it is completed.) Finally, "recognition" is the ability to reidentify the word, the object, the scene, when it reappears after some interval of time, memory being the prime example of this phenomenon. At all times, the ordering, the unifying, the synthesizing activity of the mind makes use of the pure forms of sensibility and of the concepts of understanding, which are not psychological but logical structures.

What, then, can we know about the self, the soul, the individual mind, according to Kant? No doubt, a person has a certain unified career in history. That history involves a particular bodily identity, which is expressed in the continuity and relative permanence of the person's features, appearance, and activities. My mind and my body are a unity, and that unity is expressed in my memory of past episodes, in my present grasp of my situation, and in my anticipation of and plans for the future. My experience of myself is necessarily tied up with my experience of my world. Indeed, it is the stability of that world which supplies me with records of my past and with the materials for my actions, that gives me the conviction of being an individual with a definite location in space and time, differentiated from other individuals, human and nonhuman, and pursuing my own personal goals within the total structure of my environment.

To that extent it makes perfect sense to talk about the self or the individual soul. But is the substance of the soul *permanent*, as had been argued by earlier philosophers? It is as permanent as its experience; as long as a person is alive and manifests all the typical capacities, the permanence of the human personality cannot be denied, but when he ceases to function as a person — to think, to feel, to be conscious, in other words, to be aware of the world — it is unintelligible to continue talking about the simplicity or permanence of his soul. Thus, on theoretical grounds absolute permanence, the immortality of the soul, cannot be affirmed. As we shall see in discussing Kant's ethics, there are other avenues to the questions of ultimate meaning and destiny of human beings, but these avenues are closed to us from the theoretical or scientific point of view.

In addition to the concept of the soul or self, two other concepts have been prominent in the thought of the preceding philosophers, namely, world and God. Concerning the world, Kant's position follows from his discoveries about the concept of substance. The concept of the world as a totality is a peculiar concept, for we tend to think of it on the model of objects *within* the world. We tend to think that the world is like an object, although, of course infinitely larger. Kant's comment on this is that the analogy is wrong. The notion of world totality is an illegitimate concept, because totality presupposes the possibility of the *limits* of the world, in both space and time. But given the fact that time and space are the forms without which we cannot think, it is impossible for us to postulate, say, the *beginning* of the world in time. For then we should be able to ask: "What was going on *before*?" But if nothing existed before the world began, the question would not make sense. Yet we are impelled to ask this question, because the notion of beginning as we can understand it is beginning *from* something. Hence, the concept of absolute beginning is different in kind from the concept of beginning, which we *can* understand. Similar arguments apply to specifying the limits of space. Kant dwells on these arguments at length, showing that the attempts to talk about the world totality allow us to prove opposite conclusions, thus leading us into self-contradictions or antinomies.

The main thrust of Kant's argument is relatively simple and is based on his discovery that a concept of substance allows us to unify various characteristics, properties, or processes and to view them as belonging to a single whole. There is nothing wrong with the attempt to expand this process of unification indefinitely, finally stopping with something we call the universe or the world. The only thing we should guard against is the supposition that this process of unification can be *completed*. The act of completion would be an element in an experience of some mind, but in order to function *as an experience*, it could not stop with the limits of the universe, but would have to go beyond it—hence a self-contradiction. (It may be helpful in this connection to ponder the remark of a contemporary philosopher, Ludwig Wittgenstein, who said that death is not an event in life, because if it were, its termination would be capable of being experienced, which is not the case.)

Kant recognized the natural tendency to treat the world as if it were a complete or completable object. He believed it also to be useful, but not, as he put it, in the *constitutive* way, but in a *regulative* way. World totality to him is an Idea of Reason, that is, an idea which presses the mind in the direction of possible limits of all experience. Such limits cannot be reached; hence, we cannot have an experience of an object which *constitutes* the world. However, in the interest of expanding our knowledge, we should continue to direct our investigations to regions which lie beyond our present grasp. Thus, to cover that which still lies beyond the horizon, we can speak of world totality, meaning by it all that which is within the possible ken of our experience but which is not exhausted by actual experience. As a regulative idea, the notion of world totality has a legitimate function.

In this connection it may be useful to mark Kant's distinction between transcendental and transcendent. "Transcendent" is Kant's term for supposed realities which break off from all possible experience and exist beyond it. Such "realities" are unthinkable to us. To postulate the limits of the world we must go beyond them, but this simply means that we have not reached those limits. The regulative employment of reason, while relying on all the transcendental, fundamental equipment of the mind, does not aspire to knowing the transcendent. This knowledge is not to be had, simply because it would not be knowledge.

God is also an Idea of Reason, postulating a being which is the ultimate ground and explanation of the world. This, too, is an idea which breaks with experience and postulates a transcendent reality beyond all experience. The traditional proof of God's existence which affirms that there must be a First Cause of everything is based on a conceptual mistake. There is an important logical difference between the concept of First Cause and the concept of cause as we use it in intelligible explanations: the concept of cause in these uses conceives of causes as being in turn effects of something else. This logical feature of causality makes it one of the pure categories of the understanding without which explanation of events is not possible. But the notion of *First Cause* lacks this feature; hence, it lacks explanatory power. The use of the notion of First Cause is illegitimate; it baffles, instead of illuminating, the understanding.

Kant criticized other traditional proofs of God's existence and concluded that in the realm of religion there are no theoretical or theological proofs. In his ethics, he explored a different avenue to religion as human search for ultimate meaning. His last important work was entitled *Religion Within the Limits of Mere Reason* (1793). We shall deal with that aspect of Kant's philosophy in the following chapter. Only a brief mention of Kant's other criticisms of theology must suffice at this point. Kant dismissed the ontological proof, to the effect that the assurance of God's existence is included in the concept of his essence, on the grounds that existence is not a predicate. When we describe the concept of something we do not *add* anything to the concept by saying that it exists. God may be good, wise, and all-powerful, if he exists, but his existence cannot be deduced from the analysis of his characteristics. Kant had some sympathy for the teleological argument, or the argument from design, which was very popular in his time, but he did not think that it proved enough. *That* argument can prove at most that there "is an *architect* of the world who is always very much hampered by the . . . adaptability of the material in which he works, not a *creator* of the world to whose idea everything is subject."[2] One should also note that the proofs of the existence of God as Creator presuppose the meaningfulness of the concept of world totality, a concept which Kant found to be merely regulative.

In contrast to the skepticism which emerged from the culmination of British Empiricism, Kant affirms the possibility of knowledge and gives an account of its conditions. Mind makes nature possible; that is, nature as an organized process of experience appears to us only as a consequence of the logical contribution that the mind makes to that process. This does not mean that mind *makes* nature; it only means that reality appears to us in a certain guise and that we can discover the conditions under which this reality is intelligible. Still, we may entertain the idea that reality in itself is not reality as we know it. We know only the world as it appears to us, not as it is in itself, as a thing-in-itself. Kant thought it important to be aware of this distinction, saying that we can *think* the thing-in-itself, but we cannot *know* it. We know only appearances, not things-in-themselves. But for Kant, appearances are not illusions, or *mere* appearances. In our normal perceptions, in mathematics and in science, we do have objective knowledge, which is made objective precisely by our use of categories shared by all minds. There are, of course, subjective judgments, "seemings," that is, "appearances" in the pejorative sense of the word, and they are characterized by our inability to judge by reference to common, public criteria. But for Kant appearances are objective phenomena, accessible to and knowable by everyone under normal conditions.

As far as our knowledge of the world is concerned, there is no room for skepticism. It would be a misunderstanding to construe Kant's distinction between appearances (phenomena) and things-in-themselves (noumena) as implying that some reality is inaccessible to us. It is simply a logical mistake to say: Alas, things-in-themselves cannot be known. It is not a situation which either could or should be remedied. By saying that knowledge has its conditions, Kant did not mean to say something negative. His is a positive doctrine: if something is known, it conforms to certain requirements of the mind. This means that a claim to knowledge which does not meet these requirements does not exhibit the normal features of knowledge and hence is not *knowledge*. To wish to *know* things-in-themselves is a sign of a conceptual confusion. The thing-in-itself is not of the sort to be known; hence, skepticism is out of order. Some philosophers, including Schopenhauer, drew skeptical conclusions from Kant's distinction. As for Kant himself, he believed that noumena *are* accessible to us, but not in terms of theoretical knowledge.

Things-in-themselves are noumena, realities which provide the material for knowledge, and which must be in that sense recognized as independent of the knowing minds. The fact that minds can know phenomena is a clue that the reality of minds is not exhausted in their phenomenal aspect. But this can be discovered only by going beyond the theoretical employment of reason and analyzing the nature of *practical* reason, of us as agents and not as mere knowers—a subject to be explored in Kant's ethics. In exploring our own nature more fully, we may get a hint as to the nature of noumena or things-in-themselves.

In concluding the exposition of Kant's thought, let us return to the earlier remark made that his philosophy occupies the other terminus on the spectrum of the development initiated by Descartes. As we said, Kant completes that development. If the starting focus of our inquiry is the human mind (or thinking substance, in Descartes' vocabulary), then it is desirable to make one's inspection as thorough as possible. Kant claimed to have provided such an inspection. His discovery was that the concept of thinking covers much greater territory than his predecessors had envisaged. Locke in particular was wrong in claiming that the mind, at first, is a *tabula rasa*. To being with, the mind has a *structure*: not physical, physiological, or psychological, but a *logical* structure. In his investigations of this question, Kant harks back to the Ancients and takes some important clues from both their studies of the logical form of judgments and Aristotle's doctrine of the categories. In order to think at all, the mind must exhibit a certain formal structure, and this is provided by logic, or pure critique, as Kant puts it. The inventory of the components of

that structure is quite complex and includes the pure forms of sensibility—
space and time—and the 12 categories of the understanding, all of which
are employed simultaneously when the mind makes any kind of judgment.
An important and illuminating byproduct of taking this logical inventory of
what is at the mind's disposal was the discovery that the two key concepts
which gave the empiricists so much trouble, namely, substance and causality,
are not to be looked for outside the mind, but *in* the mind, as part of its logical
equipment. "Substance" allows us to hold together an indefinite number of
available perceptual attributes. "Causality" is a relation which the mind expects
certain phenomena to exhibit if they are to be understood. In other words,
substantiality and causality are the ways in which phenomena *must* appear
to us in order to be assimilated and understood by the mind. The "must"
is logical, and not physical or empirical. This is why Hume could not find
a *necessary* connection among his impressions.

Thus, the Kantian "Copernican revolution" in philosophy disposed of the
conundrums which plagued the empiricists. It also cleared up to some extent
the confusion about interaction. "Interaction" presupposes causality, and since
causality is an aspect *of* the mind, a causal account cannot be given about
something that operates or has causal influence *on* the mind. Causality is the
way in which the mind *arranges* the perceived phenomena and hence is
applicable only *within* the realm of the mind. To ask how something that is
nonmental affects something that is mental is to suggest that the concept of
causality is applicable beyond the sphere in which alone it can operate. To
do this is to make a logical mistake, a mistake about the meaning of the word
"cause."

The qualification that Kant *to some extent* cleared up confusions about the
problem of interaction is important. With Kant as a guide, the journey toward
philosophical clarity made impressive strides. He showed that knowledge has
some conditions imposed on it by the nature of the mind and that because
of these conditions, no skeptical conclusions about either mathematics or
science need to be drawn. Mind makes nature possible, in the sense that it
shows us under what circumstances we may claim to possess objective
knowledge about the world. Yet Kant deemed it necessary to acknowledge
a kind of dualism which, while not threatening objective knowledge,
nevertheless admits that it has certain limits. What we know is the phenomenal
world, and if we do not want to land in a subjective idealism such as Berkeley's,
who claimed that the human mind can be acquainted only with its own (or
some of God's mind's) operations, we must likewise admit that all phenomena
have also a noumenal, transcendent side. That side Kant called the thing-in-
itself and believed it to be thinkable but not knowable. That it is not knowable
follows from the very nature of knowledge; it requires some specific logical
conditions. To see this, try to ask some questions about the thing-in-itself.

Suppose you ask: What is it? The very asking of this question, since it includes the words "what" and "it," presupposes the phenomena-limited concept of substance. Hence, in trying to say something about the thing-in-itself, we are treating it as a sort of phenomenon, but by its very definition it is something outside or beyond or underlying phenomena, and hence the question involves us in a self-contradiction.

As we shall see, Kant believed the thing-in-itself, or noumenon, to be accessible to us in moral experience, through our ability to act from the Categorical Imperative. He even thought that moral experience allows us to postulate immortality and God's existence. But according to him, these postulates are not objects of knowledge but merely of rational faith, in the sense that nothing we know about the world contradicts the possibility of their existence. Since morality demands that we believe in them, morality is the door to religion.

The thing-in-itself remains, nevertheless, problematic, and we may wonder whether Kant was right in claiming that it is even thinkable. Many of Kant's successors, including Hegel and Schopenhauer, found Kant unconvincing on this point. Both attempted to give a more satisfactory account of this issue.

## 2. Hegel: Reality is Rational

G.W.F. Hegel (1770-1831) occupies an important place in the history of philosophy. He wrote during a lively intellectual period, when Germany produced a host of brilliant thinkers and writers: Fichte, Schelling, and Goethe, among others. The influence of Kant was felt strongly, but his critical philosophy, because it appeared to set limits to what man can know, was at odds with the growing romantic mood. That mood was, in part, a reaction to an omnipresent emphasis on reason. The French philosopher Jean Jacques Rousseau deplored the evils of civilization and proclaimed a new man: the man of feeling. Other philosophers and poets all over Europe joined this romantic quest to break through the limitations of reason. It was Hegel's great achievement that he succeeded in constructing a system which, while preserving and indeed enhancing the role of reason, nevertheless appeared to satisfy the longing for a more intimate contact with the heart of reality.

After completing his university studies in the theological school at Tübingen, Hegel spent his life as an educator. He worked as a private tutor, a rector of a secondary school, and as a professor at the Universities of Jena, Heidelberg, and Berlin. While in Berlin he became the dominant figure in German philosophy and exerted a strong influence on the intellectual life of the Western world. His first major work, *The Phenomenology of Spirit* (1807), was followed by *Science of Logic* (1816), *Encyclopaedia of the Philosophical*

*Sciences* (1817), *Philosophy of Right* (1821), *Philosophy of History, Philosophy of Fine Art, Philosophy of Religion*, and *History of Philosophy*. The last four were published posthumously and are based on lectures delivered by Hegel between 1823 and 1827.

   Kant's notion of the thing-in-itself appeared as a stumbling block to many students of his thought. He believed that this notion was important for his philosophy, because without it the appearances would be reduced to merely mental entities, making his philosophy undistinguishable from Berkeley's subjective idealism. It seems, then, that the thing-in-itself enjoys the same epistemological status as Locke's substance; it is something I-know-not-what underlying our perceptions. While Kant cheerfully acknowledged that it is unknowable, his critics wondered whether his view is intelligible even in terms of his own epistemological conclusions. Both "existence" and "cause" are categories, applicable only *within* experience. If so, we cannot speak of the *existence* of the thing-in-itself, for it is by definition something "outside" or "on the other side" of appearances. Similarly, we cannot say that things-in-themselves cause or give rise to appearances, because causality applies only to events *in* the world. In addition, note our inability to decide whether in the case of the thing-in-itself we should resort to the singular (noumenon) or the plural (noumena) form, for these forms are also taken from one of the categories of the understanding. Whether Kant's theory can be saved from these objections is an open question, but to many of his successors they were sufficient to show that the concept of noumena or things-in-themselves was superfluous and so could and should be eliminated. Furthermore, Kant's distinction between phenomena and noumena, despite his protestations to the contrary, seems to give the latter an ontologically suspect status: in the final analysis, we don't know things as they ultimately or "really" are.
   Hegel's system was not only an attempt to "save appearances," but also a bold venture intended to show that idealism is true and that all reality is knowable and rational. His philosophy, in contrast to Berkeley's, is often called "objective idealism" or "absolute idealism," for reasons which will become apparent. Hegel's method is reminiscent of Continental rationalists; he begins with an analysis of concepts. Indeed, his logical starting point is the most abstract idea of all: the idea of being. Of everything that exists, it can be said that at least it has *Being*. Being is the most universal category applicable to everything. But since in order to talk about Being as such, we must exclude from it any and every property or characteristic; Being could also be correctly described as Nothing. This appears to be a contradiction, and Hegel admitted that the proposition that Being and Nothing are the same is paradoxical. He denied, however, that from this analysis of Being it follows that particular things both are and are not what they are. The analysis applies

only to the pure concept of Being, and it demonstrates something fundamentally important: when the mind contemplates the idea of Being, it does pass over from that idea to its opposite, namely, the idea of Nothing.

What impressed Hegel was this very tendency of thought to move from the contemplated idea to its opposite, or, as this process has been described later, to move from a thesis to its antithesis. Thus so, with the dismissal of the thing-in-itself as an illegitimate concept, it would appear that the only clue to what reality is must be found in the characteristics of thought. In this respect Kant's heritage is preserved; all knowledge must start with the examination of the nature of the mind. Also at work in Hegel's approach is an important remnant from the rationalist and the empiricist schools, namely, the belief that the mind is essentially something *active*. Bearing this in mind, it may seem plausible to identify thought with Being and to look for the ways in which that unified reality displays itself. The union of Being and Nothing is Becoming. Becoming, then, could be regarded as a synthesis in which both Being and Nothing are reconciled, overcome, or climbed over to a more adequate mode of thought. What becomes is and yet is not, because its being is on the way toward something else. All Being is on the way to Nothing, and so truly *is* Becoming.

Thus we arrive at the famous Hegelian dialectic. Everything in the world can be understood if we see it as tending to generate its own opposite, which movement, however, is taken up into a more comprehensive alternative, resulting in something which unites or brings together the two opposing positions. Here, Hegel believes to have found the key to all reality. Consider this sample of Hegel's argument that the dialectical process is essentially rational.

> *Precisely for the reason that existence is designated a genus or kind, it is a naked simple thought:* noûs, *simple abstraction, is substance. It is on account of its simplicity, its self-identity, that it appears steady, fixed, and permanent. But this self-identity is likewise negativity; hence that fixed and stable existence carries the process of its own dissolution within itself. The determinateness appears at first to be solely through its relation to something else; and its process seems imposed and forced upon it externally. But its having its own otherness within itself, and the fact of its being a self-initiated process — these are implied in the very simplicity of thought itself. For this is self-moving thought, thought that distinguishes, is inherent inwardness, the pure notion. Thus, then, it is the very nature of understanding to be a process, and being a process it is Rationality.*[3]

Recall that Kant called attention to the interplay between the self and the world in an act of perception. In this act the subject ''moves'' from himself to the perceived object. His state of mind, his subjectivity, passes over into an objective awareness. Any act of cognition is thus a synthesis of subjectivity and objectivity, for it puts the mind outside of itself and unites it with the object. Thus, again following Kant up to a point, Hegel concludes that in perception and cognition the separation of mind and nature is overcome. But Hegel also goes beyond Kant. For Hegel, the mind not only makes nature *possible*; nature itself has its being as an integral part of the whole of which mind is another integral part. That organic unity, comprising both mind and nature, Hegel calls the Notion or the Idea.

Reality is essentially spiritual. It is a *living* substance which, as Hegel puts it, exists in and for itself. It opposes one thing to another, but it also negates this opposition. What Hegel means is that nothing can be fully understood in isolation from other things, especially those things which provide their background or contrast. I may concentrate my attention on a tree, but in order to know the fuller truth about it, I must also take into account its relation to the soil from which it grows and to the sun from which it gets its light. All things form an organic unity. This means that reality does not consist of isolated bits. In time, the Whole is bound to affect the development of its parts. This leads Hegel to say that True Being is nothing but Self-restoring Identity; it is its own Becoming.

True, individual consciousness is preoccupied with its own individuality. Each person pursues his own aims as if they were the only ones that counted. When seen from the angle of dialectical development, this is understandable. In order to experience itself as infinite, reality must pretend to itself that it is finite, for only then can it set itself to *overcome* its finitude and thus become truly aware of its infinity. But this infinity is to be understood not in the sense of indefinite extension, but in the sense of being self-contained and complete; it is "at home with itself."

As we can see, Hegel's description of the Whole relies on an analogy with a thinking self. Although in actual fact I am aware of only a limited set of facts, in principle no fact need be hidden from me, and my identity would not be affected by my knowledge of these additional facts. The peculiar feature of the pronoun "I" is that there is nothing distinctive in my experience that could not in principle be in anyone's experience. I may *try* to use the pronoun "I" to stand for my single self, but I cannot *succeed* in meaning by it anything that is not public and sharable.

Keeping to the analogy between the human self and the Whole, Hegel claims that reality is to be understood not only as Substance, but as Subject as well. Properly understood, Subject turns out to be Mind or Spirit. To think of reality as mere substance incapable of self-consciousness is to leave unexplained how it can appear to us as something knowable. The fact that it is knowable allows us to speak of it as Subject, as involving self-consciousness. True reality, claims Hegel, "is the process of its own becoming, the circle which presupposes its end or its purpose, and has its end for its beginning; it becomes concrete and actual only by being carried out, and by the end it involves."[4] "The truth is the Whole. The Whole, however, is merely the essential nature reaching its completeness through the process of its own development."[5]

To characterize reality more fully, Hegel studies its character in human experience. The ego's relationship to any object, whatever the nature of the object, is a form of consciousness. Consciousness, according to Hegel, has three phases, depending on the nature of the object. That object may stand in opposition to the ego, or it may be the ego itself, or else it may be something objective which belongs both to the object and to the ego. Hegel calls this latter form, or phase, of consciousness, thought, or reason. Hence, the three phases of consciousness are: (1) consciousness in general, (2) self-conscious-ness, and (3) reason. Consciousness in general can in turn be seen as consti-tuting a triad: (1) sensuous immediacy of external objects, (2) perception, and (3) understanding.

1. An immediate awareness of an object is characterized by a "this," a "now," and a "here." The "this," the "now," and the "here" abide in our experience, even though the specific content of this experience undergoes changes. Hence, even the sensuous phase of consciousness is not determinate, but general.

2. In perception we become aware of properties inherent in things. Although properties belong to particular things and are experienced for themselves immediately in sensations, they are nevertheless related to other properties and could also be present in other individual things, hence have generality. When a thing loses its properties the thing changes, but the property itself undergoes no change by virtue of being detached from the thing.

3. When an object is seen not just from an accidental but also from an abiding side, or when the consciousness becomes aware of its essential or internal character, we have understanding. It is the consciousness which gets hold of abiding determinations of the object. (It is important to note that by "understanding" Hegel means this more limited function of the mind and regards the dia-lectical process of the mind as going beyond mere understanding.)

The second phase of consciousness, namely, self-consciousness, arises when the ego comprehends itself as that entity which can overcome the otherness of objects by being able to relate itself to them and which itself attains objectivity and actuality by virtue of being able to respond to the reality of objects. Here, Hegel seems to follow Kant, who said that in the process of becoming aware of the world, the self also becomes aware of itself. But this phase of consciousness also allows triadic differentiation, depending on the nature of objects confronted by the ego. Thus:

1. It can have the form of desire when it experiences a feeling of deficiency or want, which may be satisfied by some external object.

2. It can become aware of another ego, toward whom it may stand in a relationship of subordination or authority (Hegel calls this the relationship of master and slave). Despite this relationship to other selves, the ego nevertheless intuits its own freedom, since it also exists for itself. A slavish ego relinquishes this sense of existing for itself, while the master looks upon the slave as a canceled ego.

3. The ability of the ego to surrender its own individuality also makes possible an identification with the universal will. When this happens, self-consciousness reaches its third stage. In this stage, the separate egos mutually recognize themselves as the self-existing universal self. Pure spiritual universality is concretely experienced in the ego's sense of belonging to a family, a community, a country. The modes of experiencing this universality are the basis of such virtues as love, honor, friendship, bravery, and self-sacrifice.

For Hegel, the third phase of consciousness is the synthesis of the first two; it is the highest union of consciousness and self-consciousness. Reason combines the subjectivity of self-consciousness with the objectivity of consciousness of other things. "It is the certitude that its determinations are just as much objective, i.e., determinations of the essence of things, as they are subjective thoughts." The world is seen as not merely existing in-and-for-itself, but also as penetrated and assimilated by the ego. "The knowing of Reason is therefore not the mere subjective certitude, but also TRUTH, because truth consists in harmony, or rather *unity* of certitude and Being, or of certitude and objectivity."[6]

Note how this view disposes of Descartes' problem of the existence of the external world. External world, or Nature, is but a manifestation of the Idea; it is its external form. It is intelligible because it stands in an essential relation to the knowing mind. The reality is the Whole, but that Whole is to be seen in a constant dialectical process, generating out of itself further alternatives and thus continuing the process of self-development. Everything we know shows forth the march of reason toward its fuller self-realization. Hegel avoids falling into subjective idealism by acknowledging the independent reality of Nature, but he sees it as only an aspect of a single organic and dynamic Whole. He refers to that Whole as Mind or Spirit. Since causality applies only to one dialectical aspect of Spirit, namely, Nature, the universe is not deterministic. The march of events expresses the gradual development of the Idea of Freedom which characterizes Mind or Spirit.

A thing or an event becomes intelligible when it is seen as connected with other things and events. Everything in the universe manifests such connections. In trying to explain anything, ultimately there is no stopping point before reaching the Whole. All partial knowledge is taken up into an all-inclusive knowledge which is contained in the Absolute Idea. But the Absolute Idea is not something beyond or outside the world. As a synthesis of the finite and the infinite, it transcends the universe and yet is not absent from it. It provides both the meaning and the dynamics of the universe. The Absolute needs the world in all of its dialectical stages, nature and history included, in order to realize itself. Its perfection is both immanent and transcendent. It transcends each particular stage of the world's history, and yet gives history its direction. Although particular manifestations of the Absolute are relative and temporal, the actual life of Spirit is unending.

The work of Spirit can be seen in each human life and in the various stages of human history. Although each person regards his goals as private and personal, the pursuit of these goals fits into a larger pattern which transcends individual careers. They are directed by forces that are larger than the individual knows. Often, one is unaware of the historical aims that are being achieved through his action, and Hegel even speaks of the "cunning of Reason."

Hegel agrees with Aristotle that an individual needs others to find fulfillment; people are social animals. Family is a synthesis of the dialectical tension between individuals and allows a higher type of fulfillment for its members than they could get in isolation. But families are taken up into a larger institution of civil society, enabling them to fulfill themselves on an even higher level. The state, in turn, synthesizes the civil society or community into a still larger whole. It is a curious fact that Hegel did not project a continuous dialectical process toward a world community, in which the potential antagonism of states could be taken up into an international community. But it is clear that for Hegel individuals achieve freedom by relating themselves properly to their environment, to other people, and, as far as possible, to the entire sweep of historical development, concretely manifested in one's own past and present career.

Seen from an all-inclusive perspective, history provides a spectacle of the Absolute Spirit reaching toward and gradually attaining higher forms of its Idea. Some forms of life especially bear witness to the essential spiritual nature of reality. In art there is a movement from symbolic to classical, and then to romantic art. In symbolic art the symbol and that which is symbolized are identified and confused; the meaning is arbitrarily imposed on a sensuous medium, as in the case of an oriental statue with 20 arms. In classical art the idea of the artist is effectively rendered in a sensuous form, as in perfect renditions of the human form in Greek statues. Romantic art turns directly to inner life through music and lyric poetry.

All forms of art, however, express only the subjective aspect of Spirit. When we move to religion, subjective activity of the individual merges with objective Spirit, since individuals see themselves as created and dependent on a being external and objective to themselves. In religion there is a historical development toward higher insight, which moves from the preponderance of pictorial elements to the anthropomorphic, and finally to the religion of the Spirit. But as in all dialectical process, the earlier phases are not obliterated or canceled by the later ones. On the contrary, they are taken up, enriched, and transformed into something more inclusive and higher. Thus, finally, religion and philosophy are not separable, but form a unity.

> *Thus philosophy and religion come to be one. Philosophy is itself, in fact, worship; it is religion, for in the same way it renounces subjective notions and opinions in order to occupy itself with God. Philosophy is thus identical with religion, but the distinction is that it is so in a peculiar manner, distinct from the manner of looking at things which is commonly called religion as such. What they have in common is, that they are religion; what distinguishes them from each other is merely the kind and manner of religion we find in each.*[7]

Hegel thought of his philosophy as incorporating and spiritualizing the main insights of Christianity. Philosophy provides the highest stage in the self-development of the Absolute. The rational and systematic progress toward higher truth characterizes the history of human thought, leading us closer to the Idea of Freedom as the ultimate goal of the Absolute Spirit.

Hegel's Absolute is not outside history, including human history, in which man is striving toward greater rationality and perfection, but *in* history as such. The Absolute is timeless, but not in the sense of transcending everything that is temporal, but as being manifested in all temporality. Here, we find another example of a philosophy which rejects the two-level reality in favor of an integrated, organic reality. As Aristotle "naturalized" Plato's idealism and as Spinoza tempered Descartes' dualism with his psychophysical parallelism, so Hegel tried to avoid the difficulties with the concept of the thing-in-itself by declaring it to be nothing more than the perpetual progress of Absolute Spirit toward its own freedom. This gives every historical epoch and every individual person a definite role in their own place and time. In this regard, certain affinities to Leibniz's philosophy are evident. Similarly, Hegel's dictum that what is real is rational and what is rational is real, smacks too much of extreme Leibnizian optimism. It is still a matter of controversy as to what in the Hegelian philosophy is sound and what will not survive critical scrutiny, and it testifies to the vitality of his thought that after a long period of relative neglect it is again, in our own day, a focus of serious interest.

Hegel's influence remained strong throughout the nineteenth century and spread from Germany to other countries. It even reached England, that traditional stronghold of empiricist thought. During the second half of the nineteenth century, philosophical idealism came to dominate English universities. In the works of T.H. Green (1836-1882) it was translated into the idealistic ethics of self-realization and perfectionism. F.H. Bradley (1846-1924), although differing in some significant ways from Hegel, nevertheless saw fit to introduce the notion of the Absolute as the ultimate reference of all thought. Bradley's version of idealism sees an essential gap between any aspect of finite experience and the Absolute. He was skeptical of the ability of the intellect to give us real insight into the ultimate nature of things. Thought breaks up reality into conceptual fragments; it is of its essence to do so. Thus, in order to grasp reality, at some point thought has to commit suicide, and the person has to rise up to intuitive resources, in which task the aesthetic perception, the visions of great poets and novelists, are more promising guides than the inherently limited and limiting perspectives of abstract knowledge. "The real, to be real, must be felt." Bernard Bosanquet (1848-1923) also turns to aesthetic experiences as providing the most suitable contact with the deeper spiritual reality. For Bosanquet, each human mind "expands from its place in nature to a more or less wide and deep participation in the Absolute."

Hegelian thought also found its champions in America. The work of Josiah Royce (1855-1916) of Harvard resulted in a version of idealism which has a distinctly ethical flavor. Royce's notion of community as representing the spirit of greater harmonization, coordination, and reconciliation of initially conflicting aims and interests imbued the rest of his philosophy with the sense of moral earnestness in which the conception of loyalty provided the keynote. In one of his important books, *The Philosophy of Loyalty*, Royce declared that the highest virtue is loyalty to loyalty, the ability to embrace a worthy cause as one's practical ideal.

Surprisingly perhaps, one of the self-confessed followers of Hegel was Karl Marx (1818-1883), although his "dialectical materialism," finding Hegel "standing on his head," tried to put him right side up. Coupled with social and political revolutionary ideals, Marxism has become the official philosophy of the communist movement. Karl Marx studied Hegel's philosophy at the University of Berlin and found it convincing in many ways. Hegel's notion that all reality is a historical process in which the world moves from less to more perfect forms and becomes more and more rational as it develops struck Marx as essentially correct. He found, however, the references to the Absolute

Spirit or God as manifesting himself in the world quite useless and thought that humanity alone, in its progress toward greater perfection, constitutes the ultimate value. In this respect, there is a similarity between Hegel and Marx, for Hegel also thought of man as being the highest and unique manifestation of Spirit: to learn God's purposes we need to study human history.

Marx's study of that history convinced him that it is determined not by ideas but by material economic forces. With this modification, he subscribed to Hegel's view that all changes, including the changes in history, are dialectical in nature. A process tends to evoke a counterprocess, resulting in a new situation whereby the original opposition is eliminated and overcome. Applying this concept to social and economic developments and relying on Saint-Simon's view that history is shaped by the conflict among social classes, Marx proceeded to project the future development of mankind. According to him, human life is dominated by economic forces; all social forms emerge in the process of labor, and the mode of production determines the social relations. Having passed through the primitive, communal, slave, and feudal phases, mankind is now in the capitalist stage. As a result of inevitable historical development, this phase, in turn will be replaced, according to Marx, by the socialist and communist phases. Why is this inevitable? Marx reasoned as follows: In a capitalist society the owner class becomes ever smaller and richer, concentrating all wealth in few hands. Concomitantly, the rest of society is becoming ever larger and poorer. At last the point will be reached at which the proletariat is no longer able to subsist under these conditions, and a revolution will result, leading to the dictatorship of the proletariat and ultimately to communism.

The famous *Communist Manifesto*, issued by Marx and Friedrich Engels in 1848, formulates a set of principles according to which the Communist Party is to lead the proletariat to its victory over capitalism. The aim of communism is to establish a just, classless society in which, presumably, the dialectical process of history comes to an end. Whether this is consistent with the fundamental theme of dialectical materialism as characterizing the development of the world is an open question. History did not quite follow Marx's prediction, according to which the most highly developed, industrially progressive countries, and not the underdeveloped ones, would embrace communism first. At any rate, Marxism is an outstanding example of a philosophy that has become ideology, although Marx believed it to be the only true philosophy. But philosophy, for him, requires action. Up to now "the philosophers have only *interpreted* the world differently; the point is, however, to *change* it."[8]

# 3. Schopenhauer: Reality is Blind Will

Arthur Schopenhauer was born in 1788 and died in 1860. His father, a wealthy merchant in Danzig, was a highly cultured, broadminded person, well traveled, and liberal. He expected his son to take over the family business, but Arthur's inclination went in a different direction. For a while he was obliged to follow his father's wishes and work in a mercantile house in Hamburg. His father's death absolved Arthur from his promise to carry on the family business, and he turned his attention to philosophy, which he studied in several universities. He completed his doctoral dissertation in Jena; it was published in 1814 under the title, *On the Fourfold Root of the Principle of Sufficient Reason*. His mother was by then settled in Weimar and belonged to an active intellectual circle which had formed around Goethe. Mother and son had little understanding for each other's interests and pursuits, and their ways soon parted. Schopenhauer traveled for a while, read *The Upanishads* in Dresden, and was stirred by their content. In 1818 he finished his chief work, *The World as Will and Idea*, the publication of which, however, failed to attract any attention. The same was true of the second edition, published in 1844. In the meantime Schopenhauer settled in Frankfurt, where he led a solitary bachelor's existence. He wrote two essays on ethics, *The Basis of Morality* and *The Essay on the Freedom of the Will*, published together in 1841. A collection of essays entitled *Parerga and Paralipomena* appeared in 1851 and received considerable attention. This success stimulated interest in Schopenhauer's other works; during the remaining nine years of his life he was popular and widely read. Tourists in Frankfurt flocked to the restaurant Englischer Hof, where Schopenhauer, conscious of his growing fame, habitually dined.

It is instructive to study Hegel's and Schopenhauer's thoughts side by side, for while both of them were wont to use Kant as their starting point, their basic conclusions are antithetical. Schopenhauer believed that Kant had botched the problem of the thing-in-itself. He agreed with Kant's critics that Kant illicitly used the category of causality to describe the relationship of noumena to phenomena. But instead of concluding from this, as did the Idealists, that the unknowable surd of reality is to be dismissed as nonexistent or irrelevant, thus leaving the field fully to the manifestations of Mind or the Absolute, Schopenhauer was of the opinion that the thing-in-itself is directly accessible to us and that indeed it constitutes the essence of reality. How is the noumenon accessible? Through our *willing* side; as beings whose essence it is to will, we have an access to the very heart of the universe. The verdicts of the will and the observed fate of willing also discloses to us the essential characteristics of the noumenon.

Schopenhauer agreed with Kant that understanding makes the knowledge of phenomena possible. With some modifications and simplifications, he accepted Kant's doctrine of the categories. He also took seriously the claim that the category of causality is to be invoked when explaining all phenomena. This includes not only events in nature, but also human actions. Like the Stoics and Spinoza, he claimed that every action is fully determined by its antecedents. Hence, to speak of the freedom of the will is unintelligible. Given the person's circumstances, he cannot act any other way than he actually does. His knowledge of the circumstances will, of course, play a role in his deliberations and decisions. If he is mistaken about the actual causal relationships of phenomena around him, or if he does not understand his own motives, his actions will be infected by these misconceptions. Thus, when these misconceptions are rectified, his actions to that extent will be different.

There is, however, one element that does not change, namely, the personal individual *character*, which is inborn and constant. Schopenhauer adds that it is also empirical, that is, a person can discover the nature of his character by watching his own impulses, reactions, and goals. I find out what I am by seeing how I act.

What is the fundamental discovery behind all this? My essential reality is will. Will is the original power which, when acknowledged, reveals to us the secret of the universe. Here, we see an original treatment of the perennial problem of the ultimate basis of things. Locke, when confronted with the question of the underlying substratum of substances, gave a skeptical answer: something-I-know-not-what. Kant acknowledged the reality of noumena on the other side of phenomena, but also concluded that they cannot be known. Schopenhauer boldly announces that this is not true, that we can recognize the heart of reality most intimately, namely, as beings whose essence it is to will. A person's character is like a natural power about which no further questions can be asked. It is what it is, and it must express its own nature. Schopenhauer says at this point that one could speak here, in the Kantian fashion, of a person's *transcendental* freedom. We do feel responsible for our acts, and it is proper for a person to accept blame for his acts. But this is a way of saying that we must simply accept our character for what it is and not postulate any further causes of behavior. The circumstances will, of course, determine what aspects or sides of a character, or in the case of inanimate objects, of a natural power, will display themselves, but given the character or the natural power and given the circumstances, the outcome is inevitable. This, once more, confirms the universal applicability of the category of causality.

Natural powers are not only expressed in human characters, they are also displayed in the behavior of other animals and inanimate things. Even of natural phenomena we cannot go on indefinitely asking why they are what they are.

At a certain stage the limit is reached and we must say, for example, that it is the nature of a unit of hydrogen that when combined with two units of oxygen, it will yield a unit of water. Schopenhauer, like Leibniz, is a process philosopher; both view reality as active, dynamic, as displaying certain powers. But while Leibniz, the rationalist, thought of his monads as also displaying a capacity to fit themselves into the purposive order of the universe, Schopenhauer, the voluntarist, affirmed the absolute primacy of blind, irrational will. This is what the world is when seen from the inside.

The inside view is clearly most easily available in our own experience. Here, the primacy of will is indisputable, claimed Schopenhauer—on both the individual and social levels, and perhaps most dramatically in the arena of human history. An honest description and appraisal of ourselves will show that we are essentially creatures of desire. We are goal-pursuing beings, but we do not admit often enough that it is not we who determine our goals, but rather it is our goals which determine what we are. One desire succeeds another, one appetite appears where the previous one has been stilled or appeased. Try as we may, we cannot control the restlessness of our wills. No sooner has one goal been achieved than several others rear their heads and insist on being recognized; and so from the cradle to the grave there is no rest for the weary. All human beings are wills become visible.

The same continual pursuit of ambitions characterizes human groups from the family to the state. Indeed, if we read history impartially, we shall find it to be but one long story of strife and conflict. The aggressiveness of the naked ape, the self-assertion, the self-aggrandizement, the desire for conquest are the stock motives of political leaders. Another sober-minded student of the human race, Thomas Hobbes, in the seventeenth century, claimed that in the state of nature, life is "solitary, poor, nasty, brutish and short." But compared to Schopenhauer, Hobbes was an optimist, for he meant his description to apply only to what he called "the state of nature," prior to the emergence of political institutions. Schopenhauer, on the other hand, believed that the metaphysical nature of reality guarantees that the state of nature is the natural state of affairs for all mankind as long as it exists. Just glance at a history textbook; what does it contain? There is an account of the Seven-Year War, of the Thirty-Year War, the War of the Roses, the Wars of Succession, and so on. Only off and on do we have a couple of almost blank pages—and that is for peace.

Schopenhauer saw his metaphysical doctrine of the will as applicable to all beings and all things. Plants and animals wage a continuous struggle for survival, pushing aside and destroying obstacles, even if those obstacles are other plants and animals. The vegetative and the animal life is full of devices for defense and attack. The tall tree has no concern for its smaller fellows, whose access to life it blocks with its exuberant foliage. In spite of the Gospel's promise, the lions do not lie down with the lambs—nature is raw in tooth and claw. Even inorganic matter, through its own inertia, persists in exhibiting its fundamental natural power or has, as Spinoza called it, its *conatus*, the desire to persist in its being. Schopenhauer adds, however, that here we have nothing accidental, secondary, and potentially benevolent, but something essentially aggressive, blind, and irrational. Each existing being and thing is only an objectification of the will, for the will is essentially one. There is a problem for Schopenhauer here, analogous to the one which arose for Kant in connection with the thing-in-itself. Categories cannot be applied to the will, hence; we cannot say whether it is one or many. Schopenhauer said that it is one, but that it can be seen as objectified in existing things and beings. He also wanted to differentiate between the will in the human and the will in non-human animals. Each human character is individual, but the natural power of animals is common to the whole species. Hence, lions and cats, at least in their essential behavior, manifest the will of their species, not their own.

The will is irrational because reason and intelligence display themselves only subsequently to the operation of natural powers. Reason does not reach into the heart of the will; it is only its humble servant. Hence, the status of reason or intelligence is purely instrumental. The human intellect is but a long-distance weapon. Every being, including human beings, aims at self-preservation, and all of the universe is a tragic battle of the will, disorganized, contradictory, and blind—a welter of conflicting, reciprocally stultifying desires. No one can change his character. We can enlarge our knowledge about our surroundings and refine our self-knowledge, but in so doing, we merely help our essential, inborn, constant character manifest itself more fully and more truly. From what we do, we find out what we are. There is no escape from one's character.

The total picture, of both human life and its surroundings, including the cosmic setting, is thoroughly pessimistic. The irrational will is the true reality, relegating reason to a subordinate and ultimately ineffective role. As another preacher of wintry wisdom, George Santayana, observed in our own century, "Life is a series of little victories on the road to ultimate defeat." Schopenhauer would comment that even the little victories are merely temporary appeasements, leading invariably to pain and disillusionment.

Given this picture of reality, what does Schopenhauer, the philosopher, recommend to us as the wise attitude to take toward it? Although the will is essentially something bad, it would be a mistake to conclude that the right thing to do is to commit suicide in order to put ourselves out of the misery of being the will's blind, irrational objectification. An act of suicide would be but another assertion of the will, and hence would be a way of our remaining its obedient servant to the end. The way to defeat the will is to stop serving it. This can be done by concentrating on objects which enable us to still the insatiable surge of the will in ourselves. There are two types of objects which make this possible: aesthetic objects and the suffering of others. In contemplating the beauty of things, our own desires are arrested or neutralized; we are lost in contemplation, and so our will is at rest. The artist forgets the practical aspects of his work. In this connection Schopenhauer is reviving a version of the Platonic doctrine of forms: the objects of beauty and possibly other objects of pure contemplation—in science, in philosophy—remove the pressure of actual events and put us in touch with ideal forms alone. Ideas can become objects of knowledge only when the individuality of the knowing subject is transcended and he becomes a pure subject of knowledge.

Another avenue of liberation from the clutches of the will is to concentrate on the suffering of others. In feeling and acting compassionately, we turn away from our own desires, frustrations, and pains, which is another way of refusing to be dominated by them. We must will not to will. If human consciousness disappears, all phenomena will dissolve. This abolition of the will would not be nothingness, remarks Schopenhauer at the conclusion of his main work; it would be a positive state, a Nirvana, a bliss beyond all thought and speech.

Schopenhauer's recommendations imply that at least in such actions it is possible for the will to turn itself against itself, to deny its essential trust. Here, Schopenhauer encounters a problem. He seems to be affirming the possibility of freedom in spite of his metaphysical determinism—apparently a rather frequent philosophical predicament. We have noted it in the philosophy of the Stoics, and as we shall see in the following chapter, it is also present in Spinoza's ethics.

Schopenhauer believed that he solved the problem of the thing-in-itself. While accepting in essence Kant's epistemological views, Schopenhauer found the notion of the thing-in-itself unintelligible in terms of Kant's own doctrine. Causality is applicable everywhere in the world, and strict determinism governs human actions as well. But explanation does not reach beyond phenomena. All things display certain original powers which, given the circumstances, take their natural course. But what is the source of these original powers themselves? It is nothing but blind irrational will, and that is what Kant called the thing-in-itself, says Schopenhauer. Since we are desiring, willing, craving creatures, we know it intimately, and so does any other form of being, although of course not through the medium of consciousness which human beings possess. Every existing thing and being is an objectification of the Will to Exist, which eternally and restlessly seeks satisfaction and quietus, but never finds them. Such is the nature, the heart, of all reality. Here, ultimate skepticism is joined with ultimate pessimism, and we are reminded of the similar, but not as dismal, verdict of the Epicureans. Since Schopenhauer's verdict about

the world is based on the way he views his own experience and on the way
he understands and interprets history, the final judgment about the correctness
of this verdict must be left to each reader's response. But Schopenhauer argues
his views eloquently, forcefully, and with considerable philosophical erudition
and skill. His style is better than that of either Kant or Hegel, and some of
his specific arguments and observations on human life are often most
perceptive. His skepticism about the straightforwardness of human motivation
has fed the streams of thought which later found explicit expression in Freud's
theory of the unconscious. But it is somewhat of a puzzle that, as Thomas
Mann reports, among the devoted readers of Schopenhauer's in the last decades
of the nineteenth century were many rich, successful German merchants.

## Questions

1. What does Kant mean in saying that some concepts do not come *from*
   experience but are necessary conditions *for* all experience? What are
   the concepts that play this special role?

2. Does the statement "Some horses are not ticklish" make use of Kant's
   categories of judgment; if so, which categories are exemplified in
   this statement?

3. What does Kant mean in saying that the self and the world arise
   *together*, in the process of experience? Does this mean that there
   can be no self without the world and no world without the self?

4. What is the main point in Kant's criticism of Descartes' ontological
   proof of God's existence? Does Kant succeed in refuting Descartes'
   proof?

5. What did Hegel mean in saying that reality is a dialectical process?

6. How do you interpret Hegel's conclusion that each stage of world
   history is a manifestation of Absolute Spirit?

7. What is the role of the will in Schopenhauer's philosophical system?
   What evidence did he offer for his claim that the will is irrational?

8. What was Schopenhauer's view about the nature of human character
   and of human actions?

9. Can it be said that both Hegel and Schopenhauer were dealing, each
   in his own way, with some unresolved questions concerning Kant's
   notion on the thing-in-itself? Did Hegel and Schopenhauer go beyond
   the limits which Kant believed to have set for human knowledge?

# Notes

1 Immanuel Kant, *Prolegomena to Any Future Metaphyics,* translated by L.W. Beck, New York: Liberal Arts Press, 1950, p. 35.

2 Immanuel Kant, *Critique of Pure Reason,* translated by N. Kemp Smith, London: Macmillan, 1950, p. 522.

3 G.W.F. Hegel, *Phenomenology of Mind,* translated by J.B. Baillie, London: Allen & Unwin, 1910, pp. 54-55.

4 *Ibid.,* p. 20.

5 *Ibid.,* p. 21.

6 G.W.F. Hegel, *Outlines of Phenomenology,* translated by W.T. Harris, in *Hegel Selections,* edited by J. Lowenberg, New York: Scribner's, 1957, p. 78.

7 Quoted by J. Glenn Gray in *G.W.F. Hegel on Art, Religion, Philosophy,* New York: Harper & Row, 1970, p. 145.

8 Karl Marx, *Theses on Feuerbach,* as quoted in *The Age of Ideology,* edited H.D. Aiken, New York: New American Library, 1956, p. 195.

# Chapter Eight

# Ethical
# Theories

## 1. Spinoza: Cultivate Active Emotions

In the last chapter we noted how a certain metaphysical view may generate a corresponding ethical point of view. Schopenhauer's conclusions about what activities are worth pursuing follow from his appraisal of what the world is like. Spinoza's ethics also is a direct consequence of what he regards as the right way of understanding the nature of things. Having committed himself to the view that there is only one substance, namely, God or Nature, and that everything is but a modification of that substance and cannot be fully understood except by reference to the whole to which it belongs, Spinoza proceeds to apply this view to the human situation. He rejects the causal conception of the relation of the two attributes — thought and extension, or mind and body — to each other. The order and connection of things is the same as the order and connection of ideas, he said. This applies to the human sphere as well. Everything — every event and every action — has an adequate explanation. Since whatever happens, happens necessarily, as expressing God's reality, it would be a logical mistake to attribute to us freedom — the ability to initiate actions which do not have their origin in the total context.

In a sense, Spinoza recommends that we look upon ourselves as an action of the universe, or of Substance, seen in our individual perspective of space and time. (A similarity to Leibnitz's monadology here should not be surprising, for the two great rationalists share many basic insights.) When we do have an adequate understanding of how we act, or how the chain of events flowing from our actions has an explanation, we shall experience what Spinoza calls

169

an *active* emotion. That emotion will arise because our action or activity will be seen as adequately fitting our particular situation of which our individual characteristics are also a part. An emotion for Spinoza is not just a state of mind; it is also a modification of the body. When what we do gives an adequate expression to what we really are, we shall experience an active emotion. An active emotion can be recognized by the awareness of the increase in the active power of our body, a sense of well-being. In contrast, a passive emotion arises when we experience a sense of frustration, when we don't understand our behavior as adequately fitting our situation. Spinoza say that in the latter case we have a sense of being only a partial cause of the action and that it is being determined externally.

That persons have desires and goals is a natural state of affairs for Spinoza. Since there is a bodily aspect to ourselves and since the body's way of existing is to display power or energy, our appetites and goals call for no explanation; they are natural facts. Spinoza sees a logical connection between power and virtue. "By *virtue (virtus)* and *power* I mean the same thing; that is, virtue, insofar as it is referred to man, is a man's nature or essence, insofar as it has the power of effecting what can only be understood by the laws of that nature."[1] Everything has a natural propensity to persist in its being, a *conatus*, a desire for self-preservation. Human desires are also such natural appetites, but since to every bodily process there corresponds an idea, we are also *conscious* of our desires. As Spinoza says, "desire is appetite, with consciousness thereof." He also adds that "appetite is the essence of man, insofar as it is determined to act in a way tending to promote its own persistence." Indeed, the term "desire" is used by Spinoza to cover the whole gamut of the human mode of existence. It refers to "all man's endeavors, impulses, appetites and volitions, which vary according to each man's disposition, and are therefore, not seldom opposed to one another, according as a man is drawn in different directions, and knows not where to turn."[2]

Depending on whether one is subject to an active or a passive emotion, one experiences either pleasure or pain. Passive emotions are passions, "sufferings." They arise when there is a frustration of our normal desire to express our being harmoniously, in proper understanding of our situation and in self-understanding. This frustration is experienced as pain. On the other hand, when our action gives expression to our desires as adequately related to our propensities and our total context, we experience active emotions and pleasure.

Since the notions of pleasure and pain, and of all other value words as well— good and evil, right and wrong—have application only in the context of particular beings giving expression to their particular *conatus*, Spinoza does not think that goodness and evil have absolute meanings. They have only a

limited application and are relative to the kinds of desires and goals which
certain beings may pursue.

> *As for the terms good and bad, they also mean nothing positive in things*
> *considered in themselves, nor are they anything else than modes of*
> *thought, or notions, which we form from the comparison of things*
> *mutually. For one and the same thing can at the same time be good, bad,*
> *and indifferent. E.g., music is good to the melancholy, bad to those who*
> *mourn, and neither good nor bad to the deaf.*[3]

Good is always *a* good of some being or beings. Consciousness of appetites
gives rise to *self*-consciousness. Nature or God is not self-conscious, and as
we have seen before, to think correctly is to think impersonally, to not be
swayed by personal desires or biases. The divine intellect contains all truth
because it is not self-conscious. By the same token, the good-evil vocabulary
has no application at the boundless level of God's reality. The pursuit of desires
and self-consciousness are due to our limitations. We can still speak of God's
perfection, because His nature *is* full self-realization and unhampered free
activity. (On this topic Spinoza appears to be a bridge between Aristotle and
Hegel; his views echo some of the things Aristotle said about God and also
anticipate Hegel's conception of the Absolute.)

Spinoza sees an intimate connection between knowledge and humanly right
action. Our judgment can be influenced by undue self-assertion. While there
is nothing wrong with pursuing our normal desires—indeed by maintaining
our natural *conatus* we are realizing our good—we nevertheless may tend
to misconstrue our true good by allowing our passive emotions to dominate
the active ones. How can a passive emotion be transformed into an active
one? To every emotion there is a corresponding idea. For instance, the idea
$A$ corresponds to the emotion $a$, and the idea $B$ corresponds to the emotion
$b$. The change from $a$ to $b$ can take place only as a result of changing from
$A$ to $B$. Thus, we should strive in this way to replace passive emotions with
active emotions, such as love, kindness, and forgiveness. Hatred, fear, anger,
jealousy, and envy are the typical passive emotions because they distort the
correct understanding of things. They are rightly called irrational passions
because they make us blind to what is really happening. An irrational passion
prevents us from seeing that there are adequate causes for what happens and
that the behavior of others could not be otherwise than it is. To understand
all is to forgive all. Spinoza would go even further. He would remind the
person in the clutches of anger that he should see his anger in the full context
of the occasion which makes him angry. The occasion could not be avoided;
it fits into the rest of the situation, including the motives and the desires of
the person whom he at present tends to blame. In short, there is really nothing
to *be* forgiven.

One is reminded in this connection of the Stoic recommendation that all feelings and passions are to be extirpated, because they interfere with rational, objective understanding. Spinoza's recommendation is, however, different. He does not advocate getting rid of emotions. What needs to be done is to replace them with other emotions. How is this to be accomplished? It is to be done by taking the right view of the matter. When we see that what happens could not be avoided, when we see that there are adequate causes for what took place, we experience a transition from anger to acceptance and finally to kindness, perhaps even to love—if we manage to be affected by the thought that in spite of this incidence of pain, the restoration of the proper perspective can result in the pleasure of benevolence.

It will also help matters if in such a context we do not delude ourselves by the misapprehension that either we or the others are free. The consciousness of freedom is merely the consciousness of *wanting* to be free, but that desire arises only when we mistakenly regard our circumstances as obstructions. They need not be regarded as such, and this will happen when we accept them as belonging to the scheme of things. With this realization the sense of frustration and the desire to be "free" will disappear.

Active emotions lead to understanding and hence to happiness. Everything that enhances the growth of active emotions, the cultivation of proper dispositions, right social arrangements, and humane political institutions should be the goal of ethical endeavor. Thus, Spinoza advocated a life which was liberal, rich in pursuits, and well rounded in objectives. Such a life would be good and enjoyable. We have seen that for him pleasure is a natural sign of physical and philosophical health. In this respect, Spinoza's ethics reminds us of the ethics of the ancient Greeks, who also unashamedly proclaimed the value of natural pursuits, adequate to the human kind of being. He also agrees that we are essentially rational beings, that true happiness comes from true knowledge, and that the highest virtue is achieved in contemplation, in seeing things "under the aspect of eternity." The beauty of contemplation is also due in part to its noncompetitive character. Pursuit of knowledge naturally tends to establish a community among people; hence, it furthers the cultivation of active emotions.

In spite of the emphasis on the intuitive union with the Whole, God, or Nature, there is in Spinoza's philosophy a definite this-worldly note. It moves further away from the medieval thinker's preoccupation with supernatural salvation. The fulfillment is not to be seen beyond the grave, in some special form of existence. Although the human good is relative to the human situation, it nevertheless is the *good*, to be actively and resolutely sought, as the Renaissance figures ardently believed. Wise people meditate not on death but on life, for it is in the right living that they achieve their values and fulfill their destiny. The road to wisdom and virtue is, of course, not easy. It requires exertion, attention, and deepening of knowledge. But, as Spinoza expresses in concluding his *Ethics*, "all things excellent are as difficult as they are rare."

Spinoza's scheme emphasized the unity, the integration, of all things. Like the Greeks, he thought of the ethical ideal as harmony, proper attunement to the total scheme of things. Since knowledge is a necessary tool of such an integration into the fuller context of each human life, true understanding and insight are among the most prominent values. But knowledge for Spinoza is never merely cerebral, disembodied. Because mind and body are always *together*, as two sides of the same coin, greater understanding heightens our sense of physical well-being. Spinoza's rationalism has a definite naturalistic twist. An expansion of human awareness coincides with an increase of pleasure, which is always good. Since other human beings, by virtue of possessing similar bents and capacities, are most akin to us, it should be natural for us to feel both an attraction to and a sympathy for them. Pain is always bad whether it is experienced by us or by others. Since often it is due to passive emotions, which in turn are based on a defective understanding of our total context and of our naturally desirable objectives, we should try to transform passive emotions into active ones by a corresponding change in our ideas.

There is something very attractive about Spinoza's vision of the good life; it obviously reflects a mind that was intoxicated by the ultimate harmony of things and urged us to seek harmonious existence for ourselves and our society. In many ways, Spinoza's invitation to educate one's emotions by pointing to the unity and harmony of all things reminds one of a similar tendency in much of Eastern thought. Spinoza, "the God-intoxicated man," who is not concerned about personal immortality and is satisfied with the glimpses of eternal, impersonal Reality transcending all individuality, is not unlike the Eastern mystic who seeks to submerge his self in the large Self. Unlike some Eastern (and some Western) mystics, however, Spinoza never deprecated the value of temporal life and regarded the enjoyment of it as both possible and desirable.

## 2. Kant: Obey the Categorical Imperative of Duty

Kant's ethical theory is no less important than are his contributions to epistemology and metaphysics. He believed that all of his philosophy forms a systematic whole and that it is indeed possible to relate what he says about ethics to the other aspects of his philosophy. Although the *Critique of Pure Reason* is the most celebrated of his works, the *Critique of Practical Reason* is not far behind in its influence on subsequent thought. The notion of the Categorical Imperative is not any less famous in philosophical circles than the doctrine of the categories. It is an open question as to which of the two appeared more important to Kant. Paul Arthur Schilpp, a Kant scholar, claims that moral questions were closer to Kant's heart than was the rest of his critical philosophy, and he cites evidence that Kant set out to answer the problems of ethics before he turned to more general issues but then discovered that he needed to do some of the latter before he could do the former. This explains the order in which his books were written. Other evidence also indicates that ethical issues agitated Kant throughout his life. In his youth he was deeply stirred by Rousseau's conception of ideal humanity, and the title of his last work (written in 1795, when Kant was over 70) was *Perpetual Peace*. In that work he advocated a league of nations which would arbitrate international disputes.

It is possible, and to some extent useful, to relate Kant's ethics to his other views, and we shall do this to some extent. Kant believed, however, that his philosophical inquiries in the field of morality only bring to the surface beliefs which have always been held by the common man. If this is the case, then it should be possible to discuss Kant's views on ethics independently of his views on epistemology and metaphysics. At any rate, Kant's works on ethics can be studied independently of the rest of his philosophy. It is also an undeniable fact that those works had a powerful impact, are still read with great interest today, and continue to elicit copious commentaries.

One basic insight dominates Kant's analysis of knowledge: in a rational explanation we invoke a rule, a law, a general principle. To explain something is to see it as exhibiting a regular feature, as belonging to a *class* of things or events. A thing or event becomes intelligible when we can see it as an instance of a law or general principle. Kant's interest in *synthetic a priori* propositions came from his realization that such propositions provide epistemologically ultimate principles by means of which understanding and explanation are possible. The statement ''All events have causes'' is a synthetic *a priori* judgment. To learn that *A* causes *B* is to grasp a *universal* rule: in *every* instance of *A*, look for *B*, when appropriate conditions obtain.

Within our experience we can draw a distinction between events that happen without our participation or interference and those that are caused by us. The latter is the realm of action: actions are events which we ourselves cause. How can actions be understood and explained? They can be explained in the same way as all other events: by being seen in the light of some law or principle. But now a curious logical difficulty appears. If we regard actions as falling within a straightforward causal framework, then it appears that they are not really actions. What caused this man to steal? It was hunger. This answer, if it is meant literally, seems to establish a universal correlation between hunger and stealing: whenever there is a state of affairs called hunger, the state of affairs called stealing is also observed. But this way of putting it appears to eliminate the reference to the agent and hence to action; stealing is seen as a natural event among other natural events. This account is clearly a distortion of our normal explanation of stealing by a reference to hunger. We say instead: the man was so hungry that he could not resist stealing food. We insist on including a reference to an agent and hence to an action. Somehow, we want our account to recognize the man's own awareness of his hunger as supplying *for him* a principle of action: I steal *because* I am hungry. By presupposing this kind of intermediary, the event becomes intelligible to us *as an action* and not just as a natural event, like raining.

This sort of reflection must have been in Kant's mind when he formulated his distinction: "Everything in nature works according to laws. Only a rational being has the capacity of acting according to the conception of laws, i.e., according to principles." This distinction is crucial, and when followed out, leads to other important discoveries about human action. The phrase "acting according to the conception of laws" requires further attention. One reading of "conception" may again reduce an action to a mere event. If we think of our thief as being "detached" from his own actions, he "observes" himself stealing as he "observes" himself being in a state of hunger. The connection between the two events appears "objectively" before his mind, and he merely contemplates it, as he contemplates or cognizes the fact that it is raining outside. Is there a conception of a law? Yes. But there is no *acting according to* the conception. Thus, once more, this kind of analysis distorts what actually happens when people act.

The point Kant is making in the distinction quoted above alerts us to the fact that a person is not only a knower, a theoretical being, but also an agent, a *practical* being. Furthermore, rational explanation concerns man not only from the theoretical, spectator point of view, but also from the practical, agent point of view. This is why Kant also says that the capacity to act according to the conception of laws can also be called will. Thus, the very initial characterization of the human will involves a reference to principles, and hence to reason. Kant agrees with Aristotle that people are rational animals.

Let us return to our thief. He acts according to a principle: steal when hungry. It is *his* principle. It enables him to make his action intelligible, both to himself and others. Is it intelligible to others? Perhaps a pause is in order. How can others understand his action? They can understand it as a psychological or sociological description: hungry people tend to steal. Is the explanation satisfactory? Again, it is satisfactory if the situation is peculiar, when, for instance, the people who try to understand the explanation are "detached" from the person whose action they are trying to understand. This sort of thing happens when a social scientist reports on the mores of a group of people. His report is more likely to be accurate, or objective, when he is "detached" from the practice he is describing and when he is careful not to inject any of his value judgments.

But these are peculiar situations because they do not deal with standard cases of trying to understand the actions of other people. Normally, when we are trying to understand other people's actions, we do not detach ourselves from the situation in this "objective" way. On the contrary, bearing the situation in mind, our question is not limited to: Does the principle explain that he ought to do what he is doing? The reason for presupposing this kind of involvement or potential involvement in the situation is that the person trying to understand the action can really understand it, in the full sense of the word, only when he tries to see himself in a similar situation. This is an act of stealing, that is, depriving someone of his property. Thus, when the principle "steal when hungry" is considered, in order to understand it, one must see it as applicable also to the person trying to understand it. This means that he should be able to accept the principle when *his* property is stolen. Furthermore, he would need to understand the principle as allowing him to steal when he is hungry. When one sees that the consequences of understanding and accepting the principle involve extending it to all people who potentially can find themselves in the situation examined, including oneself, then its full meaning begins to dawn on us. It would mean that as practical agents we should have no objection to the principle's becoming a universal practice. Having reached this conclusion, we would be in the presence of what Kant calls the Categorical Imperative. "Act only according to that maxim by which you can at the same time will that it should become a universal law."

It is doubtful that the principle we used as an illustration, "steal when hungry," is enjoined by the Categorical Imperative. We are not likely to say that people ought to steal when they are hungry. At most, we may agree that under some circumstances, extreme hunger may excuse some acts of theft. But there are many other principles about which we would have no hesitation to say that they ought to be followed. "Tell the truth," "Keep your promises," "Prevent suffering," are such principles. Not that we could not find situations in which these principles should be suspended, but in such cases it would be necessary to cite *other* principles, for the sake of which one of these principles should be temporarily disregarded. It may be necessary to tell a lie in order to save a life, or it may be necessary to inflict suffering in order to prevent a serious crime.

For Kant, an action is moral if it passes the test of the Categorical Imperative. A person who acts morally acts on principles which are universalizable. Kant defends the rationality of such principles by claiming that their violation brings the person's will into conflict with itself. If I am willing to lie, to make false promises, then I am committed to condoning false promises made by others to me. But this would mean that I would never know whether their promises are to be taken seriously. Furthermore, in accepting the practice of making false promises, by either myself or others, I am in effect willing the destruction of the practice, because soon everyone will understand that any promise may be false, and in order to avoid being taken in, no one will take promises seriously. Hence, my intent to deceive others in this way undermines itself. When we try to universalize the principle "Lying is permissible," the self-contradictory consequences are even more obvious. To make lying a universal practice would undermine the basic purpose of speech—to communicate things to others. Hence, to lie is to make a subversive use of speech; it is to use it so as to contribute to the destruction of its effectiveness.

Kant formulates the Categorical Imperative in another way: "Act so that you treat humanity, whether in your own person or in that of another, always as an end and never as a means only." Kant regards this formulation as equivalent to the previous one, although he approaches the question from a different direction. Kant says that in lying to a person, we are treating her as a means. It may be to my advantage to misinform a person, but I achieve my aim at the cost of harming her. At least potentially, possession of false information harms her; she is not only ignorant, she is also deliberately misled. Even if no actual harm happens to her, I have excluded her from the circle of persons whose judgment about the meaning of my action is not distorted. I have treated her as not belonging to the circle of those who can affirm the universality of the principle on which I acted.

Kant connects the second formula of the Categorical Imperative with the idea of dignity. Since all persons are equally capable of judging morally and since this capacity goes to the very roots of human rationality, anyone who is denied participation in it is denied her dignity, her inherent worth. Nothing else can impart to man dignity or worth except morality, Kant believed. A person who takes morality seriously, who acts according to universally applicable principles, can also be described as having good will. "Nothing in the world—indeed nothing even beyond the world—can possibly be conceived which could be called good without qualification except a good will." The point of this remark is that all other human virtues and graces—intelligence, wit, composure, even good-heartedness—can be misused if not tested by the dictates of morality. Indeed, the astuteness and cool-headedness of a criminal are the more dangerous and morally despicable.

There is a third formulation of the Categorical Imperative, and it calls attention to still another important feature of morality. It contains "the idea of the will of every rational being as making universal laws." This is also called the principle of autonomy. What it says is that the source of moral action is the human rationality itself. When judging a principle universally valid, the agent stands behind and by this judgment, pledging his own serious commitment. He indicates in effect that in regard to the moral law, he thinks of himself as both its author and its subject. The authorship of the moral law is thus in persons themselves and is not merely transmitted to them from some other source. For if it were merely transmitted, we would be but a means, but if we are allowed to *judge* the validity of the principle, we take part in its moral legislation. The notion of autonomy does not imply autocracy; this is guaranteed by the first formula of the Categorical Imperative. Only when I treat others as *equally* capable of arriving at a rational judgment am I entitled to ascribe to myself the right to judge morally. Thus, in Kant's moral philosophy we see the reaffirmation of the classical faith in our ability to determine rationally our own course of action.

When Kant's ethical theory is compared with those of Plato and Aristotle, it becomes evident that he has more in common with Plato than with Aristotle. The comparison may be instructive. Kant shares with Plato the sense of opposition between nature and reason. We may remember that for Plato, the rational element had to control and direct the appetitive and spirited aspects of humanity. The latter are the natural tendencies. In yielding to them, we somehow fall short of our potential. Kant also thought that the heart of morality lies in being able to experience a conflict between one's inclinations and one's duty, between what one wants to do and what one ought to do. If I succumb to my natural desires without subjecting them to the test of the Categorical Imperative, I act like the rest of nature, and my actions are analogous to natural workings according to laws—physiological and psychological. Here, the principle of causality has full sway. But when what I do follows from subjecting it to the test of morality, the resulting action falls in a very different category, namely, freedom. It is not that the natural causal connections are denied; indeed, they still hold. But the action can also be seen as simultaneously manifesting my *conception* of a law that tells me which actions are morally worth doing.

At this point Kant sees a connection between his moral theory and the rest of his philosophy. He says that in acting morally, a person also acts as a *noumenon*, as an agent who stands outside or beyond the realm of natural causality. Actions performed out of respect for the Categorical Imperative manifest an additional and different sort of determination which is equivalent to the notion of *freedom*. It is freedom because in making the action conform to the Categorical Imperative, one is not judging from the point of view of one's personal desires, wishes, and inclinations; rather, one is performing the action for the sake of a principle applicable to all people in similar situations. This ability to act as a spokesman for and a determinant of a universally desirable order is a peculiarly human ability; it shows that we have "transcendental freedom," hence can act morally, hence have dignity and worth. In contrast, everything else in nature merely has a price; its worth is merely relative or hypothetical.

When an action is motivated not by respect for the moral law, but by the desire to satisfy some preexisting end or inclination, the principle of that action is only a hypothetical imperative. It is hypothetical because I may abandon the end or lose the inclination, and in that case the imperative, the prescription to perform the action, would also disappear. But this is not possible when the Categorical Imperative is applicable. I cannot abandon *it* with a change in my goals and inclinations, because it is valid for me, and for others, whatever my goals and inclinations happen to be.

Kant describes moral experience as a tension between the hypothetical imperatives and the Categorical Imperative, or between nature and reason. His account of that experience sometimes sounds like a description of an inner drama taking place in the soul of a person, in which the nonmoral and moral impulses battle it out. Kant also says that morality is a peculiarly *human* capacity and that it should not be ascribed to God or angels. God is not moral, because He is holy. He is not subject to inclinations, and hence for Him the notion of duty does not arise. Only a being who has the natural tendency and the possibility to ignore or disregard his duties can be described as moral.

As we have seen, the capacity to act morally is equivalent to having freedom, but freedom is not something that can be proved or exhibited in some particular experience. Freedom is a *postulate* for Kant. What we hear is the voice of the Categorical Imperative, the voice of morality. In order to think of ourselves as capable of obeying its dictates, we must think of ourselves as free of desires and inclinations which may pull us away from it; in other words, we must regard ourselves as not subject to natural causality, hence free. There are some logical difficulties here, analogous to those Descartes encountered with the problem of interaction. How can a corporeal being respond to the call of something which seems to lack any connection with the corporeal aspects of human beings? Kant tries to deal with this issue. He recognizes that the purely rational Categorical Imperative has to affect the corporeal, the feeling, side of man in order to be effective in terms of concrete action in the natural world. In order to avoid the difficulty, Kant says that the moral law can have effect on our sensibility or feelings. He believed that the very ability to see one's inclinations condemned, stricken down by the moral law, is proof of its effectiveness in our total setting, including our natural side. He also gives a description of the positive feeling that the majesty of the moral law can cause in human souls. Kant describes that feeling as *respect* and holds it to be different in kind from all other feelings which arise in connection with our natural, nonmoral desires and inclinations. He says: "But though respect is feeling, it is not received through an [outer] influence but is self-wrought by a rational concept; thus, it differs specifically from all feelings of the former kind which may be referred to inclination or fear."[4]

Although one may be inclined to ask further questions here, other contexts indicate pretty clearly what Kant has in mind. He says, for instance, that the love commanded by morality is not pathological love. By this he means that the loving attitude toward other persons should not be tied to the condition of experiencing certain definite feelings toward them. Even if the love of neighbor is required of us, we cannot be required to harbor warm feelings toward every neighbor. In fact, our natural feeling about some neighbors may be positively unpleasant. Nevertheless, we can still manifest toward them the kind of love which Kant believed is commanded by morality; we can genuinely will their welfare and express this attitude in our actions, despite our unpleasant feelings.

This distinction helps us to understand Kant's insistence that we should not regard the presence of natural benevolent inclination as a sign of moral attitude. A philanthropist may give away all of his wealth, but he may do so for a nonmoral reason—he desperately needs gratitude or the consciousness or reputation of being a benefactor. These needs are natural inclinations and have nothing to do with morality. This is why Kant regards as better illustrations of morality those instances in which a person performs an action even though all of his inclinations go the other way. Perhaps the most telling example of this connection is Kant's condemnation of suicide. He says that suicide is immoral because it is done out of concern for the particular pains and disappointments which the person is momentarily experiencing. As rational beings, we should not allow them to be the determinants of our action, but should think of our duty to promote the purposes of life which transcend our temporary disappointments.

Kant does not even trust something which one often regards as a distinctly moral trait: innocence as natural goodness. Innocence is a fine thing, but since it relies on intuitive tendencies and inclinations, it lacks the guidance of rational principles. "Innocence is indeed a glorious thing, but, on the other hand, it is very sad that it cannot well maintain itself, being easily led astray."[5] Hence, Kant prefers a steadier, more reliable and sturdier sense of duty, based not on mere feelings but on rational principles. For him, the core of moral experience is not harmony, but conflict. It is the conflict between the two aspects in us—the natural and the rational. To be moral is to be conscious of the possibility that one may *not* do what one ought to do, because one is always in danger of ignoring the voice of morality and of merely doing "what comes naturally." Spinoza had said that all excellent things are both difficult and rare, but Kant added that we never have full assurance that we are *ever* doing the right, the moral, thing. This does not mean, he continued, that we nevertheless should not try to do the right thing. If one succeeds in doing it for the right reason and from the right motive, one has risen above one's natural inclinations, and this is what morality commands.

Kant's model of inner drama accompanying all moral decisions appears to present a much less optimistic view of human motivation than does Spinoza's view. For the latter, it is the knowledge of the interconnections among things *in the world* that can induce the right ideas and active emotions. For Kant, morality consists in the capacity to lift a person above all things in the world and to impose *on* the world the morally desirable order. This difference is undoubtedly due in part to the different metaphysical pictures held by the two philosophers. Kant is closer to Plato than to Aristotle; with Spinoza, it is the other way around. According to Kant, a human being recognizes the claims of morality only as a thing-in-itself, a noumenon, which is not subject to the laws of phenomena. He thought that unless morality consists in the ability to act according to one's *conception* of a law, a person's behavior will be governed *by* some phenomenal law—physical or psychological. But if the latter is the case, neither morality nor freedom can be ascribed to us, because then we would be merely following our natural inclinations. Since Kant regarded persons not only as a part of nature but also as belonging to a rational order which can and ought to govern their behavior in nature, his view of morality was very different from that of Spinoza.

Perhaps this difference can be captured in suggesting that Spinoza did not differentiate between the theoretical and the practical uses of reason. For Spinoza, as for Socrates, knowledge is virtue, and vice is ignorance. To know how things really are is to do the good. According to Kant, the knowledge of what is (science) does not necessarily tell us what we ought to do (morality). Although it was Hume who first remarked that in ethical arguments, people proceed imperceptibly but unjustifiably from an "is" to an "ought," it was Kant who clearly insisted that our rational powers are employed in one way when we try to know nature and in a very different way when we try to determine what we ought to do. Rationality involves both a theoretical and a practical employment of reason, and it is a mistake to identify the two.

Thus, morality, rationality, and freedom are for Kant mutually supporting concepts. He grants that the fact of freedom cannot be proved; it is a postulate, derived from the undeniable call of morality in human experience. Whether or not we follow that voice is irrelevant to the fact that this voice is heard. It is very difficult for us to be sure that we actually do act out of respect for the moral law, for, acting as we usually do from mixed motives, we cannot be sure whether in any particular case it was really morality and not some secret inclination that determined our action. This determination is especially difficult to make when our inclinations and duties coincide. For all I know, Kant remarks in one place, no truly moral action has been performed in the entire history of humanity. But this does not mean that we do not have the obligation to try to obey the Categorical Imperative. Morality is not anthropology; it does not tell us what is but what ought to be. It is autonomous.

Kant upheld the autonomy of morality all the way, denying that it can be derived from any other source, including religion. In fact, he reversed the order of dependence and claimed that morality is the door to religion and not the other way around. Perhaps this is his "Copernican revolution" in the realm of theology. What are his arguments? For one, we should note that Kant sees in morality a way of connecting human beings with the noumenal order; in the realm of action, in using practical reason, we are not just a part of nature, a phenomenon—we can *dictate* to nature, can determine what should be the case. Kant's alternative version of the first formulation of the Categorical Imperative is: "Act as though the maxim of your action were by your will to become a universal law of nature."

We have also seen that the concepts of unconditional value, worth, or dignity receive their content from the moral realm. Our worth is derived from the capacity to act morally, to respond to commands which have their source in the noumenal realm. In fact, *all* we know about unconditional value comes from this dimension. If we ask *why* we should be moral, for what possible ulterior purpose, we are suggesting that there may be some other way of justifying morality, in other words, that it is not autonomous. But if we have understood that the demands of morality on us are the *highest* demands, then we will have reason to suspect that religion is but an extension of the dimension opened to us by our capacity to respond to the moral law.

Consider the notion of immortality. Like freedom, it is a postulate. A moral person does not worry whether he will be repaid for his righteousness. If his expectation of repayment was his reason for acting morally, then his action would lack morality. It would be performed out of a hypothetical imperative: I want salvation, therefore I act morally. Good people do what they do regardless of the consequences that may befall them personally. Our experience shows, however, that righteous persons do suffer, that they do not always experience the happiness of which they are worthy because of the morality of their actions. But since morality is commanded from a person's resources that go deeper than the phenomenal, it can be assumed that the worthiness to be happy will be recognized in that ultimate, transphenomenal scheme of things. To that extent, the promise of immortality is not without a point. Thus, immortality can at most be affirmed by a rational *faith*, although it is impossible here to speak of proofs or of rational knowledge. The postulate of immortality merely affirms that the consequences of morality must be commensurate with the kind of demand that it places on us. In other words, one may speak of immortality as the *consequence* of morality.

There is room in this conceptual framework for the concept of God as well. Kant thought that the same rational faith requires us to postulate God's existence. Since we all too frequently observe that moral action does not get any or full recognition in the world of appearances and since it may require immortality or transphenomenal existence to rectify the situation, it is only rational to expect that there is a being who is powerful enough to see to it that the consequences are commensurate with what is deserved. Thus, morality also includes a rational faith in God's existence.

Toward the end of his life, Kant realized that some of the language he had used in discussing the postulates of God and immortality tended to suggest meanings which he did not intend, even though he specified that his reference to faith precludes the use of images about heaven or an affirmation of some doctrinal theological statements. Nevertheless, to talk about immortality and God is still to try to say the unsayable. In addition, the belief in immortality may be seen as contributing an *incentive* to being moral. This would undermine the purity of the moral demand. Seeing this, Kant later modified his views in this area, concluding that all of these further reflections intend merely to underscore that morality is the highest form of value known to us. Religion should be recognized and respected as an expression and a deepening of this value, which in the end may fill us with a sense of mystery and awe. Two things impressed Kant as sublime — the starry sky above and the moral law within.

Kant's moral theory has received enormous attention ever since its formulation, probably because it focuses on some features of moral experience that are hard to ignore. Although the notion of the Categorical Imperative has been subjected to repeated criticisms, it has survived in one form or another in many contemporary ethical theories. Whether we must acknowledge something like Kant's Categorical Imperative as a necessary foundation of morality, or whether we can make do with imperatives of some hypothetical form alone, is still a heatedly debated question.

## 3. J.S. Mill: Follow the Principle of Utility

The inclusion of J.S. Mill among the thinkers of the modern period calls for a comment. After all, Mill's *Utilitarianism*, the work on which we concentrate in this section, was written in 1863, two centuries after Spinoza's *Ethics* and more than half a century after Kant's death. But utilitarianism can be regarded as a bridge between the modern and contemporary periods. It is one of the important alternatives in ethical theory and is still widely discussed in contemporary philosophy. What explains its appeal? The roots of utilitarianism go far back in time. The view that the assessment of desirable actions should be made by reference to pleasure was strongly defended in ancient times by Democritus, Epicurus, and Lucretius. The eighteenth century witnessed a strong revival of the concern with happiness. Indeed, one historian of that period concluded that it was the obsession of the century.

One of the earliest explicit mentions of the principle of utility, namely, that those actions are morally right which produce maximum happiness, is found in the work of the English philosopher Thomas Hutcheson. He belongs to a group of writers often referred to as the Moral Sense school of ethics. Although there are various formulations of this general view, they all emphasize the ability to discern the ethical value of an action by a special sense, or intuition. Although the "moral sense" does not necessarily exclude reason, it is closer to a feeling than to a judgment. Lord Shaftesbury, usually regarded as the first representative of this school, regarded moral discernment as analogous to an aesthetic perception. This approach was consonant with the then prevailing conviction that all of nature reveals divine design and that all beauty, including moral beauty, can be sensed as an ingredient in that design. Some eighteenth-century writers on ethics, for example, Joseph Butler, thought of moral judgment as issuing from a special source, which he called conscience or "principle of reflection." Conscience may give us direct moral verdicts which are more certain than those which the doubtful calculation of utility may provide. But even Butler was convinced that such verdicts would ultimately lead to an increase of happiness.

David Hume also believed that morality is a matter of feeling. Moral judgments occur when a sentiment of approval or disapproval is aroused. "This is good" means: "This is approved of; this is an object of esteem." "This is bad" means: "This is disapproved of; this arouses aversion." Feelings of pleasure or pain are signs of approval or disapproval. "Nothing can be more real, or concern us more," continued Hume, "than our own sentiments of pleasure or uneasiness." To discover what the right thing to do is, one must collect evidence as to how people tend to feel about the projected or contemplated action. There is a natural and universal admiration of certain social virtues among men: benevolence, humanity, friendship, gratitude, public spirit, etc. The worth of a person is determined by examining the qualities "useful or agreeable to the person himself or to others." If these qualities tend to promote the interests of our species or to bestow happiness on human society, they are morally desirable.

This standpoint is further elaborated and developed by J.S. Mill and his immediate predecessors. Mill was particularly impressed by the work of his father's close friend, Jeremy Bentham. James Mill, himself an influential utilitarian, had contributed to the dissemination of Bentham's views, especially in the area of their practical application to social needs of the time. It is generally conceded that the liberal and humanitarian reforms in nineteenth century

England were set in motion by the utilitarians. This is why it is possible to regard the ethical views of J.S. Mill as constituting a transition from the modern to the contemporary era. His thought is a culmination of a long tradition in British thought and provides a bridge to more recent developments in ethical theory.

A few words about Bentham's views are in order before we consider Mill's formulation of utilitarianism. The opening sentences of Bentham's highly influential work, *Principles of Morals and Legislation* (1789), are unequivocal: "Nature has placed mankind under the governance of two sovereign masters, *pain and pleasure*. It is for them alone to point out what we ought to do, as well as to determine what we shall do . . . . They govern us in all we do, in all we say, in all we think: every effort we can make to throw off our subjection, will serve but to demonstrate and confirm it." Bentham also gives us an explicit definition of utilitarianism. "By the principle of utility is meant that principle which approves or disapproves of every action whatsoever, according to the tendency which it appears to have to augment or diminish the happiness of the party whose interest is in question; or, what is the same thing in other words, to promote or to oppose that happiness."[6]

So sure was Bentham that this principle can tell us which actions are right and which wrong that he proceeded to propose a calculus of pleasures, a set of criteria by means of which we can determine the utilitarian consequences of each action. A unit, or, as he called it, a lot of pleasure or pain, can be ascribed to a proposed action in the light of certain estimates of pleasure to result from the action. They concern the following: (1) intensity, (2) duration, (3) certainty or uncertainty (the likelihood of its occurrence), (4) propinquity or remoteness (the interval of time between the action and its pleasurable or painful consequences), (5) fecundity (the chance of its being followed by sensations of the same kind), and (6) purity (the likelihood that it will not be followed by sensations of the opposite kind). To these six criteria, Bentham added still another one, which later will claim more of our attention, namely, (7) extent, i.e., the number of persons affected by the action in the utilitarian way.

This calculus calls attention to one important feature in Bentham's interpretation of the utilitarian doctrine: he conceives of it in a purely quantitative way. The *kind* of pleasure or pain is a matter of indifference. To quote Bentham again: "pushpin is as good as poetry," and "there ought to be a moral thermometer." This complete democracy in the realm of pleasures and pains was not appealing to John Stuart Mill, and he proceeded to amend Bentham's doctrine in his *Utilitarianism*.

J.S. Mill (1806-1873) was the world's most preeminent child prodigy. Subjected by his father to a rigorous educational experiment between the ages of three and fourteen, he was trained and drilled in subjects normally encountered only in college. In these few years Mill received, as he himself put it, "an advantage of a quarter of a century over my contemporaries." But even the young Mill's prodigious talents could not withstand the intellectual strain indefinitely. At the age of 20 he experienced a nervous breakdown from which he recovered only gradually. In the process of recovery, he received considerable help from studying Wordsworth's poetry and indulging his aesthetic sensibilities. In time, animation and enthusiasm returned to him. Like Bentham and his father, he took part in various efforts to bring about desirable social and political changes. This is reflected in the titles of his books, which also include important contributions to general philosophy — in particular, logic and the philosophy of science — *System of Logic* (1843), *Principles of Political Economy* (1848), *On Liberty* (1859), *Considerations on Representative Government* (1861), *Utilitarianism* (1863), and the posthumously published *Autobiography* and *Three Essays on Religion*.

Mill was convinced that the principle of utility can serve as the proper foundation for morality, provided that the notions of pleasure or happiness are interpreted generously. He thought that Bentham was mistaken in disregarding differences in the *kinds* of pleasure. Qualitative distinctions are just as important or perhaps even more important than quantitative ones. Here, Mill appeals to something that has been the favored refuge of many other British philosophers: experience. After all, the judgment of the value of a pleasure depends on the scope of a person's experience. Those who know only a limited number of pleasures may be acquainted only with the lower ones. One must include the higher human capacities. Utilitarianism can be easily ridiculed if one restricts oneself to pleasures of low calibre. But why should one restrict one's vision to the lower human capacities, that is, capacities which, up to a point, they share with other animals? "Socrates dissatisfied is better than a pig satisfied" is Mill's rejoinder to those who seek in utilitarianism a sanction for primitive pursuits of a greedy voluptuary. Mill's appreciation of the poet's vision of reality, of more refined feelings and attainments, speaks eloquently in his depiction of a life in which the noble attainments have their proper share. As an educational manual, spreading before us the satisfactions of a sensitive, cultivated mind, Mill's *Utilitarianism* has few equals. Like Aristotle, he is anxious to invite us to seek his pleasures in the higher realms of our potentialities.

There is still another source of happiness, according to Mill, namely, altruism. Bentham included among his criteria of right action the reference to the happiness of others. Mill expatiates on this point, arguing that "the happiness which forms the utilitarian standard of what is right in conduct, is not the agent's own happiness but that of all concerned." How do we know that the sharing in the happiness of others is preferable to preoccupation with one's own? Again, experience is the judge. There is such a thing as the conscientious feeling of mankind, and it provides the ultimate sanction of morality. To those in whom it is duly cultivated, it constitutes a sufficient proof of the truth of utilitarianism, Mill contends.

Like many of his predecessors, Mill appeals to our natural sympathies, to the capacities to feel at one with others. Eloquently and earnestly, he describes states of affairs in which this natural capacity is given proper recognition. Yet he is not unaware that the line between the "is" and the "ought" can be made to disappear. He deplores the fact that the majority of people do not follow the principle of utility, with unhappiness as the result. "Unquestionably it is possible to do without happiness; it is done involuntarily by nineteen-twentieths of mankind." This does not mean, however, that this state of affairs is desirable.

Mill's defense of the principle of utility is not as convincing as he wished it to be. Some of his arguments are logically faulty. One of them concerns his apparent identification of what is desired with what is desirable. Mill claims that just as what is seen is visible, so what is desired is desirable, not seeing that the logical function of "visible" is very different from that of "desirable." "Visible" means "can be seen," whereas "desirable" means "ought to be desired." As we have just noted, Mill admits that many people do not follow the principle of utility; they do not *desire* to perform actions that would make them and others happy. Yet he wants to claim that happiness-enhancing actions are desirable, even though many people are not motivated by that desire.

It is clear that for Mill, those who recognize the goodness of moral actions may find it highly satisfying. Morality is *capable* of cultivation, but it is not guaranteed by human nature. Mill sometimes sees this. For example, he says: "The moral faculty, if not a part of our nature, is a natural outgrowth from it; capable, like them, in a certain small degree, of springing up spontaneously; and susceptible of being brought by cultivation to a high degree of development." He adds, however, significantly: "Unhappily it is also susceptible, by a sufficient use of the external sanction and of the force of early impressions, of being cultivated in almost any direction, so that there is hardly anything so absurd or mischievous that it may not, by means of these influences, be made to act on the human mind with all the authority of conscience."[7] This admission is important, for it indicates that Mill's doctrine of utility as a moral "ought" does not follow from the facts as he sees them. Yet he builds his case on the appeal to what *is*, to the actual tendencies of human nature.

Another logical difficulty in Mill's argument can be seen in his claim that because everyone seeks his own happiness, everybody aims at general happiness. It does not follow from the fact that everyone desires his own happiness that he also desires the happiness of everybody else. Indeed, it is often the case that one person's happiness can be attained only at the cost of another person's suffering. Only when one somehow shows that that suffering is good for the person in the long run can one say that general happiness will result. The crucial issue of morality is to recognize the right of others to be happy. Only after I recognize that right can I begin calculating the likely consequences of my actions in terms of happiness. The important step is from the concern about myself to the concern about the well-being of others. Both Bentham and Mill make this step too quickly and too optimistically. They may be right in saying that *if* people act altruistically, general happiness is likely to follow, but it takes a further act of moral judgment to decide that people *ought* to act altruistically so that general happiness may result.

The logical inadequacies of arguments produced by Mill in defense of utilitarianism do not detract from his statute as an eloquent moralist, intent on showing that the moral tendency is not foreign to human nature and that morality is enhanced by envisaging in detail the attractive consequences of moral action. In that sense, Mill is an effective moral educator. In his other works, especially in the essay *On Liberty*, he champions the values of individualism and independence from social pressures. He is a true son of the modern humanistic point of view, which regards the individual human person as the source and bearer of values which make life worth living.

Utilitarianism is one of the most prominent alternatives to the Kantian approach to morality. We have seen that it appeared on the European scene long before John Stuart Mill gave it his influential formulation. We may also recall that the Ancients recognized pleasure as a desirable ingredient of life, although what was meant by pleasure varied considerably from thinker to thinker. Socrates and Plato included pleasure among the good things of life, provided it was tempered and controlled by reason. Aristotle's notion of *eudaemonia* connoted an all-around well-being which was concomitant with virtuous activities. For the Epicureans, only the immediate but moderate pleasures of the senses were worth having. Spinoza's theory, since it also recognizes the proper use of reason as the condition of happiness, is reminiscent of Aristotle's all-inclusive concept of *eudaemonia*. Of the modern utilitarians, some tend to think of pleasure as one quality present in different amounts in various experiences. This was the position of Jeremy Bentham with his quantitative calculus of pleasures. John Stuart Mill, on the other hand, thought of pleasure more along the lines of Aristotle and Spinoza. There are many kinds of pleasure, and a happy life will include those which enlist not only the senses but also the higher human capacities, including both the intellect and the sensitivity to the needs of others. The emphasis is again on harmony, on cooperation of various aspects of human endowment. To aim at such harmony is natural for us, and actions are morally right if they tend to bring about the highest degree of satisfactions for the greatest number of persons.

One of the unresolved questions about utilitarianism is the actual role of reason in the calculations preceding the choice of a course of action. Using Kant's distinction, we may ask whether morality for utilitarians is merely a hypothetical imperative and whether it ultimately rests on feeling alone. If it does, then a person who happened not to feel, for instance, any satisfaction in maximizing the happiness of others would not be obligated to do so. Furthermore, in many instances it is extremely difficult to determine just what the outcome of one's action will be in terms of personal, not to speak of general happiness. Some contemporary utilitarians try to take care of this problem by distinguishing between act-utilitarianism and rule-utilitarianism. The former is the view that the principle of utility should be applied to every individual *act* in judging its moral worth. The latter regards the principle as merely establishing what general *rules* are morally desirable. The rule-utilitarian need not worry about calculating in advance all the likely outcomes of his action, because he knows that if he and others follow general rules, the result in the long run will be beneficial to all. In some cases, to be sure, following a rule may result in more harm than good, but the general practice of following the rule will have greater utilitarian advantages than an occasional harm due to unforeseen circumstances.

As we shall see in discussing contemporary ethical theories, the controversy over utilitarianism still persists. Nevertheless, its influence on the ethical and political thought of our time has been very strong. For many people, the right to pursue happiness is one of the inalienable rights and should serve as the foundation of a just social order. By putting happiness at the very center of human consciousness, the utilitarians were acting as spokesmen for the entire age. The observation that happiness was the obsession of the eighteenth century may be applicable to the following centuries as well, our own included.

## Questions

1. What was Spinoza's distinction between passive and active emotions? By what process did he think that the former can be transformed into the latter?

2. In what ways do Spinoza's views about the role of emotions differ from the views of the ancient Stoics?

3. How did Kant propose to test whether an action is moral? How were the different versions of this test formulated by Kant?

4. Why did Kant believe that while dealing with morality we at the same time deal with rationality and with freedom? How are these concepts related in his ethical theory?

5. What were Kant's grounds for saying that it would be inappropriate to refer to God or angels as moral?

6. Why did Kant say that freedom, immortality, and God's existence cannot be proved, but that they are *postulates*? Does this point have something to do with his distinction between the theoretical and the practical uses of reason?

7. What is included in J.S. Mill's concept of happiness, and how does his concept differ from that of Jeremy Bentham?

8. Does Mill offer a description of what morality consists in, or does he offer reasons why people *ought* to follow the principle of utility? If the latter, what *are* these reasons?

## Notes

[1] From the book *Ethics* and *On the correction of the Understanding* by Benedictus de Spinoza, translated by Andrew Boyle, Everyman's Library Edition. Published by E.P. Dutton & Co., Inc. and used with their permission.

[2] *Ibid.*, p. 128.

[3] *Ibid.*, p. 143.

[4] Immanuel Kant, *Foundations of the Metaphysics of Morals*, translated by L.W. Beck, New York: Liberal Arts Press, 1959, p. 17.

[5] *Ibid.*, p. 21.

[6] Jeremy Benthan, *Introduction to the Principles of Morals and Legislation*, in *British Moralists 1650-1800*, edited by D.D. Raphael, Oxford: Clarendon Press, 1969, p. 313.

[7] J.S. Mill, *Utilitarianism, Liberty, Representative Government*, New York: Dutton, 1968, p. 28.

# Part II

## Suggested Further Reading

Aaron, R.I. *John Locke*. Oxford: Clarendon Press, 1973.

Anderson, R.F. *Hume's First Principles*. Lincoln: University of Nebraska Press, 1966.

Balz, A.G.A. *Descartes and the Modern Mind*. New Haven: Yale University Press, 1952.

Basson, A.H. *Hume*. Baltimore: Penguin, 1953.

Beck, L.J. *The Metaphysics of Descartes*. Oxford: Clarendon Press, 1965.

Bennett, Jonathan. *Kant's Analytic*. Cambridge: Cambridge University Press. 1966.

Bennett, Jonathan. *Kant's Dialetic*. Cambridge: Cambridge University Press. 1974.

Britton, K. *J.S. Mill*. Baltimore: Penguin, 1953.

Broad, C.D. *Kant: An Introduction*. Cambridge: Cambridge University Press. 1978.

Butterfield, Herbert. *The Origins of Modern Science*. Rev. ed. New York: Collier, 1962.

Carr, H.W. *Leibniz*. New York: Dover, 1960.

Chapell, V.C. ed. *The Philosophy of David Hume*. New York: Modern Library, 1963.

Findley, J.N. *Hegel: A Re-Examination*. New York: Collier, 1964.

Flew, A. *Hume's Philosophy of Belief*. London: Routledge, 1961.

Gardiner, P. *Schopenhauer*. Baltimore: Penguin, 1963.

Guyer, P. *Kant and the Claims of Taste*. Cambridge: MA: Harvard University Press, 1979.

Hallett, F.H. *Benedict De Spinoza: The Elements of His Philosophy*. London: Athlone, 1957.

Hamlyn, D. *Schopenhauer*. London: Routledge & Kegan Paul, 1980.

Hampshire, S. *Spinoza*. Baltimore: Penguin, 1951.

Kaufmann, Walter, *Hegel*. New York: Doubleday, 1965.

Kemp Smith, Norman. *A Commentary to Kant's Critique of Pure Reason*. 2nd ed. New York: Macmillan, 1923.

Kenny, A. *Descartes, A Study of His Philosophy*. New York: Random House, 1968.

Körner, Stephan. *Kant*. Baltimore: Penguin, 1955.

Loewenberg, J. *Hegel's Phenomenology*. La Salle, IL: Open Court, 1965.

Magee, Bryan. *The Philosophy of Schopenhauer*. Oxford: Claredon, 1983.

Malebranche, N. *Dialogues on Metaphysics and Religion*. London: Allen & Unwin, 1923.

Michel, P.H. *The Cosmology of Giordano Bruno*. Ithaca, NY: Cornell University Press, 1973.

Oakshott, M. *Hobbes on Civil Association*. London: Oxford University Press, 1975.

O'Connor, D.J. *John Locke*. Baltimore: Penguin, 1952.

Passmore, John. *Hume's Intentions*. Cambridge: Cambridge University Press. 1952.

Paton, H.J. *Kant's Metaphysics of Experience*. 2 vols. London: Allen & Unwin, 1936.

Paton, H.J. *The Categorical Imperative*. Chicago: University of Chicago Press, 1948.

Rescher, N. *Leibniz: An Introduction to His Philosophy*. London: Oxford, 1979.

Saw, R.L. *Leibniz*. Baltimore: Penguin, 1954.

Stace, W.T. *The Philosophy of Hegel*. New York: Dover, 1955.

Stroud, B. *Hume*. London: Routledge and Kegan Paul, 1977.

Strawson, P.F. *The Bounds of Sense*. London: Methuen, 1966.

Teale, A.E. *Kantian Ethics*. London: Oxford University Press, 1951.

Ullmann, W. *Medieval Foundations of Renaissance Humanism*. Ithaca, NY: Cornell University Press, 1977.

Warnock, G.J. *Berkeley*. Baltimore: Penguin, 1953.

Weldon, T.D. *Kant's Critique of Pure Reason*. 2nd ed. Oxford: Clarendon Press, 1958.

Wienpahl, P. *The Radical Spinoza*. New York: New York University Press, 1979.

Wilbur, J.B. *Spinoza's Metaphysics*. Assen: Van Gorcum, 1976.

Williams, B. *Descartes: The Project of Pure Inquiry*. Atlantic Highlands, NJ: Humanities Press, 1978.

Wilson, M.D. *Descartes*. London: Routledge & Kegan Paul, 1978.

Wood, A.W. *Kant's Rational Theology*. Ithaca, NY: Cornell University Press, 1978.

*John Dewey (1859-1952)*

# Twentieth
# Century
# Thought

# Chapter Nine

# Existentialism

## 1. Nietzsche: The Will to Power

Philosophical preoccupations of the twentieth century have been strongly influenced by the writings of thinkers whose work appeared just as the nineteenth century was coming to a close. This is the reason for treating such people as Nietzsche and Peirce as belonging to our century. Their seminal thought has set in motion such trends as existentialism and pragmatism, and their influence is still profoundly felt as expressed in the growing literature on their views. Twentieth century philosophical developments can be best understood if we take these views into account. Both Nietzsche and Peirce react to the ideas introduced by the pivotal thinker of the modern era: Immanuel Kant, and in Nietzsche's case, the influence of Schopenhauer is immediately present. Thus, taking our philosophical journey into the twentieth century, we see it exhibiting both continuity and change, or as Hegel might put it, identity and difference.

It should be noted that existentialism as a label for a school of philosophy did not exist when Nietzsche wrote, and both Heidegger and Sartre reject this label as not applicable to them. Furthermore, it is Søren Kierkegaard (1813-1855) who is often regarded as the first existentialist, even though some defenders of this line of thought are inclined to credit Socrates with originating it. Kierkegaard is clearly an important philosophical figure of the nineteenth century. While other philosophers were turning away from Hegel's philosophical idealism simply because they found other issues more relevant and challenging, Kierkegaard turned against Hegel because he found his philosophy excessively rationalistic. Kierkegaard rejected the entire Hegelian view of the human situation. By making the Absolute the heart of reality, Hegel's philosophy eliminated the possibility for each individual to face his own subjective inwardness. When it comes to concrete issues of life and death, of serious existential decisions, an elaborate philosophical system is a distortion and a distraction. A philosophical idealist constructs in thought a beautiful castle, but lives his real life in a desolate hovel. Kierkegaard also believed the Hegelian doctrine to be at odds with the basic message of Christianity. For Christians to follow Hegel is to betray Christ, charged Kierkegaard. To accept Christ's message is to surrender unconditionally to God's will, without the pretense of "interpreting" it in a philosophical way. Kierkegaard's views on Christianity are distinctly Augustinian. Like Bradley, although for different reasons, Kierkegaard believed that the thought of a concretely existing individual must commit suicide in order for him to be acceptable to God. Kierkegaard's emphasis on spiritual inwardness is present in the writings of many religious thinkers who regarded themselves as theistic existentialists. The Protestant theologian Paul Tillich, the Catholic Gabriel Marcel, and the Jewish philosopher Martin Buber are among their number.

On the matter of religion, Sartre proclaimed his philosophy to be atheistic, and Heidegger denied that his views leaned in the direction of theism, although some of his Christian interpreters regard his philosophy as sympathetic to theology. Nietzsche was the one who announced that "God is dead," and he entitled one of his works *Anti-Christ*. But the theism-atheism issue does not define existentialism. The selection of Nietzsche as the first spokesman for the set of ideas associated with existentialism is justified by his statement of the key themes which were the focus of interest for philosophers labeled as existentialists, in spite of their rejection of the label. These themes include: (1) the denial that there is a static human nature, (2) the discovery of deep creative resources within the concretely existing individual, and (3) the rejection of any intellectual system as capturing the essence of humanity. Regarding the last point, existentialism, like positivism and science, also rejects metaphysical speculation, but does not accept the remedies proposed by them. Instead, it finds human existence deep, mysterious, and fascinating, perhaps more adequately captured in poetry, novels, and drama than in abstract philosophical statements.

Friedrich Nietzsche (1844-1900) was one of the original thinkers whose impact on the intellectual and spiritual climate of the Western world is undeniable and yet difficult to assess. During two decades of his productive life, this explosive genius wrote books which affected not only philosophers but also artists, novelists, psychologists, and theologians. Only in this century is the fuller significance of Nietzsche's place in the history of thought beginning to be realized, as book upon book manifests indebtedness to his stimulus. For a long time he was regarded as a sort of philosopher-poet, with no clear place in the development of philosophy. More recently an examination of his strictly philosophical contributions has led to the conclusion that his epistemology, labeled "perspectivism," bears a considerable resemblance to some of the doctrines of pragmatism. Nietzsche's influence on poets and writers has been widely acknowledged—Rilke, Hesse, Thomas Mann, Shaw, Gide, Malraux, and Camus are but some of the important writers who show their indebtedness to him. Freud's views on depth psychology were fore-shadowed in Nietzsche's observations. Many noted philosophers of this century draw also on his original insights. It has been said that Nietzsche's philosophy was translated into poetry by Rilke, and Rilke's poetry was in turn translated into prose by Heidegger. Heidegger and Jaspers are the authors of books on Nietzsche, and the first name mentioned by Sartre in his main work, *Being and Nothingness*, again is Nietzsche.

Nietzsche's life was a tragic one. At the height of his powers he was struck by mental illness from which he never recovered. Since his father died when he was only four years old, he was raised entirely by women: his mother, grandmother, and two maiden aunts. After a brilliant career at the Universities of Bonn and Leipzig, he was appointed Professor of Philosophy at Basel at the age of 24, but due to failing health, partly as a result of an illness incurred during his service as a medical orderly in the Franco-German War of 1870, he resigned from his professorship in 1879. During the remaining active years of his life he traveled a great deal, spending summers in Switzerland and winters in Italy. His first book, entitled *The Birth of Tragedy From the Spirit of Music*, appeared in 1872. Some of its ideas, which created quite a stir among the scholars of Greek culture, were influenced by Richard Wagner. During the following decade Nietzsche produced several major works, thus establishing himself as a formidable figure on the European intellectual scene. These works include *The Dawn* (1881), *The Gay Science* (1882), *Thus Spoke Zarathustra* (1883-1884), *Beyond Good and Evil* (1886), and *Genealogy of Morals* (1887). In 1888 there appeared *The Case Wagner*, decisively signaling the end of friendship between Nietzsche and the musical genius Richard Wagner. Another book against the former friend, entitled *Nietzsche Contra Wagner*, was written shortly before the author lost his lucidity. Other works also written prior to Nietzsche's mental collapse but published afterward are: *The Antichrist*, *Twilight of the Idols*, and *Ecce Homo*.

While writing all these books, Nietzsche was assembling notes for a larger work which was to be called *The Will to Power*. The book was never completed, and only an uncritical collection of some notes was published by Nietzsche's sister. This, however, was not the only abuse to which his works have been subjected. Some of his ideas, in incredibly distorted form, were also used by the Nazi movement in Germany, but this linking is as justified, says Walter Kaufmann, as the linking of St. Francis with the Inquisition. Kaufmann's Nietzsche scholarship and superior translations have contributed much to a revival of interest in the work of that seminal thinker. Quotations to follow are from Kaufmann's translations.

Nietzsche believed that he lived at the time of a profound spiritual crisis. In his judgment an era was coming to an end, but it was not just the passing away of an intellectual phase; the very foundations of Western civilization were cracking. His conviction gathered momentum as Nietzsche pursued his historical studies and observed the situation around him. It is summarized in one phrase, "God is dead." Although this phrase, used by Nietzsche in his later books, has become very popular in recent decades and has even furnished a label for a new trend of contemporary theology, its meaning reaches deeper than particular theological doctrines. Nietzsche makes his pronouncement as a historian of ideas who sees ideas as forms of life, as vehicles for the articulation of central attitudes. He sees in the concept of God a summary of the highest aspirations and ideals. In the West these ideals were articulated by Christianity, but the Christian framework was indebted in many crucial ways to Greek classical thought, with its conception of the soul as the core of the spiritual and moral being of humanity. Nietzsche is both examining the meaning of the basic spiritual presuppositions and assessing their long-range consequences, especially as these consequences affected our present age.

There is a paragraph in *Gay Science* in which Nietzsche expresses dramatically the contemporary state of affairs as he sees it. He puts his verdict into the mouth of an alleged madman, itself a dramatic device. Nietzsche realized that this view would appear mad to those "normal" people who still did not see that they were living in a dying age. There may be no better way of showing what Nietzsche is trying to say than to quote this paragraph and to comment on its key passages:

> *"Whither is God," he cried. "I shall tell you. We have killed him—you and I. All of us are his murderers. But how have we done this? How were we able to drink up the sea? Who gave us the sponge to wipe away the entire horizon? What did we do when we unchained this earth from its sun? Whither is it moving now? Whither are we moving now? Away from all suns? Are we not plunging continually? Backward, sideward, forward, in all directions? Is there any up or down left? Are we not straying as through an infinite nothing? Do we not feel the breath of empty space? Has it not become colder? Is not night and more night coming on all the while? Must not lanterns be lit in the morning? Do we not hear anything yet of the noise of the gravediggers who are burying God?*

*Do we not smell anything yet of God's decomposition? Gods too decompose. God is dead. God remains dead. And we have killed him. How shall we, the murderers of all murderers, comfort ourselves? What was holiest and most powerful of all that the world has yet owned has bled to death under our knives. Who will wipe this blood off us? What water is there for us to clean ourselves? What festivals of atonement, what sacred games shall we have to invent? Is not the greatness of this deed too great for us? Must now we ourselves become gods simply to seem worthy of it? There has never been a greater deed; and whoever will be born after us — for the sake of this deed he will be part of a higher history than all history hitherto.''*[1]

Who murdered God? Ourselves — all of us. By the death of God, Nietzsche means a *cultural* event. It is a crisis of the entire culture. Thus, to say that we killed God is to say that the idea which originally was meaningful and vital is no longer so. Years before, Søren Kierkegaard had attacked Christendom for having betrayed and turned away from the original message of Christ. Nietzsche agreed, but his criticism goes deeper. The whole culture, based essentially on Christian ideals, has gone sour and is in the throes of nihilism. This includes not only the spiritual flabbiness of the church, but also the decay of all other institutions: science, education, art, morality, politics. Nietzsche levels the guns of his powerful criticism on all of these in turn.

The important point about the death of God as a cultural event is that everybody shares in bringing it about. It is not the fault of providence or of history. We have brought the crisis upon ourselves. It is *our* crisis. No external force is to blame. This is one of the things that the phrase ''God is dead'' is particularly meant to communicate. For it calls attention to the fact that a central human ideal — which makes it possible for us to seek refuge in some entity which takes up, absolves, and dissolves human disappointments and disillusionments — may not be the right ideal. Historically speaking, this ideal, originally healthy, effective, and inspiring, was a credit to humanity. At first it challenged us to put forth our best efforts. But as time went on, it gathered an increment of overtones, of concomitant notions and practices, which overshadowed and gradually killed it. So, we must perform a double task: (1) reexamine the initial impact of the ideal, and (2) expose the accretions which killed its original vitality.

Note that in the passage quoted above, the event is seen as a momentous disaster, a world-shaking catastrophe. The idea of God was immense and sublime. Its fitting images are the sea, the horizon, the sun. When these disappear, what are we to do? ''Whither are we moving now?'' What can serve as ultimate reference point, as symbolic guide? The disappearance of these potent symbols — potent because they gave us meaning, certitude, and inspiration — has left us tumbling in the void. Now we are plunging aimlessly

in all directions—backward, sideward, forward. No up or down remains.
We are in an infinite nothing. The space is getting colder and darker, we
need to light lamps, and yet all we hear in the noise of grave diggers, and
all we smell is the odor of decomposition. The crime is stupendous and
catastrophic. How can we cleanse ourselves?

The last question and the last answer in Nietzsche's paragraph complete
the picture and shift the mood. If we were capable of destroying such a noble
idea, and if we can still be aware of its nobility, we *may* survive the deed.
We may even have in us the ability to become worthy of it by creating a *higher*
ideal. Out of the agony of witnessing the death of God there may arise
something even nobler. These are Nietzsche's hope and challenge.

According to Dostoyevsky, the remarkable thing is not that God should
exist, but that such a noble idea should enter the head of such a low, vile,
despicable creature. Similarly, Nietzsche does not take the concept of God
lightly. When it first emerged, it provided us with a glorious vision, with
a source of inspiration, and the goal for aspirations. But soon it was overlaid
with other notions which in the long run have displaced the weight and the
value of the ideal. The main culprit, thought Nietzsche, was the coupling
of the idea of God with the notion of *otherworldliness*. The theme of
otherworldliness preoccupies Nietzsche, and he reserves for it his strongest
criticisms.

The essential feature of the postulation of the "other" world is that it breeds
escapism. It shifts the weight from effort, exertion, and creation to mere
receptivity, passivity, and conformity. Gift *giving* is one of the virtues Nietzsche
exalts. He contrasts it with the tendency to be a mere recipient of gifts.
Ingratitude to life is one of the pet targets of his attacks. It is a matter of
preference for the easy rather than for the difficult. Spinoza had said that
all things excellent are as difficult as they are rare. Nietzsche was not satisfied
with merely commenting on human inertia. He found it to be unworthy of
us. The tendency to seek ease may atrophy us. Since the Will to Power, as
we shall see, is the true reality of the world, self-inflicted atrophy is a perversion
of reality and of all basic values.

Nietzsche believed that the Christian religion had fallen into the hands of
those prophets and believers who advocated shortcuts to salvation; if one only
*believes* ardently, nothing else is necessary. Contrasting St. Paul with Jesus,
Nietzsche attributed to the former another vice to be transcended, namely,
resentment. Seeing that he lacked the capacity for effort, for service, for
suffering, for genuine spiritual exertion—the capacity which Jesus manifested
in abundance—St. Paul chose to "revenge" himself on Jesus and hence
advocated salvation through mere faith. This is a typical response of a small
man to a great one, concluded Nietzsche. Reflecting on this and similar
responses, Nietzsche developed his notion of slave morality. Slave morality

cherishes the virtues of submission and humility. But Nietzsche, the depth psychologist, suspected these tendencies. Too often they are ways of "revenging" oneself on those of whose superiority one is conscious. The humble and the subservient intend to gain something by manifesting these "virtues," they hope to get the attention and favor of the creative person toward whom this "humility" is displayed. All too often those who are superior are *distracted* from their creative tasks in order to console the weak and the inferior, to minister to their mediocre needs, thus squandering their own promising energies. Nietzsche depicts this phenomenon in its numerous guises and in a variety of human relationships, both personal and institutional. Friendship and marriage can be distorted by this false relationship, sapping the best energies of unlucky partners. The state, as the most inclusive and powerful social institution, may engender attitudes dominated by slave morality and allow the smallest man to run the show and kill off all creative individuals.

In *Thus Spoke Zarathustra*, Nietzsche draws a further conclusion from the failure of traditional religions to provide a meaningful form of life. With God gone, we ourselves must undertake the tasks which previously had been relegated to God. To say that the task is difficult is a gross oversimplification and underestimation, and one should try to understand the mood and the spirit, in which this task is envisioned by Nietzsche. On the surface, there is a suggestion of evolutionary thinking in his description of the new challenge. All creatures before the human species have created something higher than themselves; why should humans be capable of less and be only the ebb of this creative surge of life? *Not* to create something higher than man would be a sign of ingratitude and laziness. In one of his earlier works, an essay on Schopenhauer as educator, Nietzsche observed that a traveler who visited several continents would report this universal human trait: "men are inclined to laziness." Except for a sense of shame exhibited by a few individuals, the vast majority of people is dominated by the desire for comfort and inertia. Of course, they also suffer from bad conscience and are sheepish and timorous about their herd tendencies, but they prefer wallowing in this inertia and laziness to anything else. But this is a state of affairs which a life-affirming, creative person would find intolerable and unacceptable. Such a person could find little comfort in Darwin's theory of evolution. For all we know, those who will survive as a result of accidental mutations will be the *least* fit in the normative sense of the word. Nietzsche observed that as far as sheer adaptability is concerned, the flea beetle, or the small man who in many ways could be likened to a flea beetle, is the most likely to survive. Thus, mechanical, natural selection does not necessarily lead to the evolution of *higher* forms.

Here we touch on the theme of the "overman." Who is an overman? This expression of Nietzsche's is very inclusive. It connotes the ability to be a master of one's fate, to utilize one's talents to the highest degree, to enhance to the maximum one's creative potentialities, and to spend one's life in service to a difficult, personally chosen goal. Overman is the one who "overcomes" man as he is today, and history has no other aim than to produce superior individuals. One of the capacities which Nietzsche never repudiates and always includes among the talents to be used is reason. But he does not think of reason as some universal principle, either disembodied altogether or embodied in some dubious entity such as Hegel's Absolute. To him, reason is always *an individual's* reason, and it is not separable from other features and aspects of a living being. In this respect Nietzsche's view has something in common with the instrumentalist conception of intelligence in American pragmatism. It would not be quite correct, however, to say that to him, reason was merely an instrument. Although he does say that our task is to serve life, the quality of this service is to be judged in terms of rational discernment. The individuals for whom Nietzsche reserved highest praise were not those who excelled in action, but *spiritual* persons—artists and philosophers. Among the highest personalities that humankind has produced he lists Aeschylus, Heraclitus, Socrates, Plato, Spinoza, Leonardo da Vinci, Shakespeare, and Goethe.

For Nietzsche, the highest events in human history are related to the appearance of great, creative personalities. In fact, history for him has no other goal than the creation of superior individuals. But it is not history, not circumstances, not evolution—biological or social—that creates them. Rather, it is *they* who create all values by giving style to their lives; they seize their fate and *become*.

Note how in this view the idea of human evolution as a massive growth, progress, and gradual development is repudiated in favor of another picture. The value of the world lies in its highest creations, and these creations are individual human lives scattered across the ages. It is a prejudice to think that those who live later in history are more likely to develop into geniuses. "The Spirit moveth where it listeth," except that for "Spirit" in Nietzsche's scheme we should substitute "the Will to Power."

By now the conception of the Will to Power fits naturally into Nietzsche's framework. It is but another name for the nisus of the world's energy to seek highest manifestations in great individuals. Nietzsche would also call these individuals most *powerful*, meaning that their creative dynamism combines all the vital and rational resources available to them. A great human being is also a strong person, not in the sense of mere physical strength, but in the sense of inner resources, of the particular mastery over both herself and her total environment. In a life of such an individual, nothing is the result of an accident, and the whole life is an expression of deliberate choice and self-control. A mere "strong man," a bully, a tyrant does not qualify for greatness. This is because such a man is in fact mastered by one dominant feature or need in himself. Again, Nietzsche the psychologist observes that the need to dominate others for the sake of dominating them is pathological and in fact a sign of weakness. To demand the submission, the homage, of others, regardless of whether one *deserves* any attention at all, is a sign of dependence and insecurity. Those who lack their own individual goal seek satisfaction in what others can give them. A truly strong person will not push others around and certainly will not hurt them. Where one cannot love, says Zarathustra, there one should pass by. Zarathustra does not tell the truth to the old hermit who has not heard that God is dead. To tell him this would not be a gift, it would not add anything positive to his life. Instead, it would diminish it.

For similar reasons, Nietzsche rejects the mere exertion of political or military power. When he glorifies war, the context is usually the war against oneself, the spiritual struggle for self-mastery and achievement. Highest thoughts come on dove's feet, in our stillest hour. Nietzsche refers to the state as the new idol, as the coldest of all monsters, and adds that mud often occupies the throne. Strength alone is not enough. "Still one lies on one's knees before *strength*—according to the ancient habits of slaves—and yet, when the degree of *worthiness of being honored* is to be determined, only *the degree of reason in strength* is decisive: one must measure in how far strength has been overcome by something higher and now serves as its tool and means!"[2] Exercise of sheer physical power has its dangers. "One pays heavily for coming to power: power *makes stupid*. The Germans, once called the people of thinkers—do they still think at all today? The Germans are now bored with the spirit, the Germans now mistrust the spirit . . . . *Deutschland, Deutschland über alles*, I fear that was the end of German philosophy."[3] These lines were written at a time when Germany, under Bismarck, had achieved new political and military might.

Nietzsche's Will to Power is a very different thing from Schopenhauer's Will to Exist. Schopenhauer's will is something negative, incapable of reaching satisfaction, forever resulting in pain. Nietzsche, in spite of his great admiration for Schopenhauer, the man, had rejected the basic verdict of his philosophy. The Will to Power is essentially an affirmation of existence, a saying yes to life. The Will to Power seeks joy. Nietzsche thought that it belongs to the very essence of joy that it should manifest Will to Power. Pleasure consists in overcoming pain, in showing the possibility of mastering and transforming it. During his imprisonment Socrates mused over the fact that the removal of his chains which gave him pain was replaced by pleasure. How curiously they are connected, mused Socrates. Pleasure and potency are conceptually connected for Nietzsche. A pleasurable state is one in which we are able to satisfy a given urge or prompting. Imagine being in the process of putting a morsel of delicious food in your mouth when suddenly, an invisible hand stops the food from reaching your mouth. You will realize to what extent the pleasure consists in the ability to minister to a throbbing desire. This is why Nietzsche sees in sex another telling illustration of pleasure as potency, as Will to Power.

The coming together of the dynamic, creative impulse with its satisfaction and fulfillment is for Nietzsche the final good and value of existence. The great achievement of superior individuals is that they succeed in affirming the world through their creativity. To a creator the world looks wholesome, good, thrilling, and full of meaning. He creates the world before which he can kneel. "Only man placed values in things to preserve himself—he alone created a meaning for things, a human meaning. Therefore, he calls himself 'man,' which means: the esteemer." Nietzsche observes that those who condemn the world, who are dissatisfied with it, most likely project on reality their dissatisfaction with themselves, their inability to *bestow* value, to produce for themselves valuable experiences. Their boredom is most likely self-inflicted and testifies to their weakness.

Nietzsche uses yet another concept to show to what heights the phenomenon of affirmation may rise. This is his doctrine of Eternal Recurrence. The truth of this doctrine can dawn on a person who is capable of total, absolute affirmation, which is most likely to come in an exuberant, joyful, creative moment. It belongs to the quality of the experience that it demands its reappearance. It is such that its oblivion is unthinkable to the one bringing it into existence. If we remember both that it is the manifestation of the Will to Power and that the Will to Power ultimately is the *only* reality, there is nothing in the scheme of things that could deny the Will this right to assert itself in this eternally recurrent manner.

Nietzsche's doctrine of the Eternal Recurrence may be regarded as an alternative to other ways of affirming the ultimate meaning of the world: salvation, heaven, paradise, the City of God. It is consonant with the other features of his philosophy, especially with his repudiation of the idea of history as a linear progression to some culminating point. Culminating points are spread out over the entire circumference of the eternal circle, and to a person affirming the world it may appear as a perfect, completed, round circle, forever celebrating and returning upon itself. Nietzsche described humanity as a self-propelling wheel, and this description fits his picture of the world as well. He believed that the doctrine of Eternal Recurrence could also be confirmed by means of scientific concepts in which the law of the conservation of energy was supposed to play a part, but here he probably was exceeding his competence. His philosophical defense of the doctrine is, nevertheless, thought-provoking. Like most of his arguments, it is addressed to personal experience. He asks us to envision our lowest and our highest moments alternatively. The lowest moments of dejection, disillusionment, and pain seek oblivion. Their verdict is: if this is what reality is like, it deserves to perish, disappear.

But the highest moments, moments of exuberant intoxication and enchantment, seek perpetuation, repetition, and preservation. Pain cries out: perish, disappear! Joy exclaims: remain, return! Twelve strokes of midnight have this message to convey:

> *One!*
> *O man, take care!*
> *Two!*
> *What does the deep midnight declare?*
> *Three!*
> *"I was asleep—*
> *Four!*
> *"From a deep dream I woke and swear:*
> *Five!*
> *"The world is deep,*
> *Six!*
> *Deeper than the day had been aware.*
> *Seven!*
> *"Deep is its woe;*
> *Eight!*
> *"Joy—deeper yet than agony:*
> *Nine!*
> *"Woe implores: Go!*
> *Ten!*
> *"But all joy wants eternity—*
> *Eleven!*
> *Wants deep, wants deep eternity."*
> *Twelve!*[4]

Nietzsche's view that value arises in the process of overcoming obstacles points to the presence of a strong dialectical element in his philosophy. We noted the dialectic of pain and pleasure. More inclusively, the essence of life and history consists in challenge and response. This is the meaning of his claim that self-overcoming is the goal of human existence. We must overcome ourselves in creating *beyond* ourselves—and overman may be the product of this effort. But Nietzsche was aware that this constant drive to overcome oneself and to transvaluate prior values is fraught with danger. The reach toward higher levels is accompanied by the possibility of descent to lower depths. The higher you reach, the louder the dogs bark in your cellar. The perils of exploring unknown regions of experiences are a recurring theme in the writings of Nietzsche and many other philosophers. But Nietzsche believed that experiencing the distance between the heights and depths and the tension between baseness and saintliness is essential to appreciating what is valuable. Therefore, he welcomed the danger and hailed the daring, experimental spirit. Humanity is an experiment, and therefore must expect to live dangerously. Those who exist on the brink of disaster, who are risking the destruction of the best in them, are much preferable to the "sleepy ones who will soon drop off." Nietzsche's ardor for the daring, for the unknown and forbidden, often results in his saying some outrageous things which sound like invitations to downright immorality. But if we keep in mind the basic goals behind this exuberance, we will also sense the awareness of tragic danger. Nietzsche was aware of the likelihood that a never-ending search for higher levels of existence will result in frequent failure, but this too must be accepted as a part of the price one must pay for striving. What does it matter if in the process of making more beautiful pottery some pots may be shattered to pieces? Knowing that human vocation is dangerous, a wise person will still be able to laugh at his failures. The exuberant seriousness will never succumb to the spirit of gravity which paralyzes the sparkling dance of life.

Although the individual is the measure of all value and as such is often condemned to loneliness and isolation, the past human achievements are not indifferent to us. In fact, we should look to them for guidance and inspiration. Nietzsche tells a parable of three metamorphoses. A human life must move through three stages: a camel, a lion, and a child. The camel is a beast of burden, carrying on his back all the treasures of past knowledge and values. The lion rejects old values and creates a new freedom for himself, for even the most revered and sacred values may contain illusion and caprice. Still, the highest stage is reached when the roaring lion is changed into a child, who is lovingly absorbed in his playful activity which takes place spontaneously and innocently for its own sake. The child is the symbol of self-absorption, of abandonment to the purity of joy.

Nietzsche criticizes his contemporary culture in the light of these positive ideals. Seen in their light, much of what he perceives around him is dismally wanting. Human beings are fragmented and dissipated: here I see a monster ear, there an eye, there a nose, but nowhere a complete human soul, a *full* soul. In addition to the vice of fragmentation and onesidedness, there is also an opposite view, the pretense of false objectivity. Although it appears so very different from subjective distortion, in fact it is but a disguised attempt to hide one's bias. False objectivity is bad faith. In philosophers, Nietzsche condemns what he calls the will to a system, a desire to cut short the spirit of constant inquiry and questioning by postulating arbitrary conceptual limits in "self-evident" truths. Intellectual dishonesty prevents philosophers from examining their own axioms and presuppositions. In place of this artificial completeness and neatness, Nietzsche advocates a bold exploration of perspectives that will strike each individual thinker as convincing and possibly worth proclaiming.

Nietzsche regards reason as an instrument of life and has no use for an eternal, abiding truth; such a truth does not exist for him. Thinking is a form of acting for Nietzsche, except that a strong poetic bent in him makes him prefer such phrases as "thinking with one's blood." "Bloodless thinking" is irrelevant to human concerns and possibilities; it tends to remove itself from the actual conditions out of which any worthwhile effort has to arise. Nietzsche drives this "perspectivism" to the extreme. He was concerned primarily with individuals—as they exist in their unique situations. One always should seek *one's own* truth, that which is true for the particular person one is. In this regard Nietzsche is closer to Kierkegaard, who also exalted subjective truth, although that truth for the Danish philosopher had only one goal, namely, God. In contrast, Nietzsche's overman does not believe in preexisting values; rather, he wants to *create* values before which he can kneel.

Nietzsche observed among scholars the tendency to avoid any serious commitment, the preoccupation with trivia, which are blown up to look as if they deserved the name of science. Scholars often resemble bags of flour: when shaken, the emit clouds of dust. Here is a sample of Nietzsche's mordant satire: "They are good clockworks; but take care to wind them correctly! Then they indicate the hour without fail and make a modest noise. They work like mills and like stamps; throw down your seed corn to them and they will know how to grind it small and reduce it to white dust."[5]

The tendency to conformity, to mere imitation, sleepy comfort and self-indulgence have become the order of the day, providing the dominant values of society with all its institutions: church, education, and politics. Hence the moral fiber has become flabby and weak. This is not just a temporary disease; it has been induced through long inculcation of the superiority of the mass over the individual, of the mediocre over the superior and the unique. The "we" has been celebrated too long, says Nietzsche, and it is high time to discover the "I." This is one of the new tablets of good and evil which Zarathustra is proclaiming. Self-reliant, resolute creators of values are not helped to arise when marriage is reduced to a mutual backscratching and easy comfortableness and friends fail to say harsh things to each other for the sake of harmony and "peace of mind." Such somnolent states are to be contrasted with relationships in which the wife tries to elicit the best energies in her husband and friends are devoted to each other's perfection. Nietzsche did not expect his works to be popular—they are always addressed to those individuals for whom his writings only add another burden to the burdens they already carry. Whether they will roar like lions and then lose themselves in the childlike enjoyment of the value they create, is up to them.

## 2. Heidegger: Back to Being

Martin Heidegger was born in 1889 in a small town in southwest Germany. The family was Catholic, and after finishing high school, Heidegger joined the Jesuits as a novice. Later, he studied Catholic theology at the University of Freiburg. His interest began to shift more and more toward philosophy, especially under the influence of Edmund Husserl, the founder of the phenomenological movement, who was then a professor at Freiburg. After attaining his doctorate, Heidegger worked for five years as Husserl's assistant, until he was offered a chair in philosophy at the University of Marburg in 1923. In 1927 his best known work, *Being and Time*, appeared, and one year later he moved to Freiburg to succeed Husserl. When Hitler came to power in 1933, Heidegger was sympathetic to the Nazi movement, to the extent of joining the party. For a year he served as the rector of the University of Freiburg, but resigned from that position in 1934 in the context of a dispute about the role the German universities were to play in the new regime. Whether there is a connection between some of Heidegger's philosophical speculations and his political views is a matter of debate. After the war, instead of writing the projected second volume of *Being and Time*, Heidegger wrote a number of shorter works, shifting to a more oracular style. His writings are now widely available in translations and have been receiving a great deal of attention all over the world. He died in 1976.

To understand Heidegger one must try to place him within the total sweep of the history of philosophy. His study of the subject led him to think that the entire development from Anaximander to Nietzsche managed to dodge one fundamental question, namely, the relation of humanity to Being itself. The Pre-Socratics, especially Parmenides, had this question in mind, but after him philosophical reflection took a course concentrated on other issues, leaving the question of Being dormant. In this sense, Heidegger believed himself to be standing at a historical junction of thought, in which we must recover the kind of reflective attitude which has been lost for more than two millennia.

Heidegger's important essay "The Way Back into the Ground of Metaphysics," which was written in 1949 and to which he attached great importance, is an attempt to sum up his basic philosophical intention, especially as it was presented in his main work, *Being and Time*, published in 1927. In it he characterizes all of Western metaphysics including Nietzsche's work as concerned with beings, not Being. Even when philosophers tried to ask the most fundamental questions about reality, they thought in terms of beings. They thought of Being as Spirit, matter, energy, substance, subject, life, Will to Exist, or Will to Power, but in each case the tendency was to render Being as a kind of being. That approach, although understandable in the light of the course of historical philosophical development, nevertheless misses the main question of philosophy.

That question is man's place *vis à vis* Being itself. Heidegger does not deny the Kantian claim that knowledge has its conditions and that if we are to have *knowledge*, it must be of beings, not of Being. But he also suggests that thinking about beings is only *representational* thinking ("*vorstellendes Denken*") and that we are capable of still another kind of thinking, namely, thinking that recalls ("*andenkendes Denken*"). Once more, one may be reminded of problems surrounding the Kantian thing-in-itself. Kant was of the opinion that the thing-in-itself is not accessible to thought, although its reality is presupposed in all experience. Heidegger, however, invites us to consider some new possibilities of becoming aware of the *Ground* of metaphysics and not just of metaphysics itself.

The direction which Heidegger explores gets some initial characterization through images. He borrows a picture used by Descartes in a letter to the French translator of his *Principles of Philosophy*: "Thus the whole of philosophy is like a tree: the root is metaphysics, the trunk is physics, and the branches that issue from the trunk are all the other sciences." Heidegger finds this picture illuminating but not only by virtue of what it mentions. What it *fails* to mention is precisely the object of his philosophical interest, namely, the ground, the soil in which metaphysics, as the root of the tree, rests. Heidegger mixes his metaphors here and speaks of Being simultaneously as light which makes it possible for us to discern beings, and also as a ground or soil from which the knowledge of beings grows. "Wherever metaphysics represents beings, Being has entered into the light . . . The truth of Being may thus be called the ground in which metaphysics, as the root of the tree of philosophy, is kept and from which it is nourished."[6]

The picture is attractive and intriguing; it appeals to our sense of wanting to reach the ultimate ground of all reality. Being appears to be such a ground, and Heidegger seeks new ways of rendering our relationship to it in some intelligible way. The contrast between representational thinking and thinking-that-recalls is still to be filled out. What has been said so far is essentially negative: metaphysics represents only beings *as* beings; it does not recall Being itself. When philosophy leaves its ground, it does so by means of metaphysics. Yet even when it leaves it, it never escapes its ground. Thus, although we can no longer be satisfied with metaphysics alone, it still remains the basis of philosophy. But philosophy is not all of thinking. Thinking that recalls the truth of Being *overcomes* metaphysics.

At this point Heidegger reverses the relationship and suggests that in the relationship to Being, we are not the only active partners. Our concern with Being is possible only because Being is concerned with us also. Thus, our thinking about Being reflects that other concern. Heidegger says that Being *strikes* a man's thinking. Being itself "rouses his thinking and stirs it to rise from Being itself to respond and correspond to Being as such."[7] Here, we see a move of which theologians often make use: we can reach out toward God because God always reaches out toward us.

What Heidegger is deploring and warning against is that metaphysics should become an obstacle instead of a guide. It is an obstacle if it prevents the involvement of Being with us, if in turning our back to Being we block the radiance which may make it possible for us to belong to Being. The thinking-that-recalls is in a position to give us more than can be derived from the truths of metaphysical propositions. It can reveal the *unconcealedness* of Being (in Greek, the word *aletheia* means both "unconcealedness" and "truth"). Here, Heidegger's argument verges on paradox, for he says that the thinking-that-recalls can also become aware of the *concealedness* of Being, while metaphysics, since it presents us only with beings, can reveal to us only the unconcealed. The point seems to be that the thinking-that-recalls will also recall the concealedness of Being, in contrast to metaphysics, which keeps the concealedness away from us.

One important feature of thinking-that-recalls is that it straddles the traditional distinction between "subjective" and "objective." Heidegger observed on one occasion that "concepts taken in the modern sense are too objective (*gegenständlich*)."[8] He added that "ancient categories of Aristotle were not concepts so intended." The suggestion appears to be that we should think of thinking as a continuous creative effort to connect our human reality with the transcendent reality of Being. Max Ernst, the leader of the surrealist movement in art, believing that creative *seeing* plays a similar role, made the following remark: "As the universe loses its opacity, it blends with mankind. So to rid himself of his blindness is the first duty of man." For Heidegger, this duty consists of engaging in thinking-that-recalls. This sort of thinking, like the work of an artist, is never finished and done with; it is always *on the way* and is not satisfied with purely computational, informational verdicts of knowledge — be that knowledge scientific or metaphysical. Thinking-that-recalls insists on seeking the truth about us in a reflection that is deeper than the verdicts of objective knowledge. One of the dangers of reducing all thought to the search for objective verdicts is that it hides the truth of Being from us. On some occasions the refusal to remain on the path of reflective thought, to maintain a certain attitude of reverence toward the deeper, mysterious dimensions of human reality, may invade our consciousness with a sense of hopelessness and meaninglessness.

The lack of contact between human reality and Being may be seen, however, as a reciprocal matter; not being sought by us, Being may also turn away from us. Heidegger makes this point in the form of a question: "What if the absence of Being abandoned man more and more exclusively to beings, leaving him forsaken and far from any involvement of Being in his nature, while his forsakedness itself remains veiled."[9] He also hints that our modern age is characterized by the absence of this involvement in Being and that this situation is a result of a confusion generated by our entire metaphysical tradition. Furthermore, he foresees that the trend toward preoccupation with beings instead of Being will become more intense, thus deepening our sense of forsakedness and oblivion. To a thinker, who is still capable of recalling Being, this oblivion of Being would appear as a genuine horror. The note which Heidegger sounds here appears to be akin to those sometimes voiced in theology. This is the theme of *Deus absconditus*, a God who hides himself from us. The dread of the oblivion of Being is a "fatefully granted dread" and, for those who become aware of it, is not to be compared to any psychological mood of anxiety. That dread, according to Heidegger, is not something that haunts everybody and is not common even in those who are capable of experiencing it. In Heidegger's own words, "It is understood as extreme possibility and as such cannot be necessary."[10] Nevertheless, the onslaughts of such anxiety raise the human condition to the level of authenticity, compared with which the "everydayness" of existence is bound to appear shallow and insignificant.

Human history is not indifferent to Being; indeed, Being needs us to reveal itself. An attentive listener to human speech will discern the voice of Being in it. (This appears to be the key message of the first chapter of Heidegger's *On the Way to Language*.) The reciprocal dependence of humanity and God was celebrated in a similar fashion by the German mystic Meister Eckhart, who said: "The eye with which God sees me, is the eye with which I see Him, my eye and His eye are one. In the meting out of justice I am weighed in God and He in me. If God were not, I should not be, and if I were not, He too would not be."[11] Similarly, Nietzsche's Zarathustra greeted the sun with these words: "You great star, what would your happiness be had you not those for whom to shine? For ten years you have climbed my cave: you would have tired of your light and of your journey had it not been for me and my eagle and my serpent."[12] Nietzsche's use of the metaphor of light is especially applicable to Heidegger's thought, since the latter spoke of human existence as *Lichtung*, this German word referring to a *clearing* in the forest, where the light of the sun breaks through the trees to illuminate the path. Thinking-that-recalls creates such a clearing.

Heidegger recommends that "our thinking should become more thoughtful in its season" and that we must begin by directing it "toward a different point of origin." His objective in *Being and Time* was to open up a path of thinking that would help us find the involvement of the truth of Being in human nature. Why is Being involved in human nature? It is because Being is unconcealedness; its involvement with us is its essential feature. In developing this theme,

Heidegger makes use of terminology which justifies the application of the term "existentialism" to his philosophy. His German word for human existence is *Dasein*, literally "being there," and he proceeds to lay out its characteristic features, drawing heavily on possibilities presented by overtones of etymology. The meaning of "being there" in *Being and Time* is found, according to him, in the following key sentence: "The 'essence' of being there lies in its existence." ("*Das 'Wesen' des Daseins liegt in seiner Existenz.*") But "being there" for Heidegger also means "a mode of Being." Being and human existence are "open" toward each other. The root of "stand" in "existence" leads Heidegger to render the relationship of man to Being in almost physical, concrete terms, in which the spatial vocabulary is suffused with rich overtones of involvement, standing guard, and watchfulness. "Ex-istere" means literally "to stand out." But "standing out" is at the same time "standing in." The temporal mode of "being there" does not mean our essential separation from Being. "Out" is to be interpreted as the externalization,opening out, of the Being itself. Hence, the involvement of Being in "being there," or *Dasein*, can be recalled.

The notion of openness is important for Heidegger's rendition of the relationship. We stand in this openness, in the opening, in the clearing between Being and "being there." The German word *bestehen*, "standing it" or "enduring" is invoked to bring out the flavor of "existence." The word which Heidegger used in *Being and Time* to characterize the overall mood of being human was *Sorge*, care, a state of being engaged by projects, expectations, and anxieties. In the background of this care there is also the permanent reminder of death as the ultimate object of concern. Being-toward-death is mixed in with all our projects, even though we devise ways of concealing this fact from ourselves in ingenious and often comical ways. The tendency to escape our natural state as care-laden, death-facing beings often results, especially in our modern age, in inauthentic living; we surround ourselves by daily superficialities, trivia, and escape mechanisms, forgetting our real situation.

Heidegger stresses the essentially temporal character of human existence. But temporality is also to be understood concretely, as the experience of the *presentness* of things. Time is the presence of the present, in the manner in which Being is unconcealed. In fact, Heidegger calls time "the first name of the truth of Being" and refers to Nietzsche's view of time as eternal recurrence of the same events as the latest name of Being. Time for him is also "the horizon of every possible attempt to understand Being," and this is what his work *Being and Time* tried to demonstrate.

Metaphysics is not capable of getting at the truth of Being because it concerns itself only with beings. Therefore, a thinking which concerns itself with something other than beings may appear to refer to Nothing. From the perspective of metaphysics this is correct, but this also means that Being can be understood as Nothing and explains, given this equivalence, why Being should remain forgotten or taken for granted. Thought stops at this juncture, for, as Leibniz observed, "the nothing is simpler than any thing." However, if it is true that we are also capable of thinking-that-recalls and are not limited to mere representational, metaphysical thinking, thought must reintensify its efforts, but now in a different direction. In his later years, Heidegger found that the thinking of poets, such as Trakl and Hölderlin, was often closer to what he meant by *andenkendes Denken*, and he spent a great deal of time and effort trying to understand and interpret their way of being open toward Being.

Heidegger's objective is to recall us to our rootedness in Being. *Dasein*, human existence, is urged to listen to the voice of *Sein*, Being. Being human is a mode of Being. Human reality and Being are "open" toward each other. The relationship to Being is revealed to us in our moods of care, expectation, anxiety. It is not just our intellect, our understanding, which is being claimed by Being, but our total existence. To analyze this existence into separable components, such as feeling, willing, and knowing, is to fall into the trap of representational thinking. This is why thinking-that-recalls needs to go beyond representation and metaphysics; it must ponder moods and situations captured more faithfully in poetic utterance. It should be on guard against falling into careless, shallow concerns with the trivia of life which dominate the daily round of the average man, *das Man*. Instead, it should face the reality of crisis situations, including the final, inescapable crisis situation—death. Openly acknowledging our mortality may bring home to us the truth that temporality, being-unto-death, is the essential mark of human existence and, with this truth fully absorbed, we may lead a more "authentic" existence.

## 3. Sartre: Forward into Nothingness

As a student, Jean Paul Sartre (1905-1980) already manifested definite literary talents. After receiving his education in Paris, and for a year in Berlin, he taught in French secondary schools, but later left the academic world in order to concentrate on writing. A French soldier during World War II, he was captured by the Germans, but made his way back to Paris and fought in the Resistance. In his writing he did not limit himself to philosophic prose, but also produced novels, plays, and short stories, all of which expressed his philosophical and psychological insights into concrete human situations. Some of his better-known literary works are *Nausea* (a novel, 1938), *The Wall* (a short story, 1939), and *No Exit* (a play, 1945). His achievements as a writer were acknowledged by the Nobel Prize Commission. He was offered

the prize for literature in 1964, but refused it. After the publication of his
major work, *Being and Nothingness* (1943), Sartre's interest shifted more
and more toward social and political thought, showing a strong indebtedness
to the early Marx. Sartre's sympathies for communism as the right approach
to social economic problems, expressed in his later massive work, *The Critique
of Dialectical Reason* (1960), did not keep him from maintaining his
independent line, which often conflicted with the political lines of communist
parties, both in France and elsewhere in the world.

Sartre's chief work, *Being and Nothingness*, develops the prominent theme
of his philosophy: the basic opposition between two kinds of realities.
Borrowing Hegel's phrases, Sartre calls them the "In-itself" and the "For-
itself"; since these are technical terms, however, it is difficult to find exact
equivalents in ordinary English. But Sartre's intent in making this distinction
is not difficult to grasp. By "For-itself" he means human reality as it manifests
itself in various modes of consciousness, and it is possible to say what Sartre
wants to say by substituting in most cases "consciousness" for the cumbersome
phase "For-itself." This will be our procedure. Similarly, when he speaks
of "In-itself," we shall use the word "Being," keeping in mind that Sartre's
use of this term intends to draw attention to a contrast between human reality
and other kinds of realities not illumined by consciousness. The nature of
this contrast will emerge as we proceed with the exposition of Sartre's views.

Sartre's study of Husserl's phenomenology convinced him that in order
to characterize human reality correctly, we must concentrate on what appears
immediately before our consciousness. Phenomenology is determined to avoid
the difficulties of philosophers such as Descartes and Locke, who treated
appearances as *representations* of something beyond them. Behind the process
of thinking Descartes claimed to find a *self* that thinks. For Locke, ideas are
*copies* of objects existing outside the mind. Husserl believed that we should
give up the postulation of such independently existing realities and should
concentrate instead on the character of directly experienced appearances. Only
in such a way can philosophy become a "strict science," according to Husserl.
True philosophy, he believed, "should seek its foundation exclusively in man
and, more specifically, in the essence of his concrete worldly existence."

Husserl admitted that there is, of course, a "natural standpoint" of the
common man, who ascribes independent existence to what supposedly underlies
appearances. But this standpoint is already a *theory* about the relationship
of consciousness to something outside it. Moreover, it is a theory riddled
with difficulties and contradictions, as the whole history of philosophy, from
Plato on, amply demonstrates. Thus, the most rational procedure to follow
is to suspend, or as Husserl puts it, to "bracket" all questions or suggestions
overtly or tacitly referring to entities other than those present to consciousness

as appearances and to concentrate on describing faithfully and in detail the character of pure consciousness.

According to Sartre, however, Husserl failed to implement fully his own philosophical recommendations. For Husserl still thought that by virtue of possessing an internally connected and unified experience, consciousness calls for the recognition of the agency of a Transcendental Ego of which every particular subjective consciousness is an expression. Here, Sartre claims to discern the mistake that Descartes committed when he claimed that wherever there is thinking there must be a thinking *substance*—"I think, therefore I am." The "therefore" does not follow, believes Sartre. What needs to be done, he suggests, is to dislodge consciousness from any supposed self which provides a kind of grounding or explanation of consciousness. Human consciousness is not *caused* by Being. Causality, as Kant had already taught us, is a concept brought into being by consciousness. To say that something is a cause of something else is to have independent access to both terms, cause and effect; both would have to be available to us as appearances. But Being is not and cannot be an appearance; appearances are always modes of consciousness.

Sartre denies that consciousness knows a self which transcends its experiences and provides them with a necessary predetermined structure. *Self-consciousness* does not have a status superior to the actual appearances themselves. In fact, what we call self has merely a *derivative* status; it is a function of particular acts of consciousness. To illustrate this point, Sartre calls attention to the phenomenon of reflection or mirroring. It is more than a lucky accident that one of the ways in which consciousness can function is what we call "reflection." It may be instructive to remember that a reflection in a mirror does not have an independent existence *behind* the mirror. It shows us what is captured in the reflection itself. In an analogous way, an appearance in consciousness does not point beyond itself; it merely exhibits its own character. Consciousness acts like a mirror in the sense that it does not presuppose something *behind* appearances, some privileged subject or self performing these acts of reflection.

Wherein, then, does the feeling of substantiality, unity, and continuity of consciousness have its basis? Well, all consciousness is consciousness *of* something. Phenomenologists use a bit of technical jargon here and say that consciousness is *intentional*; it *intends* its object. Therefore, in retrospect a consciousness can say what its object of awareness was, and the ability to perform such intentional retrospective acts is also disclosed to us in a phenomenological analysis or description. A succession of performing intentional acts gives a sense of continuity, order, and relative permanence to that consciousness.

In his concept of the ''For-itself'' Sartre includes precisely this intentional directedness of consciousness at its various objects in perception, reflection, memory, imagination, feeling, and willing. This is what distinguishes consciousness from Being, which remains opaque, unilluminated, unperceived, uncognized, and hence literally meaningless. The persistent mistake of philosophy has been to treat consciousness as if it were a kind of Being. But such a reduction is the denial of the very essence of consciousness, namely, its free intentionality which endows reality with meaning.

In spite of its basic contrast to Being, consciousness is nevertheless rooted in Being and could be said to be a revelation of it. This relation, however, is experienced only on the prereflective level. On that level the obvious reality, massiveness, solidity of things—in other words, their inert, stubborn existence—intrudes itself on our senses. The human body belongs to Being. Every perception terminates in something simply *given*, and so we experience the *facticity* of the world. Our consciousness gives us only a limited, projective, intentional aspect of Being.

Wedded to the program of phenomenological description, Sartre continues to render explicit the various ways in which consciousness tries to come to terms with the Being in which it is rooted. One of his other important criticisms of the philosophical tradition is that it is strongly biased in favor of a visual model in describing consciousness. But that is not what a phenomenological description will show when properly carried out. Even Husserl, the founder of phenomenology, did not see through this habit of visualizing thought as analogous to visual perception. Heidegger had called attention to two different ways in which things are present to us. The German language has a distinction between *Vorhandensein* and *Zuhandensein*. *Vorhanden* means simply being present, available, occupying space, or standing in the field of vision. *Zuhanden* means, literally, being ''ready to hand,'' available for handling. The reference to the hand, both in German and in English, points to the tactile contact. If we really want to get the ''feel'' of reality, we should cease limiting ourselves to the more remote, indirect, abstract ways of apprehending it. What evades us in mere thought, reflection, and observation becomes accessible and palpable through touch, through tactile experience in its various modes.

Sartre's turning away from idealistic philosophies, which give prominence to thought as pure vision or pristine contemplation, is at least in part due to their unrealistic aspirations. Thought can never grasp reality as supposedly it is in itself. When consciousness tries to become Being, the result is nausea, so vividly described by Sartre in a novel by that title.[13] When contemplating its own embodiment, consciousness becomes muddied. Consciousness aspires to endow Being with meaning, but in this very attempt it is frustrated by its inability to digest its experience. When consciousness ''assimilates'' things to itself, their solid structure is dissolved into fluid images and concepts.

Conversely, when consciousness seeks the purity of concept formation, it becomes clogged by the massive, formless reality of Being. An illustration of this may be found in the experience of a somnolent person struggling with the inertia and sluggishness of his body.

Sartre's analysis of consciousness points in two directions. On the one hand, he sharpens its contrast with Being by declaring consciousness to be Nothingness. Being is massive, inert, but fully itself. Consciousness, however, always depends on negations or, as Sartre puts it, "nihilations." Consider any instance of being aware of something, say, a basket. In knowing it to be a basket, I am simultaneously aware of my consciousness as *not* being that basket and also that that basket is *not* the backdrop of other things against which I see it. This is an example of what Sartre means when he says that human consciousness has the capacity for "generating nonbeing." He pursues this line of thought through different contexts, some of which he classifies as interrogation, destruction, and negative judgment. He says that even "in posing a question, a certain negative element is introduced into the world."[14] When I am looking for a person in a room, there is a kind of "nonbeing" in my consciousness. But even when I locate that person, I can know him only by distinguishing him from all other persons in the room; he is *not* they; he is in *this* room which is known through contrast with, or elimination of, all other rooms. Similar kinds of argument are used to show that destruction and negative judgments also involve a "nihilation" of Being. Consciousness is always "on the other side" or "outside" of Being. This is why human reality, epitomized in consciousness, as set against Being, is characterized by Sartre as Nothingness.

The sharp contrast between Being and consciousness leads Sartre to conclude that human reality should also be characterized as freedom. Since there is nothing *behind* consciousness, no antecedent reality endowing it with a predetermined structure, "consciousness of being is the being of consciousness." Since there is no permanent self-determining consciousness, every mode of consciousness is freely chosen. It is free even of the burden of its own past. "Freedom is the human being putting his past out of play by secreting his own consciousness," and "consciousness continually experiences itself as the nihilation of its past being."[15]

Kierkegaard had distinguished between fear and anguish. Fear is directed toward objects in the world, whereas anguish is anguish before myself. Faced with its absolute freedom, with nothing pre-existent which shapes the modes of consciousness, a human being experiences anguish which is analogous to vertigo—as if one were confronted by a precipice. Nothing compels me to see the world the way I do or to act in the way I choose to act at any moment. Consequently, I can always say that "I *am* not the self which I will be." Or, as Sartre puts it even more paradoxically: "I am the self which I will be, in the mode of not being it.''[16] What he wants to bring out as strongly as possible is the inherent impossibility of reducing a human being to a thing. A table is only a table, a paper knife only a paper knife, a stone only a stone, and a rose only a rose. Those things persist in their being until destroyed. With consciousness it is altogether different; ''consciousness is not what it is.''[17]

Take any feature or characteristic which a person may ascribe to himself: a profession, a virtue, a vice, an attitude, or a mood. For example, he is a waiter. Sartre the psychologist observes how a person can become utterly proficient in playing a role. In *Being and Nothingness* he draws a perceptive and delightfully humorous picture of a man playing at being a waiter. The ironic thing is that the more successful the man is in playing that role, the more evident it becomes that he is obviously *not* what he pretends to be, even to himself, namely, a waiter. Here, one should overlook Sartre's obvious confusion between ''being *x*'' and ''being nothing but *x*.'' His point here is phenomenological; a person *may* deceive himself into thinking that his whole reality as a person is poured without remainder into the role he is playing. But here Sartre reminds him that his very effort to play that role to the hilt is evidence that *he* is not that role.

This example alone suffices to illustrate Sartre's claim that we constantly keep *making* ourselves into what we are at any moment. Hence, it follows that at any given moment, a man is what he is not (namely, his project, what he is making himself to be); otherwise, there would be no point in undertaking the project. On the other hand, man is not what he is, that is, his attempt to see himself as frozen in a given role is a mistake, a factual mistake. In sustaining the role of a waiter, I ''transcend it on every side,'' I ''constitute myself as one *beyond* my condition.'' To play a role is to *represent* oneself as something, both to oneself and to others. ''But if I represent myself as him, I am not he; I am separated from him as the object from the subject, separated by *nothing*, but this nothing isolates me from him. I cannot be he, I can only play *at being* him; that is, to imagine myself that I am he. And thereby I affect him with nothingness.''[18]

Similarly, my sadness is not a state of affairs to which I am related as a passive onlooker. Sadness is a conduct, *my* conduct. I cannot look at it as an object, an ''in-itself,'' finished and done with. Being sad means *making* oneself sad. A consciousness *affects* itself with sadness. ''If I make myself sad, I must continue to make myself sad from beginning to end.'' I cannot produce sadness as a ready-made thing and bestow it on myself. ''I do not possess that property of *affecting myself with being*.''[19] This means that consciousness is creating itself from nothing and that we are free, or rather, as Sartre puts it, we *are* freedom.

Or, consider my view of myself as not being courageous. I am *not coura-geous*, not in the way my pen is not a chair, but because I am capable of putting my cowardice in relation to its opposite. In other words, I am "capable of *determining* myself as cowardly." Hence the possibility of self-deception, because "human reality, in its most immediate being, in the inner structure of the prereflective *cogito*, must be what it is not and not be what it is."[20]

Since consciousness is constantly remaking itself, it is impossible to ascribe any destiny whatever to a self. Human reality is constantly in flight from itself, from its previous modes of being. Hence, the very notion of sincerity becomes problematic. To be sincere is to come dangerously close to regarding oneself as an "in-itself," as a frozen identity. People who attempt this fall into "bad faith," a form of self-deception.

Self-deception interests Sartre because it is a situation in which "the double property of the human being, who is at once a *facticity* and a *transcendence*," is not coordinated. Self-deception treats facticity as if it were transcendence, and *vice versa*. Thus, for example, a man who has an unrealistically high opinion of himself treats that imaginary self as if it were a fact, which necessitates all sorts of false excuses for the weaknesses and failures of that self. At the same time, he treats his factual self as if it were a mere possibility, not reality, and once more denies the truth about himself. Consequently, the state of self-deception is not easy to maintain; it is a perpetually disintegrating synthesis, a metastable situation. The root of the problem is that in self-deception, a person is trying, unsuccessfully of course, to constitute himself as a thing. This attempt is bound to be unsuccessful because being human is essentially being "for-itself" and never merely "in-itself."

The attempt to see human reality as primarily facticity results from a mistaken tendency, encouraged by much traditional philosophy, to look for our essence, for human nature. But there is no such nature; human existence comes before human essence. Existence is a free projection of self *beyond* its present facticity. There is nothing that limits this continuous advance into novelty and literal self-determination. Sartre, like Nietzsche, sees the concept of God as a way of denying this radical freedom to us. Nietzsche objected to the concept of God because, among other prohibitions, it imposed on us the injunction: "Thou shalt not think!" To the extent that anything is thinkable, it has been already thought by God (cf. Thomas Aquinas' Theory of Universals), and therefore no really *new* thoughts can come to us. But Nietzsche challenged human beings to make new values thinkable, to create beyond themselves. Sartre embraces atheism for similar reasons. If we are made in God's image and if our career is essentially determined for us by what *God* wants us to be, then it is a mockery to speak of human freedom. This is why existentialism prefers to see humanity as not definable. To begin with, a human being is nothing, says Sartre. First of all he exists, encounters himself, and surges up in the world. Only afterward does he define himself, but only for a time being, because otherwise he would once more fall into bad faith and would reduce himself to mere facticity. "Man simply is. Not that he is simply what he conceives himself to be, but he is what he wills, and as he conceives himself after already existing—as he wills to be after that leap toward existence.''[21] This is why for Sartre, man's existence precedes his essence.

Human existence, however, is not *just* consciousness; it is *embodied* existence. Sartre rejects Descartes' dualism. A person for Sartre is not the soul *and* the body. *"For-itself is* entirely its body and entirely consciousness: the For-itself is not united to a body . . . The body *is* entirely psychic.''[22] Sartre expresses this unitary character of human beings by using the verb "to exist" transitively and says that I *exist* my body. My body is known through the things of the world. We have already noted Heidegger's distinction between *Vorhandensein* and *Zuhandensein*. Things in the world are at a distance from my body only in a very special circumstance, namely, as objects of sight, although even to see things is to see them from a perspective, from the point of view of my body. But our relation to things is primarily instrumental; we handle them as means toward our ends. The body is revealed mainly in action, and therefore Sartre regards it as ''Being-for-itself,'' as it is in the world.

Sartre's rejection of the mind-body dualism, combined with his emphasis on the essentially active character of human reality, strikes an epistemological note which, as we shall see, was also prominent in American pragmatism. The pragmatists similarly rejected the visual model of knowing the world and emphasized the interactive, transactional character of human experience. Sartre also speaks of the *utensility* of things, of their being meaningful to us primarily as tools and instruments of action. But, as we have noted before, in place of Cartesian dualism Sartre puts an even more radical dualism, namely, that of Being and Nothingness. By equating Nothingness with consciousness, and consciousness with freedom, Sartre appears to be following the legacy of another of his philosophical predecessors, namely, Nietzsche. For Nietzsche, the outstanding, remarkable, and most valuable feature of being human was the capacity for self-overcoming or self-transcendence. Sartre also stresses the free, creative surge which Nietzsche identified as the Will to Power. Although Sartre makes no use of this label, he nevertheless sees consciousness as a will, as an activity which gives itself its own character in every decision. Sartre's view, in a sense, is more radical than Nietzsche's, for the latter lays great stress on a *style*, on carefully thought-out goals, whereas for Sartre the inherent freedom of the self to transcend itself is limited, literally, by nothing.

Like Heidegger, Sartre is concerned with authenticity, but he differs from Heidegger in that he does not see human reality in relation to Being. What is new and radical about Sartre's existentialism is that he refuses to put human reality in relation to *any* kind of transcendent reality—neither God, nor Will to Power, nor Being plays any role in describing human existence. That existence is self-creating, self-projecting, limited literally by nothing. Sartre's analysis of human consciousness convinced him of that. Consciousness consists in negations or "nihilations." So does human action, which is characterized by absolute freedom. There is no human nature, because if there were such nature, its structure would make a mockery of freedom. In this respect, the originality and novelty of Sartre's point of view are undeniable. All philosophers before him saw man in relation to some other reality—God, nature, the Absolute, the Universal Will. Sartre's account of consciousness and freedom as nothingness, as a *contrast* to Being, appears to break with the entire philosophical tradition. Whether or not that account is intelligible is an open question, but at least Sartre has tried to argue for it by stressing the negativities or nihilations at the heart of human consciousness and of all human projects, so tellingly summed up in his verdict "Man is a useless passion."

## Questions

1. Which aspects of traditional religion and of its role in contemporary civilization were criticized by Nietzsche, and what did he propose to put in place of traditional religion?

2. What does Nietzsche understand by the Will to Power? Which interpretations of it does he reject? How is this notion related to his concepts of the overman and of eternal recurrence?

3. How do you understand Heidegger's distinction between representational thinking and thinking-that-recalls? Why does he feel that we should turn to the poets in order to understand the distinction he is trying to make?

4. Are there similarities between Heidegger's notion of Being and Parmenides' notion of the One, or It?

5. What is Sartre's analysis of human consciousness? Why does he think that this analysis calls for the recognition of negations, or "nihilations"? How is his analysis of consciousness related to his concepts of the self and of human freedom?

6. What does Sartre understand by "bad faith"? Can you provide some illustrations of it from your own experience?

**224**                                                           Chapter Nine

# Notes

[1] From *The Portable Nietzsche*, translated and edited by Walter Kaufmann. Copyright 1954 by The Viking Press, Inc. Reprinted by permission of The Viking Press, Inc., pp. 95-96.

[2] Friedrich Nietzsche in *Dawn*, as quoted by Walter Kaufmann in *Nietzsche*, New York: World Books, 1956, p. 170.

[3] *Twilight of the Idols, ibid.*, p. 257.

[4] *Thus Spoke Zarathustra*, in *The Portable Nietzsche, op. cit.*, pp. 339-40.

[5] *Ibid.*, p. 237.

[6] Martin Heidegger, "The Way Back into the Ground of Metaphysics," translated by Walter Kaufmann in *Existentialism from Dostoyevsky to Sartre*, New York: Meridian Books, 1956, pp. 207-208.

[7] *Ibid.*, p. 209.

[8] Zygmunt Adamczewski, "On the Way to Being," in *Heidegger and the Path of Thinking*, ed. John Sallis, Duquesne University Press, 1970, p. 21.

[9] *Ibid.*, p. 211.

[10] *Ibid.*, p. 13.

[11] As quoted by Hegel in *Lectures on the Philosophy of Religion*, translated by E.B. Speirs and J.B. Sanderson, London: Kegan Paul, 1898, Vol. 1, p. 228.

[12] *Thus Spoke Zarathustra*, in *The Portable Nietzsche, op. cit.*, p. 121.

[13] J.P. Sartre, *Nausea*, translated by Lloyd Alexander, New York: New Directions, 1949, pp. 170-182.

[14] J.P. Sartre, *Being and Nothingness*, translated by Hazel Barnes, New York: Washington Square Press, 1966, p. 58.

[15] *Ibid.*, p. 64.

[16] *Ibid.*, p. 68.

[17] *Ibid.*, p. 105.

[18] *Ibid.*, p. 103.

[19] *Ibid.*, p. 104.

[20] *Ibid.*, p. 112.

[21] J.P. Sartre, *Existentialism and Humanism*, translated by P. Mairet and reprinted in Walter Kaufmann's *Existentialism from Dostoyevsky to Sartre*, New York: Meridian Books, 1956, p. 290.

[22] *Being and Nothingness, op. cit.*, p. 404.

# Chapter Ten

# Pragmatism

## 1. Charles Peirce: The Growth of Concrete Reasonableness

Charles Sanders Peirce (1839-1914), the brilliant and versatile originator of American pragmatism, was denied success and fame in his lifetime. Son of the noted mathematician, Benjamin Peirce, Charles received his university training at Harvard, where he studied mathematics and chemistry. His interest in philosophical problems was deepened by his participation in the activities of the Metaphysical Club in Cambridge, where papers were read and vigorously argued. (Among many other talented members of the Club were Oliver Wendell Holmes, Jr., and William James.) In spite of his definite academic propensities, Peirce failed to secure a permanent university position, reportedly because of his many eccentricities. Except for brief periods of lecturing at Johns Hopkins and Harvard, Peirce had to support himself for 30 years by working as a scientist for the United States Coast and Geodetic Survey. Peirce spent the latter part of his life fighting off financial difficulties. In these efforts he was supported by William James, and out of gratitude, he decided to add to his name "Santiago" (St. James) and signed his correspondence C.S.S. Peirce. However, his struggle with creditors which often included hiding in the attic and pulling the ladder behind him, did not prevent Peirce from working diligently on his philosophy, occasionally writing articles and reviews for which he was sometimes paid. Several of his articles appeared in the *Popular Scientific Monthly*, which, according to reports, was neither popular nor scientific, but appeared once a month. Unrecognized and poor, tended by his faithful French wife, the brilliant recluse died in Milford, Pennsylvania, at the age of 75. His writings were published by Harvard University Press as *Collected Papers*, the first six volumes of which appeared during the years 1931-1935; two additional volumes were published in 1958. Peirce's importance in American philosophy is now widely recognized, not only in the United States but also in the rest of the world. His works are now being republished in new editions and his ideas find applications in other fields besides philosophy.

As a man of science, Peirce was deeply suspicious of traditional metaphysics and managed to say some biting things about it. He believed that his pragmatism would "show that almost every proposition of ontological metaphysics is either meaningless gibberish—one word being defined by other words, and they by still others, without any real conception ever being reached—or else is downright absurd." His aim was to sweep away "all such rubbish" and to confine philosophy to "a series of problems capable of investigation by the observational methods of the true sciences." Peirce was fond of referring to his own philosophy as a "laboratory method," in which concrete, experimentally confirmed results could be obtained. As it turned out, Peirce's own researches moved in a direction of a vast architectonic and included views which are clearly of a metaphysical, speculative sort. Some scholars divide Peirce's contributions into more narrowly epistemological doctrines and metaphysical speculations, often rejecting the latter as not consistent with Peirce's pragmatism. Nevertheless, he appears to have thought that all strands of his philosophy mutually support one another and that the latter versions throw further light on his original formulations.

Peirce's "pragmatic maxim" was articulated in two early essays, "The Fixation of Belief," and "How to Make Our Ideas Clear." The new epistemological note sounded in that maxim is that knowledge is conditioned by the process of inquiry preceding the emergence of a belief. Peirce flatly states that the aim of all inquiry is the production of a belief. However, it turns out that belief for Peirce is not just a mental state; it is a disposition to act in a certain way. This key consideration accounts for the label "pragmatism," "pragma" meaning "practice," "action," "things done." As Peirce continues to develop the notion of belief, it takes more and more dimensions, finally embracing all of Peirce's "conceptual geography." Before turning to this development, however, let us consider what is involved in the view that epistemology deals essentially with a theory of inquiry. Peirce starts out with a quasihistorical characterization of the way people tended to fix their beliefs.

First, there is the method of *tenacity*, the determination to hold to received beliefs regardless of what further experience reveals about their validity or suitability. Needless to say, this method is in fact the absence of a method and consists in refusing to learn from experience. The method of *authority* consists in deferring to some persons who impose their views on others on pain of punishment. This method, although possibly a bit longer lasting than the first one, is likely to be shattered by the course of events to which it fails to respond. Philosophers have come to use still another method, which Peirce calls the *a priori* method, in which some basic self-evident truths are used as the cornerstone of all other beliefs. The trouble with this method is that what is regarded as self-evident differs from philosopher to philosopher, and so disagreements remain unresolvable. In place of all these methods, Peirce proposes the method of science, which alone can fix beliefs in a rational manner. An important feature of this comparison of various approaches is that it shifts the focus of epistemological interest from *what* is known to *how* knowledge is acquired. Methodological considerations are given priority over all other matters.

Peirce's "pragmatic maxim" is worth quoting: "consider what effects, which might conceivably have practical bearings, we conceive the object of our conception to have. Then, our conception of these effects is the whole of our conception of the object." An important word in this formula is "effect." When we believe that a substance is hard, for example, we expect that this belief will have certain consequences, e.g., that the surface of the substance cannot be easily scratched. In our dealings with that substance, we will experience certain things, and we will have certain specifiable sensations. This is what Peirce means by "practical bearings" of the effects of the object of our conception. Our belief is true when the consequences we expect the object of our conception to have actually do take place; when that conception disappoints our expectation, the belief is false. This method ties all our concepts to experience; there is a way of settling our disagreements. Two words do not differ in meaning when there is no difference in their practical bearings, when they lead to the same consequences in our experience. Thus, disputes about the meaning of our beliefs can be settled by reference to their sensible consequences. Peirce uses the example of transubstantiation. The same substance is called wine and blood, but the correctness of the description must be tested by the sensible effects the substance actually has.

The word that appears in the formula even more frequently than "effects" is "conceive" and its cognates. Many years after writing the formula Peirce felt called upon to explain and defend his prolific use of this term. He insisted on its crucial importance. The occasion for this review of the formula was Peirce's displeasure with the way it was interpreted by other philosophers, including William James, who was responsible for introducing pragmatism into philosophical discussion in America. Because of this erroneous interpretation, Peirce wanted to dissociate himself from pragmatism as it then began to gain popularity. For that purpose he coined a new name for his philosophy, namely, "pragmaticism," which he thought "ugly enough to be safe from kidnappers."

Peirce's reaction turns on a fundamental issue, which is still controversial among the interpreters of and commentators on his work. The empiricist interpreters of Peirce take the phrase in the maxim, "our conception of these effects is the whole of our conception of the object," literally, claiming that it is the *actual* effects of the conception that constitute its meaning. William James also construed the maxim in this way, thus developing pragmatism in a direction which was unpalatable to Peirce. James' interpretation opens the possibility that the meanings of words have arbitrary individual interpretations. The effects that *I* experience constitute the meaning for me; should these effects be different for you—that's your right and prerogative. Peirce sensed that this way of taking the maxim was too liberal and led in the direction of irrationalism. Therefore, he insisted that the effect of the conception is not exhausted in any number of actual experiences; it is a "would-be" which does not terminate in the experience of any given individual or even a group of individuals. He did want to connect the meaning of words with human actions and purposes, but not with just *any* action and *any* individual purpose. A conception also has a *rational* purport, in which the concept of action has to be carefully circumscribed. In criticizing those who misunderstood his pragmatism, he says: "It must be admitted, in the first place, that if pragmatism really made Doing the Be-all and the End-all of life, that would be its death. For to say that we live for the mere sake of action, as action, regardless of the thought it carries with it, would be to say that there is no such thing as rational purport." (This remark alone shows the injustice in George Santayana's later characterization of the pragmatist as a man who on a ship in a storm at sea blows into the sails to have more action.)

At this point, another aspect of Peirce's philosophy needs to be brought into play in order for us to understand why he objected to the manner in which his maxim was taken. Peirce's theory of signs can be seen as a restatement and development of the pragmatic maxim. To translate a word into a conception of its effects is to say what the word signifies. The word is a sign which stands for these effects, and they are its *interpretants*. Peirce insisted that these interpretants are *logical*, not behavioral. By that he meant that they are themselves signs and as such have further interpretants. Consider the word "apple." It is a sign of properties residing in objects covered by that term. Each of these properties—for example, roundness, sweetness, or tartness—is itself a sign. To understand "roundness," we need to know something about possible lines, diameters, shapes, spheres, etc. This explains why the word "conception" is so prominent in Peirce's formulation of the maxim. The logical interpretant of the word, or sign, carries with it its intellectual purport and *that* goes beyond any actual uses of the sign. Intellectual concepts, says Peirce, "convey more, not merely than any feeling, but more, too than any existential fact, namely, the 'would acts,' 'would do's' of habitual behavior; and no agglomeration of actual happenings can ever completely fill up the meaning of a 'would-be.' "

Thus, the whole of our language is a system of signs related to one another in multiple ways. But how does it connect with experience, with the world? Here, Peirce connects the notion of belief as a disposition to act with another important notion in his epistemology, that of *habit*. As sign-using beings, we find our way in the world with the help of successfully established habits. To have true beliefs is to be governed by habits which, in turn, are guided by uniform, regular, publicly shared perceptions. Habits are rules; they are imperatives "addressed to the future self," connecting the present experience with future action. But these habits are not blind, merely behavioral, or muscular, as Peirce puts it. "I am persuaded that nothing like a concept can be acquired by muscular practice alone." [1]

If we allow our conceptions to be checked at the gate of perception, we will operate with increasingly effective, rational habits. We will also be saved from subjectivity and idiosyncrasy. For in a gradual refinement of our conceptions, we will be getting closer and closer to what is real. Reality, for Peirce, is that state of affairs which would be approximated when an indefinite number of investigators pursue their inquiries indefinitely. The real he regarded as independent of any particular investigators. "That is *real* which has such and such characters, whether anybody thinks it to have these characters or not." Peirce was confident that "thought, controlled by a rational experimental logic, tends to the fixation of certain opinions, . . . the nature of which will be the same in the end, however the perversity of thought of whole generations may cause the postponement of the ultimate fixation." [2]

To say that the real is that which is independent of what anybody in particular thinks does not mean that our access to reality is independent of thought altogether. Peirce studied Kant long enough (according to himself, for three years, three hours a day) to have grasped Kant's main insight. There is no reason to suppose, he says, that what is relative to thought cannot be real. "*Red* is relative to sight, but the fact that this or that is in relation to vision that we call being red is not *itself* relative to sight; it is a real fact." [3] Thus, although following the Kantian doctrine in its essentials, namely, agreeing that mind makes a necessary contribution to all cognition, Peirce nevertheless rejects the doctrine of the thing-in-itself, again on purely epistemological grounds. That conception is a jarring note in a Kantian framework. The thing-in-itself does not exist as such, Peirce concluded. "That is, there is no thing which is in-itself in the sense of not being relative to the mind, though things which are relative to the mind doubtless are, apart from that relation." [4] Of the two ideas "truth" and "reality," the latter looks to Peirce as the "more occult" and hence could not be used to explain the former. When we say that a thing "has a character," we are not saying anything more than that something is true of it. We have no independent access to its reality.

Thus, Peirce could be said to have reconciled empiricism and idealism, meaning by the former the view that all experience must ultimately come back to the verdict of perception, and by the latter that mind plays an indispensable role in producing knowledge. Peirce affirmed empiricism to the extent of insisting that what is real is independent of any particular thinker, and idealism to the extent of rejecting all attempts to postulate knowledge without the activity of the mind. "All thinking is in signs," he declared. In fact, man as a constant interpreter of signs, is himself a sign. "The word or sign which man uses *is* man himself." Each sign addresses itself to my future self which will interpret that sign. "Thus my language is the sum total of myself; for the man is the thought." [5]

The conception of the thing-in-itself is one of these dogmatic concepts which block the road to inquiry, believed Peirce. He found another form of dogmatism in the rationalistic notion of intuition. Intuition is supposed to connect us directly with something which is otherwise "incognizable." Peirce believed Descartes to be the chief sinner in this department and subjected some of the Cartesian claims to fierce scrutiny. The result was further support for his theory of signs. Consider the idea of the self, something which according to Descartes is immediately available in introspection. But there is no reason to suppose that it is not derived from other cognitions. Peirce is inclined to think that infants are at first aware of the surrounding things, including other human bodies. When a child hears a bell, it is a philosophical prejudice to suppose that he thinks of himself as hearing and not of the bell as sounding. More likely, the developing mind is inveterately objectivist, not subjectivist. Only after the infant hears others called by names does he discover that he too has a name. When he disregards his mother's warning that the stove is hot and touches it, he becomes aware of ignorance, and only then does he infer that the ignorance is *his*, that "it is necessary to suppose a *self* in which this ignorance can inhere." [6] By means of such detailed criticism of the idea of self-consciousness, supposedly derived from direct intuition, Peirce concludes that there is no necessity to suppose such an intuition, but rather that the idea "may easily be the result of an inference."

Peirce's further examples show that it is also a mistake to regard the concepts of emotion, say, of anger, as having their home in the directly accessible mental realm. Anticipating some very recent discussions, he connects the idea of anger with the typical *objects* of anger: "there is some relative character in the outward thing which makes him angry." The upshot of all these examples is to show that all thought is in signs and that there is no conception of something absolutely incognizable. "To suppose that a cognition is determined solely by something absolutely external is to suppose its determinations incapable of explanation.'' This is why Kant's notion of the thing-in-itself and Descartes' intuitions block the road to scientific inquiry.

Peirce's analysis of cognition as essentially involving the use of signs opens up further aspects in his architectonic structure. A response to a sign may lie in three different dimensions. First, the response may be a mere feeling, an ''emotional interpretant''; in the case of some signs the feeling response may be exclusive and prominent. For instance, the display of a flag may convey to a viewer a feeling of familiarity or identity with his countrymen—a wave of patriotism may sweep through him. Second, the sign may be, as Peirce puts it, purely ''energetic.'' A good example may be found in the sergeant's barking out the order: ''Present arms!'' A well-trained recruit is not thinking about the meaning of the order, he just executes it, almost as a reflex. But there is a third level in the interpretation of signs which is neither mere feeling, nor a behavioral response, but understanding, taking in the cognitive scope of the sign. This third type of situation is in the nature of a logical interpretant, of a belief which takes in the rational purport of the sign and establishes a habit for future actions. The three types of response to signs Peirce also designates by technical terms: icon, index, and symbol.

Approached from this angle, the theory of signs leads to Peirce's Scotist Realism, as he chose to call it in order to indicate his agreement with the view of the medieval philosopher Duns Scotus. It amounts to the conclusion that thought connects us with ''real generals'' and that nominalism is false. ''Generality is, indeed, an indispensable ingredient of reality, for mere individual existence or actuality without any regularity whatever is nullity.''[7] Consider my action of opening a window; how can it be explained? It may be my response to a *general* fact that stuffy air is unwholesome. Peirce's realism is, then, a recognition that there are real, persistent regularities in the world and that they pour in on us from all sides of our experience. Cognition, through signs, takes account of these general regularities and enables us to establish rational habits, i.e., habits that are governed by our recognition of the fact of these regularities.

The aim of all inquiry is to lead us toward beliefs and habits that would reflect the true nature of reality. ''Accordingly, the pragmaticist does not make the *summum bonum* to consist in action, but makes it to consist in that process of evolution whereby the existent comes more and more to embody those generals which were just now said to be *destined*, which is what we strive to express in calling them *reasonable*.''[8] The aim of inquiry, then, is the growth of concrete reasonableness. It is called concrete because it is based on experimental findings, on the laboratory methods pioneered by the sciences. But if the real is defined as ''independent of the vagaries of me and you,'' then it is clear that it also involves the notion of *community*, of a joint effort of many people whose task is "without definite limits, and capable of a definite increase of knowledge."

The community, the public aspect of carrying out the inquiry, guarantees that it will also be self-corrective. Those who take part in the inquiry will be forced to recognize that as involving thought, it requires self-control. For Peirce, "thinking is a species of conduct which is largely subject to self-control." "There is no reason why thought . . . should be taken in that narrow sense in which silence and darkness are favorable to thought. It rather should be understood as covering all rational life, so that an experiment shall be an operation of thought."[9] This passage in particular brings out the central message of pragmatism: inquiry is not the inward sort of contemplation, it is as wide open as all outdoors and involves all possible instrumentalities which could further the growth of knowledge.

It may appear curious that Peirce, a scientist, sees a close connection between science and ethics. Some of his views on this issue appear extravagant. He believed, for instance, that no criminal could be a good scientist. Success in science presupposes good morals, for "the ideals of good logic are truly of the same general nature as ideals of fine conduct." Logical self-control, for Peirce, "is the perfect mirror of ethical self-control—unless it be rather a species under that genus." In fact, Peirce saw the three normative inquiries—logic, ethics, and aesthetics (the true, the good, and the beautiful)—as standing in a definite hierarchical relationship, with aesthetics being highest on the scale. This, again, may seem surprising. The explanation, however, can be found in the already discussed features of his pragmatism, if we consider them in greater detail.

How does one get at the general facts of the universe? By experiment, we were told. But this is not the whole story. Scientific progress depends on making correct hypotheses. The theory begins with a hunch, with a mere feeling that something may be the case. In fact, Peirce, the logician, believed in an additional form of argument aside from the two generally accepted: (1) deductive, in which we derive a conclusion from the premises simply on the grounds of formal logical validity, and (2) inductive, in which we conclude on the basis of statistical samples that all other things of the kind so far examined will be like them. (Peirce described induction as moving from some facts to other facts of the same kind.) His third form of argument, namely, our moving from one kind of fact to other facts of a different kind, is hypothesis, or *abduction*, as Peirce also calls it. Abduction is a kind of inspired guess. If so and so were the case, then the things we are trying to explain would follow as a matter of course. Peirce believes that here lies the creative contribution of the scientist who discovers a new theory. He is capable of making a right guess at the riddle of the universe, or at least at one of its many riddles. The fact is that scientists have succeeded in numerous instances to read the universe aright, to come up with hypotheses which attune them to the actual general features of the universe.

Peirce laid great store by this right kind of sympathetic attunement, wherein thought and reality become congruent. Once a hypothesis has been made, it can then be tested by inductive methods. But in the first hunch it is the mere feeling that must guide us. Of course, only those who have been looking in the right direction, who are familiar with phenomena under investigation, are likely to read the riddle correctly. But their original hunch will be a feeling akin to aesthetic perception.

We are able to find correct ways of interpreting the universe, through proper self-control and scientific habits, only because in the end there is a congruence between our intelligent operations and the universe as a whole. At this point the waves of metaphysics in Peirce's philosophy run rather high. Nevertheless, Peirce's doctrine of categories and his evolutionary cosmology do have obvious connections with the rest of his epistemology. Recall the three possible interpretants of signs: the emotional, the energetic, and the logical. The chief content in each, respectively, is feeling, action, thought. Now at some stage of his reflection, Peirce discovered that these three elements may be a key to the description of the most general features of the universe. Thus, he came up with his phenomenology, of which the doctrine of categories is the most important aspect.

The universe exhibits certain pervasive features: Firstness, Secondness, and Thirdness. Everything has its immediate qualitative feeling: the first blush of anything, a color, a voice, a visual pattern, even a thought, whether simple or complex, is *firstness*. It is mere quality "in its *sui-generis* suchness." It is not yet experience because all experience already involves *secondness*, a coming together of a quality and of the awareness of it. Indeed, the term "existence" is not applicable to firstness because existence is primarily a manifestation of secondness. Existence is a standing out or standing against: everything existent fights its way into reality. Secondness is a brute fact as such. A good illustration of secondness is an attempt to push against a closed door; it does not yield, it persists, it insists on maintaining itself. Hence all action, reaction, all factual manifestations partake of secondness. But there is also *thirdness*. Secondness is dyadic, but thirdness is triadic and cannot be reduced to secondness. Consider the transaction of a gift: A gives B to C. This fact cannot be broken up into mere dyadic components, say, A and B, B and C, and A and C. B must be understood as related simultaneously to A and C; otherwise, its character as a gift cannot be rendered correctly. We can see that all signs, all thoughts, are *thirds* because they involve the object, the sign, and the interpretant. Any law, any regularity, is thirdness, because it describes *relationships* among things. The very notion of relation is an example of thirdness because if two things are merely dyadic, that is, stand in no relation to each other, they are only instances of secondness. But postulate a relationship between them, then there is a third, mediating between them. Some of the other examples of thirdness, all prominent ideas in philosophy of science, Peirce lists as follows: generality, infinity, continuity, diffusion, growth, and intelligence.

The relation of the categories to one another is not quite clear. Peirce agrees that they "cannot be dissociated in imagination from each other, nor from other ideas," and that it is "extremely difficult accurately and sharply to distinguish each from other conceptions so as to hold it in its purity and yet in its full meaning." Nevertheless, he believes that his phenomenology is applicable to everything there is.

The doctrine of the categories is also connected with Peirce's evolutionary cosmology. Not only are we reaching out toward greater rationality in our habits; the whole universe, animated by what Peirce calls "evolutionary love," may be seen as moving in that direction. Human intelligence is but one form of thirdness operative throughout all reality. Peirce believed that the whole universe exhibits a growth toward more reasonableness, more complexity, harmony, and intelligence. He had even attempted to write his own chapter of Genesis in which from the primordial nothingness of mere potentiality, firstness broke through into existence, thus originating the first habit which then grew into regularities and established a pattern of constant growth toward concrete reasonableness of the universe. Our task is to contribute toward this growth, both for our own sake and for the sake of the whole order of things.

> *. . . The creation of the universe, which did not take place during a certain busy week, in the year 4004 B.C., but is going on today and never will be done, is this very development of reason. I do not see how one can have a more satisfying ideal of the admirable than the development of reason, so understood. The one thing whose admirableness is not due to an ulterior reason is reason itself comprehended in all its fullness, so far as we can comprehend it. Under this conception, the ideal of conduct will be to execute our little function in the operation of the creation by giving a hand toward rendering the world more reasonable whenever, as the slang is, it is "up to us" to do so.* [10]

In Peirce's architectonic there is even room for God, but not the God of the prophets. If the universe is moving in the direction of realizing higher values, in which process both ethics and aesthetics play a dominant role, then religion as inspiring us with the vision of ideals has its proper and desirable place. In his so-called Neglected Argument for God's existence, Peirce describes how contemplative musement about the universe in its sweeping, fascinating course through the ages can originate something akin to the belief in God. Anthropomorphic analogues need not be despised here, and Peirce uses one without apology.

> *If a pramaticist is asked what he means by the word "God," he can only say that just as long acquaintance with a man of great character may deeply influence one's whole manner of conduct, so that a glance at his portrait may make a difference, just as almost living with Dr. Johnson enabled poor Boswell to write an immortal book and a really sublime book, just as long study of the works of Aristotle may make him an acquaintance, so if contemplation and study of the physico-psychical universe can imbue a man with principles of conduct analogous to the influence of a great man's works or conversation, then that analogue of a mind—for it is impossible to say that any human attribute is literally applicable—is what he means by "God."*[11]

Peirce's philosophical evolutionism was no doubt influenced by other evolutionary theories coming into existence in his time. Among them is Darwin's biological theory, the main thrust of which was expressed in the title of his monumental work published in 1859, *The Origin of Species*. As John Dewey was to observe later, the philosophical greatness of Darwin's theory lay in the fact that it dared to speak of the *origin* of species. The idea of a species, despite Leibniz's doctrine of continuity and the great chain of being, was still regarded as connoting something stable and unchangeable. Theologians could still find in that idea a support for the view that all species were created by God and were designed to fulfill their special destinies. This was particularly important in reserving a special place for the human species, which was regarded as radically distinct from all other species of animals. Darwin's theory seemed to destroy this last vestige of humanity's privileged position in the universe. If human beings were not specially created but merely evolved from lower forms of life, then their claim to a very special cosmic role is at least exaggerated. Our kinship with apes puts us on a par with the rest of the animal kingdom, and our imperfections may suggest a possibility, as they did to Nietzsche, that a higher form of being may be more desirable.

It is not surprising that the implications of the theory of evolution frightened theological circles into wanting to question its correctness: as a result, the second half of the nineteenth century witnessed a new war between science and religion during which ecclesiastic authorities, though lacking the powers at their disposal in the days of Galileo or Giordano Bruno, nonetheless attacked and condemned the new theory with vigor. In London, T.H. Huxley, a dramatic spokesman for Darwin's theory, carried on spirited public debates with bishops, and decades later in Tennessee, a biology teacher, John T. Scopes, was tried for teaching evolution in his high school classes.

Many nineteenth century thinkers besides Peirce, found evolutionary perspectives exciting and exhilarating. Herbert Spencer (1820-1903), who in his writings appealed to the principles of evolutionary development even before the publication of Darwin's *Origin of Species*, saw in the theory of evolution a conceptual tool which could explain not only the history of life on earth but also all other processes, including the economic, social, moral, and political. Spencer's books were especially popular among those who saw in them a justification for private economic enterprise and the search for innovations. Spencer tried to provide a formulation of general evolutionary principles applicable to all reality. Here is his definition of evolution: "Evolution is an integration of matter and concomitant dissipation of motion; during which the matter passes from an indefinite, incoherent homogeneity to a definite, coherent heterogeneity." [12] One critic "translated" it "into plain English" as follows: "Evolution is a change from a no-howish, untalkaboutable all-alikeness to a somehowish and in general talkaboutable not-all-alikeness by continuous somethingelsifications and sticktogetherations." [13]

Evolution was also the chief topic of the French philosopher Henri Bergson (1859-1941). In one of his works, entitled *Creative Evolution*, he developed a metaphysics based on the conception of reality as *élan vital*, a vital urge which accounts for the emergence of continually more complicated and higher forms of living beings. Bergson coupled his metaphysics with a new kind of epistemology in which the role of reason as conceptual intelligence was subordinated to a higher form of knowledge labeled intuition. The weakness of conceptual thinking, thought Bergson, is that it breaks up experience into discontinuities. Perception provides us with only partial aspects of things and hence results in their distortion. We see only one side of an object at a time and can concentrate on only isolated sensory messages coming from it. Knowledge coming from percepts and concepts is only external and always calls for *re*construction, which once more is removed from the reality we are trying to grasp. Instead of moving around the object and getting a series of "snapshots" of it, we should try to "enter into it" by a kind of spiritual "ausculation." Even the notion of time as a succession of episodes is a distortion of experience, according to Bergson. We break up time arbitrarily into mathematically homogeneous units, thus mechanizing and distorting it. In actual experience the qualitative sense of time is very different from clock time. "I've been here for hours" may be a truer statement than the objective report, "I've waited 20 minutes." We experience duration itself and not its abstraction in conceptual time measurements. And it is in duration that we experience the continuous flux of reality, in both ourselves and the changing world of which we are in part. *Élan vital*, therefore, must be akin to our consciousness; it is a life and creativity principle which introduces novelty into the scheme of things.

The philosophy of the English metaphysician Samuel Alexander (1859-1938), expressed in the book entitled *Space, Time and Deity*, takes from modern mathematical physics a concept of space-time and declares it to be the ultimate reality. The basic character of space-time is motion, and what we call matter is composed of events or point-instants. Matter is the unity of organized motion, e.g., the movement of electrons around a nucleus constitutes an atom. Due to combinations of substances, new qualities of matter *emerge*. Also life, although depending on chemical process, is a new, emerging quality of space-time. Similarly, at a still higher level, mind and consciousness emerge as new stages in the evolution of space-time. The highest stage of this evolutionary development is the emergence of *deity*, the mind of the world. Deity does not now exist but, being the next order to evolve, it is experienced as future. By God, Alexander means "a Being which possesses deity." Our experience of deity as the emerging order of evolution leads to faith in God.

Alfred North Whitehead (1861-1947) believed that the new developments in science, especially quantum theory, the theory of relativity, and evolutionary biology, called for a thoroughgoing conceptual reinterpretation of all our experience. After a brilliant career in England (Cambridge and London) as a mathematician and philosopher of science, Whitehead came to Harvard at the age of 63 and proceeded to write his most famous books, entitled *Science and the Modern World* (1925), *Process and Reality* (1929), and *Adventures of Ideas* (1933). In these works Whitehead presents a self-contained, all-inclusive metaphysical system in which the key idea is the concept of organism. We live in a universe in which process, creativity, and interdependence are disclosed in immediate experience, and the philosophy of organism is best suited for giving these features their due recognition. The final real things out of which the universe is made up are *actual entitles*. Whitehead prefers this technical term to the traditional concept of substance. Actual entities are related to one another causally, purposively, evaluatively, and affectively. They *prehend* one another in these multiple, yet organically related, ways. They are in a process of "perpetual perishing," but as they perish they pass into other entities as actual occasions. Whitehead's universe is a constant flux, a process of becoming, in which actual entities take part in a creative advance. In addition to actual entities that are causally and affectively related to one another, there is also God, whose timeless vision contains *eternal objects*. This technical term of Whitehead's is reminiscent of Plato's Forms, which provide the goals and values for particular entities to embody. Whitehead follows Spinoza and Leibniz in attributing to each actual occasion a physical and a mental pole. Through the physical pole an actual occasion prehends other occasions; through the mental pole it prehends eternal objects which are fixed in God's primordial, timeless vision. God does not take active part in the processes of the world, but the temporal world reacts to the nature of God, and this reaction Whitehead calls God's "consequent nature." Through this reaction the errors and omissions of the past may be taken up, corrected, and transcended. Taking account of the actual process of history, God is "not before creation, but *with* all creation." God, for Whitehead, does not create the world, He saves it, or, more accurately, "he is the poet of the world, with tender patience leading it by his vision of truth, beauty, and goodness."[14] Here Whitehead seems to echo Peirce's claim that "religion is poetry, but poetry completed."

## 2. William James: The Right to Believe

William James (1842-1910) was the son of a deeply reflective, mystically inclined man of letters, Henry James, Sr., and brother of the famous novelist, Henry James. From his childhood on, William was surrounded by educated people and later became a cultural influence himself, not only in America but also in Europe, where he was a frequent visitor. Besides studying in European universities, he obtained an M.D. degree from Harvard Medical School. At first an instructor in physiology at Harvard, James branched out into psychology and then into philosophy. He was a brilliant teacher, and his tenure as professor falls into the golden age of Harvard's philosophy department, which, besides James, had on its staff Josiah Royce, George Santayana, and for a brief period, C.S. Peirce as well. In 1890 James published his famous *Principles of Psychology*. His other writings were mainly in the form of public lectures and essays and exerted a strong influence both at the time of their presentation and after publication. These writings include: *The Will to Believe* (1896), *Varieties of Religious Experience* (1902), *Pragmatism* (1907), *A Pluralistic Universe* (1909), *The Meaning of Truth* (1909), and *Essays in Radical Empiricism* (1912). It was James who was responsible for the spread of pragmatism. He developed it along his own and, in many ways novel, lines. His voluminous correspondence with prominent thinkers all over the world, published later by R.B. Perry, provides a rich panorama of the intellectual life of that period.

One short paragraph from James' *Principles of Psychology* indicates his basic position not only within pragmatism but also with regard to the history of philosophy. "Sensible objects are thus either our realities or the tests of our realities. Conceived objects must show sensible effects or else be disbelieved. And the effects, even though reduced to relative unreality when their causes come to view (as heat, which molecular vibrations made unreal), are yet the things on which our knowledge of the causes rests. Strange mutual dependence this, in which their appearance needs the reality in order to exist, but the reality needs the appearance in order to be known!'' [15]

The last sentence is an obvious echo of Kant. James is saying that in order to have a real existence, sensations or sensible appearances of things must have an independent underpinning, which Kant called the thing-in-itself. Yet, without the sensible appearance, that underlying reality would never be known. In other words, all knowledge has to fall back on sensible experience. Kant said that concepts without percepts are empty, and Peirce agreed that all concepts have to show their passports at the gate of perception. James also insists that conceived objects must have sensible effects. ''A conception, to prevail, must *terminate*, in the world of orderly sensible experience.''

But James' Kantianism has a characteristically individualistic twist. Reality for him is very generous in the modes of its appearance. It cannot be known directly, of course. Here, James joins Peirce in accepting Kant's idealistic proviso: all knowledge is mind-dependent. But whereas Kant and Peirce were inclined to interpret this dependence in terms of general logical and scientific frameworks, subject to public verification and testable in the long run by the community of investigators, James saw a possibility of individual variations on the theme, of *personal* paths to truth. This can be seen in the very way in which James sees the relation between pragmatism and truth. ''Grant an idea or belief to be true, what concrete difference will its being true make in anyone's actual life?'' Although pragmatism, for James, answers this question in terms of validation, corroboration, and verification, he also insists that truth *happens* to an idea, it *becomes* true. Its *veri-fication* means that it is *made true* by events. What are these events? They are events in a person's experience. If an idea makes a difference in ''anyone's actual life,'' truth happens to that idea.

Thus, the drift of James' pragmatism is distinctly individualistic and pluralistic. Although he is aware that this generous and accommodating conception of truth may raise some serious questions—for instance, the question of the existence of other minds, or the question, whether it does not drive him into the arms of solipsism—James is willing and ready to face such objections. Is it true that pragmatism, being concerned only with a knower's experience, precludes knowing *another person's* gladness? It is not true, answers James, if the belief in the real existence of the other person's gladness works in the believer ''the fuller sum of satisfactions.'' This means that the denial of a person's gladness as having independent existence would not yield as much satisfaction as its affirmation. This belief would result in postulating a world which is cold, dull, and heartless. Truly, belief in such a world could not be satisfying.

James is also of the opinion that the subjectivity/objectivity issue is a muddle
and that it could be overcome or eliminated by looking at it pragmatically.
Why should one presume that our subjective feelings and satisfactions cannot
yield "objective" truth? If they fit into and agree with the person's subsequent
thoughts, feelings, and actions, they get as much verification as they need.
In fact, this is the kind of verification that is needed in order to give these
beliefs validity. The demand that they be tested abstractly instead of concretely
is mystifying to James. "If our critics have any definite idea of a truth more
objectively grounded than the kind we propose, why do they not show it more
accurately?" James concludes his argument by finding a support for it in
Hegel's example of a man who wanted fruit but nonetheless rejected cherries,
pears, and grapes. Hegel's man would be satisfied only with fruit in the
abstract, and so would the critics of pragmatism, thought James.

As for solipsism, James agreed that pragmatism, seen in a certain way,
may be compatible with solipsism, in the sense that it does not prejudge any
metaphysical doctrines. One of the merits of pragmatism is that it is purely
epistemological and can be used as a foundation for most diverse metaphysics.
But James sees these further uses as less important. As long as pragmatism
is capable of testing truths which are relevant to the situation and to the
subsequent utility, it can fill "the cup of concreteness to the brim for us."

At times James speaks as if the highly individualistic uses of pragmatism
were not very likely. "As we human beings are constituted in point of fact,
we find that to believe in other men's minds, in independent physical realities,
in past events, in eternal logical relations, is satisfactory."[16] Furthermore,
"framed as we are our egoism craves above all things inward sympathy and
recognition, love and admiration."[17] This is why some states of affairs would
not be satisfactory, among them an automatic sweetheart, which, although
undistinguishable from a maiden who laughs, talks, blushes, and nurses us,
is not considered to have a soul. Thus, it is our *common* human nature and
its demands that set limits to what we can accept as true.

James believed that the universe allows the needs of human nature to be
satisfied. His position can be understood better if we see him as supplementing
Kant's logical conditions for knowledge with emotional conditions. James
himself puts it most explicitly. "The *fons et origo* of all reality, whether from
the absolute or the practical point of view, is thus subjective, is ourselves.
But, as thinkers with emotional reaction, we give what seems to us a still
higher degree of reality to whatever things we select and emphasize and turn
to *with a will*."[19] This is why the concept of the will to believe is of great
importance in James' epistemology. Recalling Locke's view of the mind as
a *tabula rasa*, we may contrast it with James' voluntaristic, expectant *tabula*.
"Any relation to our mind at all, in the absence of a stronger relation, suffices
to make an object real . . . . The mind was waiting for just some such object

to make its spring upon."[19] Mind, for James, is something essentially active and projective, fitting the world to its demand. The world does not disparage these demands; it does not deny them their right to satisfaction. James had a great admiration for Bergson, possibly because for James, reality, especially human reality, exhibits all the characteristics of *élan vital*, a vital urge. Our stance is not indifferent and neutral. Objects of our experience must appear both interesting and important. And "whatever excites and stimulates our interest is real."

This is why the concreteness of perceptions has a primacy over the abstractions of concepts. James agreed with Bergson that percepts are continuous, whereas concepts are discrete. Concepts are unchangeable, and therefore, "the 'eternal' kind of being which they enjoy is inferior to the temporal kind, because it is so static and schematic and lacks so many characters which temporal reality possesses."[20] The concepts, of course, introduce meaning into our experience. Without them, the flux of perception would *mean* nothing, it would be what it immediately is. But the way the experience is cut up by concepts is completely ideal, and here our wills make their contribution. Conceptual discernment is almost limitless, and in the multiplying of our linguistic distinctions, different universes of thought arise. "By those *whats* we apperceive all our *thises*. Percepts and concepts interpenetrate and melt together, impregnate and fertilize each other."[21] James also said that "The universal and the particular parts of the experience are literally immersed in each other, and both are indispensable."[22]

Pragmatism emphasizes the functional, instrumental, evaluative role of concepts. James did not deny that they also have what he called a "substantive content." That content could be contemplated while passively attending to the concept, or while having a corresponding image. But even such words as "triangle" or "cosine" do not merely evoke in us certain images; they also have a functional value as leading our discourse elsewhere, beyond themselves. According to James, there are also words in which the substantive concept is minimal and the evaluative dominant: "God," "cause," "number," "substance," and "soul"—these are James' examples. The more important part of the significance of each of these concepts is "the consequences to which it leads." These consequences may lie in the way they determine our further thoughts or actions. "Whoever has a clear idea of these knows effectively what the concept practically signifies, whether its substantive content be interesting in its own right or not."[23]

In the course of making his Pragmatic Rule clear, James again allows an individualistic interpretation of it. For he says: "If you claim that any idea is true, assign at the same time some difference that its being true will make *in some possible person's history*, and we shall know not only just what you are really claiming but also how important an issue it is, and how to go to work to verify the claim'' (italics added).[24] But, as we have seen, for the most part James seems to assume that concepts do provide common meanings to all possible interpreters. Without concepts we could not handle (his word) the perceptual flux. "We *harness* perceptual reality in concepts in order to drive it better to our ends." Concepts form a topographic system informing us of the whereabouts of our world and opening up practical perspectives for action. The primordial utility of the conceiving faculty, says James, is to adapt us to an immense environment. It should not be surprising to find in James' philosophy a great deal of evolutionary language.

Service to life is the main function of both percepts and concepts. James thinks that there is an analogy between percepts and touch on the one hand, and concepts and sight on the other. Perceptions are like touching, and conceptions are like seeing. Vision, as Berkeley had already observed, prepares us for contacts which are yet far off. But James would not sell short "the world of optical splendor," which is interesting and valuable in its own right. Furthermore, he seems to believe that a translation of particulars into abstractions helps us to become more idealistic. Concrete instances may appear sordid and repellant, but translated into causes such as antislavery and democracy, they become inspiring "momentous" issues. A translation of percepts into ideas may deepen our sense of life's values. Touched by a particular person's suffering, one may embark on a crusade against *all* suffering.

James thought that pragmatism assigns to concepts an epistemological status which combines "logical realism with an otherwise empiricist mode of thought." The empiricist mode of thought, according to him, "treats concrete percepts as primordial and concepts as of secondary origin." Nevertheless, the extreme nominalism of such thinkers as James Mill, who believed that things referred to by the same name have nothing in common except the name, was unpalatable to James. He wanted to affirm that we are justified in saying that two objects are the same if their comparison in perception reveals no difference and if substituted one for the other in certain operations, they yield the same result. Although the perceived shades of whiteness can exhibit some impurities, for example, we can still assign to the word "white" an unalterable meaning. We are capable of mental linguistic legislation, James appears to be saying, which is sufficient for all practical purposes. The color quality to which the word "white" always refers may not be available physically, but it is available mentally. "The impossibility of isolating and fixing this quality physically is irrelevant, so long as we can isolate and fix it mentally, and decide that whenever we say 'white,' that identical quality, whether applied rightly or wrongly, is what we shall be held to mean."[25]

This view seems to put James in the camp of epistemological conceptualists, especially since he goes on to say that many other ideas we make use of—

zeros, infinites, forces—are defined "only conceptually." Not all is clear in this position, and other contemporary philosophers will address themselves to this issue once more from another direction. In a way James anticipates this direction by sensing that language at some points sets limits to distinctions while at the same time making distinctions possible. The phrase to be noted in the last quotation from James is "whether applied rightly or wrongly." It suggests that the notion of using words rightly or wrongly depends, as Wittgenstein will say later, on the fact that we "agree in judgments." For human beings to *say* that something is true or false, they must agree in the language they use.

Seen from the pragmatic perspective, the perennial philosophical debate over the relationship of minds to bodies is misconceived, according to James. In later years of his life James moved toward a position he called "neutral monism." Reality allows characterizations from various perspectives. The same event can be seen from a mental side or a material side, and both views may be correct. This was not a new position for James. Even in the *Principles of Psychology* he thought that our universe is a pluralistic one, or that it contains subuniverses, each of which possesses "its own special and separate style of existence." (1) There is the subuniverse of qualities—heat, color, sound, and forces—life, chemical affinity, gravity, electricity. (2) There is the subuniverse of scientific theory with its various laws of nature. (3) There is a subuniverse of ideal relations—logical, mathematical, ethical, or aesthetic. Reality is a continuous flux of experience and permits alternative descriptions; it is not reducible to either matter or consciousness. But the importance and value of conscious phenomena are evident to those who undergo them. Indeed, as we have seen, the experiencers' wills may make a crucial difference to the quality of their experience.

For example, the issue of determinism and free will has a solution on the pragmatic basis. Neither determinism nor free will can be *proved*. Determinists do not have evidence for the claim that everything that happens *had* to happen that way. Their rejection of indeterminism—the view that the universe is not like perfect, interlocking machines, but rather contains some amount of "loose play"—is based on the view that the notion of chance is something positive. But it is not the case that to admit chance or indeterminism is to embrace irrationalism, the belief that the world is essentially chaotic. The concept of chance is essentially negative, merely indicating that the causes of an event could not be predicted from available data.

Since from the metaphysical point of view the issue is deadlocked, it is rational for us to decide it on what James calls "the passional grounds." The belief in free will is more satisfying than in determinism. It is also supported by our judgments of regret and of our moral judgments in general. They furnish a sufficient reason for rejecting the unprovable assumption of determinism.

As in all situations, when the human will is brought into play, the decision to believe or not to believe in free will is personal. Each individual must ask himself how the belief fits into his experience and whether it helps to make sense of this experience and to make it more satisfactory. Nothing in the universe can deny this right to believe.

A similar situation obtains with respect to religious beliefs. Here, too, real options exist. Indeed, there are some decisions we cannot escape, and in such situations our options are *forced*. Moreover, the contending alternatives must have some genuine appeal, or in other words, the options must be *live*. James believed that in his time a person living in a Christian country did not have the option of becoming a Muslim, that such an option was dead for him. In our time such an option may be live for many young people who are attracted to the "spirit of the East." In some situations the opportunity for choice must be seized, for that kind of opportunity will not come again. Such options James called "momentous."

A religious belief may become an option exhibiting these characteristics. If so, a person will be well advised to see which of the two alternatives, religion or atheism, will introduce more satisfaction into his life. James quotes with approval Professor Leuba's contention that "God is not known, He is not understood; He is used . . . . Does God exist? How does He exist? What is He? are so many irrelevant questions. Not God, but life, more life, a larger, richer, more satisfying life, is, in the last analysis, the end of religion. The love of life, at any and every level of development, is the religious impulse." [26] James believed that the doctrinal differences between the Stoic, the Christian, and the Buddhist saints do not affect the quality of their lives. Their feelings and conduct are indistinguishable. The subjective side of religious phenomena, without regard to the question of their truth, "should be classed among the most important biological functions of mankind," because of their extraordinary influence upon action and endurance.

A religious belief, coupled with genuine moral earnestness, puts a subjective self in touch with a dimension which enhances and enlarges that self. "He becomes conscious that this higher part is co-terminous and continuous with a MORE of the same quality, which is operative in the universe outside of him, and which he can keep in working touch with, and in a fashion get on board of and save himself when all his lower being has gone to pieces in the wreck." [27] So it seems that the religious belief does not really create its object; it discovers it. But in some situations a belief *can* create its object. An ardent declaration of love may cause a genuine response in the beloved. The confident conviction that I can conquer the obstacle may provide that extra push that will put me within the reach of my objective. One brave impulse of an individual will set off a spark which will energize a whole group to a resistance against an unjust or criminal act. In all of those instances the will to believe makes a real difference to what actually happens. The idea believed in *becomes* true.

## 3. John Dewey: The Uses of Intelligence

John Dewey (1859-1952) was educated at the University of Vermont and at Johns Hopkins. His long career as a teacher of philosophy at the Universities of Michigan, Chicago, and Columbia did not keep him from being strongly interested in social and political issues. While at Chicago he began experimenting with his new ideas of progressive education and put them into effect in an elementary school. His interest in educational issues broadened into an intense concern with all social issues — ethical, political, and legal. He traveled to Russia, China, and Japan, and his lectures in the Orient made a strong impression. He was the chairman of a commission inquiring into the charges against Trotsky at the Moscow trials, which resulted in the publication of a book entitled *Not Guilty*. From Dewey's pen came numerous philosophical books which articulated his version of pragmatism: *The Influence of Darwin on Philosophy* (1910), *Democracy and Education* (1916), *Human Nature and Conduct* (1922), *Experience and Nature* (1925), *The Quest for Certainty* (1929), *Philosophy and Civilization* (1931), *Art as Experience* (1934), *Logic: The Theory of Inquiry* (1938), and *Theory of Valuation* (1939). In order to have a better basis for his work on aesthetics, *Art as Experience*, Dewey became seriously interested in painting. He remained active and productive to the very end of his life. Dewey was one of the few philosophers who could write closely argued books in a living room while surrounded by playing children.

Dewey's role in the development of American pragmatism was fittingly described by himself in the early parts of his book *Philosophy and Civilization*. In it Dewey traces the development of the doctrine with which he was willing to identify himself and to which he wanted to make his own contribution. According to him, "Peirce was above all a logician, whereas James was an educator and humanist and wished to force the general public to realize that certain problems, certain philosophical debates, have a real importance for mankind, because the beliefs which they bring into play lead to very different modes of conduct." James was still preoccupied with philosophical problems generated by the war between science and religion, and he wanted to make a case for the validity of tender-minded personal values in a world where tough-minded scientific objectivity was becoming dominant. Peirce, on the other hand, was all for science, for a laboratory method in solving all issues. Dewey also found the promise of science alluring, but he believed that Peirce's

pragmatic logic needed to be applied on a much broader front and in a much
more thoroughgoing manner.

Dewey shared with Peirce the evolutionary picture of the world, although
he found no use for elaborate speculative cosmology. Darwin's work was
sufficient to show that life steadily advances into novelty and that adaptation
to a changing environment is the constant task for all living beings. The drama
of this adaptation is sufficient unto our days; it can occupy without remainder
all our energies and capacities. The most important human capacity is
intelligence, a term Dewey much preferred to the old-fashioned concept of
mind. One of the reasons why he favored "intelligence" over "mind" was
that the latter term encourages a "spectator" view of knowledge. Moreover,
the rationalists and the idealists invariably tended to lift mind from the real
processes going on in the world, thus creating for themselves the insoluble
problem of interaction, of the way mind and matter can influence each other.
This hopeless tendency can be avoided, believed Dewey, if one comes up
with a wholly different account of what knowledge is. The pragmatists are
on the right track because they see in the operation of human intelligence
an *instrument* of change.

This is why Dewey preferred to call his philosophy *instrumentalism*.
"Instrumentalism is an attempt to establish a precise, logical theory of concepts,
of judgments and inferences in their various forms, by considering primarily
how thought functions in the experimental determinations of future consequences. That is to say, it attempts to establish universally recognized
distinctions and rules of logic by deriving them from their reconstructive or
mediative function ascribed to reason." [28] One must take the words "reconstructive" and "mediative" literally in order to understand Dewey's position.
Thought does not get started, the intelligence is not engaged, until an organism
finds itself in a bind, "up against it," or "lost in the woods." One must
be in what Dewey called a "problematic situation." There must be genuine
perplexity, confusion, uncertainty. Life provides a great many of these
situations. The organism experiences an incompleteness, a blockage, a lack
which it seeks to overcome, and thus *inquiry* (another of Dewey's favorite
terms) may begin.

The puzzlement initiates a survey of what the situation is, of separating
those elements that remain stable and unproblematic from those that are the
source of the difficulty. Next comes the essential contribution of intelligence,
a leap toward a hypothesis, an imaginative reconstruction of the situation such
that the elements now blocking further smooth functioning of the organism
will be rearranged and fitted into the stable elements. The hypothesis is then
put to use, and if effective, it leads to the completion of the initial tendency
of the organism, and the problematic situation disappears.

The logical steps in a typical inquiry could be summarized as follows: (1) problematic situation, (2) ascertaining of data and identification of the problem, (3) forming a hypothesis, (4) testing the hypothesis, and (5) completion. Dewey illustrates these states by various examples. The ditch-crossing problem can be taken as typical. You walk across a field toward a destination and suddenly your progress is blocked by a stream. You stop and survey the situation: the stream is too wide to jump and too deep to wade. A short distance away lies a log. Is it long enough? You try to place it across the ditch. It reaches the other bank. You walk across, satisfied, and soon forget that particular intellectual and physical exertion, and are ready again to be engaged by other problematic episodes.

For Dewey, reflection has its home in practical situations and is explicitly adaptive in character and function. In spite of the fact that it is often indirect and complicated, "it has its origin in biological adoptive behavior and the ultimate function of its cognitive aspect is a prospective control of the conditions of the environment. The function of intelligence is therefore not that of copying the objects of the environment, but rather a taking account of the way in which more effective and more profitable relations with these objects may be established in the future."[29]

Dewey's instrumentalism assigns a new epistemological status to propositions and judgments. Propositions are not merely something entertained by the mind; they enter effectively into reconstructing and transforming the objective situation: "the proposition is itself a factor in the completion of the situation, in carrying it forward to its conclusion." Thus, when I judge that I should see a physician, I create conditions which make possible a satisfactory completion of the situation in which I find myself; I am aware both of the disadvantages of remaining in ill health and of the prospect of recovering due to the steps taken on my behalf by the physician. Therefore, my judgment that I ought to see him, when put into effect, is a concrete factor in the resolution of my difficulty.

The emphasis is on the *mediating* role of intelligence. Thus, instrumentalism means a rejection of mechanism on the one hand, and of romantic-idealistic utopianism on the other. It denies strict determinism because intelligent thought and action do make a difference in the course of events. But it also insists on attention to proximate details in order to arrange them in a desirable order. Practical ideals have nothing to do with either obscurantist emotional optimism or utopianism. "It is the recognition of the increased liberation and intelligent control of the course of events which are achieved through accurate discovery."

The notion of completeness as the aim of inquiry is also not an abstract, frozen entity for Dewey. Completeness is a relative matter, depending on the ends pursued. Given certain ends, certain means will be appropriate, and it is the task of intelligence to put the ends and means in a proper relation to each other. It is never a matter of exhaustiveness, of taking all possibilities into account, but only a matter of relative adequacy. If we include too much, we may include irrelevant data, thus vitiating our attempt to arrive at an intelligent judgment. But a right assessment of the situation leading to its satisfactory completion justifies our calling a judgment which leads up to it, a *true* judgment. It remains a mere hypothesis until it results in action. But then, "The event or issue of such action *is* the truth or falsity of the judgment."

Dewey is in essential agreement with Peirce's view that all thought is of the nature of signs. Hence, he is unwilling to ascribe cognitive significance to a mere contemplation of a datum. Percepts are only *materials* for propositions and judgments; they have no cognitive status in themselves. They may be, of course, *conclusions* from other data antecedently experienced, but in either case *inference* is necessary for a judgment to take place. Thus, the exercise of intelligence involves a transaction, a movement from data to conclusions.

In the ordinary, normal course of experience we take perceptions as signs of things to follow; we are guided by them. Dewey agrees with James that percepts do have a "surplus," a cognitively unused content which may attract our attention. Thus, a child walking down the street with his father may "take in" more from the appearance of a neon sign than does the father, for whom the sign means simply: there is a restaurant. So it is true that in his idle curiosity the child experiences more in this context than his father does. This does not mean, however, as Dewey observes, "that he is making more propositions, but only that he is getting more material for possible propositions." In other words, the child is in an aesthetic and not in a cognitive attitude. Interestingly enough, Dewey suggests that the so-called simple, thoroughly defined data of perception are not the starting point of discernment, but usually are themselves "the last refinement of perception," requiring intentionally and experimentally determined procedures for their isolation. He appears to agree with Peirce that many of supposedly intuitive, directly apprehended ideas, such as the idea of self, for instance, are in fact inferred from other ideas.

Dewey also believed that pragmatism enables us to give a true explanation of the phenomena of perceptual illusion. Take the familiar bent-stick-in-the-water phenomenon. How is one to explain it? The wrong inference from the visual perception, namely, the expectation that the stick is bent, is due to our failure to realize that we are dealing with a different medium of light transmission. The inference is correct in one medium, but wrong in another. Our mistake, then, derives from a habit which persists even though the situation is different. We overlook the different medium and allow the habit to put intelligence to sleep. The same thing happens when we see the word "pain" and, not realizing that it is given in the context of French language, make a wrong inference about its meaning.

Dewey's view of perception is in some ways reminiscent of Hume (who also emphasized the habitual association of ideas), and it illustrates one of the key points of his pragmatism. Data, whether perceptual or valuational, are only raw material, a starting point for judgment. Dewey rejects the view that any feeling or attitude, state of being, or state of mind is valu*able*. It may be valued, but this does not mean that it is *worth* valuing. The fact that we desire something does not mean that it is desirable. To declare something valuable or desirable is to make a judgment about its connection with either its antecedents or its consequences. Once more, the exercise of intelligence is found in judgment, in inference. The connections of an experience with its causes or consequences are to be established in the same way as is the truth of all other practical judgments. If our likings and attitudes lead to satisfying experiences, then they can be said to possess objective value. Feelings are notoriously fleeting, capricious, and volatile. If we were to base our judgments on them, we could not control our lives.

Emotions also do not show their significance offhand. It depends on their connection to the circumstances in which they come into play. Consider fear, for example. Under some conditions it may be cowardice: under others, reverence; and under still others, superstition. We must examine how emotional impulses are interwoven with one another and with the objective circumstances in which they occur in order to appraise their nature and value. One of the functions of intelligence is to guard us against blind impulses as well as to liberate us from the stronghold of petrified habits. Alertness, vigilance, and responsiveness to new conditions characterize a mature, truly developed intelligence.

The realm of art is no exception. Although here the "consummatory experience" is predominant, it is not passive. It is receptive and involves surrender, but this surrender, this yielding to an intense experience, involves self-control. "For to perceive," Dewey observes, "a beholder must *create* his own experience. Without an act of recreation the object is not perceived as a work of art." In creating and enjoying art there is an interplay of in-going energy, where the object of attention is seen in relation to other vital aspects of human existence. There is a carry-over into and continuity with other experiences—practical, emotional, and intellectual—which the art object merely helps to heighten and underscore. In other words, an aesthetic experience is an *integrating* experience, connecting art and life. For this reason art should become a much more integral part of our life; it should not be confined to museums, which in effect function as mausoleums. All life should become more complete, more vibrant, and art should not be compartmentalized and separated from our daily existence. If it is viewed as an end in itself, it will soon cease to affect us vitally.

The biological, evolutionary picture of the human situation leads Dewey to also take an open-ended view of desirable ends of action. Attention to the context will show us that there are no unvarying ends which man pursues. Instead, we have what Dewey calls the *means-ends continuum*, whereby means can conceivably become ends in themselves, and ends in turn can function as means toward further ends. Dewey saw in Darwin's work an effective demolition of the view that life cherishes some unchangeable forms or patterns. Organic species themselves are changeable, and since the entire life process is organic, it is prejudice and a survival of outmoded philosophies that cause us to be constant in our choice of objectives to pursue. Life is much more varied and creative than that, especially when it is guided by liberated intelligence. All progress constitutes a continuous effort to transvaluate prior values. To that extent Dewey is in agreement with Nietzsche. "Nietzsche . . . would have been within the limits of wisdom, if he confined himself to the assertion that all judgment, in the degree in which it is critically intelligent, is a transvaluation of prior values."[30]

Dewey's account of possible human satisfactions is traditional enough; he speaks of harmony, adjustment, peace, and welfare. These are thoroughly concrete concepts, tied to biological needs and physical well-being. But there are also expansiveness and hope about these multiple objectives. Furthermore, they are to be pursued not in individual isolation, but by *common* effort, utilizing scientific, publicly verifiable observations and experiments. Dewey agrees with Peirce that truth is public and that it will more likely be attained if the inquiry proceeds on a broad front, with all channels of communication open. Problems of society can best be solved by applying the methods of social engineering. A Scientific approach calls for collaboration and discussion; a problem is more likely to be solved by a committee than by an isolated individual. The American faith in the democratically conceived community effort, in voluntary organizations and associations, has its counterpart in Dewey's pragmatism. Pragmatists proposed a radical way of breaking free from the hold of dualism. Strongly influenced by the idea of evolution, it emphasized the *mediating* role of mind or intelligence. A more recent pragmatist, C.I. Lewis (1883-1964), believed that the evolutionary spirit of pragmatism could accommodate itself even to Kant's fundamental insight that knowledge involves some *a priori* structures of the mind. The only modification required, argued Lewis, is to recognize that these structures may also change in the process of experience.

> *At the bottom of all science and all knowledge are categories and definitive concepts which represent fundamental habits of thought and deep-lying attitudes which the human mind has taken in the light of its total*

*experience. But a new and wider experience may bring about some alteration of these attitudes, even though by themselves they dictate nothing as to the content of experience, and no experience can conceivably prove them invalid.*[31]

For all pragmatists, mind is the way in which the human organism copes with its environment. The display of mind is a special kind of *activity* by means of which the transition from one state of affairs to another takes place. In what is perhaps Dewey's most extreme formulation of pragmatism, the function of mind is fundamentally instrumental; thinking is on a par with walking, running, or swimming. Because of its immanence in all other natural human activities, thinking is *effective*; it transforms problematic situations into successful resolutions.

Peirce and Dewey in particular looked to science to provide us with models for resolving our difficulties and perplexities. They believed that the role of the mind is to integrate adequately all aspects of the human organism, so as to provide for its proper orientation in, and adjustment to, its environment. A human being is an organism, an integrated whole, and the task of intelligence is to make the integration as full and as harmonious as possible. If it is true that every philosopher is either a Platonist or an Aristotelian, then there is no doubt that all pragmatists are Aristotelians. They think of philosophy as enabling us to fulfill our functions in our natural setting, and they have little regard for a merely contemplative stance. Their world view is dynamic, activist, optimistic, and has little use for what Dewey calls "monkish virtues." Their conception of human possibilities is generous enough, excluding neither art nor religious attitude. Both artistic activity and a religious orientation can and should serve a fuller integration and happiness on the individual and social levels.

It may be surprising to suggest that Dewey and Spinoza have much in common. Yet in spite of great differences regarding the ultimate meaning of things, both philosophers advocate a total, natural harmony for a human person. Dewey, like Spinoza, believed that human good is dependent on the ability to see the true connections among things, to trace the antecedents and consequences of each event. "Enjoyments that issue from conduct by insight into relations have a meaning and validity due to the way in which they are experienced. Such enjoyments are not repented of; they generate no aftertaste bitterness. Even in the midst of direct enjoyment, there is a sense of validity, of authorization, which intensifies the enjoyment."[32] This is Dewey's version of what it means to experience Spinoza's active emotions. The developmental, organismic picture at work here is, of course, very strongly evident in Hegel. Dewey began his philosophical career as an ethusiastic Hegelian, but soon concluded that a more naturalistic, scientific view of human intelligence is needed to revitalize philosophy and its role in civilization.

## Questions

1. For what purpose did Peirce formulate his "pragmatic maxim?" What are its essential features? How is it related to his theory of signs and to other aspects of his philosophy?

2. What were the two ways in which Peirce defined reality? Are they in conflict with each other?

3. What was Peirce's doctrine of the categories? How would you compare his categories to those of Aristotle? Of Kant?

4. Why did Peirce object to James' interpretation of pragmatism? What are the differences between their versions of pragmatism?

5. What did James mean by "neutral monism"? Does this doctrine connect with his notion of "pluralistic universe" and with his conception of religion?

6. What was Dewey's view of the role of human intelligence? How is it expressed in his theory of inquiry? What are the salient features of that theory?

7. Do you agree with Dewey that an aesthetic experience is an *integrating* experience and that art should be connected with other aspects of life?

8. Which of the pragmatists show some indebtedness to Hegel? In what respects do they differ from Hegel?

9. Is the idea of evolution at work in American pragmatism? In what ways is it reflected in the philosophies of Peirce and Dewey?

## Notes

[1] C.S. Peirce, *Collected Papers,* edited by Charles Hartshorne and Paul Weiss, the Belknap Press of Harvard University Press, 1934, 5.479.
[2] *Ibid.,* 5.430.
[3] *Ibid.,* 5.430.
[4] *Ibid.,* 5.311.
[5] *Ibid.,* 5.314.
[6] *Ibid.,* 5.233.
[7] *Ibid.,* 5.431.
[8] *Ibid.,* 5.433.
[9] *Ibid.,* 5.419-420.
[10] *Ibid.,* 1.615. Reprinted by permission.
[11] *Ibid.,* 6.502. Reprinted by permission
[12] Herbert Spencer, *First Principles,* Par. 145, London: Watts, 1946.

[13] This "translation" can be found in P.G. Tait's review of Sir Edmund Beckett's book *On the Origin of the Laws of Nature* (*Nature,* July 17, 1879). The reviewer attributes it to the mathematician Kirkman. William James makes a reference to this "re-description" of Spencer's principle of evolution in his own, unsigned, criticism of Spencer in *Nation* **30** (1880), p. 397.

[14] A.N. Whitehead, *Process and Reality,* Cambridge: Cambridge University Press, 1929, P. 490.

[15] William James, *Principles of Psychology,* New York: Holt, Rinehart & Winston, 1890, Vol. II, p. 301.

[16] William James, *The Meaning of Truth,* New York: Longmans, Green & Co., 1909, p. 192.

[17] *Ibid.,* p. 189.

[18] William James, *Principles of Psychology,* Vol. II, pp. 296-97.

[19] *Ibid.,* p. 299.

[20] William James, *Some Problems of Philosophy,* New York: Longmans, Green & Co., 1911, p. 101.

[21] *Ibid.,* pp. 52.-53.

[22] *Ibid.,* p. 107.

[23] *Ibid.,* p. 59.

[24] *Ibid.,* p. 61.

[25] *Ibid.,* p. 105.

[26] William James, *Varieties of Religious Experience,* New York: Mentor books, 1958, p. 382.

[27] *Ibid.,* p. 384.

[28] John Dewey, *Philosophy and Civilization,* New York: Minton, Balch & Co., 1931, p. 26.

[29] *Ibid.,* p. 30.

[30] John Dewey, "The Logic of Judgments of Practise," *Journal of Philosophy* (1915), reprinted in *Pragmatic Philosophy,* edited by Amelie Rorty, New York: Doubleday, 1966, p. 234.

[31] C.I. Lewis, "A Pragmatic Conception of the Priori," *The Journal of Philosophy* (1923), p. 176.

# Chapter Eleven

# Logical
# Empiricism

## 1. Bertrand Russell: Logical Atomism

Bertrand Russell, born in 1872, belonged to a titled family. His grandfather, Earl Russell, was an eminent British statesman who introduced the famous liberal Reform Bill of 1832 in Parliament and who later served twice as Prime Minister. Orphaned at the age of three Bertrand lived with his grandmother and received a thorough education from private tutors. He entered Cambridge, where he studied mostly mathematics and philosophy and was elected a Fellow of Trinity College. Because of his opposition to the continuation of World War I, he lost that position and in 1918 was jailed for libeling American troops. Russell's strong liberal, often iconoclastic, views on politics and morals frequently put him at odds with society. In 1961, at the age of 89, he was jailed again, this time for participating in a nuclear disarmament sit-in demonstration in Trafalgar Square. At that time the bulk of Russell's energy was directed toward securing world peace and attacking those whom he believed to be leading the world to its third, and most probably final, war. Russell was then a world renowned figure. He was a Fellow of the Royal Society, a recipient of the Order of Merit, and a winner, in 1951, of the Nobel Prize for literature.

Although he wrote on many subjects, his chief contributions were made in philosophy. With A.N.Whitehead he produced a monumental work, *Principia Mathematica* (1910-1913), which showed the logical underpinnings of mathematics. Russell presented his philosophical views, which changed markedly as he developed them, and his reflections on various matters in 60 books and countless articles. His books include *Our Knowledge of the External World* (1914), *The Analysis of Mind* (1921), *An Inquiry Into Meaning and Truth* (1940), and *Human Knowledge: Its Scope and Limits* (1948). Although logic and theory of knowledge were Russell's chief philosophical preoccupations, his prolific writings address themselves to problems in ethics, psychology, education, economics, science, and political and international affairs. His *History of Philosophy*, written in the United States during World War II, has been widely read. Russell died in 1970, having lived almost a century, active and productive to the very end.

In his student days in Cambridge, Russell was under the influence of Hegelian philosophy. In England that philosophy had its own exponents and differed in some ways from the German version of Absolute Idealism. Nevertheless, the Hegelian motto that the truth is the whole dominated English philosophical idealism as well. The dominant thinker of the English school was F.H. Bradley, who published his views in a book entitled *Appearance and Reality* (1893). For Bradley, access to reality was provided by logic, by the mind's ability to make judgments. When you examine closely even the most elementary propositions from the logical point of view, you will discover, claimed Bradley, a disconcerting and startling fact, namely, that we cannot talk about isolated things or events. Suppose you are standing under a tree and say: "The blossom is white." Are you describing some particular, isolated fact? This is not so clear. "Blossom" means not only this particular blossom that you are looking at, but many others as well. Many blossoms are not white; they may be pink or yellow. To make sure that you refer to *this* blossom you would have to say other things about it, perhaps mention its size, location, fragrance, etc. But each of these attempts to pin down the object of which you are speaking would make use of general words, each of which is applicable to other objects as well. However, if this is the case, you could never succeed in securing uniqueness of reference. You would have to mention more and more qualities and relations relevant to your quest for identification, but this quest could not be completed until the whole of reality was introduced.

Moreover, the form of the simple subject-predicate sentence is logically puzzling. When we say "The blossom is white," we seem to be making a statement of identity, or at least this is what the word "is" appears to signify; but this is self-contradictory. "Blossom" and "white" are certainly not identical in meaning. Hence, for Bradley, the very attempt to speak of isolated things or events is logically impossible. Everything in the universe is related to everything else, and reality must somehow include all appearances. To *know* anything is to know *everything*.

By Russell's own account Bradley's books and McTaggart's lectures at Cambridge caused him to become a Hegelian. But he soon found himself questioning this approach to philosophy. He was stimulated by a similar rebellion by G.E. Moore, who began to ask whether the paradoxical conclusions of the idealists, such as, for instance, that time is unreal, should yield to such common-sense truths as that he had breakfast before he had lunch. The rejection of the idealist framework had for Moore and Russell a distinct flavor of emancipation. Russell himself described the dramatic nature of this breakaway:

> *Bradley argued that everything common sense believes in is mere appearance; we reverted to the opposite extreme, and thought that everything is real that common sense, uninfluenced by philosophy or theology, supposes real. With a sense of escaping from prison, we allowed ourselves to think that grass is green, that the sun and stars would exist if no one was aware of them, and also that there is a pluralistic timeless world of Platonic ideas. The world which had been thin and logical, suddenly became rich and varied and solid.* [1]

Russell's own alternative to the idealistic theory of knowledge took time to emerge from his "emancipation" and included his rejection of the initially accepted Platonic assumptions. In the course of struggling with various logical problems, he worked his way toward a view which he called "logical atomism," a comprehensive attempt to answer the question "What is there really?" To answer this question we need to reduce the apparent complexities of things to their basic components. What qualifies as basic? Certainly *things* do not, because things are complex entities, exhibiting many different characteristics which cannot be captured simultaneously in one description. In saying this, Russell already indicates that he will not accept the ordinary common-sense analysis of what we experience. By reaching beyond common sense he produced a metaphysical account, to which Russell saw no objections. To him, "the point of philosophy is to start with something so simple as not to seem worth stating, and to end with something so paradoxical that no one will believe it."

What needs to be analyzed, said Russell, are *facts*. That things in the world have various properties and stand in various relations to one another are *facts*, and these facts can be described in propositions. By "fact" Russell means "the kind of thing that makes a proposition true or false." He also says that a fact is the sort of thing that is expressed by a whole sentence, in contrast to names, which symbolize persons or things. "A name would be a proper symbol to use for a person; a sentence (or a proposition) is the proper symbol for a fact."

Most propositions describing facts are complex, as, for instance, the statement "It is raining." But some statements consist only of a *proper name* and a simple *predicate*. A simple predicate is one that cannot be analyzed into anything simpler, for example, "white." We can learn what "white" means only by direct acquaintance. A proposition which consists of only a proper name and a simple predicate Russell calls "atomic." Such propositions state *atomic facts*. Here, Russell challenges Bradley's claim that to predicate a quality of something is to distort our experience and to destroy the unity of that thing. The thing and its predicate fit together in a natural way, and the statement expressing this fitting together does not call for endless qualifications. To avoid the suggestion that the copula "is" points to the identity of subject and predicate, Russell proposed to employ his logical notation in which the predicate is placed next to the subject, *fx*, and thus avoids using the copula altogether. Bradley treated predicates or qualities as particular things and hence concluded that to identify two different things (subject and predicate) is to utter a self-contradiction. For Russell, however, a predicate such as "white" is a *general* object, ascribable to *particular* things. The same is true of relations. "London is north of Paris" describes an atomic fact, in which two objects identifiable by proper names are described by a general relational term "to the north of," *aRb*.

Qualities and relations, then, constitute separable particles which enable us to picture the world as an aggregate of separable items. Each of them needs to be known independently of the others. To understand sentences in which they occur we must first understand their particular components. Some of these we come to know directly, "by acquaintance." "You cannot understand the meaning of the word 'red' except through seeing red things. There is no other way in which it can be done."

Once we isolate atomic facts by means of atomic propositions, we can then describe complex facts by means of molecular propositions, which can be formed by means of logical connectives. Thus, two atomic facts, say, *x* is white; *y* is red, when related by a connective "and," form a molecular proposition "*x* is white and *y* is red." The truth of this proposition is a function of the truth of its constituent atomic propositions. If "*x* is white" is true, and "*y* is red" is false, their conjunction would be false; when both are true, the molecular proposition is also true. Other logical connectives, such as "or," "not," "if . . . then," reveal different ways of combining atomic propositions. Formal logic enables us to construct truth tables in which the different truth values of molecular propositions are shown to be functions of the truth values of their constituent atomic propositions.

The attraction of this analysis for Russell was that it appeared to establish a perfect correspondence between language and facts. He believed that "in a logically correct symbolism there will always be a certain fundamental identity of structure between a fact and the symbol for it."

*In a logically perfect language the words in a proposition would correspond one by one with the components of the corresponding fact, with the exception of such words as "or," "not," "if,"... "then" which have a different function. In a logically perfect language, there will be one word and no more for every simple object, and everything that is not simple will be expressed by a combination of words, by a combination derived, of course, from the words for the simple things that enter it, one word for each simple component. A language of that sort will be completely analytic, and will show at a glance the logical structure of the facts asserted or denied.* [2]

Russell adds that such a perfect language could not serve the purposes of daily life. It would be intolerably prolix, and, what is even more important, it would be "very largely private to one speaker." The latter admission will be discussed later.

In the midst of producing his reductive analysis Russell noted that it cannot be neat and simple. Not a man to hide difficulties, he proceeded to acknowledge them believing that they could be cleared up and remedied. He noted an important difference between *particular* facts, such as "This is white," and *general* facts, such as "All men are mortal." One might suppose that general facts could be represented as a conjunction of corresponding particular facts: "Adam is mortal," "Elijah is mortal," etc. But this will not quite do, observed Russell, because this conjunction still requires an additional proposition: "The list of men is exhaustive; these are all the men there are." Thus, the world cannot be described completely without reference to general facts in addition to particular ones. But neither Russell nor other logical atomists could produce a convincing analysis of general facts. Since general propositions cannot be treated as truth functions of atomic propositions, Russell felt compelled to admit general facts. But another possibility, suggested by Russell's contemporary, Frank Ramsey, was that general propositions should not be regarded as propositions at all. Instead, they express rules for using language, said Ramsey. Thus, the statement "Mercury is poisonous" is a rule telling us that we should treat anything which is mercury as poisonous.

There is also a problem with the notion of "logical particulars." According to Russell, they "stand entirely alone and are completely self-subsistent." In a sentence like "This is red," "this" functions as such a logical particular, and Russell pointed out that "this" played the same part in his philosophy as "substance" did in traditional philosophies. But he was not unaware of the problems to which the notion of substance gives rise. He discussed them in some detail in a later work, *A History of Philosophy:*

*"Substance" when taken seriously, is a concept impossible to free from difficulties. A substance is supposed to be a subject of properties, and to be something distinct from all its properties. But when we take away*

*the properties, and try to imagine the substance by itself, we find that
there is nothing left. To put the matter in another way: What distinguishes
one substance from another? Not differences of properties, for, according
to the logic of substance, difference of properties presupposes numerical
diversity between the substances concerned. Two substances, therefore,
must be just two, without being, in themselves, in any way distinguishable.
How, then, are we ever to find out that they are two?*[3]

The only positive role which the word "substance" plays, according to
Russell, is to provide "a convenient way of collecting events in bundles."
Conceived in any other way it becomes a "metaphysical mistake, due to
transference of the structure of sentences composed of subject and a predicate."

A further complication arose when Russell concluded that there must also
be negative facts. Propositions cannot be names, because they picture *two*
possible states of affairs. "To each fact there are two propositions, one true
and one false, and there is nothing in the nature of the symbol to show us
which is the true and which is the false one." Something in the world must
show us that a proposition is false. This suggests that Russell held a correspondence theory of truth. He was not sure, however, how his analysis should
treat negative facts, although he felt compelled to acknowledge them.

Still another difficulty presented itself when Russell came to deal with such
propositions as "James believes that it is raining." Is this a molecular
proposition? Here, the truth-function analysis does not work, because the truth
value of the entire proposition is independent of the truth value of "it is
raining." But if it is doubtful that the truth value of such a proposition is
a function of the truth value of its components, the atomic facts alone do not
enable us to determine the truth of some propositions. In his later works Russell
suggested that statements like "I believe" or "I think" could be reduced
to something like "it thinks in me" or "there is a thought in me." This would
enable us, presumably, to treat propositions like "I think that it is raining"
as truth functions of independently determinable facts. It also shows that Russell
was inclined toward a view analogous to William James's "neutral monism,"
according to which the distinction between mental and physical phenomena
can be made to disappear without embracing either idealism or materialism.
But the need to clarify these and other problems left the doctrine of logical
atomism far from being perspicuous and neat.

Clarity, however, is what Russell aimed at. In undertaking his reductive
analysis, he hoped to succeed where the traditional empiricists had failed.
Armed with the tools of the new logic, which he himself helped to forge,
he hoped to work out a thoroughgoing empiricism, in which the gross and
complex constituents of human experience would be reduced to their simplest
elements and thus give us a clear grasp of the facts—the true nature of reality.
Instead of speaking informally of words and "ideas," he would introduce

propositions and facts and would relate them in formal, logical ways. But Russell's admission that atomic facts by themselves do not account for general propositions seems to undermine the whole enterprise. Russell's theory does not succeed in telling us "what there is" or what "in the final analysis" exists in the universe. That he even tried to do so, that he attempted to formulate a doctrine about the "ultimate constituents of reality," shows that his objective was clearly metaphysical. Of course, Russell's metaphysics was to lean on experience, to use modern logical tools, and to harmonize with the empirical findings of natural science. Nevertheless, metaphysics as such was under attack from many directions, especially by a movement called logical positivism, to which we now turn.

## 2. The Vienna Circle: Logical Positivism

As Russell himself admitted, his views, collected under the general label of "logical atomism," were formulated in part under the influence of his pupil at Cambridge, Ludwig Wittgenstein. The extended discussions the two men held in the years prior to World War I were reflected in their subsequent writings, although after Wittgenstein left Cambridge to join the Austrian army in 1914, neither knew about the other's further philosophical development until after the war. Although Wittgenstein never became a member of the circle of philosophers who met in Vienna (and hence called themselves the Vienna Circle) in the early 1920s, he had personal contact with many of them and came to influence their views as well. Nevertheless, his own point of view, expressed in a book entitled *Tractatus Logico-Philosophicus*, published in 1921, differs significantly from both Russell's and those of the members of the Vienna Circle, as may be seen in the final section of this chapter.

Because of the views they espoused, the philosophers of the Circle became known as logical positivists. Besides its founder, Moritz Schlick, the Circle included Friedrich Waismann, Rudolf Carnap, Otto Neurath, Herbert Feigl, and Victor Kraft. Some well-known mathematicians participated in its discussions, among them Kurt Gödel and Hans Hahn. The Circle's influence spread abroad; its spokesman in Berlin was Hans Reichenbach, and in England its views were represented by A.J. Ayer. The latter spent some time in Vienna, meeting with the members of the Circle, and in 1936 he published a lucid and widely read statement of the logical positivist movement in his book, *Language, Truth, and Logic*. The following presentation of the doctrines of logical positivism is drawn mainly from Ayer's book.

The philosophical ancestor of the term "logical positivism" was a more general opposition to metaphysical thinking, articulated in the positivism of

August Comte (1798-1857). Following the lead of the *Philosophes*, his eighteenth-century predecessors in France who saw the universe freshly flooded with the light of reason, Comte proclaimed the advent of *positive* philosophy (most of his books contain the word "positive" in their titles). Comte's positivism aimed at bringing about a re-evaluation of human society by adopting methods which proved amazingly successful in physics, chemistry, physiology, biology, and zoology. He believed that the time was ripe for the emergence of a science that would put an end to the chaotic unscientific ways of organizing social frameworks, and he gave the name "sociology" to that science. Sociology, based on the scientifically oriented philosophy of positivism, would set about to reorganize society by taking into account and coordinating all of the accumulated scientific information, and this effort would result in peace, harmony, and order.

Comte defended his faith in science by reference to what he called "the law of the three stages." The intellectual development of the human race started with the *theological* stage, in which every phenomenon and every event was attributed to the work of divine powers. When the anthropocentric bias of that approach became evident, explanatory frameworks entered the *metaphysical* stage, in which explanations were offered in terms of principles describing impersonal and abstract forces, e.g., "Nature abhors a vacuum," or "Nature makes no leaps." Finally, the third stage, the *positivistic*, or scientific stage is ushered in by the realization that such principles are useless and should be replaced by a detailed scientific investigation of all phenomena.

Comte believed that his own era witnessed the emergence of the positivist stage, and he set himself the task of carrying the Scientific Revolution into the social, moral, political, and religious fields. In place of mythical divinities and metaphysical hypotheses, the concrete reality of humanity in its historical development should become the focus of concern and even of religious worship. Supernatural religion should give way to a religion of humanity in which the objects of worship are the achievements of the human race in its Progress dominated by Love and based on Order. Comte took his projected religion of humanity seriously enough to prepare a new calendar in which every day was dedicated to some humanitarian hero. Instead of apostles or saints, the persons to be celebrated during the successive days of the year were to be taken from the history of scientific and artistic achievements: Archimedes, Columbus, Galileo, Newton, Shakespeare, Bach, and 360 others. The place of God is taken by Humanity, which Comte called *Grand-Être*, the Supreme Being, and he thought of himself as the High Priest of the new religion.

Comte's positivistic philosophy is symptomatic of a new mood which began to sweep Europe during the nineteenth century, a mood which sought to revolutionize the human condition by relying on science. Philosophers were moved by the great expectation that radical changes in the social, political, and moral spheres could take place as a result of getting hold of a correct method. The dominant note of the logical positivism of the twentieth century was the reaffirmation of hostility to metaphysics. That hostility was already voiced by Kant, but he did not go far enough for the positivists. As they saw it, Kant merely contended that metaphysical knowledge is inaccessible to us. That was not radical enough. What remains to be shown, they claimed, was that propositions of metaphysics are *meaningless*—they are psuedopropositions or nonsense. No statement, said Ayer, "which refers to a reality transcending the limits of all possible sense-experience can possibly have any literal significance."

The trouble with the metaphysicians is that they do not bother to test whether their statements meet the criterion of meaningful discourse. The positivists proceeded to state what this criterion is and formulated the so-called "verification principle." "We say that a sentence is factually significant to any given person, if, and only if she knows how to verify the proposition it purports to express—this is, if she knows what observations would lead her, under certain conditions, to accept the proposition as being true, or reject it as being false."[4] Logical positivists wanted to distinguish between two senses of the verification principle. A proposition is verifiable in a "strong" sense if its truth could conclusively be established in experience. But some propositions, those stating scientific laws, for instance, do not admit of such a conclusive verification. Any finite series of observations cannot yield certainty. But they can be confirmed or verified in a "weak" sense, that is, they are rendered probable by instances of confirmation. In fact, logical positivists were committed to the view that all empirical propositions are no more than probable hypotheses, and they believed that to establish the meaning of those, the "weak" sense of verification is sufficient.

No factual proposition can be logically certain, but there are propositions which are true without being empirical. These are *tautologies*, and they provide no information about the world. The statement "Either some ants are parasites or none are" is compatible with any state of affairs. Facts do not make any difference to its truth. This holds for propositions of mathematics and of logic; they are analytically true, that is, their truth depends only on the definitions of words. Logical positivists accepted the findings of Russell and Whitehead's *Principia Mathematica*, which, according to Ayer, "makes it clear that formal logic is not concerned with the properties of men's mind's, much less with the properties of material objects, but simply with the possibility of combining propositions by means of logical particles into analytic propositions, and with studying the formal relationships of these analytic propositions, in virtue of which one is deducible from another."[5]

Analytic propositions make no assertions about the empirical world; therefore, they cannot be either confirmed or confuted by experience. "They simply record our determination to use words in a certain fashion.'' They are conventions accepted by the speakers of a language. The truth or falsity of more complex analytic propositions of pure mathematics or of logic cannot be determined at a glance and often may surprise us. But this is due to the limitation of our reason and perhaps to a lack of training. A person familiar with deductive systems would be able to tell quickly which propositions are tautological and which are self-contradictions. Ayer cites approvingly Hans Hahn's remark that an omniscient being needs no logic and no mathematics.

Where does this leave the propositions of metaphysics? Are they tautologies, or can they be verified? Neither is the case. According to Ayer, a metaphysical sentence may be defined as ''a sentence which purports to express a genuine proposition but does, in fact, express neither a tautology nor an empirical hypothesis.'' Consider, for instance, the concept of substance, so dear to metaphysicians. They use it to refer to the thing itself, over and above its appearances or properties. But we should not be victimized by the linguistic convention which makes it possible for the sentence to leave open what exactly it refers to when we attribute a property to a thing. Logical analysis will show that that something is not some ''simple entity,'' inaccessible to sense perception, but all other sensible properties which go together with the property first mentioned in a sentence.

A material thing is a *logical* construction. Sense data attributed to a material object are not *parts* of that object; they are elements in the logical construction which can be expressed in a definition, itself a linguistic convention. Hence, it is language that provides the clarification of sentences which at first blush appear metaphysical.

So the task of philosophy becomes one of clarifying language. In Ayer's words, ''the propositions of philosophy are not factual, but linguistic in character—that is, they do not describe the behavior of physical, or even mental, objects; they express definitions, or the formal consequences of definitions. Accordingly, we may say that philosophy is a department of logic.'' Philosophy still has a useful function; it can analyze and clarify the concepts which figure in our use of language, both in daily discourse and in science. The scientific use is of special interest to philosophers, and indeed philosophy should become the logic of science. Instead of regarding philosophical statements as belonging to a special category, we should see them as scientific statements refined by logical analysis. The objective is not to establish a set of philosophical propositions, but to make other propositions clear.

There was a further consequence of making the verification principle the exclusive arbiter of meaningful statements. The statements of ethics became problematic, for they are neither tautologies nor empirical statements. What sense experience verifies the judgments of ethics or of other values? None. They are not empirical or scientific and hence have no cognitive meaning.

They cannot be translated into statements of empirical fact. To say "You acted wrongly in stealing that money" is not to say any more than "You stole the money." The statement merely expresses the speaker's feelings of disapproval. "For in saying that a certain type of action is right or wrong, I am not making any factual statement, not even a statement about my own state of mind. I am merely expressing certain moral sentiments." The implication of this is that when two people disagree on the rightness or wrongness of an action, there really is nothing about which they disagree. In formulating their stand on the question, neither of them is asserting a genuine proposition. They merely voice opposing feelings on the matter.

What is, then, the function of ethical language? It is to express feeling, to arouse feeling, and to stimulate action. Moral judgments do not say anything, and hence they do not come under the category of truth and falsehood; they are pure expressions of feelings and attitudes. To be sure, something can be found out when moral language is used, namely, that the users of that language do have certain feelings and attitudes about actions done or contemplated. To find this out is the task for psychologists and sociologists. In this sense, "ethics, as a branch of knowledge is nothing more than department of psychology and sociology."

What is true of ethics is true of aesthetics as well. "Aesthetic terms are used in exactly the same way as ethical terms." The only way in which aesthetic judgments are open to empirical study is that which determines what caused aesthetic feelings or why various societies admired the works of art they did. These, too, are either psychological or sociological questions. The object of aesthetic criticism is not to yield knowledge but to communicate emotion. The information we get from ethics or aesthetics is only about our own mental and physical makeup.

Propositions of theology also admit of a similar analysis. They are pseudopropositions, incapable of verification, hence neither true nor false. A believer admits that much when he says that the nature of God is a mystery transcending human understanding, which means that it is unintelligible. A mystic produces no intelligible propositions—his intuition does not reveal to him any verifiable propositions. Religion, like ethics, is of interest to the psychologist or the psychoanalyst who may want to examine various kinds of feelings people have, either about particular things and actions or about the universe as a whole. In neither case can we speak of knowledge, because empirical information is lacking.

Thus, the logical positivists arrived at the conclusion that the propositions of metaphysics, ethics, aesthetics, and religion lack any cognitive, empirical, or theoretical sense. They convey no knowledge, and their function is essentially and exclusively expressive. Rudolf Carnap believed that there is a similarity between metaphysics and lyrics. He expressed his antimetaphysical thesis as follows:

> *This thesis asserts that metaphysical propositions — like lyrical verses — have only an expressive function, but no representative function. Metaphysical propositions are neither true nor false, because they assert nothing, they contain neither knowledge nor error, they lie completely outside the field of knowledge, of theory, outside the discussion of truth or falsehood. But they are, like laughing, lyric, and music, expressive. They express not so much temporary feelings as permanent emotional or volitional dispositions. Thus, for instance, a metaphysical system of Monism may be an expression of the emotional state of someone who takes life as an eternal struggle; and ethical system of Rigorism may be expressive of a strong sense of duty or perhaps of a desire to rule severely. Realism is often a symptom of the type of constitution called by psychologists extroverted, which is characterized by easily forming connections with men and things; Idealism, of an opposite constitution, the so-called introverted type, which has a tendency to withdraw from the unfriendly world and to live within its own thoughts and fancies.* [6]

There are, of course, other problems that the logical positivists had to work out. One of them involved making clear in what empirical verification itself consisted. What is the character of experience on which empirical verification finally rests? In a large and loose way, the position was phenomenalistic: the ultimate appeal was to sense experience or sense data. But what is the ontological status of sense data—what kind of being do they have? Two possibilities which presented themselves and were sometimes accepted had questionable consequences. One of them was the view that verification has to fall back on the knower's personal, private experience. Concepts were to be defined in terms of remembered similarity among sense data. Carnap admitted that this was a form of solipsism, but claimed it to be only methodological solipsism, analogous to Descartes' methodological skepticism. But this did not really show how the gap between the private and the public, the merely subjective and the objective, was to be bridged. If my experience is private to me and yours to you, how can we speak of *facts* which are to be true for both of us? Moritz Schlick thought that the difficulty can be overcome by recognizing the presence of a common structure in the content of our private worlds, for we do discover that we apply the same words on the same occasions. To this one may reply that two people, each being immured in the fortress of his own experience, could not possibly verify how that common structure is experienced by the other.

Another recourse was that communication of empirical facts ultimately rests on "protocol statements," such as an observer's report, "Red spot here now"—possibly refined by a more specific indication of space and time at which redness occurs. But if such statements are to be intersubjectively verified, then they cannot be lodged in the observer's experience alone. So some positivists concluded that they must refer to physical events. Instead of referring to the observer's private experience, the protocol statements are referring to the state of his body or his behavior. In other words, everything is to be reduced to the language of physics—as Neurath concluded. The attraction of this physicalist doctrine was that it appears to support the idea of the unity of science. But on the other hand it does away with all mental phenomena; the old doctrine of materialism reemerges, albeit in modern guise.

In addition, there was the annoying question of the epistemological status of the verification principle itself. Is it a tautology, true by definition, or is it an empirical statement, to be verified by observation? Neither appears to be the case. But if so, is it meaningful? It will not quite do to claim, as did Ayer, that the principle was not meant to be verifiable. According to him, it was put forward as a definition, but not as an arbitrary definition. Nevertheless, to most philosophers, the principle was an arbitrary denial of the meaningfulness of some propositions, in particular those of ethics. Even if one goes along with Ayer's claim that the verification principle "purports to lay down the conditions which actually govern our acceptance or indeed our understanding, of common sense and scientific statements," it certainly is not the case that common sense rejects ethical discourse as meaningless.

There was a further consequence that contributed to the demise of logical positivist doctrines, a consideration which perhaps cuts deeper than all others. It was put forward by a thinker who in many ways agreed with the philosophers of the Vienna Circle and may have been partly responsible for some of their views. That consideration is brought to light in Wittgenstein's *Tractatus Logico-Philosophicus* and has since that time acquired considerable notoriety: "Whereof one cannot speak, thereof one must be silent." And, as Frank Ramsey added, one cannot whistle it either.

## 3. Wittgenstein of the *Tractatus*

Ludwig Wittgenstein's philosophical views were expressed in two important books: *Tractatus Logico-Philosophicus*, published in 1921, and *Philosophical Investigations*, which appeared posthumously in 1953. In the first book, Wittgenstein articulates concepts and ideas which have much in common with Russell's logical atomism and with the Vienna Circle's logical positivism. In his second book, he repudiates some of his fundamental early views and strikes out in a new direction, thus giving a powerful impetus to a different emphasis in philosophy, which we shall explore in the following chapter. The main feature of this new direction is that it sees language as a much more complex phenomenon than philosophers, including the author of the *Tractatus*, had realized.

Ludwig Wittgenstein was born in Vienna in 1889. His initial interest was engineering, but after studying it for several years in Berlin and in Manchester, England, he became attracted to some mathematical problems and then to philosophy. From 1911 to 1913 he studied in Cambridge, mainly with Bertrand Russell. At the outbreak of World War I he enlisted in the Austrian army, underwent officer's training, and was captured by the Italians. Released after the war, Wittgenstein returned to Vienna. Heir to a large fortune left to him by his father, he proceeded to give away all of his money and lived very simply and frugally for the rest of his life. Believing that he had solved the important problems of philosophy in the *Tractatus*, he worked for six years as a schoolmaster in a small Austrian village and later as a gardener's assistant in a monastery. Gradually, his interest in philosophy reasserted itself, and Wittgenstein returned to Cambridge in 1929. The following year he was made a Fellow of Trinity College, and he remained in England until his death in 1951, except for several sojourns in Norway and in Ireland. During World War II he worked as an orderly in a London hospital and later in a medical laboratory in Newcastle. After the war he was appointed to a professorial chair in Cambridge, but resigned two years later.

Wittgenstein's manner of doing philosophy was unconventional. He did it with extreme concentration. His lectures, usually to a small group of students, were extraordinary occasions. Although he prepared his lectures carefully beforehand, their presentation elicited from him intense concentration; he actually rethought every single point. Those who attended these lectures found them exhausting, but extremely penetrating and exhilarating. There was something in Wittgenstein's personality that tended to evoke veneration and even fear. The amount of intellectual labor he had put into his philosophical exertions is evident in the many books which gradually appeared after his death, each bearing witness to his relentless struggle with difficult questions: *Remarks on the Foundations of Mathematics* (1956), *The Blue and Brown Books* (1958), *Notebooks 1914-18* (1961), *Zettel* (1967), and *On Certainty* (1969). *Ludwig Wittgenstein: A Memoir* (1958) by Norman Malcolm gives a moving portrait of that unusual man whose style of life was strongly influenced by figures whose views Wittgenstein hardly mentions in his writings: Schopenhauer, Kierkegaard, Dostoyevsky, and Tolstoy.

In the *Tractatus*, Wittgenstein asserts seven propositions and discusses their meaning and import in further propositions which are numbered so as to indicate their place in the explicatory scheme. The key ideas of the entire system are introduced immediately. "The world is all that is the case." What is the case is referred to as the facts. Hence, like Russell, Wittgenstein contends that "the world is the totality of facts, not of things." Of course, in mentioning facts we may also be mentioning things, but to mention a thing is not necessarily to mention a fact. Furthermore, most things are complex, and in giving an account of the world we should start with something simple. How do we get at something simple? When we deal with a simple fact, or a simple state of affairs. "What is the case—a fact—is the existence of states of affairs." What characterizes the existence of a state of affairs is that it is a fact but itself does not consist of facts. How are facts accessible to us? Through language. Language makes it possible for us to picture states of affairs to ourselves; it makes them thinkable. "A logical picture of facts is a thought."

Here, we come to Wittgenstein's famous picture theory of propositions. Thoughts are propositions, and propositions are pictures of facts. Language also makes it possible for us to name things. But to name something is not to state a fact, and hence not to produce a proposition. To describe something, however, is not to name, but to picture, a fact. Suppose that there is an object $A$, and that $A$ is red. Its being red is a fact, expressible in a proposition. But in the proposition, $A$ is merely named, not pictured. An elementary proposition is a picture of an atomic fact. Wittgenstein also claimed that "An elementary proposition consists of names. It is a nexus, a concatenation of names." Furthermore, the names in elementary propositions must refer to simple objects. This means that Wittgenstein uses the word "name" in a technical sense. Ordinary names such as "cat," "square," or "Fido" do not qualify as "names" in Wittgenstein's special sense, because they admit of further analysis; they refer to complex objects. He also believed that simple objects are colorless; the color which an object has, is a fact about it; hence, the color cannot belong to the object. The objects cannot be thought of except in the context of a possible atomic fact.

For Wittgenstein, "A name cannot be dissected any further by means of a definition: it is a primitive sign." Therefore, an elementary proposition must contain names which are not further analyzable. What would qualify as such a name, Wittgenstein never says, nor does he give examples. When asked about this a long time after he had repudiated some of the key doctrines of the Tractatus, he confessed that he regarded the determination of what constitutes a simple object as a purely empirical matter, in which he needed to take no interest, since he was concerned only with the *logical* structure of language.

This is an important point for determining the affinity of Wittgenstein's views with those of the logical positivists. One may be tempted to introduce here the notion of observation or of sense data. In using simple names we are referring to the immediate data of sensation; hence, the foundation of all meaningful statements must be observation statements. But the text of the *Tractatus* gives little support for this interpretation. In one place Wittgenstein says the following: "The references of primitive signs can be made clear by elucidations. Elucidations are propositions containing the primitive signs. Thus they can only be understood, if one is acquainted with the reference of the signs."[7] Further reading of the passage indicates that by "primitive signs" Wittgenstein does mean "names." But it does not follow that he is referring here to acquaintance with a sense datum. Hence, it cannot be argued that the *Tractatus* embraces the phenomenalist doctrine of perception.

Whatever the status of simple objects named in an elementary proposition, the proposition, when asserted, affirms that a given state of affairs exists or that the proposition is true. The proposition is not itself a name because, as Wittgenstein had pointed out to Russell, to each proposition there correspond *two* states of affairs. If the state of affairs pictured by the proposition does not exist, then the proposition is false. But if it does exist, the proposition pictures truly the given facts. Language shows how the world is structured. Hence, the general form of proposition is: "This is how things are." There are objects to which names correspond. There are atomic facts to which atomic propositions correspond, and there are facts expressible in complex propositions.

Why does Wittgenstein think that propositions are pictures of facts? The idea came to him while he was reading in a magazine a description of how a car accident had taken place. The diagram of the collision suggested to him that a proposition, like a diagram or a map, is also a kind of picture. To the fact that the watch is on the table there corresponds a proposition which shows the structure of that fact. The names in the sentence are combined in a similar way to the way the objects are concatenated. "The fact that the elements of a picture are related to one another in a determinate way represents that things are related to one another in the same way." This means that the proposition is also a fact, but it is a fact which has a logical form which makes it a picture (true or false) of another fact. In other words, the structure of the fact is reproduced in the logical form of the proposition. The proposition *shows* its sense. But we cannot tell from the form of the proposition alone whether it is true or false. "In order to tell whether the picture is true or false we must compare it with reality." The elements of a proposition must have a one-to-one correspondence with the elements of the situation. Thus, for the proposition "London is north of Paris" to be true, the object "London" must be to the north of the object "Paris."

Another central thesis of the *Tractatus* is that "A proposition is a truth-function of elementary propositions." Russell's logical atomism also accepted this thesis. If a proposition is composed of elementary propositions, then to determine the truth of that proposition we must examine the truth of the elementary propositions which make it up. Given the logical connectives between two propositions and given the truth value of each proposition, we can determine the truth value of the complex proposition. $p$ & $q$ is true if and only if $p$ is true and $q$ is true. $p$ v $q$ is false when and only when neither $p$ nor $q$ is true.

There are propositions which are always true no matter what truth values their component propositions have; for example, "It is raining or it is not raining." Or, consider the form of argument which the logicians call *modus ponens:*

If $p$ then $q$

$p$

———————

Therefore $q$

The form of this argument is always valid; it is a tautology. Why? The first proposition, "If $p$ then $q$," tells us that if $p$ is true, then $q$ is also true. The second proposition tells us that $p$ is true. Hence, it follows logically that $q$ cannot be false. No matter what the truth values of $p$ and $q$ are, the conclusion always follows validly from the premises.

What is to be noted about tautologies, or the truths of logic, is that they tell us nothing about what the case is. To be told that it is raining or not raining is not to get any information at all, although what was said is true, necessarily true. Hence, elementary propositions are the key to the truth about the world; they connect us with reality and determine the outcome of truth-functional analysis, in which we determine the truth of molecular propositions by analyzing them into elementary propositions. Nevertheless, the fact that propositions when analyzed truth-functionally can yield truth or falsity does tell us something about the world. Tautologies have no subject matter, but they "describe the scaffolding of the world," says Wittgenstein. If the names have meaning and if elementary propositions have sense, then logical relations among elementary propositions also tell us something about the world. It is difficult to follow Wittgenstein here, and the interpretation of his statements is controversial. The minimum claim that he makes, however, is that we need the propositions of logic in order to determine the truth values of nonelementary propositions; hence, the propositions of logic, although they have no content, are nevertheless not meaningless. They are senseless, that is, they have no sense, but they are not nonsense. Therefore, the assertion of tautologies, even though they convey no information, is nevertheless possible.

The situation is quite different, however, when we ask this question: What is the relation of propositions to the facts which they depict? Here, we encounter the famous paradoxical conclusion of the *Tractatus,* namely, that all of its propositions are nonsense. How so? Well, consider what can be said, according to the views of the *Tractatus.* We can meaningfully assert (1) elementary propositions which depict atomic facts, and (2) propositions which are truth

functions of elementary propositions. Note that a proposition which would
tell us *how* a proposition connects with the fact it depicts is not among the
two possibilities. Such a proposition would attempt to transcend language and
tell us something which cannot be said. This means that philosophy, which
tries to tell us how language connects with the world, is also trying to say
what cannot be said. The propositions of philosophy are neither empirical
nor logical. Hence, they cannot be true or false; they are simply nonsensical.
This is true of all propositions of the *Tractatus* as well. Nevertheless, they
are not useless. They can be used as a ladder which a person throws away
after climbing to the position from which he can see what he set out to see.
"My propositions are elucidations in the following way: anyone who
understands me eventually recognizes them as nonsensical, when he has used
them—as steps—to climb up beyond them. (He must, so to speak, throw
away the ladder after he climbed up it.) He must transcend these propositions,
and then he will see the world aright."[8]

Like the logical positivists, Wittgenstein believed that language is essentially
used for *one* purpose, the stating of facts. When we attempt to go beyond
these limits and talk about ethical or religious values, or about the world as
a whole or its meaning, we attempt to say the unsayable. Not that these things
do not matter; it is only that we cannot speak of them. Life in space and time
*is* a riddle, but we can neither express it nor solve it; the solution lies outside
space and time. It is the same with ethical values. Everything that happens
in the world is accidental and merely happens, but since value is nonaccidental
it cannot lie in the world. "It must lie outside the world." So while there
are inexpressible things, they cannot be put in language. They merely show
themselves. "They are what is mystical."

Since Wittgenstein has already told us that all the propositions of the
*Tractatus* are nonsensical, those dealing with the inexpressible also fall in
that category. Nevertheless, they invite us to give up efforts to say the
unsayable. Instead, we may try to get "the feeling of the world as a limited
whole," which "is the mystical feeling." Here, the uses of language are of
no avail; but if so, what guidelines can we have? Metaphysics may be *important*
nonsense, as it was for Wittgenstein, but it is still nonsense, nonetheless. Is
the inexpressible showing us something about the world in the same way the
propositions of logic show us the formal-logical properties of language in
the world? The comparison would not lead us very far, for the properties
in question are formal-logical, and we at least can learn a good deal of logic
from studying deductive systems. Logic is, in Wittgenstein's words, a kind
of scaffolding *of* the world. Ethics, aesthetics, and religion are wholly *outside*
the world. Using Kant's distinction, we might say that logic is transcendental;
it provides necessary conditions for understanding the world. Since the
propositions of logic are not transcendent, they are not unsayable, but the

propositions of ethics or of religion *are* unsayable. "Whereof one cannot speak, thereof one must be silent."

The "mystical" side of the *Tractatus* remains a controversial matter. Considering his other views, his admiration for Schopenhauer and for some religious thinkers, it can be argued, against logical positivists, that the book is not wholly and decidedly antimetaphysical. But there are many things in the *Tractatus* that Wittgenstein subsequently decided were quite wrong and that he proceeded to replace by fresh philosophical explorations. It is doubtful that his later work resolves the questions about the inexpressible, but it is interesting to note that his later work has stimulated some novel explorations in theology and philosophy of religion.

Some historical comparisons of contemporary empiricism with its predecessors may be helpful. The empiricism of the twentieth century shares a basic ambition with the British empiricism of the eighteenth century; starting with discrete items directly available in experience, the eighteenth-century empiricists hoped to show how the entire edifice of knowledge is built up. But whereas the British empiricists were relying on a psychological description of how simple ideas are combined to yield more complex ones, the empiricists of the twentieth century wanted to use the recently discovered tools of logic. Locke started from simple ideas, and Russell and Wittgenstein began with elementary propositions. From atomic propositions, by means of logical operations, one can arrive at molecular propositions. The truth or falsity of molecular propositions depends on the truth or falsity of elementary propositions. Given certain elementary propositions and certain logical truths, one can determine which combinations of elementary propositions yield truths and which do not.

Thus, the ideal of perfect clarity is attainable, provided we know which elementary propositions are true and provided we are careful not to make any logical mistakes in producing truth functions of these propositions. Since the truths of logic are purely formal, or, as Wittgenstein showed, tautological, the only thing needed for perfectly certain knowledge is the knowledge of the truth or falsity of elementary propositions. Hence, it appears that the goal of logical empiricism was rationalistic, in the sense that the truth of propositions is to be tested deductively, by means of logic. This is not surprising, for the model for the empiricist ̈philosophy was natural science, which relies on mathematical procedures to prove the truth of its theories. Given certain data, certain laws or generalizations are established logically, with the help of mathematics.

As we have seen, the Achilles heel for logical empiricism turned out to be the uncertainty about the elementary propositions and the nature of the objects to which elementary propositions supposedly refer. Russell's "this red here" or the logical positivists' "protocol statements" or Wittgenstein's "simple objects" turned out to be harder to make sense of than it at first appeared to those who appealed to them. In addition, Russell admitted having difficulties with negative and general propositions; the logical positivists couldn't quite make up their minds in what verification was supposed to consist; as we shall see in his *Philosophical Investigations*, Wittgenstein concluded that the notion of a simple object is a nest of confusions.

Thus, the dream of modern empiricism to construct an edifice of philosophy on the model of science began to fade. Even as it was being entertained, it became evident that the cost of turning philosophy into strict science involved the need to declare as nonsense a great many kinds of propositions. At first, the positivists thought that they had finally led philosophy out of a conceptual wilderness by showing the propositions of metaphysics to be meaningless, but it then became clear that the propositions of ethics and aesthetics, of religion, and even of philosophy itself, would have to go as well. The price appeared to be high, but more sanguine souls tried to patch up things by providing alternative accounts of at least some forms of discourse which would fit the theory. In this way, the notion of emotive meaning was born.

## Questions

1. What are the main features of Russell's logical atomism? Why did he think that it should enable us to construct a logically perfect language?

2. What was Russell's difficulty with general propositions and with propositions of the form: "John believes that it is raining?" How did these difficulties affect the theory of logical atomism?

3. What was the philosophical aim of the verification principle?

4. What is a physical object, according to logical positivists? How did they interpret the statements of metaphysics?

5. What were the problems which the logical positivists themselves regarded as unresolved?

6. Why did Wittgenstein think that propositions are pictures of facts and that molecular propositions are truth functions of elementary propositions?

7. What was Wittgenstein's interpretation of the laws of logic?

8. On what grounds did Wittgenstein conclude that all of the propositions of the *Tractatus* are nonsensical?

# Notes

1 *The Philosophy of Bertrand Russell*, edited by P.A. Schilpp, Evanston: The Library of Living Philosophers, Northwestern University, 1944, p. 12. Reprinted by permission.

2 Bertrand Russell, "The Philosophy of Logical Atomism," in *Logic and Knowledge* edited by R.C. Marsh. New York: Macmillan, 1956, pp. 197-198. Reprinted by permission of George Allen and Unwin.

3 Bertrand Russell, *A History of Western Philosophy*, New York: Simon and Schuster, 1945, p. 201. Reprinted by permission.

4 A.J. Ayer, *Language, Truth and Logic*. London: Victor Gollancz, 1950, p. 35.

5 *Ibid.*, p. 81.

6 Rudolf Carnap, *Philosophy and Logical Syntax*, as quoted in *Introduction to Philosophy* by A. Smullyan, P. Dietrichson, D. Keyt, and L. Miller. Belmont, CA: Wadsworth, 1962. p. 22.

7 Ludwig Wittgenstein, *Tractatus Logico-Philosophicus*, translated by D.F. Pears and B.F. McGuinness. London: Routledge & Kegan Paul, 1961, 3.263.

8 *Ibid.*, 6.54.

# Chapter Twelve

# Language Analysis

## 1. Wittgenstein of the *Investigations*

There is good reason for discussing Wittgenstein's philosophy in two different chapters. His later thought initiates lines of inquiry which break not only with his earlier views, but also with some basic conceptions of philosophy as it has been traditionally practiced. Logical atomism, of both Bertrand Russell and Wittgenstein's *Tractatus*, is still obsessed with the notion that the key philosophical problem is to describe the relation between thought and its object. Hence the search for elementary propositions which would "picture" atomic facts for us. The underlying assumption was that somehow there *must* be simple objects and that true propositions name or "picture" them. What could be a candidate for such an object did not interest the early Wittgenstein; he believed this to be an empirical question. But as he later focused his attention on this question, he noticed that this may be the source of a basic philosophical confusion. The confusion has two levels — the specific and the general. The specific level concerns the relation of a name to its "simple" object. If there are no "simples" to which a name can be attached, the relation itself is obscure. On the general level, the confusion is even more disastrous, for it appears that philosophers, including the author of the *Tractatus*, were obsessed with making the notion of a proposition as a picture of facts the exclusive paradigm of a meaningful proposition. Recall that all propositions were to be regarded as truth functions of elementary propositions. But if elementary propositions are themselves problematic, if they do not give us "pictures" of any simple facts, then *all* of our language becomes problematic.

To get at the root of the difficulty, Wittgenstein examines what happens in so-called ostensive teaching. Try to imagine a primitive language in which one person teaches another how to use the word "trowel." Suppose that you happen not to know the meaning of the word. So I point to a trowel and say "trowel." How do yo know what I am pointing to? You may think that I am referring to the object's color, or to its shape, or to its position. Even more fundamentally, how do you know that I am teaching you something and not commanding you to do something or complaining about something? It appears that in ostensive teaching, a connection between the thought and its object is not directly and unmistakably grasped. Even ostensive teaching presupposes some previous knowledge of words, a previous mastery of some uses of language. Without such a mastery I cannot get the meaning of words taught by ostension.

It became clear to Wittgenstein that the words "simple" and "composite" are relative to context. What is simple in one context can be composite in another. Is the color white simple, or does it consist of the colors of the rainbow? What could be regarded as simple constituents of a chair? Would they be bits of wood, molecules, or atoms? "Simple" means "not composite." Yet "composite" may have many different senses. A chessboard is composed of 32 white and 32 black squares. But Wittgenstein points out that we could also say that it is composed of the colors white and black and of the schema of squares. Is a sentence composed of words or of a combination of sounds or letters? Questions like these indicate that the search for the absolutely simple is misguided.

It is a mistake to think that we always get a better understanding of a sentence if we analyze its referent into simpler components. Instead of saying: "Bring me the broom," I may say: "Bring me the brush and the handle which fits into it." Do we understand the second order better than the first? The second "analyzes" the object of our reference into simpler components, but this analysis does not create a better understanding of the order. This example shows that understanding does not involve latching on to some simple objects of thought and somehow keeping them together before the mind.

One favored way of going around the difficulty of identifying the simple object of thought was to "remove" it from the objective world and place it in the subject's experience. This tendency has been clearly prevalent at least since Descartes, one of its latest versions being the sense-data theory. To be sure, William James and Bertrand Russell theorized that sense data are neither mental nor physical, but that they could be "ingredient" in either realm—this was their so-called "neutral monism." Nevertheless, as perceived by the subject, sense data are directly given to him in sensation. Wittgenstein wanted to know what exactly happens when a person identifies and refers to such an item of private experience. Suppose you have a sense datum, or a sensation, and you want to refer to it. How can you identify it? You can identify it by some word or symbol. Suppose you call the sensation *E*. The next day you think that you have *the same* sensation. Are you right in calling it *E*? On what grounds do you do so? Well, it *seems* to be the same; you remember yesterday's sensation, "compare" it with the one you have today, and *are inclined* to say that they are the same. Now, is it enough for you to claim that you have identified them correctly? Note that the only grounds on which you judge here is what *seems* to you to be the case. Would you therefore be prepared to say that what seems to you, or what you are inclined to say, is equivalent to *being* correct, right? If you would, then the distinction between seeming to be right and being right is eliminated. What seems right *is* right.

This consequence is unacceptable because we do want to distinguish between seeming to be right and being right. How do we do this? Suppose that the sense datum in question is a familiar one. Suppose you see a red flower. How do you know that you have identified the color correctly? Here, you do not rely on memory alone. It is doubtful that you even try to "look into your mind" to "compare" the perceived color with other instances of redness you had seen in the past. But suppose I raise a doubt as to whether the flower is red. What do you do? You point to other red things, you bring samples, color charts, etc. You refer to a great many other things which you and anyone else who speaks English and is not color-blind call red. It is this possibility of exhibiting your mastery of this segment of language in objective, public contexts that entitles you to claim that your identification was correct. Normally, of course, you would not even need to produce other samples and make comparisons; you simply could say: "I've learned English."

This reply to a "doubting Thomas" need not be taken as a sort of rebuff. It points to an important facet of using language. "I've learned English" calls attention to the fact that to use words correctly is to manifest a certain mastery, a linguistic competence, which was probably acquired a long time ago and included an early childhood stage when mistakes and misidentifications of colors in all likelihood were frequent. A small child's descriptions of colors and sounds are taken with a grain of salt, because the mastery of words is not yet to be expected. But the time soon comes when we do not doubt that even children when they report their perceptions to us see the same colors as we do. There are, of course, special situations, such as color blindness or jaundice, but in these we can *explain* the discrepancy between normal and abnormal vision.

How do we know then, that our perceptions are correct? We *agree in judgments*, says Wittgenstein; we discover that teaching language is *successful*, that a child in being taught the uses of words at a certain stage demonstrates that he *can go on in the same way*, produce *correct* identifications of colors, sounds, and objects. In other words, the very fact that communication by language occurs shows that we do agree in judgments and that skepticism about knowing what others perceive is out of place. The supposition that someone may always be seeing blue while I am seeing red is confused, because there is no way for a person to find out what he sees except by means of publicly accessible objects. The words I am inclined to use in my descriptions are the words I have been taught by others when they described what *they* saw or heard. Even if I try to "point with my attention" to my inner sensation, I cannot give it a correct name without being able to also give that name to other objects which other people can perceive as well.

An important conclusion from this is that the very idea of a private language, i.e., language that only *I* can understand, is incoherent. Such a "language" could not even get started, for it would lack any criteria of correct application. Every "use" of its supposed "vocabulary" would be compatible with its misuse, and hence no one, including the speaker, could know what he was "talking" about. Wittgenstein gives numerous examples which show how we can have an illusion of understanding an expression without it actually being the case that we do understand. Suppose I say "It is five o'clock on the sun." The words used are familiar enough. Yet does the expression make sense, can one understand it? Although each word in it has meaning, the whole locution itself, as it stands, cannot be understood. It looks like the proposition "It is five o'clock in Rome," but the surface similarity is misleading. We have no idea how the "time of day" on the sun is to be determined, because we do not even know what could possibly be meant by "day" on the sun.

Following this line of thought Wittgenstein also remarks that if a lion could talk we would not understand him. The very idea of talking presupposes knowing how the words we use are connected with things we normally, *as human beings*, do. Consider our example of identifying colors. What would it take for us to make sense of a lion identifying colors, or making reference to them? We would have to give him *human* purposes and capacities; he would have to be transformed into a human lion. Furthermore, it may be instructive to ponder the differences in physiological structure between men and lions, including the structures of the throat, tongue, and mouth, and their possible bearing on *our* concept of talking. Reflections of this sort led Wittgenstein to say that to imagine a language is to imagine a form of life. Language gives expression to particular needs, capacities, and abilities which the speakers of language have. Language emerges as the form of life is defined, articulated, and developed. Words have meaning only in the stream of life. Language is not tacked on to culture as something which takes shape independently of language; language and culture develop simultaneously or side by side. Similarly, it is a confusion to say that language causes or determines certain forms of life. The relationship between language and culture is not causal. Language *shows* what the given form of life *is*.

This view of the nature of language steers us past the long-standing temptation to see it as operating on one single model, traditionally favored by philosophers: name and its object. To break the hold of this misleading picture, Wittgenstein wants us to reflect on the many *different* functions which the use of language has. Compare the items in the following set of linguistic activities.

- *Giving orders and obeying them*
- *Describing the appearance of an object, or giving its measurements*
- *Constructing an object from a description (a drawing)*
- *Reporting an event*
- *Speculating about an event*
- *Forming and testing a hypothesis*
- *Presenting the results of an experiment in tables and diagrams*
- *Making up a story; and reading it*
- *Play acting*
- *Singing catches*
- *Guessing riddles*
- *Making a joke; telling it*
- *Solving a problem in practical arithmetic*
- *Translating from one language into another*
- *Asking, thanking, cursing, greeting, praying* [1]

If we but reflect for a moment on what actually takes place when we are engaged in such activities, we no longer will be tempted to say that in each case we are doing *the same* thing. Wittgenstein thinks it helpful to see the situation as analogous to using a great variety of tools. Things we do with hammers are very different from what we do with saws, or screwdrivers, or glue, or sandpaper. To say that every word in a language signifies something is to say nothing at all; it is equivalent to saying that each tool *modifies* some material. In either case we get no information.

Do uses of language have nothing in common, then? Is there no such thing as the nature or essence of language? Wittgenstein's answer to this is original and revealing. He introduced the conception of "language-game," an expression which should be understood as a technical term. The question "What is the essence of language?" may be answered in the same way as the question, "What is the essence of games?" Do all games have something in common? Well, look and see. There are all sorts of games: board games, card games, ball games, Olympic games.

*Look for example at board-games, with their multifarious relationships.*
*Now pass to card-games; here you find many correspondences with the*
*first group but many common features drop out. When we next pass to*
*ball-games, much that is common is retained, but much is lost. —Are*
*they all "amusing?" Compare chess with noughts and crosses. Or is*
*there always winning and losing, or competition between players? Think*
*of patience.*[2]

Wittgenstein concludes that this examination yields the following result: "We
see a complicated network of similarities overlapping and criss-crossing:
sometimes overall similarities, sometimes similarities in detail."

Here, we have the notion of "family resemblance," which Wittgenstein
believed to be helpful in breaking the spell of the picture: if we are to understand
a concept, we must somehow get hold of its "essence," something that all
instances of that concept must share. It should be noted that Wittgenstein is
taking another look at the question which a long time ago generated the picture
of Platonic Forms and all the subsequent controversies about the relation of
particulars to universals and the ontological status of the latter. Are universals
real, or are they mere names? Perhaps there is another, more plausible way
of explaining how the same word can apply to an indefinite number of instances,
without all these instances having any *one* feature in common. Consider still
another illustration. Here is a cable made of metal fibers. Does there have
to be a single fiber running through its entire length in order for it to be a
cable? Not at all! The fibers overlap with other fibers for a given length and
then are replaced with others which overlap with still others, but no fiber
needs to run through the whole length. Similarly, members of a family may
show resemblances in build, features, color of eyes, gait, and temperament,
but none of these features has to be present in all members in order for them
to belong to the family.

The notion of "family resemblance" enables us to break the hold of the
persistent temptation to say that concepts must have an essence, a universal
form which is present in all instances of the concept. One of the facts about
human beings is that they can learn the use of words which are connected
not through some one element of common essences, but through overlapping
similarities of certain features. Of course, some features may be regarded
as essential. For example, ordinarily we learn that the word "bed" is connected
with "sleep"; beds are things that are normally used for sleeping. But there
are beds—those in museums, for instance—that are no longer used for
sleeping. Still, they share other features with things we call beds—certain
basic structure. But, again, does the structure always have to be the same?
A mother, after arranging a mattress on the floor, may say to a visiting relative:
"Your bed is ready."

Furthermore, the "family resemblance" analysis of concepts helps us see what is involved in borderline cases. Some things may share some features with one class of objects and other features with another class of objects. Is this a chair or a sofa? Is this a window or a door? Is this a tree or a bush? In some respects it is one and in other respects the other. No clash of essences is taking place. Rather, to use the image of the cable, at a certain point the color or the texture of the fibers changed, but it may be difficult to decide at what point the change justifies a different name.

This analysis of the nature of concepts also affects the concepts of meaning and understanding. To understand a word is not to have grasped its meaning in a flash, as it were. Indeed, Wittgenstein wants to lead us away from the idea that understanding is a kind of mental occurrence or process. How do I show that I understand the word? I do so by being able to use it correctly, by applying it in right situations. This I have learned from other members of my linguistic community. Having understood a word or a locution has consequences: I can make appropriate verbal and behavioral moves. If understanding consisted in the occurrence of some inner processes, then presumably these consequences could be regarded as inessential. Yet this is not the case. A person may profess repeatedly that he understands something, that he has the right meaning in mind, but if he "does not go on" in the way in which his claim to have understood the locution would entitle us to expect, then we are justified in saying that he does not understand.

All of this should not be taken as a denial that some mental processes occur as a person tries to follow someone's words or is trying to learn something. Of course, many physiological, psychological, and emotional phenomena may and usually do go on. But the point is that they, in themselves, do not constitute understanding, because, as Wittgenstein insists, they do not have the *consequences* of understanding.

It is not incorrect to say that a person who grasps the meaning of a word or an expression follows the *rules* of their application. There are some rules to follow here, in the sense of learning the boundaries of application. We *can* make mistakes in applying words, we can *mis*understand them, either in the learning stage or afterward. We may be *corrected*; someone can point out to us that the words do not apply to the situation or that it is not clear how they are to be applied. But rules do not proliferate *ad infinitum*. At some stage rules give out; there are no rules for the application of rules. One is not *guided* by any further rules or interpretations. When I identify an object as a spoon, for instance, I am not interpreting anything—sense data, visual impressions, or whatever. In ordinary perception we do not see something *as* something. I see a knife, not some object *as* a knife. In contrast, I can see a flat piece of metal as a knife, but only if it is *not* a knife.

The lesson here is that the mastery of language is expressed in some definite abilities and performances—at some point one proceeds *without rules*. One cannot be asked indefinitely: Why do you say this and not something else? Are you justified in calling this flower red? At a certain point justification is neither necessary nor possible. Why do you call this red? "I simply do— and so do you" is the right answer. As Wittgenstein puts it, "To use a word without a justification does not mean to use it without right." This right is earned by being able to exhibit one's correct understanding of a word.

Wittgenstein's view of language enables him to conclude that in sharing language, people also share a form of life. It is possible for people to understand one another, to communicate their thoughts, their sensations, their feelings, to guide one another through appropriate locutions which, as we have seen, include much more than naming objects and stating facts. When language is used properly, with its familiar, established meanings, nothing is hidden; we can say what we want to say without fear of being misunderstood. Of course, attention is never directed just to words, to language, because language is not *mere* language; it is rooted in the total context of various natural facts, facts about ourselves and about our surroundings. As we observed before, language could not become language unless it developed in the context of attention to facts and events which supply the material for the appropriate use of words.

This analysis also provides an explanation of how things can go wrong. When we depart from familiar, established, shared expressions and begin to coin locutions for which there are no accepted applications, language goes on holiday, it idles. Wittgenstein believed philosophers to be especially susceptible to this malady because they have a tendency to *extend* the uses of language without making clear how these extensions are to be understood. It is evident that Wittgenstein did not think that extension, growth, change, and development of language is either impossible or undesirable. In fact, he compared language to a city in which some streets and sections are clearly and neatly laid out, with other streets meandering with little regularity, with new suburbs and individual structures being built. Linguistic change does take place; some words lose currency or disappear altogether, others come on the scene, or some old words and expressions gain new, often surprising connotations. But all this happens "in the stream of life," in close relation to the corresponding changes in the form of life of a given community. Things go wrong only when a new use of a word is suggested *without* it being clear how it is to be applied or why it is to replace or supplant the familiar, accepted, sharable uses of it. When a philosopher uses an expression in a new way, side by side with the ordinary, familiar way, his statements may take on the flavor of paradox. He may appear to be saying strange things. Sometimes the discrepancy between the philosopher's way of speaking and that of the ordinary man may be so great as to lead to bafflement. Such situations prompt Wittgenstein to say: "When we do philosophy we are like savages, primitive people, who hear the expressions of civilized men, put a false interpretation on them, and then draw the queerest conclusions from it."[3] Inattention, lack of concern for avoiding conflicts between the philosopher's language and established usage, is a constant danger for a philosopher: bewitchment of intelligence by means of language. Referring in part to his own misconceptions in the *Tractatus*, Wittgenstein says: "We have got onto slippery ice where there is no friction and so in a certain sense the conditions are ideal, but also, just because of that, we are unable to walk. We want to walk: so we need *friction*. Back to the rough ground!"[3]

This call is to be understood as a call to examine the particular ends, objective purposes which the various uses of language are intended to secure. This is not, however, a narrowly pragmatic doctrine. Among the uses of language is science, but so are poetry, technology, and religion. Although understanding poetry presupposes a grasp of the prosaic meanings of words employed, the writing and reading of poetry have their own special objectives. A "family resemblance" analysis of the word "understanding" would uncover some strands that are prominent in the poetic range of it. There are not *two* meanings of "understanding," one for prose and one for poetry; both belong to the fuller explication of the word. There are some special ways of leading a person to comprehend a poem.

It would be an error to conclude from Wittgenstein's assorted criticisms of philosophers that he finds the activity of philosophizing useless or unimportant. The mistakes the philosopher makes are not silly. His understanding suffers bumps from running against the limits of language, but these are not to be ridiculed. The desire to clarify our concepts is often a *deep* concern, a disquietude resulting from the unclarities and uncertainties of many concepts. Although the familiar workings of language can provide us with clear paradigms and criteria of correctness, language itself may mislead and confuse us. Often, we may become clearer about the meaning of what is said by looking under the surface grammar to what Wittgenstein calls depth grammar, a meaning which is laid over by the superficial form of the locution. "He runs a race" looks on the surface very similar to "He wins a race," but the similarity of form hides an important difference between the two verbs. Winning is not a process, an activity; rather it signifies achievement, result.

Similarly, one should be on guard against mistaking a grammatical remark for a factual remark. For instance, it may seem that one is getting a bit of information in the statement: "One plays patience by oneself." But this is not an empirical statement. It is merely an explication of what the word "patience" means. "One plays patience by oneself" gives expression to the rules of usage of the word "patience." Another example of a purely grammatical statement would be, "Every rod has length." This statement is always true, because it is true by virtue of the definitions of the words "rod" and "length." If we were to begin calling objects which had no length "rod," the linguistic rules would change as well.

Some of the debates which philosophers and scientists are carrying on today turn on the way in which the rules for the use of words are laid down. "Machines cannot think"; is this a grammatical or an empirical proposition? If one regards thinking as something tied to activities of human or humanlike beings, machines do not think. Wittgenstein was inclined to take this view. "We only say of a human being and what is like one that it thinks." But one may, of course, dissociate the concept of thinking from some of the phenomena of thinking which are attributable only to what is like a human being. Thus, the proposition "Machines can think" can be *made* true by this shift of grammatical rules. The point is that it is not a matter of *discovering* some new empirical fact.

The account of meaning in terms of use may raise further questions and problems. It has been observed that "use" is not any less vague than "meaning." Therefore, to explain meaning in terms of use still leaves many difficulties. One of the problems is to decide whether the mere fact that a language game is played guarantees that there is nothing wrong with the playing of that game. Wittgenstein's views have inspired some people to adopt a rather strongly relativistic view of language. They claim that the determination of the validity of statements can be made only from *within* any given linguistic practice. For instance, religious statements can be evaluated only from the point of view of those who agree in some fundamental judgments within that religious discourse. Thus, an atheist cannot criticize a believer, because he does not share the form of life of the believer, a form of life which includes an acceptance of some key tenets and convictions. Therefore, it seems that an external criticism, that is, a criticism by one who does not share these basic tenets, is impossible. This point of view, sometimes labeled "fideism," attributes to Wittgenstein some such theses as the following: Each form of life is in order as it is. Forms of life are *given*; taken as a whole, they are not amenable to criticism. Each distinctive form of life has a logic of its own. The philosopher's task is not to evaluate or criticize forms of life, but only to describe them.

It is true that Wittgenstein thought that the grounds on which religious believers affirmed their faith were different from other types of evidence and that indeed it was not a matter of evidence with them at all. On the other hand, there is no evidence that he thought of language as separable into independent compartments: language of science, language of religion, or language of poetry. Words used by religious believers, including such words as love or forgiveness, still have to brought back to their normal, everyday uses in order to be understood. Because the vocabularies of daily life, of science, and of religion overlap at many points, the crisscrossing of different applications still can be examined and described. It is not clear what it would be like to engage in a *purely* religious discourse, with its own set of special standards of meaning. Furthermore, if within some discourse claims made are presented as factual, then it should be possible to indicate which facts are being appealed to, so that not only those already convinced but also those who are not convinced could understand the claims. Believers do not claim to speak an esoteric, only internally valid language. If they did, there would be no point in their saying that they thought their beliefs true. On the other hand those outside the circle will fail to understand the believers altogether if they cannot share at least some of the experiences to which the believers want to call attention.

A similar debate is going on about the possibility of declaring any form of life to be more or less rational than others. Can a primitive society which does not use the scientific methods of testing beliefs be declared to be irrational? Are there criteria of rationality common to *all* activities, pursuits, and forms of life? Here, again, the issues are not clearly defined. Some critics see Wittgenstein leaning in the direction of cultural relativism. Others find this conclusion unwarranted. The debate is going on in a lively fashion. This indicates that Wittgenstein's later approach still leaves many philosophical problems unresolved. What he aimed at was *complete* clarity, a situation in which "the philosophical problems should *completely* disappear." He added, however, that "The real discovery is the one that makes me capable of stopping doing philosophy when I want to." But this does not mean that when a thinker stops doing philosophy, it will not be carried on by others.

In his early work, Wittgenstein, like the logical positivists, tried to bring absolute clarity into our descriptions of the world by relying on discoveries of modern logic. For a while the idea of the possibility of a perfect language, organized on the principles of logic, animated many gifted thinkers. In a manner reminiscent of Descartes, they began to eliminate from language everything that could not be said clearly and verified distinctly. The dream proved to be short-lived, but was in many ways instructive.

Wittgenstein's career can be studied as an example of waking from such a dream and facing reality again. But facing it with a difference, for the dream was not useless. Having recognized the pointlessness of arbitrary and restrictive demands on language, it was now possible to appreciate the many different things language can do, namely, to relate us to the world in a variety of important and interesting ways. To some extent, this conclusion can be seen as a Kantian legacy. More radically than Kant's categories, *language as a whole* allows us to experience the world in various dimensions and forms of life. That in the house of language there are many mansions (each entitled

to careful attention) may be a genuine philosophical insight not unworthy of
its predecessors in the history of human thought.

## 2. Ryle: The Concept of Mind

Gilbert Ryle (1900-1976) has exerted a powerful influence on philosophy
in the English-speaking world. He was educated at Brighton College and at
Queens College, Oxford. He remained at Oxford and taught there for 44 years
as lecturer, tutor, and from 1945 on as Waynfleete Professor of Metaphysical
Philosophy at Magdalen College. After retiring from his post in 1968, he
continued as editor of *Mind*, one of the prestigious philosophical journals.
His *Concept of Mind* appeared in 1949, has been reprinted several times since,
and is now available in Spanish, Italian, German, and Polish translations.
It has been a must for anyone wanting to follow the main developments of
English philosophy. One review, by another eminent philosopher, became
literally prophetic. "This is probably one of the two or three most important
and original works of general philosophy which have been published in England
in the last twenty years . . . Professor Ryle writes with Aristotelian pregnancy,
and almost every paragraph contains observations which require and will
certainly be given, thousands of words of discussion"[5] Ryle continued to
develop his views in articles, many of which have been published as collections
(*Dilemmas*, 1954, *Philosophical Papers*, 1971, *On Thinking*, 1979), leaving
an important imprint on the career of philosophy.

The objective of *The Concept of Mind* is to be critical and constructive at
the same time, but one may tend to underestimate the latter aspect because
of the far-reaching character of the former. When Ryle attacks what he calls
the Cartesian myth, he also calls into question the pervasive influence which
that myth has had on the entire subsequent course of Western philosophy.
The Cartesian point of view is so deeply entrenched that Ryle finds it proper
to refer to it as "the official view," not only endorsed by most philosophers
since Descartes, but also adopted in its essentials by the man in the street.
A concentration on the negative, critical side of Ryle's philosophy may divert
the reader's attention from the positive account he has to offer. In this exposition
I shall try to present both sides of his contribution.

What is the "official doctrine" of Cartesianism? Ryle calls it "the dogma
of the ghost in the machine" and describes its essential features. It is the view
that every human being is both a body and a mind. What goes on in the mind
is wholly distinct from what happens to and is done by the body. When the
body disintegrates, the mind may continue to exist and function in its own
separate way. The behavior of the body is a wholly public affair and is subject

to mechanical laws, as are all other bodies in space. But since minds are not in space, their operations are not subject to these laws. The workings of the mind are not publicly accessible; they are wholly private. The working of each person's mind is perfectly transparent to him; each subject is directly and immediately conscious of the content of his own mental life. But this mental life of a subject is accessible only to him; for others it remains a closed book. Each person's life career proceeds on two separate tracks—the bodily and the mental, the public and the private.

The relationship between the two realms is sometimes described in spatial metaphors: the mental life is inner and the bodily life outer; one is internal, the other external. But if we press the metaphor we will see that its explanatory power is illusory, for "inside" or "inner" are still spatial notions—and we were told that minds are not in space at all. This points up once more the perennial problem of interaction, which in spite of many valiant efforts by Descartes' successors has never been solved to anyone's satisfaction. The problem, to restate it briefly, is as follows. How can something intrinsically private become public? What are the actual transactions between the private and the public episodes in the history of an individual? It seems that the language referring to such transactions would contain unavoidable self-contradictions: something nonspatial breaks out into space, something immaterial causally affects matter, and the other way around.

That the connection between a person's body and his mind becomes inexplicable and mysterious is but one absurd consequence of the insistence on the intrinsic privacy of the mental. Another consequence is the inevitable isolation of minds from one another. For the only "evidence" in support of the existence of such minds comes to us in the form of their bodily manifestations. But how do we know that they are manifestations of *minds*? If in our own case such a connection cannot be established, how can we say that it holds in the case of others? We observe a person's body and its various ways of behaving, but being shut up in our private consciousness we cannot get at the mind of someone else. We cannot know the individual characteristics of the other alleged mind, because these characteristics are locked up in the other person's private realm. Thus, the conclusion must be solipsism. As Ryle puts it: "Absolute solitude is on this showing the ineluctable destiny of the soul. Only our bodies can meet."

The separation of the private from the public would mean that we could never give any verdicts about other people's mental characteristics. When judged on the basis of what we can observe him to do or say, a person may appear to be a genius, but for all that, it is not impossible that in reality, in his private mental realm, he may be an idiot. Or conversely, idiotic behavior does not preclude the possibility that behind that behavior there resides a brilliant mind. Thus, the theory precludes our offering even everyday normal estimates of other people's personal characteristics. Furthermore, it makes it hazardous for a person to claim sanity even for himself, for after all, being denied access to the rational qualities of real others (not just their bodies), he could not compare his characteristics with theirs.

Ryle offers some conjectures as to the motives behind the emergence of the theory of mind as a ghostly theatre behind the bodily scene. Descartes was obviously impressed by the success of the new physics and its mechanical laws. On the one hand, he was attracted by the explanatory powers of the materialistic doctrines. On the other hand, he could not follow Hobbes in adopting them wholeheartedly as applicable to all phenomena, including the mental. Therefore, he began to talk about the mind in *para*mechanical terms. If mental conduct should not be described in terms of mechanical processes, then we must describe it in terms of nonmechanical processes. If matter obeys causal laws, then the workings of minds must be regarded as results of some nonmechanical causes. Ryle observes that the Cartesian description of the workings of the mind is given by mere negatives: "They are not in space, they are not motions, they are not modifications of matter, they are not accessible to public observation. Minds are not bits of clockwork, they are just bits of not-clockwork." Ryle concedes that the *para*mechanical theory of mind may be an advance over the *para*political model which it replaced and which regarded the mind as a series of hierarchical faculties, where ruling, obeying, collaborating, and rebelling were the accepted idioms.

The paramechanical model is clearly at work in the concept of will which represents volitions as inner mental thrusts. According to the theory, the inventory of the inner also includes special episodes called volitions, which are supposed to link the mind with its "expressions" in the public world. But these episodes, being essentially mental in character, cannot provide a link to bodily processes. They are said to provide links between minds and bodies, although the theory itself forbids such transactions. Again, the problem of interaction comes to plague us.

Moreover, if every bodily action, to be called voluntary, must issue from a mental volition, then every volition, if it is to claim voluntary status, must issue from another voluntary volition—and so on *ad infinitum*. The causal model of voluntary action, relying as it does on a paramechanical explanation, cannot explain how action comes about. It strikes Ryle as significant that the language of volitions is never used by ordinary people, for instance, no one ever says that one performs a few difficult and many easy volitions a day.

Another area in which philosophers, leaning on the dogma of the ghost in the machine, have introduced conceptual confusion is the theory of perception. In this area philosophers introduced another dubious term, namely, the notion of sensation, thus writing several chapters in paraoptics—a pseudoscience of mental life—of which the British Empiricists were especially fond. The key mistake, says Ryle, was to assimilate sensation to observation. According to the theory, sensing is a kind of seeing, and since each seeing has an object, then every sensation has to have an object. Thus Locke concluded that we really do not experience objects but rather their qualities—primary and secondary. Hume believed that the foundation of knowledge is impressions, verdicts of the senses of which we are directly aware in perception.

Ryle's criticism of the doctrine of sensations begins with a confession of a certain uneasiness even in talking about them. For to talk about them is already to accept the philosopher's theory that there are such entities and that there are mental acts of "observing them." But the philosopher's talk about sensations clearly deviates from that of ordinary people, who do not say that looking at a yellow flower gives them a sensation of yellow. Ordinary perceptual reports do not refer to sensations but to objects. Sensations are typically described by employing the vocabulary of common objects and cannot be described otherwise. As Ryle puts it, we never talk about sensations "neat," in isolation from the common context in which colors, sounds, shapes, and tastes are experienced. Sensation words draw their significance from the objects in the presence of which the sensation may be had, objects like fleas, needles, and stoves. Moreover, the description of sensations often includes the way they strike us—as pleasant, painful, disturbing, exciting, or annoying. Because pain is something I mind having, the expression "unnoticed pain" does not make sense.

If sensations were something one could observe, then it would be possible to do it more or less successfully. We make mistakes in observation, but having a sensation is not something concerning which one could either make or avoid a mistake. Sensations can be neither correct nor incorrect. No mental powers of discrimination are employed in having sensations; hence, Ryle thinks it is quite correct to say that there is nothing "mental" about sensations. Furthermore, one does not witness them; there can be a witness or several witnesses to a fire, but no witness to a qualm. It is also incorrect to say that sensations are something that we *feel*. When grit gets in your eye, you may rightly report a strange or unpleasant sensation in your eye, and when the grit is removed it makes sense to ask "How does your eye feel now?" But when you switch your gaze from one object to another it would make no sense to inquire: "Did the feeling in your eye change when you switched your gaze from the table to the chair?"

The sense-datum theory, which claims that we do not see objects but only sense data out of which the mind "logically constructs" objects, also assimilates the concept of sensation to the concept of observation. It has borrowed verbs applicable to the latter, e.g., "observe," "scan," or "savor," and transplanted them into the shadowy realm of inner episodes called sensations, so that words like "intuit," "cognize," and "sense" are supposedly referring to special cognitive relationships in which the mind stands to sense data. But this is sheer mystification, concludes Ryle. "Sensations then, are not perceivings, observings, or findings; they are not detectings, scannings, or inspectings; they are not apprehendings, intuitings, or knowings. To have a sensation is not to be in cognitive relation to a sensible object. There are no such objects nor is there any such relation."[6]

Another area in which the dogma of the ghost in the machine does epistemological damage lies in the analysis of imagination. Imaginings, too, are supposed to be ghostly seeings. Although it is true that imagining occurs, it is false to say that images are seen or scanned by an inner eye. Once more, one is victim of a wrong assimilation. Hume's account of ideas as copies of impressions is a most typical example of such a mistake. For one to fancy to hear, he must *not* hear. "An imagined shriek is not ear-splitting, nor yet is it a soothing murmur, and an imagined shriek is neither louder nor fainter than a heard murmur. It neither drowns it nor is drowned by it." This illustration shows that the kinds of characterizations we apply to sights seen and sounds heard cannot be applied to sounds "heard" or sights "seen" in the imagination. Only *within* imagining can we distinguish between vivid and hazy pictures, but Humean impressions cannot be described as vivid at all. We may picture vividly, but we do not see vividly. Hence, the assimilation of "ideas" or images as copies to their originals is based on a misleading analogy. Ryle shows this mistake by drawing another analogy. "One actor may be more convincing than another actor; but a person who is not acting is neither convincing nor unconvincing, and cannot therefore be described as more convincing than an actor."[7] The temptation to construe imaginings as a kind of seeing is strong for those who have accepted some version of the sense-datum theory of perception. If one can "see" sense data, then one can also contemplate one's imaginings. But if it is wrong to say that I can witness myself sensing, i.e., seeing or hearing, then it is also wrong to say that I can observe my imagined seeing or hearing.

One thing needs to be kept in mind while following Ryle's criticisms. He is not denying that people have minds and exhibit mental characteristics. What he is attacking is the *description* of these phenomena in terms of what has become an official doctrine. Only those who are victims of this doctrine may mistake his criticism of their account of volition, sensation, or imagination for a denial of the aspects of experience about which they are theorizing. In the very first chapter Ryle insists that he is not "denying that there occur mental processes." However, he thinks that the account of them in terms of the Cartesian myth is wrong or misleading. It does not square with what we know to be true about minds and mental processes and with what is already embedded in linguistic distinctions which each of us actually makes in daily life. It is not just the conflict between the philosopher's theory and the ordinary people's way of speaking. Ryle, himself a philosopher, sees his job as one which requires pointing out the confusions and absurdities in a philosophical theory by utilizing distinctions which, as far as we can tell are not themselves problematic. This does not mean that the ordinary people's distinctions could not be wrong—they are not immune to criticism, should such criticism be in order. This only means that we cannot ignore the working distinctions and discriminations of which we avail ourselves in making sense of our experiences. What Ryle proceeds to say about the nature of minds in a positive way is based on what he believes to be acknowledged as true and correct in our familiar ways of referring to mental operations and characteristics.

There is one type of mistake to which philosophers are especially prone. We have encountered it in some of the critical remarks discussed above, namely, the assimilation of a mode of speaking in one area of experience to another area where this mode of speaking is inapplicable. Ryle calls this a category mistake and gives numerous illustrations of it. A person watching the march of a division of soldiers may wonder why he does not see the division marching by but only battalions, batteries, and squadrons. He thinks that a division must be something *in addition* to the elements which make it up. Similarly, a team's *esprit de corps* is not exhibited alongside the particular performances; a player cannot display it as something separate from his actual playing of the game. The American Constitution is not one of the items parallel to the executive, legislative, and judiciary branches of the government; none of them is related to the Constitution in the ways in which it is related to the other branches of government. It would be a category mistake to regard the Constitution as one of the institutions which it delineates.

The warning against the category mistake is a warning against improper linguistic assimilations. This is what happened when the theory of mind was couched in paramechanical and paraoptical terminology. The consequence was a displacement of our attention from concretely available facts of experience to a ghostly realm of inner mental processes. The way to correct this mistake is to return our attention to situations in which the presence of mental operations and characteristics is acknowledged in our actual use of language.

In the chapter entitled "Knowing How and Knowing That," Ryle reminds us that the notion of human intelligence is much broader than the overintellec- tualized account given of it by philosophers. In a very important sense "knowing how" is logically prior to the more sophisticated "knowing that." It is also a more appropriate context in which to explore the nature of mind. To know how to do something is to display a certain capacity and competence; it is a disposition, an exercise of a skill. When we say that a person knows how to do something, we are not referring to any processes or acts or episodes going on in him—in his mind, in his brain, or in his head. A disposition is not an act and not a series of acts. To think of it in this way would be, again, to make a category mistake. To refer to something as a mental process is not to ascribe to it some special cause. Here, an analogy may help. When a pane of glass breaks, two kinds of explanations could be given: (1) it was hit by a stone, and (2) glass is a brittle substance. When we speak of mental capacities, the second kind of explanation is in order. Why did the student give the right answer? She knows arithmetic. She has mastered the skills of arithmetic and therefore *can* give right answers in this area. Her knowledge, then, is a dispositional property. "To possess a dispositional property is not to be in a particular state, or to undergo a particular change; it is to be bound or liable to be in a particular state, or undergo a particular change, when a particular condition is realized."[8]

When we think of mental phenomena in dispositional terms, we avoid the pitfalls of the dualistic picture. Being intelligent does not consist of two operations: doing something and thinking what one is doing. When a clown trips on purpose his action is both physical and mental, and there are not two separate processes going on. Intelligent performance satisfies the criteria of competence which the agent knows how and when to apply. This does not necessarily mean that he needs to state what these criteria are: he may know how to tie a knot correctly without being able to give verbal accounts of how it is done.

Skills and competencies are acquired by learning, but we should not equate learning with mere drill. This would be another category mistake. Human learning is typically *training* which involves more than mere mechanical habituation. "It is of the essence of intelligent practices that one performance is modified by its predecessors. The agent is still learning. . . . Drill dispenses with intelligence, training develops it."[9] Furthermore, intelligent dispositions are not one-track responses. A polite person is trained to respond politely in infinitely heterogeneous situations. He also manifests the ability to recognize situations in which politeness is in order, which may involve saying and doing things, or refraining from doing them.

Ryle calls attention to the fact that we have adequate linguistic devices to capture the meaning of dispositional descriptions. When we say that glass is brittle, we are making a lawlike statement; we are saying that under certain conditions glass is likely to shatter. It can also be described as a hypothetical statement: if such and such conditions obtain, glass will shatter. We understand the meaning of such statements quite adequately and we use them daily. Only an epistemologist's prejudice would confine the use of sentences to the job of reporting facts actually obtaining at the time of utterance. We get information when we are told that a substance is soluble or that a person knows Latin. The former means that if the substance is placed in a liquid, it will dissolve; the latter means that if the person is shown an original text by Cicero, he will understand and translate it. The "would" or "could" words can also convey information and should not be relegated to an epistemological limbo. With their help we can formulate statements which function as "inference licenses" allowing us to predict or expect some things in the future.

Ryle also observes that many statements, especially those used to describe mental characteristics, fall into the border area between categorical and hypothetical statements. He calls them "semi-hypothetical" or "mongrel-categorical." Such a statement functions in some respects as a statement of brute fact and in others a license to inference. It is both narrative and predictive. As an example he gives the colloquial accusation "you *would* miss the train." The statement refers to both the particular error for which a reproach is made (the categorical aspect) and also the propensity which makes the error predictable (the hypothetical aspect). This hypothetical aspect allows us to conclude that other similar actions could be predicted of that person. The recognition of mongrel-categorical statements also helps to account for such celebrated perceptual puzzles as the elliptical appearance of round plates or the bent look of sticks in water. "The plate has an elliptical look" is also a mongrel-categorical statement, whereby we apply a rule about untilted elliptical plates to the actual look of the plate. A proposition is complex yet not mysterious.

So the topic of mind is "not the topic of untestable categorical propositions, but the topic of sets of testable hypothetical and semi-hypothetical propositions." It is an inquiry into capacities, skills, habits, propensities, liabilities, and bents. We discover that there are other minds in understanding what people say and do, but this discovery is not an inference from some operations behind the scenes. When I follow your speech, appreciate your joke, or understand your chess move, I am in the presence of your mind and you are in the presence of mine. Of course, we can misunderstand each other, but misunderstanding makes sense only against a background of a possible understanding. We follow other people's minds when we follow their styles and their procedures.

The topic of mind is concerned with the "characterization of such stretches of human behavior as exhibit qualities of intellect and character." Here, the typically dispositional words, such as "know," "believe," "aspire," "clever," and "humorous," have determinable meanings. Similarly, when we refer to inclinations and motives, dispositional accounts are in order. Explanations by motive are inquiries into the agent's character, or at least into his temporary bent or propensity. This is the procedure of novelists and biographers, who stick to describing what *persons* do and undergo instead of limiting themselves to "descriptions" of what goes on in people's minds. In this respect their example is to be preferred to that of epistemologists. Here is Ryle's account of what we understand by "conceit," a mental characteristic *par excellence*. "To be conceited is to tend to boast of one's own excellences, to pity or ridicule the deficiencies of others, to daydream about imaginary triumphs, to reminisce about actual triumphs, to weary quickly of conversations which reflect unfavorably upon oneself, to lavish one's company upon distinguished persons and to economize in association with the undistinguished."[10] This certainly is not a single-track disposition.

Another thing to keep in mind is that even when describing what is personal to ourselves, we have to describe it in neutral and impersonal terms. Even the words referring to sensations, if they are to be understood, by either ourselves or others, must be granted the meanings commonly ascribed to them. How else could we identify and describe our sensations, feelings, and moods? Even secondary qualities are public. When we identify something as green, we indicate that it would look so to anyone in a position to see it properly. When Kant says that perception involves subsuming something under a concept, he suggests that some special process is going on, some ghostly wheels are going round. But he is on the right track if he wants to call attention to the fact that a person who does not know, for example, what mosquitoes are and what they sound like could not identify the whine of one circling close by.

Returning to the concept of *intellect*, which he has described as a sophisticated species of mental competencies, Ryle winds up his positive account by granting the intellectual powers a certain primacy, namely, cultural primacy, which is obviously connected with education, instruction, with didactic discourse. Intellectual work is an activity of a specific sort, with its own criteria of achievement and excellence. But it is wrong to think of it as having causal anteriority to all intelligent activities. People learn how to argue logically and coherently without taking a course in logic. Again, it was the epistemologist's prejudice that construed "judgment," "deduction," "inference," and "abstraction" as kinds of processes. These words do not refer to processes; rather, they indicate verdicts. They are the referees', not the biographers' words. Mastery of arguments is also a skill in which one can be instructed. To grasp an abstract idea, e.g., the concept of contour, is to learn how to execute certain tasks with the help of maps. Although the cultural primacy of intellect as the ability to perform certain specialized sophisticated tasks is undeniable, each human being displays the characteristics of minds in numerous ways, such as attending, trying, wanting, fearing, perceiving, recollecting, learning, pretending, and many others.

Ryle concludes his analysis of mind by indicating that the abandonment of the dogma of the Ghost in the Machine can be indeed liberating.

> *Abandonment of the two-worlds legend involves the abandonment of the idea that there is a locked door and a still to be discovered key. These human actions and reactions, those spoken and unspoken utterances, those*

*tones of voice, facial expressions and gestures, which have always been the data of all the other students of men, have after all been the right and the only manifestations to study. They and they alone have merited, but fortunately not received, the grandiose title "mental phenomena."* [11]

The workings of people's minds are studied not only by psychologists but also by "economists, criminologists, anthropologists, political scientists, and sociologists, by teachers, examiners, detectives, biographers, historians, and players of games, by strategists, statesmen, employers, confessors, parents, lovers, and novelists." [12]

Ryle's positive account of the nature of mind rests on his recognition that our actual talk about mental phenomena and characteristics does not exhibit the character of concealedness ascribed to it by Cartesian philosophers. He shows this particularly in the section entitled "Unstudied Talk," where he reminds us that learning to talk is at the same time learning to make oneself understood. If I know what "depression" means, I can refer by this term not only to your depression but to mine as well. The normal feature of unstudied talk, in contrast to more sophisticated forms, including pretending and dissembling, is that it is not guarded but is based on candor. "We have to take special pains to keep things back only because letting them out is our normal response." Unstudied talk can be contrasted with studied conversational talk and other forms of unstudied talk, including the didactic, pedagogical, and homiletic talk. Nevertheless it is the basis of all other forms of talk. We make the mistake of concluding that because some of our use of language involves concealments, *all* of it does. "But the fact that concealments have to be penetrated does not imply that non-concealments have to be penetrated." Some utterances are direct avowals and could be described as coming from the heart and not from the head. My saying "I am depressed" or "I am bored" may be a way of *showing* that I am depressed or bored. Such utterances, Ryle remarks, require no sleuth work.

This way of seeing the functioning of our language will not appear surprising if we but remember how language is learned. A child does not begin by learning words which are of no interest to her. On the contrary, language is injected into interest already present. A child is told the names of things in which she is taking interest, and taking interest at the time the word is uttered. Therefore, the name attachment does not occur in an abstract vacuum; it is an integrating transaction where language and life meet. This is particularly true when the "mental" phenomena—emotions, moods and feelings, instructions, rebukes, and counsels—are predominant. Consequently, when we follow the talk of a person who has mastered a language, there is no reason for separating the reported experience from the linguistic vehicle by means of which the report is made:

> To say something significant, in awareness of its significance, is not to
> do two things, namely to say something aloud or in one's head and at
> the same time, or shortly before to go through some other shadowy move.
> It is to do one thing with a certain drill and in a certain frame of mind,
> not by rote, chattily, recklessly, histrionically, absentmindedly, or
> deliriously, but on purpose, with a method, carefully, seriously, and on
> the qui-vive. Saying something in this specific frame of mind, whether
> aloud or in one's head, is thinking the thought. [13]

Philosophy as language analysis is never the analysis of *mere* language.
Language is never *mere*.

## 3. Austin on Speech Acts

John L. Austin (1911-1960), is regarded as an original and seminal thinker
among analytic philosophers. While brilliantly pursuing his studies of classics
at Balliol, he became interested in philosophy and in 1933 became a Fellow
of Oxford's All Souls College. Later, he served as a Fellow, a Tutor, and
finally as a Professor in Magdalen College. During World War II he was
head of a section charged with intelligence work in preparation for the invasion
of Western Europe. His expertise and judgment were highly valued by his
military superiors, some of whom expressed the opinion that the life-saving
accuracy of the D-Day intelligence was due largely to Austin's work. After
the war he returned to Oxford and became one of the most influential
philosophers of the postwar period. Concentrating mainly on teaching, he
wrote relatively little, but his few published essays were immediately recognized as breaking new and important ground. The essays were posthumously
published as *Philosophical Papers* (1961) by J.O. Urmson and G.J. Warnock.
Warnock also published *Sense and Sensibilia* (1964), a skillful reconstruction
of Austin's lectures and notes on the theory of perception. Urmson was the
editor of *How to Do Things with Words* (1962), which was originally delivered
as a series of lectures by Austin at Harvard University in 1955. All three
volumes are recognized as classics in analytic philosophy.

Although the focus of Austin's interest was language, his view of what
language is certainly differs from that of a grammarian or lexicographer. Austin
believed that attention to the distinctions already existing in language is
indispensable to the clarification of philosophical problems. When dealing
with a concept, it is first necessary to make an inventory of variants of its
meaning, of its cognates, and of the differences of its application. The interest
in these investigations, which may at first appear superficial, has a deeper
rationale. This rationale has been expressed by Austin in one of his most
influential essays, "A Plea for Excuses," published in 1956:

*When we examine what we should say when, what words we should use in what situations, we are looking not merely at words (or "meanings," whatever they may be) but also at the realities we use the words to talk about: we are using a sharpened awareness of words to sharpen our perception of, though not as a final arbiter of, the phenomena. For this reason I think, it might be better to use, for this way of doing philosophy, some less misleading name than those given above ["ordinary language," "linguistic" or "analytic philosophy," or "the analysis of language"]— for instance, "linguistic phenomenology," only that it is rather a mouthful.* [14]

Austin's "Plea for Excuses" deals with the traditional problem of responsibility for actions. But he does not think that much will be gained by examining the concept of responsibility by itself. After all, there are other words which are commonly used when the question of someone's responsibility is considered, such as doing something "knowingly," "deliberately," "intentionally," "voluntarily," "inadvertently," "by mistake," "under duress," etc. In describing actions we naturally employ such expressions because they do throw further light on the nature of the action discussed. The words used have not appeared in our vocabulary without reason; they acknowledge differences and nuances which are important for us to take into account if we are to describe correctly what is taking place. In this way, the richer vocabulary at our disposal may tell us something important about the phenomenon we are trying to understand and explain. Linguistic phenomenology enables us to appraise facts more accurately.

Austin had seriously considered the possibility of carefully classifying the different kinds of sentences and expressions we use. In this respect, he differs from Wittgenstein, who was merely calling our attention to the fact that there are "*countless* kinds" of sentences. Wittgenstein probably thought that an attempt to classify them would be useless, but to Austin this looked like a promising venture. Shortly after the war, he, together with a group of Oxford philosophers, conducted sessions during which they endeavored to establish and clarify existing linguistic distinctions, aiming at a thorough inventory of things which language allows us to say. Austin thought that this painstaking, quasiscientific approach could serve as either a preliminary to solving some philosophical problems or self-justifying clarificatory activity. The value of such a venture remains controversial, and Austin himself believed that it would call for a prolonged monumental effort to survey the domain of the existing linguistic distinctions. Nevertheless, he entertained the hope that such a project was feasible. This invitation to study language carefully does not imply that language is static. It need not be denied—and Austin did not deny this—that language can be modified and improved. He merely observed that we must be clear about what language is like before we try to improve it.

One of the results of paying attention to already existing linguistic distinctions is that we do not fall victim to premature and rigid dichotomizing, that is, dividing all phenomena into mutually exclusive classes. One such celebrated dichotomy is the distinction between appearance and reality. Austin believed that this distinction loses much of its metaphysical appeal if we recognize that the word "real" does not denote some special ontological realm, on the other side of all possible appearances. In *Sense and Sensibilia* Austin argued that if we look closely at the little word "real," we will be less tempted to discuss such topics as "the Nature of Reality." For one thing, when trying to decide whether or not something is real, the negative use of the word seems to be more important. We say that something is real in order to mark it off from the specific ways in which it may be found to be *not* real. A duck is a real duck if it is not a dummy, a decoy, a toy, or a picture. Therefore, "the function of 'real' is not to contribute positively to the characterization of anything, but to exclude possible ways of being *not* real."

Furthermore, "real" belongs to a group of other words which fulfill the same function, among which are: "proper," "genuine," "live," "true," "authentic," and "natural." Words which are often used as a contrast to "real" also fall in this general linguistic dimension: "artificial," "fake," "bogus," "makeshift," and also names such as "dream," "illusion," and "mirage." The opposite of a makeshift theater is not a real but a proper theater; natural silk is opposite to artificial silk; and the opposite of dummy ammunition is not real but live ammunition. Adulterated cream is no less real than pure cream. The wearers of false teeth find them to be nonetheless real. Sometimes "real" may mean "good," as in the exclamation" "This is a *real* carving knife!"

Austin calls the word "real" an *adjuster* word. We use it to adjust other words "to meet the innumerable and unforeseeable demands of the world upon language."[15] In this respect it performs the same function as the word "like." When we run across an animal that looks like a tiger but isn't one, we may say that it is not a *real* tiger but only *like* a tiger. Of course, sometimes it may be convenient to invent a new word for the newly discovered thing or phenomenon, but we are not linguistically helpless without a new name; we may make use of an adjuster word, such as "real" or "like." Having become aware of these various different possibilities of making a significant use of the word "real," we will no longer insist on one uniform meaning of "reality."

A similar point can be made about another pet distinction of philosophers, namely, that between material objects and sense data. The notion of a sense datum depends on its contrast to material objects, but if we look at various candidates for "sense data" we note that they are a mixed bag indeed. The main contention about sense data is that they are *directly* perceived—what we are aware of are our own ideas, impressions, sensa, sense perceptions, percepts, etc. "Perceiving directly" is to be marked off from "perceiving indirectly." But this is not easy. When I look through binoculars, do I see *indirectly*? When I look at myself in the mirror, do I see myself indirectly? If I touch your hand through a glove, is this indirect touching? What can be said about messages transmitted through telephone, television, or radar? Still another case of perceiving indirectly is observing electrons in a Wilson cloud chamber.

When a phenomenalist says that we perceive material objects indirectly, via sense data, does he say any of the things referred to above? If not, what does he say? It is not clear. Austin concludes that the only role which the phenomenalists' notion of material object plays is that of a foil for "sense datum." But if we try to make a list of things that we can perceive, the list will not be limited to any *one* sort of things. We perceive not only people, people's voices, rivers, mountains, but also flames, rainbows, shadows, vapors, gases, and pictures on a movie screen. Not all of these items can be split into two aspects, a sensation on the one hand and a material object on the other. Thus, close attention to what we can say about our perceptions gives little support to the phenomenalist's dichotomy.

Austin's other philosophical investigations bring to light further important discoveries. In many cases we use words not just to *say* something but also to *do* something. A typical example is the expression "I promise." The utterance of these words is an *act*; when spoken under appropriate conditions it *introduces* a new fact into the situation, namely, that the person who spoke these words is subsequently under an obligation. The utterances which signify a doing of some sort Austin called "performative" and initially contrasted them with "constatives," utterances whose primary function *is* to say something, to convey information. Here are other examples of performatives: "I acquit you," spoken by a judge in a trial; "I bequeath . . . ," written in a last will and testament; "I apologize," spoken by anyone in countless situations; "I do," spoken by a bride in a marriage ceremony. Such doings are of course *also* sayings, but the saying in itself does not reveal the *whole* phenomenon of which saying is a part. We must look beyond the saying to appreciate the *force* of the utterance.

Indeed, in his later investigations of the distinction, Austin came to adopt the term "force" as providing a useful linguistic tool. In *How to Do Things with Words* he argued that every total speech act or utterance has three aspects, or can be examined from three different perspectives. First, there is the locution itself which consists of speaking (or writing) certain words which have meaning in a language, that is, have sense and refer to something. Second, in addition to the meaning of the locution, it may have a certain force, which Austin calls "illocutionary force." The illocutionary force of an utterance shows what a person *does, in* saying something. For instance, the locution "The door is open" may not be just a comment; it may also have the force of a request, or of an order—if spoken by someone in authority and in a certain tone of voice. Third, the speaking of some words may have a further consequence: the door will actually be shut by the hearer. This consequence Austin calls "perlocutionary force"; *by* saying something, the speaker has brought about certain results. For example, the illocutionary force of a statement may have been only to warn, but the actual consequence, or the perlocutionary force of the utterance, was that the hearer became alarmed. Similarly, the illocutionary force may be merely to argue a point; whether the perlocutionary force will also be to *convince* the hearer is an open question.

Austin believes that to call attention to the illocutionary force of utterances is to make us more fully aware of the different functions language performs. To understand what is being said one needs to know more than the meaning of locutions; one must also appreciate their point and purpose, the kind of role they play in a given context. It is a prejudice to regard the *statement* form as the paradigm of the successful use of language. Logical positivists had concluded that statements expressing ethical judgments are meaningless because they cannot be true or false. But Austin reminds us that for some utterances the demand for verification is misguided; their function calls for a different standard of appraisal. The determination of the truth or falsity of an utterance is in many cases simply not called for. This does not mean, however, that the utterances could not be wrong or go wrong in other ways.

So far, philosophers have tended to recognize only two kinds of infelicities (Austin's term) in using language. A statement is out of order when it is found to be either self-contradictory or factually false. But consider the defendant's lawyer saying to his client during a trial: "I acquit you." The utterance is "infelicitous," it "misfires" because the lawyer is not the person entitled to utter the words with the force with which the judge can use them. Think of the notorious incidents in which the Brooklyn bridge was sold to unsuspecting dupes who assumed that anyone who offers to sell the bridge can be presumed to own it. Or consider Austin's example: "When the saint baptized the penguins, was it void because the procedure of baptizing is inappropriate to be applied to penguins, or because there is no accepted procedure of baptizing anything except humans?"[16]

What indicates the standards by which the use of language, or performance of speech acts, is assessed? The total context of their utterances, answers Austin. The purely verbal, or locutionary, considerations are, of course, relevant. The words used must have accepted meanings, and their reference must be clear. But in addition there are other conventions of which the speakers are normally aware and which make clear whether or not the utterance was felicitous, successful. Sometimes the point of an utterance cannot be seen from just its form: "This is yours" may be used as information, but also as making a gift. The speaker's being committed by his promise is a matter of convention, and this convention enters into the illocutionary force of "I promise." Here, it is useful to remember Austin's claim that what needs investigation is not *mere* language but also the various ways in which it connects with the world and with what we do. "The ice is thin," when spoken in appropriate circumstances, can be rightly taken as a warning. "The door is open" may be a report, an order, a request, or a hint. "I declare war," said by the chief of a state who does not intend to fight, is a misuse of language. Its illocutionary force may have bad perlocutionary consequences. Some historians believe that when the Secretary of State declared that the United States would not intervene militarily if South Korea should be attacked, he thereby encouraged the North Koreans to proceed with their aggressive designs against South Korea.

Whether there are rules governing the conventions by means of which the illocutionary force of utterances can be determined is an open question, although one philosopher, J.R. Searle, defends such a conclusion in his book *Speech Acts*. Austin limited himself to saying that there are conventions governing the illocutionary forces of utterances, although he warned that it is often difficult to decide where conventions begin and where they end. But he urged that we determine the happiness or unhappiness (his words) of utterances while keeping in mind the total context. Locutions and illocutions are abstractions; "every genuine speech act is both."

Furthermore, we should not draw arbitrary boundaries around the use of such words as "true" and "false." These words, like "free" and "unfree," do not stand for anything simple at all, believes Austin. They stand "only for a general dimension of being a right or proper thing to say as opposed to a wrong thing, in these circumstances, to this audience, for these purposes and with these intentions." [17] There are utterances which look like constatives, or factual statements, but which the use of the word "true" does not really help to characterize. Austin's example is "France is hexagonal." Is this description true or false? Neither, remarks Austin; the description is merely *rough*.

On the other hand, it is not quite correct to say that the utterances which appear to be primarily performative have no connection with truth. When we infer *validly*, argue *soundly*, or judge *fairly* we are moving within the dimension of assessment in which truth and falsity are relevant. Upon scrutinizing the performative-constative distinction, Austin began to wonder whether it could survive. In some sense, stating, affirming, concluding, and identifying are also expressive of illocutionary forces and hence have a performative dimension. "Surely to state is every bit as much to perform an illocutionary act as, say, to warn or to promise." By saying "The cat is on the mat," I indicate that I believe it to be true. The statement would be infelicitous, it would be wrong for me to make, if I didn't believe it to be true. When we ask: "Is it a fair statement?" we are not interested merely in its truth or falsity. "The truth or falsity depends not merely on the meaning of words but on what act you were performing in what circumstances." In trying to understand what is said we must bring to bear on utterances all the dimensions of assessment which would do justice to the total speech act. This includes standards of logic and of factual correctness, but also other considerations and conventions of which the speakers of language can normally be expected to be aware.

Austin's analysis shows that philosophers who concentrate on the meaning of words and utterances are likely to ignore other dimensions of language use. Meaning is an abstraction and cannot capture all that language is and does. Hence there is the need to examine the total speech act and the conventional standards by which it is governed. The notion of illocutionary force may be regarded as an umbrella term covering various types of assessment criteria: true/false, right/wrong, fair/unfair, correct/incorrect, good/bad. Whether what is said is a proper thing to say depends not only on the facts but also on the purposes and other circumstances of the speech act. For instance, a command is "unhappy," or out of order, if the speaker has no authority to command, that is, if he is not entitled to obedience. But even if he does have such authority, the command could be assessed on yet other grounds. Is it *fair* for him to exercise this authority, in this way, at this time, with respect to such and such objects? The hearer may say: "I understand that you are commanding me and that you have a right to do so, but I don't understand your command. It does not make sense to me—in these circumstances." In assessing the command it is also relevant to consider its objectives, the motives it involves, the values which it would realize or fail to realize. All of these things may be necessary to understand in order to assess the command. If so, the dichotomy between facts and values would be difficult to maintain. Uttering such expressions as "I promise," "I bet," or "I do" in appropriate circumstances may have consequences of not only a logical but also a moral sort. According to Austin, "Accuracy and morality alike are on the side of the plain saying that *our word is our bond.*"

One of the reasons for concentrating on language analysis was the realization that the program of logical positivism was just too reductionist. The picture of the world it painted, even if true up to a point and under certain restricted conditions, did not provide an acceptable account of the full sweep of human experience. Referring to his *Tractatus*, Wittgenstein at a later date remarked that there was nothing wrong with it as such; it was like a clock that functioned faultlessly, except that it failed to show the right time. Nevertheless, this way station in the journey of philosophy was interesting and instructive. Besides showing that a temptation to produce a neat, elegant, simple, and all-inclusive account of the world is extremely hard to resist, its latest failure helped to prompt explorations in new directions. Wittgenstein discovered, for instance, that it is a serious mistake to think of language as always working on one model: a name and its object. This is how he began to turn toward the thoughts which led to his *Philosophical Investigations*.

Closer attention to the way language actually works, to distinctions it makes and to functions it performs, opened up new territories for philosophical exploration. The change brought about by the pioneering efforts of Wittgenstein, Ryle, and Austin was enormous, as evidenced in the philosophical literature of the last three decades and in the discussion carried on in journals and in professional meetings. The change was frequently referred to as a revolution in philosophy, and it is undeniable that the analytic approach became dominant in the English-speaking world—England, America, Australia. As more translations became available, the interest in language analysis began to spread to other countries as well.

One of Whitehead's maxims was: seek simplicity and distrust it. Wittgenstein was struck by the fact that the quest for simplicity, for one simple model, is harder to resist than we think. He would qualify Whitehead's maxim by adding that the very *impulse* to simplicity is to be distrusted, because usually it leads to oversimplification and distortion. The philosophers' persistent tendency to think that all language involves naming, that to every word there must correspond an object, is the prime example of such an oversimplification. A truly empirical attitude would be to look and see just *how* language functions. If we do so, we will discover that we do a great many *different* things by means of language and that those things need not have one common denominator. This is how Wittgenstein was led to conclude that to imagine a language is to imagine a form of life.

Wittgenstein believed this discovery to be applicable to one age-long philosophical problem, namely, universals. Must the things we classify under the same concept have some *one* thing in common, a form, an essence? If this need not be the case, then the Platonic quest of the Forms was a misguided venture. Wittgenstein thought that the things we refer to by the same name need not have any *one* thing in common, but may belong together because of "family resemblances." (Recall his example of a cable in which no single fiber runs throughout the entire length of the cable.) How do we know that people mean the same things as we do when they use the words we do? When examined carefully, the question answers itself. It contains the word "the same." How do we know that we use the expression "the same" as others do? By noticing that we actually succeed in communicating, that we report the same sensations and perceptions, or, as Wittgenstein puts it, that we agree in judgments. This is one of the natural facts about human beings; at a certain point they develop a common vocabulary, a common set of responses when certain words are spoken.

But the kinds of responses and reactions vary indefinitely. Requests differ from statements, expressions of regret from expressions of joy, congratulations from threats, promises from expectations, appraisals from verdicts, apologies from contracts, etc. The consequences of paying attention to the many different things we do with, or by means of, language have immediate consequences for what is to be understood by mind or intelligence. Here, language analysis picks up the line of thought already taken up by the pragmatists, who in their own way refused to accept the view that the mind is to be understood as something which merely contemplates preexisting truths. Perhaps the line goes even farther back, at least back to Kant, who wanted to distinguish between the theoretical and the practical uses of reason—between statements that report what is the case and statements that tell us what we should do. But language analysts go beyond both Kant and the pragmatists and want to call attention to a *great many* different uses of language, not just two.

In Ryle's main work, *The Concept of Mind*, this recognition of the human mind as a rich, multifarious matrix of dispositions, bents, and capacities started from his criticism of Cartesian dualism. But the negative program to expose Descartes' doctrine of "the ghost in the machine" was in fact but a vehicle to defend a positive picture of the human mind. Because of their constrictive, reductionist categories, speculative epistemologists give us a distorted picture. The full-blown workings of the human mind are shown in the accounts which are faithful to all the different kinds of purposes, interests, and dispositions which people exhibit in their verbal and nonverbal behavior. Here, we can learn much from the novelists, biographers, and historians, and not just from philosophers and psychologists.

Austin's notion of a speech act also includes a reference to the total context in which language is used. He advocated a detailed study of different kinds of locutions because he thought it natural to suppose that linguistic distinctions did not arise arbitrarily, but rather in order to express or to facilitate the great variety of pursuits in which human beings engage. Language did not arise spontaneously full-blown, but developed gradually within the context of natural human needs, desires, interests, and aspirations. To treat human experience with respect is also to treat *language* with respect. Although one cannot imagine a greater gulf in philosophical temperament than that dividing Austin and Heidegger, one may see in Austin's plea the same message as Heidegger's: the language *speaks*—it tells us some important things about human beings. Although Austin would certainly stop short of saying that to know about *Dasein*, the human existence, is to get at the unconcealedness of Being, he thought it philosophically important to let language *be* as it reveals something worth knowing about ourselves not just as individual subjects but as participants in a development which is larger than any given person. The thing to remember is that language is not *just* language—it is also a form of life to which it gives expression.

## Questions

1. How did Wittgenstein's dissatisfaction with the notion of a simple object lead him toward the view of language expressed in *Philosophical Investigations*? What are the main features of that view?

2. When Wittgenstein speaks of "family resemblance" among objects falling under the same concept, does he touch on Plato's problems when the latter formulated his Theory of Forms? What takes place when a person understands the meaning of a word—according to Plato, to Peirce, and to Wittgenstein?

3. What is the distinction between grammatical and empirical statements, according to Wittgenstein? Is that distinction similar to that between analytic and synthetic statements?

4. How does Ryle criticize Descartes' mind-body distinction?

5. What is Ryle's positive account of the nature of the human mind? How does he distinguish between intelligence and intellect?

6. Why does Austin say that what is often referred to as analytic or linguistic philosophy could just as well be called "linguistic phenomenology?"

7. What are Austin's reasons for suggesting that the expression "the nature of reality" is confusing and misleading? How does he criticize the sense datum theory of perception?

8. Why does Austin claim that philosophers should not confine themselves to the study of the *meaning* of words and sentences but must also pay attention to the illocutionary forces of utterances?

## Notes

[1] Ludwig Wittgenstein, *Philosophical Investigations*. Oxford: Basil Blackwell & Mott Ltd., 1953, par. 23. Reprinted by permission.

[2] *Ibid.*, par. 66. Reprinted by permission.

[3] *Ibid.*, par. 194.

[4] *Ibid.*, par. 107.

5 Stuart Hampshire in *Mind*, LIX, 1950, pp. 237-255.

6 Gilbert Ryle, *The Concept of Mind*, New York: Barnes & Noble, 1949, p. 214.

7 *Ibid.*, p. 250.

8 *Ibid.*, p. 43

9 *Ibid.*, pp. 40-41.

10 *Ibid.*, p. 171.

11 *Ibid.*, pp. 320-321. Reprinted by permission.

12 *Ibid.*, p. 322.

13 *Ibid.*, p. 296. Reprinted by permission.

14 J.L. Austin, *Philosophical Papers*, 2d ed., edited by J.O. Urmson and J.G. Warnock. Oxford: The Clarendon Press, 1970, p. 182. Reprinted by permission.

15 J.L. Austin, *Sense and Sensibilia*. New York: Oxford University Press, 1964, p. 73.

16 J.L. Austin, *How to Do Things with Words*. Cambridge, MA: Harvard University Press, 1962, p. 24.

17 *Ibid.*, p. 144.

# Chapter Thirteen

# Ethical
# Theories

## 1. Sartre: Existentialist Ethics

Sartre's *Being and Nothingness* discusses many themes which normally fall within the province of ethics, but at the time of writing the book he promised to discuss them explicitly "on an ethical level" in another work to be written later. That work was never written. Indeed, in an interview in 1964, Sartre confessed that by then he regarded the task to be impossible. "From the period when I wrote *La Nausée* I wanted to create morality. My evolution consists in my no longer dreaming of doing so." In spite of Sartre's disclaimers, it is difficult not to see his existentialism as recommending a certain stance toward life. Many books have been written about existentialist ethics, and this would not have been possible if that philosophical position contained or implied no recommendations as to how human beings should act. Although it is true that both Heidegger and Sartre were primarily concerned with offering a philosophical *description* of the "human condition," that description was meant to affect our conception of our possibilities and of the ways they could be expressed in life.

In *Being and Nothingness*, Sartre discusses in some detail one of the central topics of ethics, namely, the concept of value. He says that "human reality is that by which value arrives in the world." Sartre precedes this definition by relating the notion of value to his general point of view. He complains that the moralists have not adequately explained some prominent phenomenological features of value—its unconditionality and its nonbeing. This statement has a paradoxical ring akin to those we encountered before, e.g., that consciousness is what it is and is not what it is. Here, Sartre is being quite consistent and has a similar message to convey. He rightly observes that *qua* normative existent, that is, as something merely aimed at, value does not exist. "Its being is to be value, that is, not-to-be-being." But farther on in the same paragraph he clarifies this dark saying by adding that value does not reside in human acts as redness resides in some objects. "Value is given as a beyond of all acts confronted, as the limit, for example, of the infinite progression of noble acts. Value is beyond being."[1]

Invoking his general view that consciousness is nothingness, Sartre tells us that value is "the lacked." We experience value as that which we do not possess but merely aim at. Since every act of consciousness transcends the facticity of a person, the consciousness of value is a perpetual self-transcending. "The supreme value toward which consciousness of every instance transcends itself by its very being is the absolute being of the self with its characteristics of identity, of purity, of permanence, etc., and as its own foundation. . . . It *is* as the meaning and the beyond of all transcending; it *is* as the absent in-itself which haunts being for-itself." But we also know from Sartre that consciousness, or for-itself, is also freedom. Hence, he concludes that "Value haunts *freedom*."[2]

One of Sartre's chief objectives is to lead us away from the tendency to think that there is something called human nature. When Aristotle said that to understand anything is to know its proper function, he encouraged philosophers to look for this proper function. This can never be found, concludes Sartre. To ask what the nature or essence of humanity is, is to misunderstand it fundamentally. The misunderstanding consists in assimilating a human being to a thing, an "in-itself." An "in-itself" is a finished, completed object. Knowing what the essential features and function of a paperknife are, I can make one. But a person is not an artifact; she continually makes herself what she is by successive decisions. These decisions are not determined by any preexisting structures, essences, or models. This is due to the very nature of human consciousness. Consciousness is a way of introducing a gap between oneself and the world. Thinking a thought involves already being at a distance from the object of one's thought. When I think of something, I am also aware of myself as being related to that something by my act of thinking. But the very fact of consciousness, in which the thinker finds himself not *determined* by the object of his thought, also testifies to the fact of human freedom.

This conclusion has a direct consequence for the characterization of human actions. To be guided by thought, to be conscious of what one is doing, means to be always in a position to either choose or reject what one is doing. This applies to every type of human activity and behavior. Suppose I take a job as a waiter. This means that I have decided to play the role of waiter. But at any moment of playing that role I could cease playing it; the possibility is open to me to give up this project. Of course, I may tell myself why it is important for me to keep playing it, and thus I can convince myself that I really have no choice about it. But my deciding that "I have no choice about it" is my decision to view the situation in this light, and hence it is not true that I am determined to remain in that state by something other than my decision; I have simply chosen to persist in my initial choice.

The same is true about my moods, emotions, and states of character. It would be an act of "bad faith" on my part to say that my acts of jealousy are simply due to my being a "jealous type." The explanation is the other way around; because I persist in giving myself over to emotions of jealousy, I can say of myself that I am jealous. Jealousy does not belong to me as say, the odor of an onion belongs to that onion. If I am jealous, sad or envious, it is only because I continually *make* myself jealous, sad, or envious. For Sartre, I am free not to be what I am in these respects.

Sartre regards emotions as ways of responding to the world and therefore as analogous to actions. Like actions, emotions give expression to our projects. A girl who does not want to make a painful confession breaks down in tears in order not to be able to speak. Although she knows that she still can speak if she chooses, she is pretending, by crying, that this is impossible. When we are angry, we are angry *about* something, and it fits our purposes to see that something angrily—this is the way we want it to appear to us. Thus, emotions are the ways in which we want to perceive the world. They show how we choose to use our freedom.

Acting on principles also invokes choice. I am denying my freedom when I succumb to the authority of a moral principle or adopt a moral code. Actions which stem from the belief that one is morally *bound* to follow certain standards, norms, or precepts are in bad faith. A person who deludes himself into thinking that he has no choice in such situations, that he has to accept the moral verdicts of his social and cultural group, does not realize that any system of values can be dissolved in the "nothingness" of his freedom. Not necessity, but the free decision not to make some other use of his freedom keeps him from setting aside whatever claims or principles he actually accepts. A person whose actions are governed by a moral code or a set of principles has surrendered his fundamental capacity to act freely, and this is bad faith, a form of self-deception.

The contention that it is a mistake to look for some common human nature or for a set of functions, goals, or values to be sought by every human being is expressed in the principle: existence precedes essence. This principle points up the independence of the existing individuals of any presumed structures within their psyche, conscious or unconscious. A human individual is not "massif," solid, as a being that is "in-itself." "The in-itself has nothing secret." In contrast, a person cannot be analyzed away into a sum of his knowledge, his beliefs, and his convictions, moral and otherwise. At every moment he is choosing himself; he is condemned to be free.

The principle "existence precedes essence" should also remind us of Sartre's rejection of Cartesian dualism. Acts of consciousness are not only constructions of what a person is conscious *of*, but they are also her aspirations to *be* something. Choices are not only contemplative but also practical; they transform, revolutionize the self. In this sense, Sartre subscribes to the view that the aim of thought should not be just to describe the world but also to change it. As the continual restructuring of our experience, consciousness plays a revolutionary role; it provides both the form and the matter, the theories and the methods of practical implementation. Every decision involves a transformation of facticity or environment into a *situation*. As we have seen, Sartre rejects all forms of determinism. "The environment can only act on the subject to the extent that he understands it; that is, transforms it into a situation."[3] But this transformation does not invoke preexistent rules or principles, nor does it mean to serve as a precedent to be followed by either oneself or others. Each new situation has to be faced afresh, allowing the prereflective consciousness of the agent to make a new, free decision.

As Nietzsche found existence without God difficult and trying, so Sartre reminds us that the absolute freedom of a person to make herself what she wills carries with it the sense of anguish and abandonment. But this is a price which we, having discovered our deeper sense of dignity and responsibility, should be willing to pay. In fact, Sartre believes that the consciousness of being the fashioner of human reality should imbue us with the sense of utter responsibility. My commitments and my actions are always on behalf of all humanity. "In fashioning myself I fashion man."[4] Sartre echoes Dostoyevsky's claim that everyone is responsible for everyone else. He does not make sufficiently clear what precisely he means by responsibility in such contexts, but he seems to interpret the phenomenon of abandonment and anguish as coupled with the realization that the actual human choices will become the future facticity of which the further acts of transcendence will have to take account. "Everything happens to man as though the whole human race had its eyes fixed upon what he is doing and regulated its conduct accordingly."[5] Considerations like these prompt Sartre to assimilate his brand of existentialism to humanism. In 1946 he published an essay entitled *Existentialism and Humanism*, in which he wanted to answer the critics who viewed existentialism as a philosophy of despair. Afterward he regretted its publication and believed its claims to be misleading; the essay, nevertheless, was taken by many readers to state Sartre's ethical views. It has been noted that the views put forth in that essay bear a strong resemblance to Kant's ethical theory. Although every choice is personal and subjective, Sartre says, in choosing for himself each person is choosing for everyone else as well. Each person's responsibility for his free choice "concerns mankind as a whole." My choices are my "commitment on behalf of all mankind." In using my freedom I am endorsing the use of freedom of all other persons, and it would be self-contradictory for me to recognize my freedom without granting the freedom of others.

Although this position resembles Kant's, it also differs from it in important respects. Kant viewed the Categorical Imperative as enabling us to judge morally how the *conflicts* between or among human wills are to be resolved. Recognizing the claim of the Categorical Imperative entails for Kant the curbing of one's freedom as subjective choice insofar as it is based on one's own merely individual desires. Morality, while an expression of human rational freedom, is incompatible with the individual's *arbitrary* choice on behalf of al humankind. Moral responsibility involves recognizing the right of others to judge my acts morally. This is incompatible with Sartre's view of freedom, which must ultimately be lodged in the subjective choice alone, if it is to be authentic and not in bad faith. Therefore, when Sartre speaks of each person's responsibility for humanity as a whole, he means in fact the sense of responsibility to oneself and not to others. But responsibility to oneself, like duty to oneself, is a morally problematic concept. There is an important *contrast* between responsibilities which one has only to oneself and those one has to others. I can release myself of responsibilities I owe to myself, but this alternative is not open to me when I owe them to others; only *they* can release me. Thus, it appears doubtful that Sartre's attempt to assimilate his ethical views to the Kantian position succeeds in expressing Kant's main concern as an ethical theorist.

Some of Sartre's statements make it clear that his views cannot possibly fit into an ethical theory such as Kant's. According to Sartre, even in what we call love only three behavior patterns are possible: indifference, masochism, and sadism. Since love depends on being freely given, it is always in danger of lapsing into indifference. Needing another person's love, we may allow ourselves to be dominated by him or her, to be treated as a thing. The remaining possibility is to control the others by various forms of violence, which is equivalent to sadism. All three forms of relationship are, of course, undesirable and are based on inevitable conflict, and all three indicate that Sartre thinks it impossible to regard other human beings as ends in themselves.

One of the chief difficulties in evaluating the ethical implications of Sartre's view lies in his treatment of the Other, of other people. Sartre's phenomeno-logical analysis concentrates heavily on the subjective side of experience. He shows himself to be a follower of Descartes when he says: "Before there can be any truth whatever, then, there must be an absolute truth, and there is such a truth which is simple, easily attained and within the reach of everybody: it consists in one's immediate sense of one's self."[6] The analysis of human beings as manifesting an absolutely free consciousness, as setting and choosing for themselves their individual destinies with each single decision, seems to be concerned only with the personal aspect of ethics. The insistence on the absolute freedom and human autonomy may appear liberating and exhilarating, and it has so appeared to many readers of Sartre. But the fact that we are also social beings is also of interest to ethics. One may even argue that moral problems arise primarily out of human social settings. If our actions had no effects on others, the scope of ethical inquiry would be much narrower than it is, and one may even wonder whether it would not be radically different. After all, when we speak of a person's moral obligations, we assume the presence of other persons to whom these obligations are due. We do sometimes speak of duties to oneself, but when we stop to think about this expression, we may see that it is not very clear. In the case of a duty to another person, we are bound by that duty until released from it by the person to whom it is owed; it is not within our own power to release ourselves from that duty. But in the case of a duty which is owed to ourselves, we *are* in a position to release ourselves from that duty. This is a morally important difference. Therefore, an adequate analysis of ethics must address itself to interpersonal relations as well, and since our objective is to examine the ethical import of Sartre's views, we should pay some attention to what he says about this aspect of the human condition.

Sartre does recognize the importance of other people in one's experience. Others play a fundamental role in the way we experience our freedom. While my own reality is disclosed to me in my consciousness, others know me only as an object of perception or attention. They see me only from the outside and refer to me by some description, and sometimes by my proper name. Observing my character traits, my habits, my activities, they treat my reality as predictable, as if it were an in-itself. Thus, in their way of viewing me I may appear as a thing, in which my fundamental reality as freedom is either denied or ignored. Even to be looked at is to be reduced in status from a subject to an object. Another person's subjective world, or the way the world looks to her amounts to disintegration of *my* world, as I construct it for myself in my consciousness.

In addition, there is always the temptation to accept the others' view of oneself and thus to lapse into bad faith. Since others may think me a thief or a coward, I *am* what they think me to be. The acceptance of such a reduction of status is, of course, self-deception, because we need not choose to persist in any given role or state. But the way in which others are aware of me can also show me the character of my projects, of my freely chosen self. Imagine yourself peeping through a keyhole of someone's room, believing yourself unobserved. You are so absorbed in this act of looking and listening that you are not even aware of your "self." But then you are jolted into this awareness by suddenly realizing that someone is looking at you, is observing you in your activity. At this moment your intimate selfhood is suddenly disclosed, and you may feel shame or guilt. Since such self-awareness brings into the open what we are up to and discloses our actual desires and wishes, what we are at that moment is made evident through the reality of other people.

The knowledge that the way we manifest ourselves to others is always open to change since this way is conditioned by our freedom and theirs, is not a comforting knowledge. In fact, it is a source of agony and repeated disillusionment. Seeking constantly to fill the "gap in our being," the ever-present nothingness at the heart of our subjective reality, we turn toward projects which promise us stability, solidity, satisfaction. For instance, to be loved by someone may be a source of fulfillment and satisfaction. But if we think that it is something reliable, something we can regard as a permanent possession, we are again in bad faith, self-deceived. The very fact of freedom makes it impossible for any person to achieve a permanent state of satisfaction. The other person's love for us is his or her project, freely given and always open to cancellation. The loving gaze may be withdrawn at any moment, and our dependence on it makes us all the more vulnerable. Knowing our mutual dependence, we frequently use this knowledge to hurt others. "Hell is other people," exclaims Garcin in Sartre's play *No Exit*, when he has realized that there is no greater punishment than that human beings can inflict by denying to others what they desperately need. Garcin, having been branded a coward by his fellow revolutionaries, needs some reassurance by Inez, a person he respects, that the verdict is not just. But Inez, being denied what *she* needs, pronounces her decision: "You are a coward, because I wish it." In the context of the play's action, Inez's choice has a powerful impact on Garcin's self-esteem and drives him to the conclusion that hell is other people.

It would seem, then, that in Sartre's view the fact of human freedom has two faces. Seen from the direction of each individual, it opens up unlimited possibilities for choice, for selection of personal projects. But seen as the freedom of others, it is a constant threat and potential obstacle to all our goals and projects. Because other people have their own intentions, form resolutions, and pursue their own plans, it is natural to expect failure in interpersonal relations. It is precisely the *freedom* of others that is a perpetual outrage to us. Still, to expect this to be different would be an act of bad faith, for this expectation would entail treating others as things, as incapable of exercising their freedom any longer. I cannot get hold of another person's freedom, because I cannot control what she thinks, feels, or intends to do. This is an unfortunate situation if I am dependent on her love or good will. So the human condition is indeed hopeless, and Sartre speaks of man as "useless passion."

There are situations, admits Sartre, in which individuals can participate in common projects. When pursuing some common objective, they can bring their freedom in line with the goals of others. But this relationship is not a genuine sense of unity. It cannot be, because that unity is only the result of a temporary coincidence of goals pursued by separate individuals. As Sartre puts it, "the experience of the 'we' remains on the ground of individual psychology and remains a simple symbol of the longed-for unity of transcendences. It is, in fact, in no way a lateral, real apprehension of subjectivities as such by a single subjectivity; the subjectivities remain out of reach and radically separated.''[7] The group may resort to some special devices to keep the common effort alive. Such a device may be the creation of an external threat or the demand of an oath. But given the ultimate separation of individual subjectivities, such devices are not really effective in linking the individual wills, in giving them a genuinely common goal. Sartre was quite explicit on this point and claimed that the essence of the relation between consciousnesses is *conflict*. It follows from this that if morality consists in the presence of a bond uniting a group of individuals by commitment and loyalty, the existentialist point of view precludes the possibility of morality. Perhaps this is why Sartre decided to give up the thought of "constructing a morality."

The passages in which Sartre appears to invite a Kantian interpretation of right decisions must be taken in some other way. For Kant, a moral person decides not as an isolated individual but as a spokesman for, and a legislator of, the universal society of rational agents. For Sartre, the agent is not in a position to legislate morally for others and can express only his own subjective freedom. How can such decisions be characterized? What Sartre says in other contexts indicates that he thinks of moral decisions as akin to works of art, or rather that human actions are hybrid phenomena, at once aesthetic and moral. When an agent acts he is *making* something of himself. (The ambiguity of the French word *faire* may have conditioned Sartre's thought: *faire* covers both doing and making.) As such, all consciousness is unstable, transitory, and equivocal; it never becomes an object for itself. But in a work of art which embodies a conscious intention, the self achieves something: consciousness secures a symbolic self-expression.

One feature seems to be common to the ethical views of all three existentialist thinkers: their skeptical attitude toward the possibility of a genuine community with others. Nietzsche exalts the individual; his whole philosophy aims at encouraging a person to say "I," because the "we" has dominated the human scene far too long. Even a friend is good only when he helps a strong "I" to emerge. When Heidegger speaks of *Mit-sein*, being with others, he acknowledges only the *fact* that human reality is social. This fact, however, is not seen as a value, as something that adds a dimension of fulfillment to the solitary individual; his primary objective, after all, is to find his way back to Being. Sartre repeatedly points to the impossibility of establishing a mutually fulfilling relationship with another person; on the whole, other people are—

hell. Sadism, masochism, temporary group solidarity (cemented by explicit oath) to gain a specific goal—these are the only kinds of interpersonal relationships that can be realistically envisaged. As we have seen, this conclusion appears to follow from the very fact of freedom as Sartre understands it: the freedom of others robs me of mine, their freedom limits and threatens me at every moment. If so, how can I feel wholly secure in the presence of another?

The contemporary appeal of existentialism probably lies in its explicit interest in the subjective aspects of human existence. When Sartre claimed that his existentialism is a form of humanism, he was not altogether wrong. Even the theistic versions of existentialism aroused interest and attention because, following Kierkegaard, they acknowledged the centrality of individual human existence. Paul Tillich proclaimed that Christianity, in order to remain vital, must keep reaffirming "the Protestant principle," must grant the individual his right and freedom to reinterpret symbols and find his own way to God. Nontheistic or atheistic existentialists have a similar appeal in that they encourage the individual to reject all restraining structures—physical, cultural, or metaphysical—which would constrain the individual's desire for self-expansion and self-fulfillment.

Since all acts of consciousness are intentional, the ways in which an agent handles his situations may be regarded as artifacts, and so all human actions can be seen in terms of artistic symbolism. What we make of ourselves through actions can be referred to as something which we *have*, is our own, a fact which is perhaps captured, by means of a hyphen, in the English word "be-havior." But we should never forget that the meaning of what we do or achieve can be judged *objectively* only from the outside, by others. Thus, a writer, for instance, cannot judge his novel objectively. He must leave this to his readers. Moreover, to be effective, he must address himself to the freedom of others. But if the structure of society tends to deny this freedom, the novelist can only point out roads to freedom to his readers. (*The Roads to Freedom* is the title of one of Sartre's novels on this topic.)

There is also existentialist psychoanalysis, with Sartre as its chief "patron saint." By denying that there is something Freud had called the unconscious, Sartre opened the door to a more direct way of facing self-deception and self-delusion. If everything a person does is due to his or her own free choice, then repressive mechanisms are a myth. The very idea that the mind can be represented by a mechanical model is contrary to the entire existentialist view. Wholly new concepts of the human self have begun to emerge, displacing the Freudian interpretation. Today, a variety of existentialist approaches to psychiatry and psychoanalysis appear to be flourishing, ranging from professional direct psychotherapy to innumerable do-it-yourself encounter groups.

In his later writings Sartre was increasingly preoccupied with the way in which society prevents and oppresses freedom. He began to regard the individual's lack of identity as sociologically and not just ontologically grounded. If the scope for individual freedom is conditioned by the presence of others, the economic conditions, the relationships of property and production cannot be ignored. The fundamental fact of human existence which Sartre wants to exhibit in his latest major work, *Critique of Dialectical Reason*, is economic *scarcity*. As in the earlier works, individual consciousness finds itself *de trop*, superfluous. But now that sense of lack, of being deprived, is heightened by the scarcity of things on which existence depends. In *The Nausea* the chief metaphor was indigestion, the resistance of things in our attempt to assimilate them ontologically; in *The Critique* the main metaphor is actual hunger. Herein lies Sartre's "conversion" to Marxism. But if we keep in mind the original negative accent of his dialectic, we will also notice a basic continuity of his philosophical development. He saw existentialism as a contribution to the emergence of a new social order within the framework of Marxism. Sartre believed that existentialist thought could make Marxism less orthodox and less dogmatic, enabling individuals to see how their choices can contribute to a revolution aimed at the elimination of scarcity and injustice. But whether this continuous effort will lead to success remains forever uncertain; here, Sartre's view differs from the dogmatic verdict of orthodox Marxism. The only thing we can be sure of is that the future will judge us, and since the meaning and outcome of our actions will forever elude us, we should concentrate on the immediate significance of the present and keep to the making and remaking of our own destiny. That destiny is in our hands. "We are left alone, without excuse."[8]

## 2. Dewey: Pragmatic Ethics

Dewey's ethical theory is naturalistic. To him, *any* inquiry is a *natural* process whereby intelligent organisms rearrange their experience in order to achieve a given goal. Inquiry begins, we are told by Dewey, when our natural needs and wants are blocked, when our goals cannot be achieved because of some obstacle or interference. The aim of thought is to restructure the organism's environment in such a way that the blockage disappears and the satisfaction of the goal is possible. Dewey begins by assuming that human organisms *value* certain things and activities. He adds, however, that at the level of mere valuing we are not yet at the level of ethical inquiry. There is a difference between valuing and *evaluating*; only with the latter do we reach the stage of ethics. Dewey agrees with Mill's critics who do not accept his easy transition from "desired" to "desirable." One can value something without evaluating it, that is, without judging whether it is valuable, as one can desire something without considering whether it is desirable.

Questions of ethics deal with the way the transition is made from valuing to evaluating, or from merely valuing something to *judging* something to be valuable. Since this is a matter of judgment, Dewey does not think that problems of ethics can be solved by recourse to feeling or emotion. Valuings themselves, of course, involve feelings and attitudes. It belongs to the very occurrence of valuing that it involves feelings and attitudes. But more belongs to the description of valuing; not only do we feel in a certain way, but we also *behave* in certain ways toward the objects we value, and this behavior shows that we indeed do value them.

Dewey was very concerned about stressing the importance of what he called "behavioral prizings," because at this level we can offer objective descriptions of our values. We can point to things and actions in the world instead of speaking of amorphous inner processes, accessible only through introspection. If we want objective knowledge and not mere subjective impressions, then we should take cognizance of the factual, objective aspects of our valuings. Feelings, or "internal states," are not only fleeting, perishable, and uncontrollable, they are not even publicly accessible. Regarded as an immediate organic state, a feeling is an incomplete datum; in isolation from the objective situation in which it arises, it cannot be ascribed any definite meaning. Feelings always arise in the organism's interaction with its environment and are identifiable only in reference to environmental conditions. They belong to both the subject and its environment at the same time, and not to the subject alone. Dewey believed, therefore, that value theory should study such behavioral transactions as "nourishing, caring for, looking out after, fostering, making much of, being loyal or faithful to, clinging to, holding dear, maintaining in existence, etc." A mother's love for her child is expressed not just in the feelings she harbors, but also in the way she goes about caring for the child in countless daily actions.

A value judgment is called for when the values sought cannot be realized either because of unfavorable circumstances or because they conflict with other things and activities which we also value. The aim of inquiry is to find ways to change the circumstances so as to remove the blockage or to discover how the conflicting values can be harmonized. The former is the simpler case, for it does not raise the question of the desirability of the initially pursued value. The latter case is more difficult, for it may call for a possible revision of the objective to be sought. Seeing that a certain value is not compatible with others which I also cherish, I may need to revise my estimate of its importance. Although I like to eat green apples, it would be unwise for me to discount the likelihood of indigestion if I eat them. It may be natural for me to have others recognize my superior athletic prowess, but should I be the one to call attention to it, my peers will be less willing to acknowledge my talents. My desire for fame or recognition is one of my ends, but it is not the only end; I must keep an eye on other values as well. Furthermore, all ends are also means to other ends, and there are no "ends-in-themselves." In one context something may be an end; in another, a means.

Dewey's attack on the concept of ends-in-themselves is connected with his view of experience as adjustment to continually changing, fluid conditions. He criticizes the persistent tendency of philosophers to universalize values. This philosophical fallacy, says Dewey, "consists in the supposition that whatever is found true under certain conditions may forthwith be asserted universally or without limits or conditions." But this would suggest, he continues, that "because a thirsty man gets satisfaction in drinking water, bliss consists in being drowned."

If we remember that all satisfaction is specific satisfaction and that all success is success of a specific effort, we shall shy away from trying to universalize and to absolutize values. "Success and satisfaction become meaningless when severed from the wants and struggles whose consummation they are, or when taken universally." History shows, observes Dewey, that when some special ends are set up as ultimate and universal, the results are fanaticism, arrogance, and hypocrisy.

Principles and standards are not directly discerned from the depth of conscience or some other special moral faculty. Principles are only the intellectual equivalent of naturally acquired habits, and their generality is due to the accumulation of wisdom in action. They are "methods of inquiry and forecast which require verification by the event." They "exist as hypotheses with which to experiment. . . . All principles are empirical generalizations from the ways in which previous judgments have practically worked out."[9] As such, they are not "fixed rules for deciding doubtful cases, but instrumentalities for their investigation." Experimentation and constant revision by consequences are involved in all moral judgment. "Morality is a continuing process, not a fixed achievement. . . . In the largest sense of the word, morals is education."[10]

Moral education consists in learning how to anticipate by thought and imagination various possible consequences of action and in adjusting it to actual circumstances. In this way we minimize failure and disaster. The value of imagination lies in the fact that a chain of imagined consequences is retrievable; when overtly tried out, they are irrevocable. The goal of thought is to find a way "fully open." This happens when habits and impulses work harmoniously together, or as Dewey puts it, "when there is a picture of open seas, filled sails and favoring winds." The impulses and preferences are always there; they are not born of bloodless cogitation. The task is only to avoid their incompatibility and conflict. The optimum solution in deliberation is that which "most fully releases activities." What is wanted is "the emergence of a unified preference out of competing preferences."

To get the full flavor of what, according to Dewey, constitutes the goal of moral deliberation, nothing will serve better than a sample of expressions actually used by him to describe the achievement of successfully operating moral intelligence. The agent will be capable of "vibrating response" to the situation; the solution will be characterized by "order, perspective, proportion"; it will "connect satisfactorily with surrounding conditions," "coordinate, organize" every function and factor of the situation; it will result in a "more generous and comprehensive scheme of action." Rationality in conduct is the capacity to "widen the life of strong impulses while aiming at their happy coincidence in operation." The action of a person of cultivated intelligence will be "generously conceived and delicately refined," the result of a long process of selections and combinations. Forethought and flexibility will be our chief weapons in the business of living.

According to Dewey, it is not merely a thought of a future state but the *present attitude* of the organism to the object of thought that is the determinant of action. We don't know what our future feelings will be, but we do know in what way the prospective outcome affects us *now*. Therefore, theories based on the calculation of future pleasures or pains pursue a delusive task. Utilitarians are among those who make this mistake. They fail to see that "in truth, a man's judgment of future joys and sorrows is but a projection of what now satisfies and annoys him."

> *Some objects when thought of are congruent to our existing state of activity. They fit, they are welcome. They agree, or are agreeable, not as a matter of calculation but as a matter of experienced fact. Other objects rasp; they cut across activity, they are tiresome, hateful, unwelcome. They disagree with the existing trend of activity, that is, they are disagreeable, and in no other way than a bore who prolongs his visit, a dun we can't pay, or a pestiferous mosquito who goes on buzzing.*[11]

The most important part of the human environment is other human beings. The sociality of human activities is the outstanding fact of which morality must take account. All morality is social, says Dewey. In dealing with inanimate nature or the organic part of it, we rely on our technical skills, and the appropriate inquiries are physics, chemistry, biology, zoology, etc. In dealing with the social environment we develop psychology and moral science. Our activity sets up reaction in our surroundings. Among such reactions will be the approval, disapproval, encouragement, or resistance of other people. This interhuman response is a matter of fact. Therefore, it is meaningless to say that conduct *should* be social. It *is* social. Conscience, remarks Dewey, is literally knowing *with* others. It is taking into account that our actions will be imputed to us together with blame or praise of those who will be affected by these actions.

Again, approval or disapproval is not a mere feeling on the part of our critics; it is manifested in concrete behavior. Those manifestations modify our future actions, and this is their aim. Responsibility and accountability are also directed toward the future. Social conditioning and pressure are a fact which cannot be ignored or brushed aside. We *must*, not merely *ought*, respond. Our actions, habits, and traditions are saturated with what society demands. They are reflected in our behavior, as the language of our fathers is reflected in our speech. "Morals is as much a matter of interaction with his [man's] social environment as walking is an interaction of legs with a physical environment."[12] To introduce the idea of "ought" into morality implies that morality depends on something apart from social relations. But this means that one leaves the actual social sphere, which alone is the field of morality. The ideas of blame and praise, exhortation and punishment have no meaning apart from the concrete facts of interaction among human beings. The idea of Right signifies nothing but "the totality of social pressures exercised upon us to induce us to think and desire in certain ways."

An individual behaves morally because he knows that otherwise he would be made uncomfortable by his fellows. "He recalls that if he acts this way or that some observer, real or imaginary, will attribute to him noble or mean disposition, virtuous or vicious motive. Thus he learns to influence his own conduct."[13] Undoubtedly this attribution will not have the form of mere feeling, but will manifest itself in some overt reaction. To behave morally is to reflect the commonly accepted ways of behavior and to view one's acts as others view them.

The authority of morality turns out to reside in social sanctions and pressures. According to Dewey, "The community without becomes a forum and tribunal within, a judgment-seat of charges, assessment and exculpations."[14] Because others actually *do* respond to what we do, the meaning of what we do is affected by this response. Thus, modification of our behavior is just as inevitable as that due to our interaction with the physical environment.

Dewey also believed that scientific and moral intelligence can flourish only in a free, democratic society. Liberalism relies on experimental intelligence in adjusting without violence the existing conflicts between social groups. "The method of democracy is to bring these conflicts out into the open where their special claims can be seen and appraised, where they can be discussed and judged in the light of more inclusive interests than represented by either of them separately."[15] In all of these activities of social engineering, people should aim at "softening rigidities, releasing strains, allaying bitterness, dispelling moroseness," and Dewey is anxious to acknowledge the values of cheerfulness, companionship, curiosity, courage, sensitivity, generosity, and impartiality. But he does not seem to realize that here he is not speaking of facts alone. He is not speaking of mere factual findings, established impartially and scientifically. He is invoking moral norms and principles. What he describes are not findings of what is already the case, but conclusions of what is morally desirable. Life does not guarantee that people will always recognize morally desirable norms, and Dewey is reading his own moral impulses and convictions into the actual course of human affairs.

Furthermore, his contention that human activity carries within itself its own standards and normative principles does not answer the question of how to discriminate among them. The question turns on the content to be given to such high-sounding and undoubtedly well-meaning terms as "liberating activity," "vibrating response," and "releasing fully all capacities." They seem to function normatively in Dewey's theory. But normative in what sense? What would a proponent of some new policy appeal to if he were to point out that it would release human capacities? Dewey's theory rests on his faith in the democratic process and is based on the expectation that scientific intelligence will always be the instrument of healthy moral impulses. His optimism is often quite explicit.

> *Suppose, for example, that it be ascertained that a particular set of current valuations have, as their antecedent historical conditions, the interest of a small group or special class in maintaining certain exclusive privileges and advantages, and that this maintenance has the effect of limiting both the range of the desires and their capacity to actualize them. Is it not obvious that this knowledge of conditions and consequences would surely lead to revaluation of desires and ends that had been assumed to be authoritative sources of valuation?*[16]

History is an eloquent witness to the fact that the mere discovery of unfair special privilege does not lead to its immediate elimination. The need for its elimination is obvious only to those morally responsible people who believe that the maintenance of unfairness and injustice is something that *ought* to be done away with. No doubt this is for Dewey so true that it hardly needs to be mentioned. Nevertheless, it does need mentioning and one ought to be clear about it and that it requires more than just faith in the effectiveness of the procedures of "social engineering." Dewey assumes that intelligence is moral *per se*, i.e., that nature and human nature provide moral lessons intrinsically. Because of this, his theory was viewed by some critics as encouraging moral conservatism.

## 3. Emotivism and Prescriptivism

One of the persistent themes in contemporary philosophy is the concern with the different *kinds* of propositions. This concern is not new. We have seen that Locke, Leibniz, and Hume emphasized important differences between statements which refer to matters of fact, and statements which merely exhibit the relation of ideas to one another. Philosophers wanted to call attention to the interesting fact that the *methods* of showing the truth or falsity of these two types of sentences are very different; in one case we point to, or exhibit, some facts, in the other case we show a logical connection between the subject and the predicate of the sentence. Contemporary philosophers, especially the logical positivists, found this distinction extremely important and proceeded to draw some metaphysical conclusions from it.

The epistemological status of propositions expressing ethical judgments also began to be scrutinized more sharply. Already Kant's ethical theory raised the question of how the truth of ethical statements is established. Statements expressing what *ought* to be, claimed Kant, are not reducible to statements of what *is*. In his view, the knowledge of the truth of an ethical statement has to connect with a dimension which lies outside all particular facts. If we regard nature as the collection of all facts, then the examination of nature cannot tell us what we ought to do. In that sense, the answer to questions of right and wrong does not come from nature; it must be derived from other, nonnatural sources. What these sources are Kant proceeded to tell us in his analysis of moral experience in which the notion of the Categorical Imperative was central.

Mill's ethical theory provides an interesting contrast to Kant's. Following the lead of his utilitarian predecessors, Mill was prepared to affirm that it is quite unnecessary to leave the realm of natural, empirical facts in order to get an adequate account of what ethical statements mean and what they refer to. There is no mystery about them, says Mill. Ethical discourse is concerned with the maximization of pleasure and the minimization of pain. Ethical judgments report the results of calculating the consequences of our actions on general happiness, or the estimate of the kinds of feelings which will result from what we propose to do. The meaning of ethical statements is made clear when we translate them into statements of the likelihood or unlikelihood of some states of affairs coming about. To put it in simple terms, when we ask the question "What is good?" the answer is "Pleasure." What is in fact desired is desirable. In other words, such ethical terms as "good" or "right" can be analyzed by reference to natural events, such as the occurrence of some kinds of feelings.

Mill's theory is a good example of what in the contemporary period has come to be known as *naturalism* in ethics. Closer attention to what is communicated in ethical language, however, convinced at least one influential philosopher that there is something fundamentally wrong with any kind of naturalistic ethics. In his famous book, *Principia Ethica* (1903), G.E. Moore (1873-1958) describes what he called the "naturalistic fallacy," which consists in identifying the meaning of a word like "good," when it is used in ethical statements, with some particular natural properties. Suppose we assert that "good" *means* "pleasant." To this move Moore responds with his "open question" argument. If you identify "good" with "pleasant," then it is impossible to ask whether a given pleasure is good. But we do ask such questions; it is an open question whether something which is pleasurable is also good. Since this question can be asked, the meaning of "good" cannot be identical with "pleasant."

Moore called this mistake in analysis the "naturalistic fallacy," because in his view the ethical property, referred to by "good," is nonnatural. It is simple and indefinable and known by direct intuition. Moore's use of "naturalistic" in "naturalistic fallacy," however, has a broad meaning. What he wants to affirm is the impossibility of defining ethical properties by reference to any nonethical properties. But pleasure is only *one* of the properties by which a philosopher might want to analyze good. The history of ethics is replete with attempts to give an analysis of "good" which would not stand up to Moore's open question argument, but which would not necessarily be naturalistic in a straightforward sense. "Morally good" may be identified with the "interest of the stronger," or with the "object of any interest," or with "survival," or with "most evolved," or with the "will of God." It has been suggested by Professor W.K. Frankena that what Moore had in mind was really a "definist fallacy," the fallacy of trying to define the indefinable. If "good" is indefinable, then every attempt to define it is self-defeating.

Moore's inquiries have focused the moral philosophers' attention on epistemological issues. What is the philosopher doing when he examines the meaning of such words as "good" or "right" and offers his analysis of them? Is he still doing ethics, in the sense of telling us what things, actions, practices, or principles are good? It appears that he is interested in a different question. He wants to settle the question of what kinds of propositions are expressed in ethical statements; he is doing *metaethics*. This does not mean that he is no longer prepared to say what things or activities he regards as good. As an ethical person he will be prepared to affirm some ethical norms or goals, but as a philosopher he is interested primarily in determining the epistemological status of ethical propositions. Moore himself believed that "by far the greatest goods with which we are acquainted include personal affection and esthetic enjoyments," but his questions shifted the philosophers' interest to the *method* by which we arrive at ethical judgments. Since for Moore the ethical properties to which these judgments refer are nonnatural and indefinable, the presence of such properties can be determined only by intuition.

Among the better-known intuitionists in ethics were E.F. Carritt (*Theory of Morals*, 1928), W.D. Ross (*The Right and the Good*, 1930, and *The Foundations of Ethics*, 1939), and H.A. Pritchard (*Moral Obligation: Essays and Lectures*, 1949). One of Pritchard's famous essays is entitled "Does Moral Philosophy Rest on a Mistake?" The answer to the question was: Yes, it does. When we wish to reassure ourselves that our calculation in arithmetic is correct, we only have to reexamine the content of our consciousness. Thus, "to remove the doubt, it is only necessary to appreciate the real nature of our consciousness in apprehending, e.g., that $7 \times 4 = 28$, and thereby see that it was no mere condition of believing, but a condition of knowing." Similarly, when confronting a moral obligation, we cannot doubt that it has a claim on our recognition of it. Therefore, we should "realize the self-evidence of our obligations, i.e., the immediacy of our apprehension of them." Pritchard and Ross found the concept of right or obligation to be more fundamental than the concept of good. To experience the full force of morality is to recognize the objective claim which our moral obligations have on us.

Although intuitionism enjoyed considerable vogue, especially in England, its conclusions appear to preclude moral arguments. Ethical properties must be simply "seen" or cognized. Of course, the intuitionists regarded the appropriate moral training as a necessary prerequisite to having right moral intuitions, but that still did not help to decide how one could settle a difference of opinion as to whose intuitions were correct. This was one of the chief reasons why intuitionists failed to make many converts among philosophers. Nevertheless, the very problem which gave rise to intuitionism, namely, how to analyze the special features of ethical statements, remained at the forefront of philosophical inquiry.

On the whole, contemporary ethical theories reflect the particular epistemological point of view with which their authors are identified. This is certainly the case in regard to Dewey's pragmatic ethics and Sartre's existentialist ethics. The impasse of intuitionism and the arguments of logical positivists have opened a new line of inquiry, to which we now turn.

Emotive theories of ethics arose in response to the discovery that ethical propositions differ significantly from other propositions. Two contributions were especially important, that of G.E. Moore and that of logical positivism. Moore's argument from the "naturalistic fallacy" convinced him that an ethical statement refers to some special nonnatural property grasped by direct intuition. The criterion of meaning set forth by the logical positivists left no room for ethical statements among meaningful propositions. Yet, since ethical language is obviously used, it appeared only natural to ask whether ethical statements have a function which is altogether different from that of cognitive propositions. The emotive theory set out to show that the function of ethical statements is not cognitive but expressive and dynamic. Ayer believed that moral judgments express the feelings of the speaker. Carnap thought that they are really disguised commands; "You ought to tell the truth" is just a misleading way of saying "Don't lie." Still another philosopher who defended this noncognitivist approach to ethics is C.L. Stevenson. In his influential book *Ethics and Language* (1944), he presented a carefully worked-out emotive theory of ethics.

According to Stevenson's analysis, ethical statements have two components: descriptive and emotive. He presents this distinction by means of "working models":

1. "This is wrong" means "I disapprove of this; do so as well."

2. "He ought to do this" means "I disapprove of his leaving this undone; do so as well."

3. "This is good" means "I approve of this; do so as well."[17]

The declarative clauses in these working models are descriptive; the imperatives have emotive meaning. Their combination in a statement results in a function which is neither descriptive nor imperative. Moral judgments are used "more for encouraging, altering, or redirecting people's aims in conduct than for simply describing them." People who use moral language are not merely expressing their feelings, as Ayer thought, nor do they just utter commands, as Carnap believed; rather, they resort to a "characteristic and subtle kind of 'emotive meaning.'"

> *In virtue of this kind of meaning, ethical judgments alter attitudes, not by an appeal to self-conscious efforts (as in the case of imperatives), but by the more flexible mechanism of suggestion. Emotive terms present the subject of which they are predicated in a bright or dim light, so to speak, and thereby lead people, rather than command them to alter their attitudes.*[18]

Moral disagreements have two components: disagreements in beliefs and disagreements in attitudes. Disagreements in beliefs can be clarified and settled by attention to facts. When people argue about the merits or demerits of a course of action, it is important to determine just what each of the parties believes to be factually true about the situation and about the consequences to be expected from the actions to be taken. Very often this factual clarification will remove the disagreement, for with the change in beliefs the change in attitudes is likely to come about. Some words used in descriptions have emotive connotations built into them. When a person is described as industrious, it can be expected that the description will generate a favorable attitude in the hearer of the description. But of course some factual conditions must hold in order for the description to be applicable, and there usually is agreement as to what these factual conditions would have to be. It is clear that a person who is trying to change his hearer's attitude toward someone or something will use adjectives and descriptions which have appropriate emotive meaning.

The change in beliefs is not the primary objective in the use of moral judgments; the main objective of such judgments is to influence attitudes and conduct.

Stevenson sees a continual interplay between the descriptive and emotive functions of language. In the course of time a word may change its emotive meaning without undergoing a parallel change in descriptive meaning. Sometimes a change in one respect will reflect a change in the other.

> Suppose, for example, that a group of people should come to disapprove of certain aspects of democracy, but continue to approve of other aspects of it. They might leave the descriptive meaning of "democracy" unchanged, and gradually let it acquire, for their usage, a much less laudatory meaning. On the other, they might keep the strong laudatory meaning unchanged and let "democracy" acquire a descriptive sense which made reference only to those aspects of democracy (in the older sense) which they favored.[19]

At any given time, however, the emotive meaning of democracy may be sufficiently firm to be used dynamically, that is, to influence the attitude of the hearer. Thus, in our time, to refer to a procedure as "democratic" indicates one's positive attitude toward it. In contrast, in Plato's time a claim that a political change would lead to a democratic form of government would have elicited a negative attitude.

It should be noted that the intent of the defenders of the emotive theory was to rescue ethics from the apparent limbo into which it has been thrown by the intuitionists and logical positivists. A recourse to special intuitions and nonnatural properties was highly unconvincing, but so was the claim that moral discourse is meaningless. The emotivists have at least shown that we should look in a different direction to determine the function of moral language. It is not difficult to see, however, that the dynamic function of language discovered (or rediscovered) by the emotivists is not limited to moral discourse. It is much more general. We find it in advertising, commercials, in political speeches, in propaganda. If the objective is to influence attitudes and conduct, then the instruments for control, redirection, and modification of attitudes are indeed numerous and may include threats, blackmail, and bribes. These considerations make it clear that the dynamic function of language is much wider than moral discourse. There is also the obvious possibility that some dynamic uses of language may conflict with morality.

The latter difficulty is a serious complication for the theory. It is analogous to the difficulty to which Moore called attention in his naturalistic fallacy. Granted that a moral argument aims at changing the hearer's attitude, could the hearer not ask why the change is desirable? It seems that Stevenson was concerned merely with the *effectiveness* of moral language and not with its *justifying* function. He viewed moral discourse as essentially nonrational, as aiming at efficacious manipulation through psychological pressure or suggestive persuasiveness. His theory commits him to the view that when people argue morally, they are in fact working on each other's emotions, and when they mention facts, these facts have no rational bearing on the argument. As long as the facts I mention happen to connect with the attitude of the hearer, they are the right facts to mention, according to the emotivists. But this makes the connection between facts and attitudes arbitrary and nonrational. Granted that changes in beliefs may lead to changes in attitude, it should still be possible to show why a change in belief *warrants* a change in attitude. Saddled with its descriptive-emotive dichotomy of meaning, the theory was not prepared to deal with this question.

In addition, having begun by yielding to the temptation to oversimplify, the emotive theory ended in exaggerating the importance of the dynamic aspect of moral discourse. It is not true that when people use moral language they always address themselves to one another's feelings or attitudes. Sometimes one is not interested in bringing about a change in anyone's attitude; one merely wants to indicate what one's own attitude is. This situation does not appear to be covered by the theory at all. On some occasions the use of language with clear emotive overtones may be inappropriate for a moral discussion; instead of producing understanding, it may result in exacerbating and inflaming feelings. Such words as "bad" or "wrong" should be distinguished from "vicious" or "blackguard," and moral problems may be resolved more effectively by refraining from discussing them in emotively charged terms of the latter kind. Moral advice may be given in entirely dispassionate terms and may for that very reason be *better* advice than some highly emotional plea. All of this shows that there need not be anything emotive about moral criticism or approval.

R.M. Hare's two books, *The Language of Morals* (1952) and *Freedom and Reason* (1963), continue the search for a correct account of moral discourse. Hare agrees with Stevenson that the moral philosopher is concerned with metaethics, with the description of the salient features of moral language. But this enterprise also has practical consequences. In his second book, Hare describes the relationship between metaethics and ethics as follows:

> *Ethical theory, which determines the meanings and functions of moral words, and thus the "rules" of the moral "game," provides only a clarification of the conceptual framework within which moral reasoning takes place; it is, therefore, in the required sense, neutral as between different moral opinions. But it is highly relevant to moral reasoning because, as with the rules of a game, there could be no such thing as moral reasoning without this framework, and the framework dictates the form of reasoning.* [20]

Hare agrees with Stevenson that the function of moral discourse is to guide action, but he rejects Stevenson's analysis of this guidance. An ethical judgment is not equivalent to a verbal push, and to do justice to it we must look more closely. It is important to distinguish between *getting* someone to do something and *telling* him to do it. A person assenting to a judgment "I ought to do X" is also assenting to the command "Let me do X"; to that extent there is a connection between moral judgment and action. But there is a difference between persuading and prescribing, says Hare: "Persuasion is not directed to a person as a rational agent, who is asking himself (or us) 'What shall I do?,' it is not an answer to this or any other question; it is an attempt to *make* him answer in a particular way." In contrast, prescribing does not aim at *influencing* a person one way or another. It consists merely in telling him what to do, which is a linguistic performance and not a causal one, and certainly not a verbal shove. When you raise the question "What shall I do?" I can answer without in the least trying to move or induce you to do it. These are *further* matters, and I could resort to some sort of persuasion or psychological pressure, but in merely telling you what to do, I need not resort to anything like that at all. Austin had a similar distinction in mind when he said that what I am doing *in* saying something (illocutionary force) is very different from what is brought about *by* saying it (perlocutionary force).

Hare's prescriptivism, then, rejects the view that moral judgments are essentially emotive, but he does not regard them as primarily conveying information. Their function is to indicate that the speaker who accepts them is also committed to doing something. For instance, if I accept the proposition "I ought to return his car," I also accept the imperative, "Let me return his car." My not returning the car would amount to rejecting the proposition "I ought to return it." It is this connection of a moral judgment with an imperative that makes it prescriptive. The special function of the word "good" is that it is used to *commend* the thing or action in question, and to commend something is to indicate that it is worth choosing, that a certain kind of response or action is appropriate with regard to it. But moral judgments have yet another feature which distinguishes them from other value judgments. Imperatives conveyed through moral judgments are also universalizable; that is, they are applicable to other situations which share the same relevant features. To regard a judgment as universalizable is not only to regard it as covering all other similar cases, but also to treat it as applicable to oneself. Thus, to assent to the proposition "you ought to repay your debts" involves agreeing to obey the imperative "Repay the debt," when I myself become a debtor. An opportunist is a person who does not subscribe to the universalizability of moral judgments. The best answer to the question about a person "What are his moral principles?" would be contained in a study of what he *did*.

Hare also wants to distinguish between universal and general principles. Moral principles are always universal, although they can be either general or specific. "The moral principle 'One ought never to make false statements' is highly general: the moral principle 'One ought never to make false statements to one's wife' is much more specific. But both are universal; the second one forbids *anyone* who is married to make false statements to his wife."[21] Hare believes that moral development consists in making our moral principles more and more specific. As we grow, we learn what exceptions and qualifications need to be written into general moral principles in order to make them more responsive to the complexities of particular situations. As long as our social environment remains more or less stable, we seldom need to make significant qualifications of our principles; should the social and cultural context change radically, however, such a modification may be called for.

In arguing morally, people make use of principles which for those who invoke them entail corresponding imperatives. In acting on such imperatives, a person shows his serious commitment to such principles. But at all times the commitment involves rational reflection. Every time a qualification of a general principle is accepted, that is, every time a general principle takes a more specific universal form, a person is said to make a decision *of* principle. This is a time when the moral agent makes *his* decision prominent; he sets a precedent for himself and for others. When asked for a justification of his decision, he may invoke other relevant principles and mention facts which so far have escaped notice. But at a certain point the chain of reasons will stop and the commitment will no longer rest on further reasons.

> *Thus, if pressed to justify a decision completely, we have to give a complete specification of the way of life of which it is a part. This complete specification it is impossible in practice to give; the nearest attempts are those given by the great religions, especially those which can point to historical persons who carried out the way of life in practice. Suppose, however, that we can give it. If the inquirer still goes on asking "But why should I live like that?" then there is no further answer to give him, because we have already,* ex hypothesi, *said everything that could be included in this further answer. We can only ask him to make up his own mind which way he ought to live; for in the end everything rests upon such a decision of principle. He has to decide whether to accept that way of life or not; if he accepts it, then he can proceed to justify the decisions that are based upon it; if he does not accept it, then let him accept some other, and try to live by it.*[22]

Such a decision, continues Hare, would be far from being unfounded or arbitrary; on the contrary, it would take into account all that is relevant to it.

The role of decision in subscribing to moral judgments is not quite clear in Hare's prescriptivism. On what grounds are decisions of principle made?

Is inflicting unnecessary suffering morally wrong because some persons *decide* that it is wrong? It seems that my deciding for or against cruelty is quite a different matter from discovering that it is a valid moral principle. Similar questions arise with regard to the universalizability of moral judgments as Hare understands it. Is Hare advocating anything more than *consistency* in one's own behavior? That something is a universal moral principle is certainly not dependent on my or anyone else's prescribing it as morally desirable. Apart from these fundamental questions one may also wonder whether, as in Stevenson's theory, too much emphasis is laid on one sort of moral discourse, to the exclusion of other types. Hare seems to have concentrated on situations in which one wants to know explicitly "What shall I do?" But this certainly does not exhaust moral discourse. We criticize, commend, or express distaste, but we also offer advice to others which does not immediately connect with anyone's action. We profess aspirations and formulate ideals, we form resolutions and, as parent or teachers, for instance, help others to form and to execute their resolutions. Hare's theory certainly corrects some of the emotivists' oversimplifications and distortions of moral discourse, but his analysis has problems of its own.

## 4. Arthur Murphy: The Language of Justification

The philosophers' interest in metaethics, which prompted attempts to determine the special features of moral discourse, ultimately had fruitful consequences. Perhaps it is inevitable that striking out in a completely new direction initially results in one-sided and exaggerated findings. Although the discovery of the emotive and prescriptive aspects of moral language was a useful one, it tended to blind the proponents of this new analysis to other features of moral discourse. We have noted that the interest in metaethics paralleled a more general interest in what could be called metaphilosophy, an investigation of the function of philosophical statements. This in turn alerted many thinkers to the need to pay closer attention to the different uses of language. The preceding chapter presented the results of philosophical investigations which were dominated by the desire to be fair to the many kinds of distinctions which language makes possible.

The theory with which we conclude this brief survey of contemporary ethics is also animated by this desire to be as fair as possible to all the important aspects of the moral uses of language. In his book *The Theory of Practical Reason* (1964), Arthur E. Murphy acknowledges the influence of the later Wittgenstein on the way Murphy sees the task of moral philosophers. What needs to be done, thinks Murphy, is to describe as faithfully as possible all the important features of the way we use moral language. He thinks it helpful to regard practical discourse as *the language of justification*, of presenting reasons which can serve as grounds for action. The clarification of that language, although in a sense a metaethical enterprise, is nevertheless important, if it is the case that a clear-headed use of that language secures for us certain objectives which could not be attained otherwise. Murphy sees the connection as follows: "The point of a better understanding of the use of practical discourse is to use it better for its own practical purposes so that men, in the light of it, may know better how to live."

What needs to be done, thinks Murphy, is to examine not just the meaning of some special terms or typical phrases used in moral discourse, but also the total background of this practice, the conditions which disclose its point and purpose. People who use the language of justification wish to call attention to many different things. Among these things will be found those to which previous philosophers called attention while excluding or ignoring *other* relevant things. Thus, a moral judgment will involve a reference to facts, to attitudes, to universal norms, to the common good, and to the moral status of people taking part in that discourse. By acknowledging the contribution of each component in its own specific way we will come closer to giving a correct account of what happens when people argue morally.

It may be helpful to see the relevance of all these factors is we consider a concrete example. Suppose a person says to someone "You ought to make this trip." From the discussion preceding and following this statement we construct the following context.

1. *Facts*. The brother of the hearer is stranded ten miles from home, due to a car breakdown, and the trip in question would rescue him from the predicament.

2. *Attitudes*. It is assumed that the hearer is, on the whole, well disposed to his brother, that is, is inclined to take an interest in his welfare.

3. *Universal norms*. The speaker would give this advice to anyone in a similar situation, and even more importantly, would accept the judgment if *he* were in the hearer's situation.

4. *Common good*. It is assumed that there is a common bond between the two brothers, that they share certain goals — in this case, the desire to be helped out of a tight spot.

5. *Moral selfhood*. The hearer is presumed to be the kind of person with whom the preceding four points would carry weight, i.e., that he is a responsible moral agent.

This analysis may appear unduly complex, but this is no objection, provided that all these factors *are* relevant if we are to understand the meaning and force of the utterance "You ought to make this trip." Our analysis merely spells out the items that would usually be mentioned in order to make the situation explicit. Should the hearer not be quite convinced and should he ask "Why ought I?," the speaker could justify his statement by making the following replies: "Because he is stuck ten miles from home, perhaps without money, in the dark, in the blizzard, and there is no way for him to get home (factor 1), or "Because he is your brother (factor 2 and/or 4), or "Because one should help people who are in trouble" (factor 3), or "Because you are someone he can count on for help" (factor 5).

To use the language of justification is to participate in the form of life in which the conditions mentioned in the analysis of our example are presupposed. The questions of what one should or should not do have to connect with some facts in the world. In our example the discussion began with the recognition of certain factual circumstances: the car broke down, a person is stranded and the victim happens to have a brother who hears about the problem. Therefore, the problem arises out of a concrete context of human needs about which people are not indifferent; they have some attitudes toward them, positive or negative. Without the presence of such attitudes moral discourse could not be initiated. As Murphy puts it:

> *Men do indeed come to hunger and thirst after righteousness, but if they did not hunger and thirst after other things, food, shelter, security and affection, for example, which can be reliably attained on humanly liveable terms, only on the condition that they deal righteously with each other in the pursuit and enjoyment of them, righteousness would have no content and its dictates no normative cogency.*[23]

The reference to wants, needs, and attitudes in a moral judgment is made, however, in a special way. To mention a want, an interest, an attitude *as a reason* for action is to imply that it is *entitled* to this status. This means that it should be *generally* applicable; *anyone* who has this need or is in that situation is morally entitled to be helped. A person who points to a want as a ground of action should be prepared to treat this want as deserving this status, regardless of who has the want.

> *Reasons are public essentially; they must be common grounds for action, if they are warrantably to be grounds at all, and it is in the establishment of such community of understanding that they prove their cogency as reasons. All reasons are in this sense universal, that if they are valid grounds for one man's actions they must be no less for any other man whose situation is, in all morally relevant circumstances, the same.*[24]

But the universal validity of a reason cited may not be quite enough. The moral rule "Help others in distress" is a universally valid moral rule, but it is not equally binding on everyone in all circumstances. If in the example given above the hearer were a complete stranger to the stranded person, he could have rightly replied: "I agree that one should help others in distress. I subscribe to this moral principle. Nevertheless, it is not *my* obligation to rescue that person." The case in which the person addressed is a brother, a relative, or a close friend of the victim is clearly different. Why? Because one may presuppose the existence of a special common bond among brothers; they have certain obligations to each other that are not shared by people who are not thus related or who do not share more specific common ends. This is why Murphy emphasizes the importance of *community* in a moral relationship. Moral community exists when a group of people treat some universal norms as constituting a concrete moral bond among them. The distinction helps to demarcate situations in which we accept certain moral beliefs without being thereby obligated to do anything in particular about them from situations in which we are so obligated. In the former case it is simply not *up to us* to act, and it may not be morally fair to expect us to act. If we fail to act on such an abstractly valid principle, no one can accuse us of acting immorally. The situation is different when in addition to subscribing to a moral rule, we are also situated in such a way that it *is* up to us to apply it. Standing in a special relationship to other persons—as a father or a brother, or occupying a certain position as an officeholder, a member of an organization sharing certain goals and objectives—I will have corresponding obligations not applicable to others.

Murphy continually reminds us that moral language is always addressed "to whom it may concern." Creating and maintaining a moral community is not the work of disinterested parties; it calls for initiative and constant support by moral agents. "There are no communities save as actual men in social groups are so related as to share in rights and goods that *in common* they can recognize as their own. It is as persons or moral agents that they can be thus related."[25] Only *for* a moral self can there be universally valid, justifying reasons and common good. The set of the person's reasoned commitments and concerns constitutes the content of his moral character. "A man's character is at least as important to us as his actions, and one of the most important things about his actions is that they in some way shed light upon his character or nature or person."[26] A person is what he stands for, and stands by, as an agent.

As users of moral language we indicate that we are aware of the various conditions which make this use credible and effective. Of course, we do not always live up to what our use of that language implies. Our facts are not always correct, our attitudes not fairly conveyed, our acceptance of a norm and our commitment to the common good may be doubtful. But to the extent that we fail to abide by what is indicated by the very use of language we employ, we also show ourselves deficient or untrustworthy. Murphy is aware of the fact that morality is not an endowment but an achievement. Seldom is it fully secure; we are capable not only of moral growth but of backsliding as well. Yet, if we understand the role of the language of justification, we will see why it is important to keep that role intact.

> *If this kind of thinking were rejected, this way of acting would go with it, for the thinking is the conceptual structure of action, and the action, practically, makes no sense without it. There can be a society of sorts without this kind of action. Ants and bees appear to have no use for it. And as Ionesco's* Rhinoceros *points out, if we all became rhinoceri we should no longer use it either. To say that in that case something of great worth would have been lost is to make an assertion whose cogency no rhinoceros would understand.*[27]

One should also keep in mind that practical judgments are by definition relevant to situations in which something is to be *done*. This means that we ought to distinguish the contexts of their use from the situations in which no action at all turns on the outcome of a judgment. We can, of course, offer "moral remarks" about certain events in history or about the practices of some far-off tribes. These remarks may play a useful role, say, in an "evaluative" contemplation of history, in our reflections about the ways of the world, or about the evolution of morals. Such activities may even play an important role in our general and moral education. But because in such contemplative observations no practical issue needs to be resolved, they should be demarcated from the strictly normative use of language. This distinction needs to be underscored because in talking about ethics, we frequently move from one level to the other without noticing that in so doing we are really changing the subject. If we keep in mind that a reference to a moral community is a necessary move in an attempt to solve a practical problem, we shall not confuse the issue by continually shifting the boundaries of that community. One begins to consider a concrete problem of concern to, say, New Yorkers, and all of a sudden one is confronted with unusual customs of the Trobriand Islanders. This does not mean that a moral issue could not arise for a Trobriander among the New Yorkers or vice versa, but then the problem would need to be solved within the compass of agreements to which both could morally assent.

In general, one cannot stand outside the practice of normative discourse and *merely use the language* characteristic of such discourse. The judgments of an uncommitted, uninvolved bystander acquire practical validity only when he hypothetically assumes the validity of relevant concerns and speaks from the point of view of such hypothetical assumption. Expressions such as "If I were you" or "If I were in your situation" (meaning, "having the obligations and opportunities that you actually have") usually preface the judgment or advice of an uncommitted observer. His moral relation to the hearer is at least characterized by good will, by a desire to help him solve his practical problems. We ask a "third party" for an opinion not because his noninvolvement makes him a better judge, but because we are sometimes *too* involved to see the situation clearly. Yet, we would be foolish to accept his advice unless we had grounds for believing that he understands the purpose and the point of the language of justification and is willing to respect its concrete conditions (both factual and normative) in the particular case.

According to Murphy, the entire practice of the language of justification can be maintained at its adequate level only if the users of this language are clearly aware of its aims and objectives. His theory is addressed to us as the users of that language in order to elucidate what we are actually doing when we participate in the practices of normative discourse. We are also invited to consider what would be *missing* from the human scene if the practices of the language of justification were to disappear from it. Obviously, some familiar ways of addressing one another—advising, admonishing, encouraging, or criticizing by producing reasons for our judgments—would either disappear or be transformed into something *less* than what they now are. This would be a severe handicap, eliminating from our daily life countless familiar moral transactions without which our life would surely be impoverished. Morality, as Murphy reminds us again and again, is not the whole of life; it leaves room for purposes of other sorts. Not all our problems are moral problems. Where no actual obligations exist, it is a mistake to use moral language. Moral diversity—the presence of different values and life styles—is often compatible with mutual forbearance and tolerance. "Moral diversity *becomes* moral disagreement only when the diversity itself is made a moral issue."[28] But when we do make a moral issue of it, we fall back on a use of language with its own special rules and purposes. Whether we are to participate in this use is not a matter of indifference to us. When moral considerations become relevant, we ignore them only at the risk of damaging a vital part of ourselves. As with the Ten Commandments, if we break them, they break us. Morality as a search for justifiable, common rational grounds for action is a particular kind of enterprise, but without it, in Murphy's words, "we literally should not be ourselves."

Murphy sees the human self as essentially dynamic and developing:

> The self that, if he is a self at all, he can recognize he ought to be, is always to some degree an ideal. The "choice" to be this self, or to live up to this ideal, in his conduct is not made once and for all in a supertemporal world and irrevocable thereafter. It must be made continually in quite mundane circumstances, in the way that responds to the requirements and opportunities of his situation as a self or agent.[29]

The importance of the initiative of responsible agents clearly emerges from Murphy's description of contexts in which practical reason is called upon to do its work. He reminds us that the actual communities of which we are members suffer from tensions and disharmonies which cry out for relief. The groups in which we live

> are incomplete, onesided and in many ways parochial in the range and level of their moral understanding. The good reasons we have learned in them are sometimes not good enough for the achievement of an effective moral order in our social relations. The communities in which their moral intent could be adequately fulfilled has still in large measure, and under great difficulties, to be built.[30]

Murphy also tells us that the building of communities in which the intent of moral norms is more adequately fulfilled is not an impersonal natural process determined by sociology or "social engineering." It is always the work of *people* who are concerned to bring about whatever changes appear morally desirable.

The moral bond is not of an abstract, disembodied sort. Nor does it appear on the human scene automatically, wherever and whenever human beings happen to interact. It is, like moral selfhood, an achievement. It becomes effective only when there is a willingness to govern one's behavior in terms of some mutually binding rules. When no such rules are recognized and respected, a moral community does not exist. The practice of the language of justification depends on the active support of practical agents who participate in it.

One may well understand that in the circumstances under which Sartre formulated his philosophical view, it would have been difficult for him to maintain an optimistic stance *vis-à-vis* science and its promise to solve all human problems. Both the economic depression of the 1930s and World War II raised the question whether the gains on scientific fronts are likely to be translated into moral gains. Existentialism as a whole appears to be a protest against all attempts to objectify, to naturalize, human existence. The values worth bothering about are, as Kierkegaard proclaimed long ago, not those found in objective, publicly accessible relations, but in the experiences of the solitary individual who seeks inward purity and subjective truth. Existentialism appealed to many people because it stresses the personal side of life, calls attention to crucial decisions and crisis situations and to the devious devices by means of which people deprive themselves of authentic existence. Sartre dwells on phenomena of bad faith and self-deception because these are the ways in which people prevent their freedom from expressing itself. Existentialism appeared to be a champion of liberation of the human psyche in all its possible forms, and in this respect it has exerted a strong influence on all aspects of our contemporary culture: art, theater, psychiatry, and religion.

The word "existential" has acquired a distinctly positive ring and is often used as a contrast to merely academic or irrelevant aspects of life. But the emphasis on the personal, individual, and unique aspects of existence seems to submerge questions which, since Socrates, were also at the very center of moral inquiry. Socrates, we may recall, recognized the importance of moral community. For him, a person needed to take the step from "I" to "we" in order to live up to his full humanity. When, how, by what sorts of actions does a person acquire moral status? This question seems to set moral philosophy in motion, and a philosophy which tries to bypass it may have to do without ethics, as Sartre discovered in his own case when he concluded that it was impossible for him to create an ethics. Kant's moral philosophy, which enjoins a person to treat other persons as ends in themselves, followed Socrates' lead in not separating the notion of a moral self from the notion of a moral community. Nietzsche, on the other hand, set in motion the existentialist reaction by declaring the "I" to be higher than the "we." Following this lead, Sartre saw the fact of human freedom as an insuperable obstacle to the emergence of a genuine community among persons.

Dewey's pragmatic ethics moves within the framework of his general epistemology, according to which intelligence is an instrument of action. Consequently, for him, intelligence as such is a moral force. To behave morally is to put one's whole intelligence to use, to look before and after, to connect the contemplated action both with its antecedents and with its likely consequences, and to aim at the greatest harmonization of existing needs and interests. The model for moral behavior is the behavior of a scientist, who is not satisfied with staring at his data but makes them intelligible in terms of the connections they have to other data — in other words, when they are subjected to controlled imagination and experiment. If we follow the example of science and if we govern our interpersonal relations in terms of intelligent social engineering, our problems will find adequate and satisfying solutions. As we have noted, this kind of ethics puts a great deal of faith in the inherent reasonableness of man and exhibits considerable, even exaggerated, optimism about the uses to which science can be put. On the epistemological level, it appears to commit Moore's "naturalistic fallacy" in assuming that the predominant social goals of any epoch are *eo ipso* good. In other words, it has no provision for judging whether the direction in which society actually moves is morally desirable.

As our brief discussion of the distinction between ethics and metaethics indicated, contemporary theorizing about morality was affected by the general realization that philosophy must return to basic questions of meaning. Language analysts in particular have concluded that it will no longer do to assume that the key verbs of epistemology, such as "to know," "to believe," "to will," "to feel," "to intend," "to value," and "to justify," carry their meaning on their faces. To describe how they function is one of the central topics in contemporary philosophical psychology, a study of the concepts traditionally regarded as inhabiting "the mental realm." Emotivist theories reflect this wider preoccupation.

The career of the emotivist school of ethics exhibits in an interesting way that the two poles of morality, the personal and the social, need to complement each other. The emotivist ethical theory was an offspring of logical positivism. Since ethical statements have no cognitive meaning, as the positivists have declared, moral utterances either express an emotional attitude of the speaker or intend to evoke a similar attitude int he listener. But it is not evident that there is anything moral about either having a certain attitude of feeling or wanting to elicit it in others. In fact, some feelings may not be worth having, and some attempts to work on the feelings of others may be downright immoral. There is nothing moral about either part of Stevenson's two-part analysis of an ethical statement: "I like it; do so as well." This is why Hare thought it necessary to move away from the purely emotivist view to what he called prescriptivism, in which the imperative contained in the prescription is regarded as universalizable. My subscribing to a judgment, "You ought to do X,"implies my acceptance of "Let me do X" in similar circumstances. This move introduces a moral dimension into discourse. But, as his critics point out, Hare's process of justification stops with the "decisions of principle," by which a person merely affirms what his values happen to be and that he is committed to them.

Arthur Murphy believed that more can and should be expected from the language of justification. None of our commitments need to be seen as ultimate irreducible data perceived by an intuition or emotively embraced. Every moral action and every moral rule is open to rational scrutiny and should be capable of justification. We do not stop with saying "This is what I happen to believe" or "This is the way I was brought up" or "These are my culture's values." In each case we can offer a rational defense of *why* we accept the values on which we act. When we do offer such a justification, we address ourselves to the capacity of others to judge for themselves. In other words, we respect their capacity to judge rationally and impartially, i.e., morally. The willingness to give a fair hearing to principles invoked in good faith by others makes a moral community possible. Thus, the Socratic and Kantian demands that no one person can arrogate to himself ultimate moral authority, but must also make room for the judgment of others, are justified. In Murphy's own view, Socrates was closer to the realistic appraisal of morality, because he recognized that he had to appeal to the concrete community of his fellow Athenians, whereas Kant, in Murphy's view, ultimately appealed to a noumenal, disembodied rationality of man. This is a point of interpretation of Kant's theory, and the dust of controversy has not yet settled on this issue. But Murphy accepts the basic Kantian provision that moral reasons are never merely personal or private and that they apply equally to all persons similarly situated. The moral self and the moral community are mutually dependent. "On moral issues a man who judges for himself speaks for the moral order of a community, however widely or narrowly he conceives it."[31]

## Questions

1. How do you understand Sartre's claim that "value is beyond being?" How does this expression connect with Sartre's views on human freedom?

2. What does Sartre mean by responsibility? How do you interpret his statement: "In fashioning myself I fashion man?" Is Sartre's position here similar to that of Kant? What roles can other people play in a person's life, according to Sartre?

3. What was Dewey's distinction between valuing and evaluating? Does this distinction reflect his general philosophical point of view?

4. Do you agree with Dewey that all morality is social and that "in the largest sense of the word, morals is education?" How would you criticize his ethical theory?

5. To what did G.E. Moore call attention when he formulated his "naturalistic fallacy?" Must one be an intuitionist in ethics to recognize the importance of avoiding this fallacy?

6. What is the purpose of ethical statements, according to Stevenson, and how does he analyze them? Do you find that this analysis renders correctly what you do when you use ethical language?

7. What is the function of the word "good," according to Hare? Do you agree with him?

8. On what grounds does Hare claim that moral principles are always universal, although they can be either general or specific? What is a "decision of principle?"

9. What are the components of an ethical judgment, according to Murphy?

10. Why does Murphy claim that moral language is always addressed "to whom it may concern?" What is he trying to convey by saying that where no actual obligations exist, it is a mistake to use moral language? Do you agree with this conclusion?

# Notes

1 J.P. Sartre, *Being and Nothingness*, translated by Hazel Barnes. New York: Washington Square Press, 1966, p. 550.

2 *Ibid.*, pp. 144-45.

3 *Ibid.*, p. 731.

4 J.P. Sartre, *Existentialism and Humanism*, translated by P. Mairet and reprinted in Walter Kaufmann's *Existentialism from Dostoyevksy to Sartre*. New York: Meridian Books, 1956, p. 292.

5 *Ibid.*, p. 293.

6 *Ibid.*, p. 302.

7 J.P. Sartre, *Being and Nothingness*. New York: Washington Square Press, 1966, p. 550.

8 J.P. Sartre, *Existentialism and Humanism, op. cit.*, p. 295.

9 John Dewey, *Human Nature and Conduct*. New York: Holt, Rinehart and Winston, 1950, pp. 239-40.

10 *Ibid.*, p. 280.

11 *Ibid.*, pp. 200-201. Reprinted by permission.

12 *Ibid.*, p. 318.

13 *Ibid.*, p. 315.

14 *Ibid.*, p. 121.

15 John Dewey, *Liberalism in America*. New York: Putnam's Sons, 1935, p. 79.

16 John Dewey, *Theory of Valuation*. Chicago: University of Chicago Press, 1939, p. 59. Reprinted by permission.

17 Charles L. Stevenson, *Ethics and Language*. New Haven: Yale University Press, 1944, p. 21.

18 *Ibid.*, p. 33. Reprinted by permission.

19 *Ibid.*, p. 72. Reprinted by permission.

20 R.M. Hare, *Freedom and Reason*. New York: Oxford University Press, 1963, p. 89. Reprinted by permission.

21 *Ibid.*, p. 40.

22 R.M. Hare, *The Language of Morals*. New York: Oxford University Press, 1952, p. 69. Reprinted by permission.

23 Arthur E. Murphy, *The Theory of Practical Reason*. LaSalle, IL: Open Court, 1964, p. 97. Reprinted by permission.

24 *Ibid.*, pp. 114-15. Reprinted by permission.

25 *Ibid.*, p. 378.

26 *Ibid.*, p. 132.

27 *Ibid.*, p. 56. Reprinted by permission.

28 *Ibid.*, p. 339.

29 *Ibid.*, p. 180. Reprinted by permission.

30 *Ibid.*, p. 220. Reprinted by permission.

31 Arthur E. Murphy, *The Theory of Practical Reason*. LaSalle, IL: Open Court, 1964. p. 283.

# Chapter Fourteen

# The Present:
# The Contending
# Trends

## 1. The New Empiricism

From its very beginnings philosophy was fascinated by the distinction between being and being known. The question "What can be known?" inevitably dragged behind it its twin: "What *is* there?" Parmenides and his followers took a radical stand on these questions and declared that Being must remain on the other side of knowledge. Plato concluded that apart from the soul's direct contact with the World of Forms, knowledge of objects and events in the world is no more than opinion, unreliable commerce with mere appearances. John Locke, the first modern empiricist, paradoxically believed that there can be "no science of bodies," while accepting, in a Cartesian fashion, the certainty of the relations between ideas. Likewise, Leibniz, distinguishing between truths of fact from truths of reason, regarded only the latter as directly knowable by human minds (in virtue of the self-evident principle of non-contradiction), reserving the complete knowledge of any fact for God alone. Hume was skeptical about the idea of causality on which all factual claims are based. Kant's division of judgments into analytic and synthetic, while paralleling the distinction between truths of reasons and truths of facts, allowed the possibility that the "synthesis" can signify a contact not only with sensory experience but also, in the so-called 'synthetic a priori,' with something that encompasses all experience.

We have seen, however, that logical positivists argued that what Kant regarded as synthetic a priori judgments were really analytic and, by invoking the verification principle, favored the position of their empiricist predecessors.

343

An interesting and innovating twist to the empiricist saga was given by a pair of twentieth-century thinkers, Pierre Duhem (1861-1916), a French historian of science, and Willard Van Orman Quine (1908-), an American philosopher, in whose work that twist blossomed into a comprehensive and influential theory. Duhem suggested that an *isolated* hypothesis cannot be tested empirically. To test, for instance, the hypothesis that the earth is flat, we not only need to observe the ships moving away from us toward the horizon but also must presuppose, among others, the truth of the theory that light travels in a straight line. In contrast, classical empiricists, including logical positivists, assumed that individual sentences are sufficient to provide the needed verification.

Following Duhem, Quine argued that not single isolated sentences, but *systems* of sentences are needed to provide empirical evidence for factual assertions. The assumption that individual sentences can be examined for empirical content, Quine called "the dogma of reductionism." "The dogma of reductionism" survives in the supposition that each statement, taken in isolation from its fellows, can admit of confirmation or infirmation at all. "My counter suggestion. . . is that our statements about the external world face the tribunal of sense experience not individually, but only as a corporate body."[1]

The far-reaching consequence of this claim is *holism*: the view that no empirical statement is sufficient unto itself, and that the primary vehicle of empirical significance is the system as a whole. "The totality of our so-called knowledge or beliefs, from the most casual matters of geography and history to the most profound laws of atomic physics or even of pure mathematics and logic, is a man-made fabric which impinges on experience only along the edges. Or, to change the figure, total science is like a field of force whose boundary conditions are experience."[2] This conclusion applies to a priori knowledge as well. All of its purported instances, including logic and mathematics, presuppose background assumptions and are in principle open to revision, in other words, are subject to what C.S. Peirce called "fallibilism." Likewise, science, with all its background assumptions is a web of interconnected sentences. No sentence has non-refutable status and, conversely, every threatened statement can be saved by introducing requisite changes elsewhere in the system.

Rejecting the dogma of reductionism, Quine proceeded to criticize the classical empiricist distinction between analytic and synthetic statements. Analytic statement depend on the synonymity of expressions which comprise it. But the synonymity question is confused by the failure to distinguish between the meaning of an expression and its reference. "Evening Star" and "Morning Star" both refer to Venus, but their meaning is not the same. An alternative way of describing the difference is to say that both expressions have the same extension (both refer to the same object—Venus) but have different intensions.

We can explain what is going on without talking about intensions or meanings and *their* alleged synonymity. To investigate synonymity, we can limit ourselves to the way people use and correlate linguistic expressions. For that purpose we need to appeal only to such entities as sentences, predicates, singular or general terms, and the human behavior with regard to these linguistic entities. This admittedly sparse ontology is sufficient to explain what is going on; we can eliminate meanings or intensions by an application of Ockham's Razor. Linguistic expressions can be only *comparatively* synonymous, and the comparative differences can be established by noting the respective behavior expressed toward them. To invoke the notion of analyticity is to prejudge this task. Individuals can be said to be identical when whatever is true of one is true of the other; and this can be established without talking about meanings or intensions. Similarly, classes are identified when they have the same members or the same extension. When the linguistic function of particular expressions is unclear we fix it by pragmatic considerations. "Beyond those conditions of partial agreement, dictated by our interests and purposes, any trait of the explicans comes under the head of 'don't cares.' Under this head we are free to allow the explicans all manner of novel connotations never associated with the explicandum." [3] But we can extend familiar meanings and stipulate new ones when linguistic innovations appear to improve our theories. Even such venerable candidate for a synthetic a priori principle as "Every event has a cause" appears to lose its a-prioricity in the face of quantum theory, which in effect questions the self-evidence of the principle.

To describe reality we begin, according to Quine, with what he calls a "stimulus meaning," a disposition to assent to a sentence uttered. Language is our avenue to reality; there is no such thing as language-independent meaning. The linguistic behavior of speakers in the face of stimulus conditions provides us with information of what there is. "The stimulus meaning of a sentence for a subject sums up his disposition to assent to or dissent from the sentence in response to present stimulation." [4] Sentences will presuppose varying degrees of background information, and those which are least dependent on idiosyncratic background information Quine calls observation sentences. "This is a helicopter" presupposes much more background information than, say, "This is a table."

If the description of reality begins with observation statements, one must examine the degree of assurance that two speakers understand each other, that is, speak a *common* language and describe *the same* reality. Here we can expect to run into what Quine calls indeterminacy of translation. It is most clearly evident when we try to follow a completely unfamiliar speech. By resorting to the now famous example of the sound "gavagai," uttered by a native whose language the hearer does not know, Quine shows that it is open to the hearer to take the expression as referring either to a rabbit, or to a rabbit segment, or to a temporal rabbit stage. If the linguist-hearer leaps to the conclusion that "gavagai" is a whole enduring rabbit, he is being guided by the background information which the native does not share. Quine claims that this indeterminacy of translation affects all language use and that the agreement in use rests merely on pragmatic considerations expressed in behavioral criteria.

What this assumption shows, concludes Quine, is that reference to objects is inscrutable and is shot through with ontological relativity. In practice we deal with it by settling the question of reference in terms of our home language and its background assumptions. When we ascribe truth to some statements we do so in relation to the object language we employ. But any object language can be talked about in a metalanguage, and every perspective on truth is relative to some metalinguistic vantage point. Nevertheless, the fact that language can be learned and intersubjectively used indicates that human organisms have certain neurologically based dispositions which enable them to perceive similarities. Their disposition to utter observation sentences does not require background knowledge; it is behavioral through and through and involves the physiological equipment of sensory receptors and nerve endings. Consequently, for Quine, epistemology "simply falls into place as a chapter in psychology and hence of natural science."[5] Science and philosophy are not discontinuous; they belong together. In characterizing his position Quine said, "I see natural science as continuous with the mathematics that it uses, just as I see all this as continuous with philosophy. It all goes to make up our inclusive system of the world."[6] The insistence on the continuity of science and mathematics is in part supported by Quine's questioning the defensibility of logical truths, a position already embraced by Alfred Tarski when he pointed to the arbitrariness of logical connectives. But Quine also believes that to make a serious science of behavior possible we need to modify significantly our present ways of talking and to translate our descriptions into a purely extensional language in which references to meanings and propositions would disappear.

Accepting the view that a sentence is true if it corresponds to the facts which it purports to describe (the view usually referred to as "convention T" and exemplified by such a formula as "snow is white" if snow is white), and embracing Quine's holism (the view that not isolated sentences, but systems of sentences provide empirical confirmation), Donald Davidson, a student and follower of Quine, has proposed an alternative solution to the problem of indeterminacy of translation. What people say is connected with their beliefs, desires, and intentions. Language users can be attributed the intention to communicate what they believe, that is, hold to be true. At least in some situations we can assume without any qualms that linguistic expressions of natives stem from the desire to tell us what they hold to be true. The events we witness, i.e., a string of words, are caused by the motive to express what the speakers believe to be the case; for instance, that the stuff referred to is snow and that it is white. The presence of reasons for such linguistic events makes them into actions, thus leading Davidson to say that in human behavior reasons can act as explanatory causes. When an agent gives reasons for his actions, he *rationalizes* it, and Davidson argues that "rationalization is a species of causal explanation."[7]

Davidson accepts a notion made famous by Quine, namely, the so-called "principle of charity," according to which a great many beliefs of people coming from different cultures and speaking different languages are the same; human beings share many true beliefs, and interpret these beliefs in ways that optimize agreement. "Charity is forced on us, whether we like it or not, if we want to understand others, we must count them right in most matters."[8] The assumption of the principle of charity goes hand in hand with Davidson's questioning the idea of conceptual schemes, dividing languages into incommensurable structures. The appeal to conceptual schemes rests ultimately on the assumption that alternate discourses are not even *languages*. If we deny the *possibility* of translation, we have no reason to suppose that the series of sounds we hear constitutes speech behavior. A partial failure of translation is possible only in the context of successful translation. Translatability, one might say, is a criterion of something being a language. The dualism of scheme and reality strikes Davidson as a dogma, responsible for the dubious notion of conceptual relativity and of truth as relative to its scheme. Without this dogma, he concludes, "this kind of relativity goes by the board. Of course truth of sentences remains relative to language, but that is as objective as can be. In giving up the dualism of scheme and world, we do not give up the world, but re-establish immediate touch with familiar objects whose antics make our sentences and opinions true or false."[9]

Davidson's rejection of the scheme-content distinction has as its consequence the removal of the suspicion that because of subscribing to different conceptual schemes people live in "different worlds." That suspicion, however, is nurtured by the work of Thomas Kuhn who has examined the history of science in his book *The Structure of Scientific Revolutions*. Kuhn's study is at odds with the views of an influential philosopher of science, Karl Popper, who defends what he calls "methodological falsificationism." What makes theories scientific is not that they produce confirmation of their predictions and generalizations based on such confirmation, but that they state conditions under which they would be falsified. Science, then, is the search for disconfirmation and rejection of conjectured hypotheses. This critical process goes on *within* the scientific inquiry which develops inherent criteria by which theories can receive their "corroboration." Apart from the fact that the epistemological status of Popper's principle of falsification is unclear, Kuhn's historical work shows that the development of science does not bear out the importance ascribed to the principle by the Popperians.

Kuhn distinguishes between the "normal" and the "revolutionary" periods in scientific development. During "normal" periods the basic presuppositions, assumptions, and key concepts which define the framework of inquiry remain stable. But when that framework runs into anomalies which it cannot solve, new paradigms may be brought from *outside* the framework, creating altogether new procedures and experiments and sometimes producing results that are not commensurate with beliefs accepted before the new paradigm was introduced. There is some uncertainty as to what is to be covered by the notion of paradigm; it seems to be applicable to general metaphysical frameworks, to disciplinary matrices, or some new crucial experiments. Whatever the precise use of "paradigm," its function is to lead scientific development in a "revolutionary" direction, not implied in anything known and suspected beforehand. This feature, claim some critics of Kuhn, amounts to condemning science to irrationality or at most to a *post hoc* rationalization of theories. Rather than being a logical progress from theory to theory, history of science turns out to be merely a history of changes, many of them explicable only sociologically or as due to fortuitous circumstances. It also raises the specter of untranslatability of the terms of one paradigm into those of another. Although Kuhn's views are controversial and are being reformulated by him in the light of such criticisms, they have proved highly stimulating, especially with the regard to the relation between natural and human sciences.

The connection between knowledge and human interests, clearly recognized in the empiricist views of Quine and Davidson, comes more emphatically into view in the work of the German philosopher, Jürgen Habermas. His objection to all forms of positivist thinking, articulated in his book *Knowledge and Human Interests*, is that in analyzing the connections of knowledge and human interests they disavow critical reflection.[10] Habermas believes that the present task of philosophy is to counter the cumulative and massive disillusionment of European culture, caused by the deterioration and distortion of Enlightenment ideals into mere instrumental thinking, called by Max Weber *Zweckrationalität*. Such thinking limits itself to satisfying piecemeal, fragmented social purposes, thus neglecting their coordination which would foster the growth of science, rationality, and universal human freedom, as envisioned by the spirit of the Enlightenment. The headlong pursuit of material production, coupled with near-sighted business mentality and industrial technological zeal, have reduced the Enlightenment ideals to an ironic illusion and contributed to the emergence of Marxist and Fascist ideologies. The vaunted Western rationality, instead of leading to the emancipation of the human spirit, wound up in the disenchantment of the world, echoed in the "iron cage" of Weber's *Zweckrationalität* and in the "negative dialectics" of Theodor Adorno and Max Horkheimer in the Frankfurt Institute for Social Research, in which Habermas began his intellectual career.

Thoroughly conversant with intellectual developments not only in Germany but also in the rest of Europe and in the Anglo-American philosophical circles, including pragmatism and language analysis, Habermas proceeded to develop the theory which acknowledges the legitimacy of all cognitive interests. Among them are: 1) the technical approach of the empirical-analytic sciences, and 2) the practical, moral, and aesthetic concerns of the human sciences, persuasively articulated by such hermeneutic thinkers as Hans-Georg Gadamer. The hermeneutic-interpretive approach, by stressing the importance of humanistic and aesthetic concerns, aimed at correcting the bias of modern cultures in favor of natural science, technology, bureaucracy, and external control, neglecting what was labelled as the "lived world."

What is needed, believes Habermas, is a critical social science which would synthesize the empirical-analytic and the historical-hermeneutic approaches, because such syntheses would further what he calls the *emancipatory* interest. That interest is satisfied through participation in an open, free, reciprocal, non-coercive and non-manipulative communication. Habermas' Theory of Communicative Action is designed to articulate the conditions of satisfying the emancipatory interest. It would take into account not only the need for testing, revising, and corroborating all kinds of inquiries but would also involve participants in non-distorted communication in the process of validating mutually accepted procedures, practices, and institutions. They would not be delivered to anonymous forces, "ideological frozen forms of dependence," but would arise out of the process of self-reflection. Communicative action is intersubjective and dialog-like in character, allowing for interaction and interrelation among independent subjects, recognizing the need to accommodate their genuine plurality.

In the critical activities of the constructive sciences, such as Chomsky's generative grammar or Piaget's theory of cognitive development, Habermas discerns the presence of a thrust toward universal validity. This thrust is not to be identified with any a priori tendencies of the mind, but it nevertheless animates any empirical demand for confirmation and the willingness to accept the verdicts of falsification. All particular reconstructive moves in any science further the aims of communication, which encompasses all such moves in what Habermas calls "universal pragmatics." Although hypothetical and fallible, human search in restricted domains presupposes an unrestricted and general competence of unforced communication. The various structures of intersubjective communicative competence ground the success in any particular reconstructive project. Universal validity claims arise from respecting the demand for comprehensibility, truth, sincerity, and normative rightness inherent in the acknowledged aims of a given discourse. Argumentation of this sort is, according to Habermas, not an artificial invention but a part and parcel of our everyday, pre-theoretical communicative interactions. In making this claim, Habermas seems to be close to Davidson's observation that whenever we try to understand an unfamiliar locution, the principle of charity recommends the assumption that the speaker intends to communicate what he believes to be true.

The Theory of Communicative Action intends to bring into contact anonymous social systems with the "life world" of participants, giving each component a legitimate role and thus encouraging social hope. The individual actors as "place holders" in the system can perform creative functions in negotiating and reconstructing the social meanings of their world. This function is a part of an overall rationality of which the empirical-analytic rationality is also a component, but which does not dominate or deform the more encompassing and balancing communicative rationality.

Habermas sees his position as avoiding the extremes of pure historicism and pure transcendentalism, while allowing that "a moment of *unconditionedness* is built into the *conditions* of actions oriented toward reaching understanding." [11] This demand for unconditionedness makes it possible to see social practices of justification as more than just such practices. But the universalism Habermas aims at is not abstract and has an empirical component. In his view, "philosophy shares with the sciences a fallibilist consciousness, in that its strong universalist suppositions acquire confirmation in an interplay with empirical theories of competence." [12] He hopes that the Theory of Communicative Action will enable us "to cope with the entire spectrum of aspects of rationality—and with the historical fate of reason that has been arrested again and again, ideologically misused and distorted, but that also stubbornly raises its voice in every inconspicuous act of successful communication." [13]

## 2. The New Dialectics

The label of "new empiricism" applied to the thinkers just discussed is appropriate because of their faith that experience provides access to some realities that *settle* the question of what is to be believed, of what is true. They see through the inadequacies of classical empiricism and of logical positivism but nevertheless undertake to construct philosophical theories that are at least quasi-scientific. They favor epistemological realism and even some forms of materialism, because these positions point to the possibility of settling the question of truth by some non-linguistic realities.

In contrast, the thinkers we are about to discuss represent an approach in which this possibility is no longer taken seriously. The term "dialectics" seems appropriate here because it *suspends* the idea of arriving at a closure. Closure is neither possible nor desirable. To embrace dialectics is to be wedded to a process of endless experimentation and invention, in which nothing encountered or invented has an enduring nature or essence. There is no such thing as human nature or the purpose of history. Like empiricism, dialectics has a venerable ancestry. The Presocratics looked to experience to determine what there is: water, air, earth, fire. But when Socrates invented the dialectical method, he planted in Plato the idea of the first fundamental opposition: appearance and reality. The primary task of the human being on earth is to be mindful of the unresolved tension between the two, until, liberated by philosophy, the soul can escape into the eternal companionship of Forms, fully enjoyed only by Aristotle's God. When Hegel transformed God into the dialectical adventures of Absolute Spirit, he prepared the ground for a historicism without purpose. That kind of historicism appears to have won the day, when, following Nietzsche's announcement of the death of God, philosophers were set free to articulate non-theological versions of dialectics. Some of them, like the dialectical materialism of Marx, were ideological in character. But ideologists of various stripes still have a theological residue, in the sense that they attribute to history and to social movements some static ends, some essential objectives, which would *end* the dialectical movement. Marx, for instance, envisioned a "withering away of the state." The "new dialectics" has no such illusions.

Contemporary empiricists and dialecticians have something important in common: fascination with language. Both have made what has been called the "linguistic turn." French structuralism, which played a role in Foucault's and Derrida's intellectual development, was modelled on language. Claude Lévi-Strauss, who made the wider movement known as structuralism possible, treated anthropological phenomena — systems of kinship, totems, and myths — as embodiments of certain codes embedded in human minds. Cultural artifacts resemble language: customs and practices are modes of communication and are signs of underlying structures given expression in cultural transactions.

Lévi-Strauss' method was based in part on the work of the Swiss linguist Ferdinand De Saussure, who produced a seminal theory about the components of a sign. Its acoustic component he called the *signifier* and its mental or conceptual component he labelled the *signified*. There is some obscurity about the connotation of the signified: it does not seem to distinguish between the sign's meaning and reference but instead calls attention to what is happening in the mind of a hearer when the appropriate signifier is used and when a certain neural event in the brain occurs. Signifiers and signifieds are inseparable in practice but can be separated into their components by a linguistic theorist.

What is important about Saussure's theory is that it regards linguistic signs as not natural but arbitrary and merely conventional. Particular languages use different sounds for signifiers and divide the total field of what is expressed in words in different ways. Often a close translation from one language to another is possible, but sometimes a language may lack a concept available in some other languages.

Saussure's theory of signs gave rise to what is called "semiology" in Europe, while in America the label "semiotics" is associated with the theory articulated by C.S. Peirce. As we have seen, Peirce's theory, in his "pragmatic maxim," gives a more detailed account of the meaning of signs. For Peirce, the meaning of a sign consists in its interpretation by other signs. Saussure embraces a more radical view and claims that the meaning of a sign depends on its *difference* from other signs; he says that without differences there can be no meaning. Any phonetic or semantic unit derives its meaning from the system to which it belongs; it has no meaning of its own. Since the individual units in the system are arbitrary, there is no stability in language; it is "a form and not a substance."

Saussure distinguishes between what he called *langue* and *parole*. By the former he means the system or structure of language, the corpus of linguistic rules followed by language users. The latter refers to speech in the actual use of individual speakers. A similar distinction was made by Noam Chomsky who contrasted linguistic *competence* with linguistic *performance*. For both theorists the task for a linguist is not to study speech or performance but *langue*, the structure of language. But the connection between structure and event as actual linguistic practice requires further attention and generates important philosophical questions. By looking at linguistic and cultural structures as having their own life and exerting their power over individuals or societies, structuralists seem to put in question the very reality of individual subjects as independent entities. The ontological status of intentional human agency, or even of humanity as such, tends to disappear from sight.

Michel Foucault (1926-1984) began to look at cultural history as a sequence of *discourses*. But seeing that the use of language is not just intent on depicting the "way things are," he became interested in the ways in which "desire and power" permeate discourse. What is said in language reflects the prevailing interests and oppositions. Although desire and power are expressed in terms of knowledge and truth claims, speech acts in fact mask the presence of power relations. The originator of this view of language and knowledge, which could be labelled "dialectics of power," is Nietzsche who saw in the will to truth the *will to power*. Social life unfolds within the context of external restraints, fraught with impulses to dominate. They take the form of "rules of exclusion" and determine what can be said and not said, who is allowed to speak on behalf of what causes. Even what is regarded as true or false, as reasonable or foolish, proper or improper, sane or insane is embedded in the controlling features of discourse, which of course differ from place to place and from time to time. Foucault's historical studies are pursued in his many books. *The Archeology of Knowledge, Madness and Civilization, The Birth of the Clinic, The Order of Things, Discipline and Punish: The Birth of the Prison,* and *The History of Sexuality,* probe and diagnose mechanisms of control governing discursive and non-discursive activity alike. Applying a "genealogical method," Foucault finds that history displays more discontinuities than continuities. It does not reveal any unchanging truths nor universal moral progress, but presents a spectacle of conflict, subjection, and domination, in which rituals and other cultural practices disguise the play of power and enforcement.

The rules and norms of society, its organizational and hierarchical order, reflect an interplay of desire and power struggle among groups, resulting in prohibitions and entitlements prevailing at any given time. All signifiers are given forms which define privileges and exclusions and are reflected in connotations given to such concepts as "sanity," "health," "sexuality," and "knowledge." By pointing to some events and developments ignored by traditional and conventional historians, Foucault undertakes to expose the dark underside, the deception, the injustice and duplicity underlying all discourse. By giving a single name to things which are different in their actual make-up and by emphasizing certain selected analogies, resemblances and metaphors, the discourse determines what can be seen in the world and what can be known about it, thus giving each historical period, after a series of formation shifts, its dominant *epistémé.* The reform of the European prison system in the nineteenth century, for example, was carried out within the context of an *epistémé* which aimed at making *everyone* docile, hard working, self-regulative, productive, and conscience-ridden. Education, discipline and punishment are aimed at producing a "normal" person. Modern legal and penal systems, demanding conformity and adjustment, make the society as a whole akin to a prison.

People living under the dominance of an *epistémé* are not likely to be aware of its configuration, but in a transitional period, such as ours, they may become conscious of living in a gap between radically different discourses, without being able to foretell just what will take the place of the dying one. One symptom of being conscious of living in such a gap, where an *epistémé* undergoes a "mutation," will be the disappearance of a distinction between literal and figurative meanings, thus testifying to the arbitrary nature of all social forms. At such a time the boundary between the use and *abuse* of language is difficult to draw. Because language is not a *representation* of anything, does not provide transparent and unambiguous signs of reality, its fragmentation is its likely fate, and humanity, lacking essence or objectivity, finds itself living "in the interstices of that fragmented language." Human beings experience themselves as unstable, replaceable forms in a changing impersonal structure.

Foucault's historical work and its philosophical application have met with a good deal of criticism. His skepticism about objective truth is seen as an obstacle to identifying any historical facts, even though he claimed that his studies were "of history," not of a "historian." Since his method was to appeal to documents, which provide *evidence* for his conclusions, he opens himself to criticisms based on other documents. But central to Foucault's historicism is his seeing it in terms of power relations. "Power," he said, "is everywhere": it comes "from below" and underlies all kinds of relations—economic, political and those manifest in other forms of discourse. It is effective and accepted even when some parts of it are hidden. It can be analyzed only in the moments of its manifestations, "on the wing," so to speak. Since it comes and goes, it is perceivable only indirectly.

Because discourse reveals power concatenated with knowledge, one inseparable from the other, Foucault makes use of a unitary term Power/Knowledge. He sees knowledge as a system of correction and control. Indeed, there seems to be a pun in the word "discipline" in the title of his book *Discipline and Punish*. Knowledge is a kind of mastering as reflected in referring to fields of knowledge as disciplines. Thus one might say, punningly, that disciplines (say, social science) make discipline (social control) possible. Such an interpretation does not confine power to repressive, exclusionary connotation; it can also be positive and creative as enabling and empowering, the way it was understood by Francis Bacon in *his* claim that "knowledge is power," Bacon thought of knowledge as truth-generating, and so does Foucault, although for him the regime of truth is not of universal validity but relative to a given age, manifesting itself in multiple forms of constraint. Missing from Foucault's analysis (and from some of his own political behavior, which struck some critics as anarchic) is the acceptance of a possibility that in a liberal state society as a whole can, through its elective representatives and the governmental machinery, exert *its own* power, counterbalancing the power of "special interests." The absence of this function of power looks to Foucault's critics as catastrophic for his political theory. His dialectics seems to be confined to analyses which expose the repressive and exploitive phenomena of human history. On that reading, he is to be counted among cultural pessimists, in the company of Oswald Spengler who saw our century as manifesting the decline of the west. Even Nietzsche's nihilism found a relief in his hope for the Overman.

Since men and women are for Foucault always social creations, the products of codes and disciplines, some critics conclude that there is no room for freedom in his dialectics. But this is not what he himself seems to have believed. In an interview shortly before his death, he gave an account of how he understood the notion of "relationships of power" and "games of truth." That account seems not too far from what Wittgenstein meant by "language games." In Foucault's words: "When I say 'game' I mean an ensemble of rules for the production of truth." [14] He did not mean to limit the notion of power to "a political structure, a government, a dominant social class, the master facing the slave, and so on." Power, he continued, is always present whenever one communicates verbally, is involved in the love relationship, or speaks as a participant in some institution. It is present whenever "one wishes to direct the behavior of another." [15] But he adds immediately that "there cannot be relations of power unless the subject are free," and "if there are relations of power throughout every social field it is because there is freedom everywhere." [16]

While in his earlier works Foucault tried to discuss how human subjects are defined in institutions and practices of control, in the final volume of his *History of Sexuality* he wanted to articulate what he called "the care of the self." His historical model comes from ancient classical texts, as compared with subsequent Christian writings. He favored "an exercise of self upon self by which one tries to work out, to transform oneself and to obtain a certain mode of being." [17] Echoing Kant, he claimed that "liberty is the ontological conditions of ethics. But ethics is the deliberate form assumed by liberty." [18] In the light of this view of the self, the notion of truth acquires a meaning hardly present in Foucault's earlier discussions of it. "Who says the truth?" he asks, and answers: "Individuals who are free, who arrive at a certain agreement and who find themselves thrust into a certain network of practices of power and constraining institutions." [19] It is a pity that Foucault did not live long enough to put these views about ethics, freedom, and the self into a clearer relation to his earlier views.

While the focus of Foucault's work are power relations, justifying us in applying to his thought the label "dialectics of power," Jacques Derrida (1930-) has a more encompassing view of the way human discourse can be dispersed or disseminated, enabling us to call his philosophy "radical dialectics." Since among the targets of his criticism is structuralism, he is sometimes referred to as a post-structuralist. But this label, like post-modernism, often applied to him and to some other thinkers on the present scene, is rather uninformative and has no positive content. Deconstructionism, another term of Derrida's own making, has become widely popular, especially in the context of literary criticism, which has responded in a lively fashion to some of his conclusions about the nature of literary texts, especially to his slogan that there is "nothing outside the text."

Derrida's chief philosophical target is what he calls "logocentrism" or the "metaphysics of presence." What he means by it may be best illustrated by an example. If we take Descartes to be the originator of modern philosophy, Derrida could be plausibly put at the end of it (thus in a way justifying the label "post-modern"). Descartes' view of the self is a paradigmatic instance of what Derrida calls the "metaphysics of presence." For Descartes the human self is a constant presence, a *res cogitans*, an unchanging substance that underlies all experience. We have seen how in Kant's philosophy the thinking self becomes somewhat desubstantialized or formalized, constituting no more than "transcendental unity of apperception." But Kant, according to Derrida's view still subscribes to the "metaphysics of presence," when he says things like, "the 'I think' accompanies all my perceptions," or "the world and the mind arise together."

Among the more recent targets of Derrida's attack is Saussure's view of the signifier as something present to the consciousness of the speaker in a sign situation. Derrida interprets Saussure's linguistic theory more radically than its author; perhaps because he draws its full implications. If it is the case that the meaning of a word is nothing positive but depends on how it differs from the meaning of other words, then there is no easy way to close off the play of differences an interpreter can initiate. This in a nutshell is Derrida's "deconstruction." He takes seriously the observation, as ancient as Zeno and Heraclitus, that nothing is ever simply present. Putting this point paradoxically (echoing some Heideggerian and Sartrean locutions about Nothingness), we can say that the absence *haunts* the present. What is absent are the dialectical changes we can ring on possible significations. Among them of course is the possibility of resorting to the play of opposites (Socrates relied on it in his proof of the immorality in the *Phaedo*, Hegel made it the center piece of his process philosophy, Marx used it to justify revolutions, and Lévi-Strauss described cultures in terms of binary oppositions).

Derrida starts at a more fundamental level—the elementary material under-pinnings of language. When we hear the sound "bet," it comes to us in the aura of similar sounds like, "pet," "net," "pat," "rat," etc. One sound carries "traces" of others, says Derrida, which shows, according to him, that Saussure was wrong in privileging speech over writing. What is true of phonemes is true of the meaning of words, written or sounded. If, as Saussure says, and Derrida agrees, "in language there are only differences, without positive terms," then every word or concept carries with it "traces" of such differences. Meaning comes to us in terms of an underlying system of differ-ences. In this connection we may think of Wittgenstein's claim that meaning of a word consists in the explanation of meaning and of Quine-Davidson holistic approach to this questions, but Derrida may suspect these accounts of still gravitating toward some kind of logocentrism, the supposition that each word or concept has a definite center of gravity. In contrast to Wittgenstein's idea that understanding involves a mastery of a technique, Derrida would favor a view that the play of language can never be mastered, that it is always opened to radical dialectics. "The absence of the transcendental signified extends the domain and the interplay of signification infinitely."[20]

It would not do to fall back on the familiar notion of ambiguity, for as the very etymology of this term indicates, we are not in the presence of a choice between only two possible interpretations. The descriptive term Derrida favors is *dissemination*, a kind of semantic dispersal where resemblances and differences can be played off against one another endlessly. But of course, even if the freedom of interpretation is larger than philosophers have supposed, it is not the case that anything goes, that our choices of interpretation of meanings can be wholly arbitrary. Words have their history and not all "traces" are equally plausible. Nevertheless, the traces, or what Derrida also calls supplements, are both backward- and forward-looking. To make this point he introduces a neologism whose difference from its derivation cannot be detected in speech but only in writing. The word is *différance*. The substitution of the letter "a" for the letter "e" calls attention to the circumstance that in French *differer* means both to differ and to defer. Differing is to be understood as deferring an interpretation to a possible modification of meaning, suggesting that that modification is not foreclosed by any preexisting *center* of original meaning.

Derrida also uses the word *espacement*, spacing, to make the same point. A word can be spaced differently in the dimension of possible meanings. According to Derrida, *différance* "is a structure and a movement which cannot be conceived on the basis of the opposition presence/absence. *Différance* is the systematic play of differences, of traces of differences, of the *spacing (espacement)* by which elements refer to one another."[21] Notice that the neologism is meant to avoid being frozen into a structure, for it is said to be both structure *and* movement. Nor does Derrida want the analogy to space to be too literal, for he claims that even "classical thought concerning structure could say that the center is, paradoxically, *within* the structure and *outside it*." He reasons that a complete meaning is *totalized* and as such perceived as frozen. "The center is at the center of the totality, and yet since the center does not belong to the totality (is no part of the totality), the totality *has its center elsewhere*. The center is not the center."[22] This "contradictorily coherent" notion characterizes all *epistémé* in philosophy or in science, observes Derrida, reminding us perhaps of Hegel's view of contradiction as not limited to purely formal logical opposition but as living out its dense career in multiple dialectical guises.

Derrida finds an illustration of this linguistic phenomenon in Rousseau's claim that education supplements nature. The locution suggests that nature as such is incomplete or insufficient and must be supplemented in order to be truly itself. Here we have an instance of the "logic of the *supplement*."

Similarly, masturbation, which while being a substitute for heterosexual activity, nevertheless shares something of its nature. The logic of supplementarity, however, does not apply merely to special cases; it is pervasive and powerful and is found in all typical human activities and states: passion, language, art, society. *Différance*, rather than being anomalous marginal case, is at work in all acts of communication.

Philosophy in particular had shown a predilection for logocentrism. Derrida finds the constant of presence in such heavy-duty words as *"eidos, arché, telos, energeia, ousia* (essence, existence, substance, subject), *aletheia,* transcendentality, consciousness God, man, and so forth."[23] Thus, his criticism of the "metaphysics of presence" turns out to be an attack on all metaphysics, which he finds to be befuddled by its own language, and Derrida believes himself to be merely completing the task begun but not decisively accomplished by his philosophical predecessors: Nietzsche in his undermining of the concepts of being and truth, Freud in his critique of self-presence in consciousness, Heidegger in his frontal assault on onto-theology. Following them, Derrida concludes that "there is no transcendental or privileged signified and that the domain of play of signification has no limit."[24] He presented his key ideas first in a paper read at the University of Johns Hopkins in 1966 and subsequently published in the volume entitled *Writing and Difference*. His other books include *Speech and Phenomena, Of Grammatology, Positions, Glas, Margins,* and *Dissemination.* All of his works display a vigilant practice of radical dialectics or deconstruction.

## 3. Philosophy Democratized

This philosophical travelog will end by considering the work of a thinker who followed closely the Western intellectual journey and came up with a challenging estimate of where it might be heading. Richard Rorty has been a diligent student both of the history of philosophy and of the shape it has taken in the hands of its contemporary professors. Actively involved as a competent practitioner in the work of Anglo-American analytic philosophy, some of whose representatives we have considered under the heading of "New Empiricism," he also made a serious effort to become acquainted with the work of so-called "Continental Philosophers" of Europe, including those of Foucault and Derrida. When Rorty's *Philosophy and the Mirror of Nature* was published in 1979, it drew attention to itself in part because its philosophical heroes turned out to be three thinkers hardly thought to be likely bedfellows. They are Dewey, Wittgenstein, and Heidegger. It is as if Rorty decided to mix apples, oranges, and nuts. But the attention and discussion the book received quickly showed that Rorty knew what he was doing.

*Philosophy and the Mirror of Nature* is an attack on philosophy's predilection for epistemology, especially favored by analytic philosophers who would like to model philosophy on natural science. Epistemology still seems obsessed with the search for a "philosopher's stone," when this image is taken to stand for some hard foundation of all knowledge, or to change the figure, some essence or elixir that would dissolve all problems. One reason for Rorty's choice of his models was their abandonment of the view that knowledge represents or corresponds to some non-linguistic reality. Heeding their message, and the message of people like Quine who also took this notion to heart, Rorty urged that philosophers should give up the "myth of the given," together with other theories which looked upon "the mind" as a receptacle ready to receive "the given" in whatever shape it reveals itself. As we have seen, many other thinkers besides Rorty have begun to accept some form of holism as inescapable. Meanings, they concluded, do not come in atomic bits but as parts of a system.

That is why contemporary philosophers, European and American alike, have begun to take *language* seriously. Like Wittgenstein, Ryle, and Austin, they have realized that language does not come "neat," is never "mere," but functions as a "form of life." Whatever we encounter—be it atoms, galaxies or sense data—comes under *some* description even though this circumstance saddles scrupulous thinkers like Quine with the problem of the "indeterminacy of translation," which Quine sought to resolve— unsuccessfully, believes Rorty—by an appeal to "observation sentences." Observation or not, they are still *sentences*, and every attempt so far to ground them in non-sentences by making a direct connection of language with Reality Itself, with something non-linguistic, has been incoherent.

To give up this discredited epistemological ideal, however, does not mean to cease trying to cope with the world as rationally as we can. One of Rorty's other intellectual heroes is Thomas Kuhn, who in his historical work showed that science did not adhere to its professed ideals in getting to where it is today. The course scientific development actually took reveals many paradigm changes; much deviant, oddball experimentation; and often just sheer luck, the play of contingencies shrewdly exploited by ingenious minds. One of the lessons drawn in *Philosophy in the Mirror of Nature* is that all progress in thinking, be it about nature or human affairs, includes a reactive, interpretive or hermeneutic component, leading Rorty to endorse what he calls "edifying" thinking. He chose this word over its possible rivals, such as "education," (which strikes him as too flat) and the German word "Bildung" (which sounds too foreign). The connotation of "edification" he emphasizes has little to do with elevation or inspiration, but is preserved in *Bildung*, the German word for education. In Gadamer's use of it (whom Rorty also admires) we are invited to respect the broader cultural tradition as a depository of multi-dimensional skills and practices, which include art and what the Germans call *Geisteswissenschaften*, translated into English prosaically as "human sciences." These cultural goods can be easily accommodated under Wittgenstein's umbrella term, the "form of life," which also covers what other European thinkers, following Dilthey, prefer to call "life-world." One of the consequences of taking this larger view is that the distinction between the natural and human sciences becomes questionable. To think hermeneutically about both is not to employ an epistemological method but to "muddle through" problematic situations. To be sure, the muddling through doesn't occur in an intellectual vacuum but presupposes expert background knowledge in a given area. Productive thinking successfully marries analytic-constructive and creative-reactive resources of people who try to cope with their problems.

If we can cope better when we bring together the systematic-constructive and innovative-hermeneutic thinking, the question can be raised what contribution, if any, philosophy can make to this process. Alarmed by his questioning of the central position of epistemology, some philosophers took Rorty to be advocating "the end of philosophy." This he emphatically denies. But he does suggest a change in our expectations. In his more recent work, especially in his latest book, *Contingency, Irony, and Solidarity*, he recommends what could be called a "privatization" of philosophy. The search for "what it all means," for some set of settled answers to what is possible in human life is essentially a private matter. It does, of course, have a "public" dimension in a sense that what has been thought before is on record and can be further disseminated in books and journals. One can more intensely participate in the search for knowledge and wisdom when requisite institutions, especially educational ones exist. But to sum up confidently in a finished package what one ultimately comes to believe is to present to others something that may look to them as a highly contested matter, quickly generating debate and controversy. No doubt out of such debates much good may come, and many controversial ideas, systematically and convincingly articulated, have proved to be useful to the cultural life of societies and traditions, including natural science. Nevertheless, Rorty warns that the step from private conviction to public acceptance and implementation is a large one. Often it is fraught with peril, as the effect of many a philosophical or ideological doctrine has shown. It is therefore important to make a distinction between the private and the public uses of philosophy. *Contingency, Irony, and Solidarity* is an attempt to clarify this distinction. The three words in the title are recommended as a replacement for words which so far were favored to define our epistemology-dominated philosophical tradition, words such as "rational," "criteria," "foundation," and "argument."[25] Rorty believes that we will be better off if we begin to describe our situation in alternative ways.

The word "contingency," when applied to language, selfhood, and community, gets us off the well-trodden but demonstrably unprofitable path of looking for their "nature" or "essence." Leaning on the work of many thinkers who have helped us to see the hopelessness of this search: Hegel, Nietzsche, Freud, Kuhn, Davidson, Rawls and others, Rorty goes a step further and shows that together with the recognition of contingency entering the life of language, persons, and communities there also comes the possibility of redescribing them in more promising, indeed, liberating ways. He sides with those who take historicism seriously, summarizing his position in suggesting that we "substitute Freedom for Truth as the goal of thinking and of social progress."[26]

Rorty thinks that we are more likely to make progress if we stop emulating priests and instead try to become poets. The priesthood he has in mind is that represented by a theologian (who has lost his undisputed prominence as the result of the Enlightenment), by a still worshipped scientist, or by a would-be super-scientist—the metaphysician. What all three have in common is their claim to tell us "how things really are" on the basis of descriptions which they put forward as corresponding to some non-linguistic reality. Rorty keeps reminding us that *all* our descriptions of how things are must be in *some* vocabulary and that there is an incoherence in claiming that one's present vocabulary mirrors Reality Itself or captures Reality's Own Language. People who aspire to that condition are trying to divinize (or re-divinize) their language, selfhood, or community. Having painted themselves in the corner, they freeze these aspects of the human form of life into abstractions, ignoring phenomena which fail to fit these abstractions. It is also not surprising that those who are wedded to such programs should resist the pragmatic advice not to ignore the growing edge of experience but to welcome the invention of new vocabularies, new paradigms and metaphors, which respond to causes still outside the province of established distinctions and descriptions.

That's why the model of a poet looks to Rorty as preferable to that of a priest. It points to the importance of leaving room for the reactive, creative, or edifying processes which, with some luck, may enable us to make our language, our persons, and communities better than they are. Rorty points out that changes taking place in the frontier areas of discourse, including science, cannot be judged by the already accepted standards of rationality because the appeal to reason or to common sense insists on judging all novelty in terms of current criteria, thus denying beforehand the transforming power of re-textualization. Although *caused* by something preexisting, metaphors do not *express* anything preexisting.[27] The charge of irrationality and the insistence on argument and logical demonstration are legitimate only within the framework of established meanings, but they are out of place where the vocabulary as a whole is being changed or when a metaphor, when successful, *introduces* a new meaning. Whenever such an introduction helps us to see ourselves in a new light, we are in the presence of an activity which is more akin to that of an experimenting poet than to that of a law-invoking priest. The constructive and progressive changes that are taking place in the Western intellectual climate, in all fields and disciplines, including science and philosophy, are due to such contingent creative, innovative activities.

That's why Rorty recommends the ironic stance toward what he calls one's "final vocabulary," a set of words which at any given time we are comfortable with and on which we rely when explaining or justifying what we believe. An ironist is a person who suspects that his final vocabulary may be not quite right. Aware of other beliefs, couched in different vocabularies, he takes seriously the possibility that there may be better ways of describing what is important to him; he worries about the adequacy of his vocabulary. Rorty shows that that suspicion is behind what has been happening in philosophy ever since Hegel's *Phenomenology of Spirit*. Metaphysicians at first turned into ironic theorists (Nietzsche, Heidegger), and, as seems to be the case with Derrida in his later writings, began to see through the pitfalls of trying to put an end to metaphysics by creating another metaphysics.

It should be noted that this development does not put "an end to philosophy." What Rorty sees in this change is merely the unmasking of the pretension that there *must* be a carry-over from private philosophical reflection to public concerns. We should have learned by now, he intriguingly suggests, that the work of philosophers is of great importance primarily to people seriously engaged in the process of self-creation, if among the aims of that project one counts a utilization of concepts, theories, and narratives to which thinkers across the ages, up to most recent ones, have made significant contributions. In this way, the philosophical writings from Plato to Habermas can be a rich and stimulating resource. Rorty admits to be profoundly affected in this way by writers like Nietzsche, Heidegger, and Derrida.

But if one looks for advice and guidance on matters of public concern neither Nietzsche nor Heidegger has anything credible to say. If we look to them for help in this domain, we will be disappointed and disillusioned. On questions having to do with social and political matters we get more help from such novelists as Nabokov and Orwell. In analyzing some of their works Rorty discovers that they were deeply sensitive to one phenomenon of special importance to morality and politics: cruelty. Accepting Judith Shklar's claim that cruelty is the worst thing we do, he carefully traces Nabokov's awareness of the possibility of humiliating others in virtue of one's own greater creative talent. *Lolita* and *Pale Fire* explore situations in which characters with superior intellectual and poetic gifts are wholly incurious about the suffering that goes on around them and to which they themselves at least partly contribute. Rorty notes the fact that in his formal definition of art Nabokov listed *curiosity*, morally understood, as the first condition of a successful work of art. Since Nabokov was widely perceived as a literary aesthete, advocating art for art's sake, his linking of art and morality may come as a surprise. Nevertheless, it supports Rorty's own recommendation that such blurring of distinctions is to be welcomed; he counts among Freud's achievements that he blurred the distinction between morality and prudence.

The third part of Orwell's *1984* struck many of his readers as odd and puzzling because in the figure of O'Brien he dwells on the possibility that cruelty, "torture for torture's sake," can be the primary motivating force in a person's behavior. According to Rorty, "Orwell managed, by skillful reminders of, and extrapolations from, what happened to real people in real places—things that nowadays we know are still happening—to convince us that O'Brien is a plausible character of a possible future society." [28] Rorty agrees that this is the really scary part of Orwell's book, because there is nothing in human nature that guarantees that O'Briens cannot happen. This is one of the contingencies of which the book warns us.

Among other contingencies, *not* facts of human nature, is solidarity. Rorty prefers this term to objectivity as description of what we should aim at. The latter term suggests that the goal of intellectual activity—in science or in morality—is to *discover* something preexistent. In contrast, Rorty thinks that solidarity is something *made*, not found. Relying on Wilfrid Sellars' notion of "we-intentions," he shows that moral progress consists in extending the scope of a particular "us" to some particular group so far treated as "them." We should keep trying "to expand our sense of 'us' as far as we can," and "to *create* a more expansive sense of solidarity than we presently have." [29] Here the motivating force should not be the discovery of something that dictates a convergence of beliefs and desires, but rather a response to the suffering of others.

The three concepts—contingency, irony, solidarity—in Rorty's use of them, are interconnected. Because freedom lies in the recognition of contingency, including the contingency of intellectual structures, ironism, as a persistent worry that our final vocabulary stands in need of improvement, is a sensible attitude to cultivate. It is an expression of intellectual humility (Peircian fallibilism) and of the willingness to credit other outlooks as potentially including candidates for one's self-criticism and further self-creation. Since this is a matter of reflection and respect for considered opinions of others, a liberal ironist will always prefer persuasion to force, reform to revolution. And he will be on the lookout for the danger of humiliating others by rhetorical displays of one's own intellectual or artistic powers. To think that the wish to be kind can be bolstered by argument is to court this danger, because to present one's preferred alternative as having a rational foundation, or being lodged in some facts of "human nature," is to load the dice in one's favor, thus opting to speak "from authority" — a form of force. Among the most moving parts of Rorty's book is the chapter "On Private Irony and Liberal Hope," in which he distinguishes between a liberal metaphysician and a liberal ironist. "The liberal ironist just wants our *chances of being kind*, of avoiding the humiliation of others, to be expanded by redescription. She thinks that recognition of a common susceptibility to humiliation is the *only* social bond that is needed . . . Her sense of human solidarity is based on a sense of common danger, not on a common possession or a shared power." [30]

It would be churlish not to be touched and inspired by such a hope for the future. Behind Rorty's recommendations one can imagine a kind of vision, a utopian vision at that. It is a picture of a society in which people desire to be thoughtful about themselves and about the way the world strikes them. Heidegger complained that the most depressing thing about us is that we still are not given to thinking. Without agreeing with him that our thinking must try to recall what he called Being, we may nevertheless grant that thoughtfulness and reflection can make us more interesting and more vibrant people — to others and to ourselves. To be sure, devoting a considerable time and effort to philosophizing may interfere with doing other things, and Plato was largely right in concluding that a healthy society needs contributions of people with different talents and propensities. Indeed, to function well a society needs experts, and it may take all of one's physical and intellectual energy to become and work as a physician or engineer. As compared to people who are absorbed in daily living, philosophically-minded people may look peculiar, not much different from poets.

But to cut poetry and art out of human life is to impoverish it severely. To obliterate from a culture all traces of poetry, or art or of philosophy, unquestionably diminishes its scope for good life. Among our social ideas should be therefore the aim to encourage in everyone a latent desire to have a personal point of view and to include some esthetic pursuits in the round of life. A free, democratic society will respect this aim. It will not ostracize, exile or ignore its poets, artists, or philosophers, and will welcome in its midst even the oddballs whose creative desire seems especially intense. A result of allowing this to happen may be the invention of new, unheard of ways of thinking and feeling and of providing for the society some useful new concepts and vocabularies, new disciplines, new forms of art.

When philosophers, as all-purpose intellectuals, attach themselves to some discipline or some domain of social and political life, and after learning its special discourse contribute to the resolution of some of its problems, the whole society benefits. Likewise, by becoming more reflective and philo-sophical, specialists in some area of knowledge, some branch of science or economics, may help to advance the frontiers of its knowledge and under-standing. One of the significant changes in professional philosophy is the emergence of the field of applied ethics, distributing analytic and creative talents among different professional fields: medicine, engineering, business, and law. Experts in these fields have recognized that such a collaboration is needed and is useful. What we are seeing is perhaps what Dewey had in mind when he declared that the problems of philosophers should become the problems of human beings. Preferring Dewey's path, Rorty faults Foucault's philosophy for being devoid of social hope.

All useful thinking, Dewey insisted, is *ad hoc*, addressed to problems actually pressing at a given time. Similarly, resources that can be brought to the task of coping with the problems cannot come from anywhere else except from the norms and values which seem most reasonable and justifiable. This is one consequence of taking historicism seriously; in that sense we have no other rational choice than to try to lift ourselves by our own bootstraps. In commending a recent influential ethical theory, one articulated in John Rawls' book *The Theory of Justice*, Rorty observes (and Rawls agrees) that its two principles of justice — 1) each person has a right to the most extensive basic rights (right to vote, to hold office, to own property, to enjoy freedom of speech, conscience and thought, et al, compatible with the same liberties for others; and 2) social and economic inequalities are justifiable only when their existence makes the least advantaged better off than they would be if these inequalities were eliminated — are not historical constants but are a distillation of the social and political experience of a certain group of people living at a certain period of Western civilization. A liberal society will stand by these principles unflinchingly, without claiming for them transcendent universal validity. It will welcome and advocate the enlargement of human solidarity couched in their terms, without claiming for them a divinely sanctioned validity, believing that moral progress can rely only on persuasion and not on force. To look for more than such a voluntary solidarity is to court the danger of distraction and divisiveness when people begin to argue about their candidates for universal or theological foundations.

Mindful of the injunction to look out for the possibility of willful or unintended infliction of pain on others, and accepting the moral truth of the observation that cruelty is the worst thing we do, a sensible society will allow people to devise their own philosophies of life and their own interpretations of the meaning of the universe. To push any one point of view on everybody else, to expect everyone to agree on some philosophical doctrine — theological or metaphysical — is to be engaged in unwarranted interference, which is unworthy of a democratic state. Philosophy privatized is also philosophy democratized. Privatization of philosophy liberates the imagination, allowing those familiar with a given intellectual territory to increase their delight by engaging in the play of deconstruction. Rorty admires Derrida for his special talent to do this successfully in the vineyard of the history of philosophy, limiting himself to the observation that Derrida's earlier attempts to give special status to such alleged "non-concepts" as *différance* and "trace" smack too much of metaphysical thinking that Derrida himself urged us to disavow. The plea for the privatization of philosophy is a plea to avoid intellectual one-upmanship and the possibility of humiliating others.

Rorty is sensitive to the fact that "most people do not want to be redescribed," especially when what seems most important to them is made to look futile and obsolete. But every articulated point of view contains in it a power of redescription. Since the exercise of that power can cause humiliation, such redescription should only take place when it is invited and is conducted in the spirit of enlarging a potential solidarity, not conversion.

This reminder is worth heeding especially at our stage of language-dominated civilization, when it seems easier, and natural, for people to be guided by the "final vocabulary" of a religion or of some other emotionally buttressed and rhetorically reinforced world view adopted from some segment of one's immediate cultural tradition. Most people, absorbed in the cares of living or making a living, simply do not have either the resources, or the inclination to spend more than the minimum of time on what Heidegger grandiosely called "thinking that recalls," and what other philosophers more modestly recommend as a reflective attitude toward one's basic beliefs. Philosophy, like the spirit, "bloweth where it listeth," and to many folk—busily engaged in getting, begetting and spending—cultivated reflectiveness looks like an alternative if unenviable way of being different. But no one can deny that this rarefied interest has produced a corpus of books that, in addition to being a component of other intellectual pursuits, is a source of delight and enlightenment to those who have the leisure and predilection to become acquainted with them. Societies that still cherish the intellectual and poetic dimension of life continue to make institutional provisions for access to such creations of the human spirit.

Rorty prefers to make this point in a more modest, mundane vocabulary when he says about the aims of edification: "To say that we become different people, that we 'remake' ourselves as we read more, talk more and write more, is simply a dramatic way of saying that the sentences which become true of us in virtue of such activities are often more important to us than the sentences which become true of us when we drink more, earn more and so on."[31] As long as this distinction is still felt and where it is felt, philosophy departments will not disappear from universities, nor philosophy books from library bookshelves. Indeed, under auspicious conditions philosophy can become democratized, in the sense that more people will try to make themselves more interesting, or at least will not bypass opportunities to do so. It does not seem overly optimistic to end this brief account of philosophy's journey on the note of such a hope.

## Notes

1 W.V. Quine, "Two Dogmas of Empiricism," in *From the Logical Point of View*. Cambridge, MA: Harvard University Press, 1953, pp. 40-41.
2 *Ibid.*, pp. 42-43.
3 W.V. Quine, *Word and Object*. New York: John Wiley and Sons, 1960, pp. 258-59.
4 *Ibid.*, p. 34.
5 W.V. Quine, "Epistemology Naturalized," in *Ontological Relativity and Other Essays*. New York: Columbia University Press, 1969, pp. 82-83.
6 Bryan Magree, *Men of Ideas*. New York: Viking, 1978.
7 Donald Davidson, "Actions, Reasons, and Causes," in *Actions and Events*. Oxford: Clarendon Press, 1960, p. 3.
8 Donald Davidson, "On the Very Idea of a Conceptual Scheme," *Proceedings and Addresses of American Philosophical Association*, Vol. XVVII, 1973-74, p. 19.
9 *Ibid.*, p. 20.
10 Jürgen Habermas, *Knowledge and Human Interests*. Boston: Beacon Press, 1971, p. vii.
11 R.J. Bernstein, ed. *Habermas and Modernity*. Cambridge, MA: MIT Press, 1985, p. 195.
12 *Ibid.*, p. 196.
13 *Ibid.*, p. 197.
14 James Bernauer and David Rasmussen, eds., *The Final Foucault*. Cambridge, MA: MIT Press, 1988.
15 *Ibid.*, p. 11.
16 *Ibid.*, p. 12.
17 *Ibid.*, p. 2.
18 *Ibid.*, p. 4.
19 *Ibid.*, p. 17.
20 Jacques Derrida, "Structure, Sign, and Play in the Discourse of Human Sciences" in *Writing and Difference*, translated by Alan Bass, 1978, p. 280.
21 Jacques Derrida, *Positions*, translated by Alan Bass. Chicago: University of Chicago Press, 1981, p. 27.
22 *Writing and Difference*, p. 279.
23 *Ibid.*, pp. 278-80.
24 *Ibid.*, p. 281.
25 Richard Rorty, *Contingency, Irony, and Solidarity*. Cambridge: Cambridge University Press, pp. 6, 9, 49, 75.
26 *Ibid.*, p. xiii.
27 *Ibid.*, p. 36.
28 *Ibid.*, p. 183.
29 *Ibid.*, p. 196.
30 *Ibid.*, p. 91.
31 Richard Rorty, *Philosophy and the Mirror of Nature*. Princeton: Princeton University Press, 1979, p. 359.

# Part III

# Suggested Further Reading

Achinstein, P. and Barker, S.F., eds. *The Legacy of Logical Positivism.* Baltimore: Johns Hopkins University Press, 1969.

Alexander, Samuel. *Space, Time, and Deity,* 2 vols. New York: Dover, 1966.

Alston, W.P. *Philosophy of Language.* Englewood Cliffs, NJ: Prentice-Hall, 1964.

Anscombe, G.E. *Introduction to Wittgenstein's Tractatus.* London: Hutchinson, 1959.

Armstrong, D.M. *A Materialist Theory of Mind.* New York: Humanities Press, 1968.

Aune, Bruce. *Rationalism, Empiricism, and Pragmatism: An Introduction.* New York: Random House, 1970.

Ayer, A.J., ed. *Logical Positivism.* New York: Free Press, 1959.

Barnes, Hazel. *An Existentialist Ethics.* New York: Knopf, 1967.

Bernstein, R.J. *John Dewey.* New York: Washington Square Press, 1966.

Bernstein, R.J. *Habermas and Modernity.* Cambridge, MA: MIT Press, 1985.

Bernstein, R.J. *Beyond Objectivism and Relativism.* Oxford: Blackwell, 1983.

Bernstein, R.J. *Philosophical Profiles.* Philadelphia: University of Pennsylvania Press, 1986.

Blackham, H.J. *Six Existentialist Thinkers.* London: Routledge, 1952.

Brandt, R.B. *A Theory of the Good and Right.* Oxford: Clarendon Press, 1979.

Breisach, Ernst. *Introduction to Modern Existentialism.* New York: Grove Press, 1962.

Buber, Martin. *Between Man and Man.* Boston: Beacon Press, 1958.

Carnap, Rudolf. *The Logical Structure of the World.* Berkeley: University of California Press, 1967.

Chomsky, Noam. *Language and Mind.* New York: Harcourt, Brace, 1968.

Cummings, R.D. *The Philosophy of J-P. Sartre.* New York: Random, 1965.

Danto, A.C. *Jean-Paul Sartre.* New York: Viking Press, 1975.

Davidson, Donald. *Actions and Events.* Oxford: Clarendon Press, 1980.

Davidson, Donald. *Truth and Interpretation.* Oxford: Clarendon Press, 1984.

Derrida, Jacques. *Dissemination,* translated by Barbara Johnson. Chicago: University of Chicago Press, 1981.

Derrida, Jacques. *Writing and Difference,* translated by Alan Bass. Chicago: University of Chicago Press, 1981.

Finch, H.L. *Wittgenstein: The Later Philosophy.* Atlantic Highlands, NJ: Humanities Press, 1977.

Flower, E. and Murphey, M. *A History of Philosophy in America.* 2 vols. New York: G.P. Putnam's Sons, 1977.

Foucault, Michel. *The Archeology of Knowledge.* New York: Pantheon, 1972.

Foucault, Michel. *The Birth of the Clinic,* translated by M. Sheridan Smith. New York: Pantheon, 1973.

Foucault, Michel. *Discipline and Punish*. New York: Pantheon, 1977.
Frankena, W.K. *Ethics*. Englewood Cliffs, NJ: Prentice-Hall, 1963.
Gadamer, Hans-Georg. *Truth and Method*, translated by G. Barden and J. Cumming. New York: Seabury Press, 1975.
Gallie, W.B. *Peirce and Pragmatism*. Baltimore: Penguin, 1952.
Gewirth, Alan. *Reason and Morality*. Chicago: University of Chicago Press, 1978.
Geiger, G.R. *John Dewey in Perspective*. New York: Oxford University Press, 1958.
Greene, M. *Introduction to Existentialism*. Chicago: University of Chicago Press, 1959.
Gustafson, D.F. *Essays in Philosophical Psychology*. Garden City, NY: Doubleday, 1964.
Habermas, J. *Knowledge and Human Interests*, translated by T. MacCarthy. Boston: Beacon Press, 1971.
Habermas, J. *The Theory of Communicative Action*, translated by T. McCarthy, Boston: Beacon Press, 1987.
Habermas, J. *The Philosophical Discourse of Modernity*. Cambridge, MA: MIT Press, 1987.
Hacker, P.M.S. *Insight and Illusion*. New York: Oxford University Press, 1972.
Hampshire, Stuart. *Thought and Action*. London: Chatto and Windus, 1959.
Heidegger, Martin. *What is Called Thinking?*, translated by F.D. Wieck and J. Glenn Gray. New York: Harper & Row, 1968.
Heidegger, Martin. *Poetry, Language, Thought*, translated by Albert Hofstadter. New York: Harper & Row, 1971.
Heidegger, Martin. *The Basic Problems of Phenomenology*, translated by Albert Hofstadter. Bloomington, IN: Indiana University Press, 1982.
Hollinger, Robert. *Hermeneutics and Praxis*. Notre Dame, IN: University of Notre Dame Press, 1985.
Hospers, John. *An Introduction to Philosophical Analysis*. 2nd ed. Englewood Cliffs, NJ: Prentice-Hall, 1967.
Hospers, John. *Human Conduct*. New York: Harcourt, Brace, 1961.
Hoy, D.C., ed. *Foucault: A Critical Reader*. Oxford: Blackwell, 1986.
Husserl, Edmund. *Ideas*, translated by W.R. Boyce Gibson. New York: Collier, 1962.
Husserl, Edmund. *Phenomenology and the Crisis of Philosophy*, translated by Quentin Lauer. New York: Harper & Row, 1965.
Jaspers, Karl. *Reason and Existenz*. London: Routledge, 1963.
Joad, C.E.M. *A Critique of Logical Positivism*. Chicago: University of Chicago Press, 1950.
Kekes, John. *The Examined Life*. Lewisburg: Bucknell University Press, 1988.
Kenny, A. *Action, Emotion and Will*. London: Routledge, 1963.
Kenny, A. *Wittgenstein*. Baltimore: Penguin. 1973.
Kerner, G. *The Revolution in Ethical Theory*. London: Oxford University Press, 1966.
Kerr, Fergus. *Theology After Wittgenstein*. Oxford: Blackwell, 1986.
Kripke, S.A. *Wittgenstein on Rules and Private Language*. Cambridge: Harvard University Press, 1982.
Lewis, C.I. *Mind and the World Order*. New York: Scribner's, 1929.

LePore, E. *Truth and Interpretation: Perspectives on the Philosophy of Donald Davidson*. Oxford: Blackwell, 1986.

MacIntyre, A. *After Virtue*. Notre Dame, IN: University of Notre Dame Press, 1983.

Malcolm, Norman. *Ludwig Wittgenstein: A Memoir*, 2nd ed. London: Oxford University Press, 1984.

Malcolm, Norman. *Knowledge and Certainty*. Englewood Cliffs, NJ: Prentice-Hall, 1964.

Malcolm, Norman. *Thought and Knowledge*. Ithaca: Cornell University Press, 1977.

Malcolm, Norman. *Nothing is Hidden*. Oxford: Blackwell, 1986.

Manser, A. *Sartre: A Philosophic Study*. London: Athlone Press, 1966.

Marcel, Gabriel. *The Philosophy of Existence*. New York: Philosophical Library, 1949.

McGinn, Colin. *Wittgenstein on Meaning*. Oxford: Blackwell, 1984.

McGuinnes, Brian. *Wittgenstein and His Times*. Chicago: University of Chicago Press, 1982.

Megill, Allan. *Prophets of Extremity*. Berkeley: University of California Press, 1985.

Mehta, J.C. *The Philosophy of Martin Heidegger*. New York: Harper, 1971.

Moline, F. *Existentialism as Philosophy*. Englewood Cliffs, NJ: Prentice-Hall, 1962.

Naess, Arne. *Four Modern Philosophers: Carnap, Wittgenstein, Heidegger, Sartre*. Chicago: University of Chicago Press, 1968.

Nagel, Thomas. *Mortal Questions*. Cambridge: Cambridge University Press, 1979.

Nehamas, A. *Nietzsche: Life as Literature*. Cambridge, MA: Harvard University Press, 1985.

Norton, David L. *Personal Destinies*. Princeton: Princeton University Press, 1976.

Nozick, R. *Anarchy, State, and Utopia*. New York: Basic Books, 1974.

Olafson, F.A. *Principles and Persons: An Ethical Interpretation of Existentialism*. Baltimore: Johns Hopkins Press, 1967.

Orenstein, Alex. *Willard Van Orman Quine*. Boston: Twayne, 1977.

Passmore, John. *A Hundred Years of Philosophy*, 2nd ed. Baltimore: Pelican, 1968.

Pilkington, A.E. *Bergson and His Influence*. Cambridge: Cambridge University Press, 1976.

Pincoffs, E.L. *Quandaries and Virtues*. Lawrence, KS: Kansas University Press, 1986.

Pitcher, George. *The Philosophy of Wittgenstein*. Englewood Cliffs, NJ: Prentice-Hall, 1964.

Popper, Karl. *The Logic of Scientific Discovery*. New York: Basic Books, 1959.

Popper, Karl. *Conjectures and Refutations: The Growth of Scientific Knowledge*. New York: Harper & Row, 1963.

Popper, Karl. *Objective Knowledge*. Oxford: Clarendon Press, 1972.

Prado, C.G. *The Limits of Pragmatism*. Atlantic Highlands, NJ: Humanities Press International, 1987.

Quine, W.V. *From a Logical Point of View*. Cambridge, MA: Harvard University Press, 1953.

Quine, W.V. *Word and Object*. Cambridge, MA: MIT Press, 1960.

Rawls, John. *A Theory of Justics*. Cambridge: Harvard University Press, 1971.

Reichenbach, Hans. *The Rise of Scientific Philosophy*. Berkeley: University of California Press, 1956.

Rorty, Richard. *Philosophy and the Mirror of Nature*. Princeton: Princeton University Press, 1979.

Rorty, Richard. *Consequences of Pragmatism*. Minneapolis: University of Minnesota Press, 1982.

Rorty, Richard. *Contingency, Irony, and Solidarity*. Cambridge: Cambridge University Press, 1989.

Ryle, Gilbert. *Collected Papers* (2 vols.). New York: Barnes and Noble, 1971.

Santayana, George. *Character and Opinion in the United States*. New York: Scribner's, 1920.

Santayana, George. *The Life of Reason*. New York: Scribner's, 1954.

Searle, John. *Speech Acts*. Cambridge: Cambridge University Press, 1969.

Searle, John. *Intentionality*. Cambridge: Cambridge University Press, 1983.

Sellars, Wilfrid. *Science, Perception, and Reality*. New York: Humanities Press, 1963.

Singer, M.G. *Generalization in Ethics*. New York: Knopf, 1961.

Sleeper, R.W. *The Necessity of Pragmatism*. New Haven, CT: Yale University Press, 1986.

Smith, J.E. *The Spirit of American Philosophy*. Revised edition. Albany, NY: SUNY Press, 1983.

Staten, Henry. *Wittgenstein and Derrida*. Lincoln, NE: University of Nebraska Press, 1984.

Strawson, P.F. *Individuals*. London: Methuen, 1959.

Sturrock, John. *Structuralism and Since*. New York: Oxford University Press, 1979.

Tillich, Paul. *The Courage to Be*. New Haven: Yale University Press, 1952.

Urmson, J.O. *Philosophical Analysis: Its Development Between the Two World Wars*. Oxford: Clarendon Press, 1956.

Urmson, J.O. *The Emotive Theory of Ethics*. London: Hutchinson, 1986.

Warnock, G.J. *English Philosophy Since 1900*. London: Oxford University Press, 1958.

Warnock, Mary. *Existentialist Ethics*. New York: St. Martin's Press, 1967.

Warnock, Mary. *The Philosophy of Sartre*. London: Hutchinson, 1965.

Whitehead, A.N. *Adventures of Ideas*. New York: New American Library, 1955.

Wiener, Philip P. *Evolution and the Founders of Pragmatism*. Cambridge, MA: Cambridge University Press, 1949.

Williams, Bernard. *Ethics and the Limits of Philosophy*. Cambridge, MA: Harvard University Press, 1985.

Winch, Peter. *The Idea of a Social Science*. London: Routledge, 1958.

# Index